The Committee

*In memory of Brian Raymond
and with gratitude to Geoffrey Bindman*

The Committee
Political Assassination In Northern Ireland

Sean McPhilemy

Roberts Rinehart Publishers

Published in the United States and Canada by Roberts Rinehart Publishers,
6309 Monarch Park Place, Niwot, Colorado 80503, USA
Tel 303.652.2685 • Fax 303.652.2689

Distributed to the trade by Publishers Group West

Library of Congress card number 98–65007

ISBN 1–57098–211–2 (hardcover)

© Sean McPhilemy 1998

10 9 8 7 6 5 4 3 2 1

Printed in the United States of America

Contents

Acknowledgments

I had no idea what I was stepping into when, early in 1991, I began to investigate the escalating Loyalist assassination campaign in Northern Ireland. It never occurred to me that I was embarking on a project which would, between then and now, turn my life upside down and virtually destroy the successful television production company I had formed in 1986. Back in 1991, I would certainly have refused to believe what I now know to be the truth—namely, that most of the murders of Catholics and Republicans committed in 1989, 1990 and 1991, crimes which in 1998 remain officially "unsolved," were in fact sanctioned and organised by senior police officers belonging to the Royal Ulster Constabulary.

My first debt is to Ben Hamilton who, as a young television researcher, suggested this topic for a television documentary. His magnificent work in 1991 resulted in *The Committee*, which revealed the existence of a then unknown Loyalist terrorist body. I also wish to thank everyone involved in making that film. I hope that, one day, the documentary will be shown again and that my colleagues will receive the recognition they deserve.

I was helped with my investigation into collusion between the Loyalists and the "security" forces by quite a few people in Northern Ireland—friends, journalists, lawyers, librarians and, most especially, the relatives of the murder victims. I am advised that it would be unwise to identify any of them publicly. I hope they realise how grateful I am to them all.

During the past seven years, I have also relied heavily and constantly on my English friends for advice and support. When I assured them that I had been followed by MI5 or RUC agents during my research trips to Northern Ireland, that my telephone was tapped by the security services or that I was working on the biggest story of my professional life, they did not roll their eyes, shake their heads or avoid my company. They encouraged me to persevere. So I am pleased to be able publicly to thank John Plender, David Cox, Omar Hemeida, David Melvin, Sarah Brook and Ian Tomlin.

I am especially grateful to Tim Laxton who, since 1994, has helped me in countless ways to complete the investigation I began in 1991.

Tim's first career as a City accountant has left him with few illusions about what seemingly respectable people are capable of doing; so he found no difficulty in believing that the Loyalist assassination campaign was being run by affluent and well-connected individuals, including a banker, a lawyer, an accountant, a clergyman and the owners of some of the largest businesses in Northern Ireland.

During the lengthy legal proceedings which followed the broadcast of *The Committee*, I had some of the finest legal brains in England on my side. Publication of this book may, I suspect, lead me to call on their services again. I am deeply grateful to Jonathan Caplan QC, James Price QC, Lord Williams of Mostyn QC and to my solicitors at Bindman & Partners—Geoffrey Bindman, Verity Danziger, Lynn Knowles and Anna Rowland. They have all taught me that the law holds no terrors for anyone who has acted in the public interest and who has told the truth.

Finally and ironically, I wish to thank one of the murder conspirators whose elaborate attempt at deception, which lasted for almost eighteen months, served only to intensify my resolve to persevere until I had uncovered the full story. Committee member Ken Kerr appeared to be experiencing a death-bed conversion, his imminent demise from colon cancer being—supposedly—his reason for "helping" me. Sadly, his expressions of remorse proved to be bogus, his "revelations" to be false and his tape-recording of the Committee planning a murder to be a fake. His duplicity is significant only as an illustration of the lengths to which the "security" forces in Northern Ireland have been prepared to go in their efforts to sabotage this book.

Sean McPhilemy
Oxford
February 1998

Chapter 1

THE MURDER OF DENIS CARVILLE

Friday, October 5th 1990 has no particular significance for most people in Northern Ireland. Nor is it a memorable date for people in Britain or elsewhere. But for Denis and Jean Carville, the memory of what happened on that Friday will haunt them to the end of their lives. For it was on that day that the youngest of their three children, also called Denis, went out for the evening, never to return. The nineteen-year-old youth had come home from work, had tea with his family and then, after resting for a few hours, had gone out to enjoy the weekend. He set off in the white Ford Fiesta his father had bought him, picked up his girlfriend who lived nearby and drove for a few miles to a local beauty spot, popular with courting couples.

Denis was a happy young man. He had been born and raised in the small town of Lurgan in County Armagh, where he still lived with his parents and his sister Una. His only brother, Michael, had married and moved to live nearby. The Carville home was a modest, pebble-dashed house across the street from their local Catholic church. Denis had trained as a carpenter and was employed as a joiner by a local building firm. He enjoyed his weekends, which were spent on his hobby, fixing and tinkering with his car, and in the company of his girlfriend Lynn Hughes, whom he planned to marry before long.

When Denis parked his car at the beauty spot on the shores of Lough Neagh, he was totally unaware that he had driven into the middle of a murder plot that had been drawn up just one week earlier by a gang of Ulster Loyalists, a group incensed by the Provisional IRA's terror campaign and determined to resist any move towards the creation of a united Ireland. Denis did not realise he was placing himself in danger because he had no interest in politics and no involvement in the sectarian strife that had raged in his native land from before he was born. He and his mother had just returned from an autumn holiday in Spain and, therefore, Denis would probably not have known that two weeks earlier, while he had been abroad, another local youth and his girlfriend had also chosen to park their car at the very same beauty spot. Colin McCullough, a soldier in the Ulster

Defence Regiment, had been shot dead by an IRA gunman as he sat talking to his girlfriend in their car.

A week after that murder and a week before Denis parked his car close to where it had occurred, a group of Loyalists had gathered in a Lurgan pub, the Dolphin Bar, to plot their revenge. They decided to send a chilling message to the IRA. An eye for an eye; a Catholic youth for a Protestant youth; a tit-for-tat retaliation against any Catholic youth whom they might find at the beauty spot over the coming weekend. The Loyalists agreed that the planned murder would be carried out by one of their most experienced killers, Billy Wright, whose notoriety as a Loyalist assassin had already won him the nickname, "King Rat." As the conspirators departed from their meeting on Saturday, September 29th 1990, they knew it was likely that, one week later, local news bulletins would be reporting that vengeance for Colin McCullough's murder had been visited on the Catholics of Lurgan.

The conspirators could feel confident because they were, in fact, key members of a larger organisation, which had been running a secret campaign of political assassination for some time, directed mainly against IRA terrorists and Republican activists. They were part of an unprecedented Loyalist coalition which had formed in response to the IRA's twenty-year terror campaign and to a growing fear among Ulster's one million Protestants that the British Government could not be trusted to prevent further moves towards the creation of a united Ireland. This coalition had come together in the Ulster Loyalist Central Co-ordinating Committee— "The Committee"—which had a membership of around sixty people, drawn from the business community, the professions, Loyalist paramilitary groups such as the Ulster Volunteer Force and the Ulster Freedom Fighters and, most significantly, from the higher ranks of the locally recruited security forces, the Ulster Defence Regiment [UDR] and the Royal Ulster Constabulary [RUC].

This secret terrorist organisation, whose existence in October 1990 was totally unknown to the public in Britain and Ireland, had already sanctioned and organised many murders. It was the brainchild of William "Billy" Abernethy, a manager in the Head Office in Belfast of the National Westminster Bank's subsidiary in Northern Ireland, the Ulster Bank. Abernethy combined this respectable position within the Belfast business community with an apparently selfless commitment to his community, through his past part-time membership of the local police force, the RUC.

Abernethy had a strong personal motive for creating a new Loyalist organisation to wage war on the IRA. His younger brother Colin, an uncompromising advocate of the Loyalist cause, had been the victim of a particularly cold-blooded IRA assassination in 1988. Shortly after his brother's murder, Abernethy had decided that the best way to deal with the Republican menace was to unite the forces of the entire Loyalist family; he set his new Loyalist coalition, those who had formed the Committee, the task of eliminating IRA activists and Republicans. The Committee was given the job of sanctioning and organising assassinations based on accurate intelligence and effective logistical support provided by high-ranking RUC and UDR officers devoted to the Loyalist cause.

The Committee had suddenly emerged in mid-1989 as the most important Loyalist terror grouping because it was able to call on the active support of these senior police officers within the RUC and UDR. Many members of the local security forces had grown increasingly disillusioned with the British Government's policy towards Northern Ireland and with what they saw as a half-hearted effort to defeat the IRA. These disaffected RUC and UDR officers had formed themselves into another unknown and illegal body within the security services, called the "Inner Force." Though the disgruntled and subversive officers continued to wear the uniform of the British Crown and to take the Queen's shilling, they routinely supplied official intelligence information to Abernethy's terrorist committee so that the Loyalists could identify and eliminate those deemed suitable targets for their assassination campaign.

Abernethy had forged a particularly close relationship with one of the most senior officers in the RUC, a former Head of Special Branch and an Assistant Chief Constable, Trevor Forbes OBE. Forbes—the effective head of the unofficial Inner Force—had emerged in the 1980s as the RUC's most controversial officer because his "shoot-to kill" policy had put him at the centre of the notorious Stalker Affair. Although he had succeeded in sabotaging an official investigation by a team of English detectives under John Stalker, he had subsequently been "let go" from the RUC and had decided to occupy himself in retirement by continuing his war against the IRA in an entirely unofficial but equally effective manner. Forbes's access to high-level RUC intelligence and his intimate knowledge of police operating procedures, acquired over a life-time career with the RUC, enabled Abernethy's Committee to function smoothly. Thanks largely to Forbes and the Inner Force, the Loyalist death squads were able to remove their targets with ruthless efficiency and to do so without any serious risk of detection.

Naturally, Forbes was careful to avoid being seen in the company of the Loyalist paramilitaries who carried out the killings. He never attended the meetings where the logistical details on specific attacks were discussed and settled. So he did not attend the meeting in the Dolphin Bar in Lurgan on Saturday, September 29th 1990 when the conspirators reviewed the crucially important intelligence information received from the Inner Force about police deployment in Lurgan over the coming weekend. He left the planning of the forthcoming murder to his friend Billy Abernethy and other Committee members, including the chosen assassin, King Rat.

And so it came about that, exactly one week after the sub-committee meeting in the Dolphin Bar, two on-duty RUC police officers belonging to the Inner Force in Lurgan began, on the night of Friday, October 5th 1990, to search for a Catholic youth who would satisfy the designated criteria for the planned assassination. The officers drove to the beauty spot and began to check car number plates in an effort to establish the identities of the drivers parked on the lough shore. After a time, they selected their intended victim, who was sitting in a parked car registered to someone living in a Catholic area of Lurgan. Satisfied that they had found a suitable target, someone who met all the criteria that had been explained to them by their Inner Force superiors, the two RUC men then drove the short distance to the car park of the Silverwood Hotel on the outskirts of Lurgan, where King Rat was awaiting their arrival. They guided the gunman back to the beauty spot and pointed out the car in which Denis and his girlfriend were sitting.

King Rat, his face covered with a mask, walked up to the car, tapped the window with the barrel of his gun and demanded identification from Denis. After the frightened youth had produced his driving licence the gunman, careful to avoid any mistake, sought confirmation of the youth's religious affiliation by asking him to provide the name of his priest. Once Denis had confirmed that he was a Catholic, King Rat told him to turn his head away and to look out the front window of the car. Then, without uttering another word, the gunman fired a bullet through the back of the young man's head. Denis died instantly. Lynn Hughes, the horrified and terrified girlfriend, now experienced what Colin McCullough's girlfriend had suffered after the IRA murder two weeks before. Lynn, shocked and distraught, fled from the scene and kept running until she reached a farmhouse where she reported what had happened. By this time, the two police officers had guided King Rat out of the murder area and helped him make good his escape. Then, their mission completed, the RUC men went back on duty.

Shortly after the murder, the dead youth's parents were roused from their bed to learn the terrible news. In the days that followed, the killing was universally condemned. A photograph of the smiling innocent boy, taken at his brother's wedding not long before, was flashed on television screens around the world. For a brief moment the name, Denis Carville, encapsulated the primitive and hate-filled conflict that had lasted so long and inflicted so much misery on so many. After the funeral, which was watched by the gloating assassin, attention quickly moved on to a fresh atrocity and the Carville family was left alone to grieve for the son they had lost.

Although seven years have passed since the murder, the Royal Ulster Constabulary has neither arrested nor charged anyone with the crime. Officially, the case remains open and under investigation. Yet, long before his retirement in December 1996, the then RUC Chief Constable Sir Hugh Annesley and other senior officers were informed that Denis Carville was murdered by King Rat, Billy Wright, at the behest of Ulster Bank manager Billy Abernethy and his Ulster Loyalist Central Co-ordinating Committee.

In October 1991—just a year after the killing—two high-ranking RUC detectives were handed a dossier containing the first-hand testimony of a member of the murder conspiracy, someone who had been present when the full Committee had met, shortly after the murder, to review how the assassination had been carried out. This testimony revealed that Billy Abernethy, Billy Wright and other Committee members had met in the Dolphin Bar, where they had initiated the sequence of events which led to Denis Carville's murder a week later. From the day the dossier was given to the RUC by Britain's Channel 4 Television, October 7th 1991, the RUC Chief Constable and his most senior officers have known the identities of those responsible for the Loyalist assassination campaign which, in 1989, 1990 and 1991, ended the lives of many Republicans and Catholics in Northern Ireland. The dossier contained the names of nineteen key members of Abernethy's Committee, including those of the former RUC Assistant Chief Constable Trevor Forbes OBE, a prominent Belfast solicitor, an apparently respectable Presbyterian Minister and the richest car dealer in the province.

Instead of arresting, interrogating and charging these murder conspirators, the RUC allowed them to remain at liberty and to continue their murder campaign. Why? For what reason did the RUC's Chief Constable disregard the confession of one of the murder conspirators? Why did he allow the RUC to suppress the truth about collusion between members of his police force and Loyalist terrorists? Why did the British Conservative Government, which also received a copy of the Channel 4 dossier on Abernethy's Committee, assist the RUC in containing the scandal? And how many more innocent Catholics in Northern Ireland were subsequently murdered by Loyalist death squads as a result of the failure to arrest those involved?

This book will answer these questions by telling, for the first time, the full story of collusion between the British security forces and the Loyalist death squads, between the RUC and the secret terrorist body which organised the assassination of numerous Catholics and Republicans in Northern Ireland between 1989 and 1996—the Committee.

Chapter 2

ULSTER SAYS NO

Ulster, the Six Counties or, in the absence of a name all can agree on, Northern Ireland has been a thorn in the British State for a generation and a monument to the failure of Westminster's ruling elites. With the territory's one and a half million inhabitants unable to agree even on what to call the land they share, it's hardly surprising that successive British governments have failed to reconcile the two conflicting nationalisms and deliver an overall settlement. Prime Minister Margaret Thatcher's instinctive conviction that "Ulster is as British as Finchley," her north London constituency, was shaken by her experiences in office and especially by her narrow escape from death when the IRA bombed her hotel in Brighton in 1984. Gradually and reluctantly, she came to see the weakness in the Unionist claim that the Northern Ireland conflict could be solved by security measures alone. In 1985, Cabinet Secretary Sir Robert Armstrong persuaded her to break with the past and embrace a bold political initiative which would—he hoped—produce a lasting settlement.

Sir Robert played a central role in the intense diplomatic effort which culminated in the signing, in November 1985, of an historic agreement between the British and Irish governments. It was historic because London agreed, for the first time since the creation of the Northern Ireland state in 1921, that Dublin should be granted a say in affairs north of the border; London accepted that Dublin could represent the Catholic population within the troubled and disputed province. Throughout the delicate diplomatic negotiations, Sir Robert had been conscious that the Prime Minister was deeply ambivalent about the emerging deal with Dublin, her Unionist heart resisting her realpolitik head; and he feared that she might, at the very last moment, recoil from the deal he had brokered and refuse to grant Dublin a role after all. So when the Irish Taoiseach, Garret Fitzgerald, arrived at Chequers for the final negotiation before the scheduled signing ceremony, he was taken to one side by a nervous Sir Robert, just before he entered the British Prime Minister's room. "Go easy on her, Garret," whispered a worried Cabinet Secretary, "or she'll rear up." Wisely, the

Taoiseach took the advice and the Prime Minister gave no sign of any reluctance to proceed.

A short time later the two Prime Ministers met at Hillsborough Castle and signed the Anglo-Irish Agreement which, despite claims to the contrary, was a dramatic turnaround in British policy towards Northern Ireland. Although Mrs. Thatcher insisted that British sovereignty over the province had not been compromised, she could not deny that another sovereign government—and one which claimed jurisdiction over the entire island of Ireland—had been formally granted a say over how the province was to be governed. London's new agreement with Dublin left no room for doubt that Northern Ireland, whatever its eventual political status might turn out to be, was as British as Finchley no more.

Ironically, the agreement designed to bring the two communities closer together drove them further and further apart as the years went by. On the Catholic side, though the Republican movement scorned the accord as an entrenchment of the British presence in Ireland, mainstream opinion viewed it as a significant advance for the Nationalist people. While the agreement would not reverse the effects of discrimination or quickly produce a more equitable balance of wealth between Catholics and Protestants, it guaranteed that Protestant domination would never return. Champions of the agreement within the Catholic community were also able to point to the physical presence of Dublin civil servants at Maryfield, outside Belfast, as tangible proof that the minority would get a fairer deal in the future.

On the Protestant side, there were no similar divisions. Virtually every politician and public figure shared their community's shock and outrage at the betrayal of the cherished union with Britain. Nearly half of the adult Protestant population converged on Belfast's City Hall to hear their leaders denounce the agreement. The crowd roared its approval for Ian Paisley's thunderous response to Dublin's involvement in his province, "Never, never, never." Margaret Thatcher's effigy was set on fire and, as the angry crowds dispersed in disbelief at London's treachery, their leaders began the difficult task of devising a strategy for undermining the agreement and preventing any further surrender to Dublin.

Protestant Ulster had entered a crisis that it could scarcely comprehend and certainly could not solve. The IRA's relentless terrorist campaign had already succeeded in securing the abolition of the Stormont Parliament, the symbol of Protestant supremacy. Direct rule from London had brought laws to abolish discrimination in employment, which resulted in a steady increase in the numbers of educated, confident and assertive Catholics in public positions. And finally, unbelievably in Protestant eyes, the British Prime Minister who had sent a task force half way around the globe to defend a few barren islands in the South Atlantic, had now signed away Ulster's birthright in an effort to appease militant Republicans.

The Whitehall mandarins, who had negotiated the deal with Dublin, framed the agreement so that it could not be wrecked by Ulster Loyalists in the way they had destroyed a previous effort to reach a settlement, the Sunningdale power-sharing deal agreed in the 1970s. Indeed, the Thatcher-Fitzgerald accord was devised in such a way that Dublin's influence would be reduced in direct proportion to the willingness of Ulster Protestants to make the agreement work. Yet such was the hostility generated by the agreement that no Protestant politician dared to propose any approach other than outright opposition to Dublin's involvement. The result was political deadlock, with sullen and resentful Unionist leaders raging against Thatcher's betrayal, their only comfort coming from former Conservative cabinet minister and subsequent Unionist MP Enoch Powell who, with his characteristic reserve, accused her of "treason."[1]

With the IRA's terror campaign continuing unabated and no sign from London that the agreement would be set aside, relations between the two communities inside Northern Ireland continued to deteriorate. Yet Protestant fury caused the two governments to tread warily, with the result that the agreement delivered little that Catholics could point to as evidence of progress towards a fairer society. The ensuing deadlock enabled the IRA to claim that its early denunciation of the deal had been justified. Protestant opinion hardened against both London and Dublin, and the prospects for a just and peaceful settlement receded beyond the horizon.

Unionist leaders, once so reassured by Thatcher's deep emotional attachment to the union and by her steely resolve in defeating the IRA hunger strikes a few years earlier, were humiliated by the Prime Minister's decision to give Dublin what it wanted. They discovered, too late, that they had misjudged their standing in London, that they had underestimated their Nationalist opponents on both sides of the border and, most serious of all, that they had not appreciated how much their intransigence, inarticulacy and intimidating conduct in Parliament and on television had damaged their cause. They found themselves isolated and friendless at Westminster, discredited and shamed in the eyes of their constituents at home. A gulf began to open up between the traditional Unionist leadership and the voters who had loyally followed their advice ever since the troubles began. It wasn't long before new faces appeared to challenge those who were seen to have failed, new voices to offer a more direct and effective way of coping with Ulster's enemies, and new organisations to ensure that Ulster Protestants seized control of their destiny before the ultimate betrayal, Britain's eventual withdrawal in favour of a united Ireland.

The Ulster Hall in Belfast was the venue, in November 1986, for the inaugural meeting of the body created to secure these two vital objectives for Ulster Loyalism, the elimination of the IRA and the destruction of the Anglo-Irish Agreement. Ulster Resistance, as its name implied, would preserve the Protestant way of life by resisting all those with alternative plans for the constitutional status and character of their province. Just one year after the agreement had been signed, around a thousand Ulster Loyalists, many of them former members of the security forces, gathered in the Ulster Hall to pledge their commitment to the new body. It was a solemn occasion, marked by angry speeches, grim faces and the marching rituals which signalled the essentially military character of the new organisation. The message sent out was that Ulster Loyalists were preparing "to use all means necessary to defeat the Anglo-Irish Agreement." Mere talking, diplomacy, negotiation and the political arts had failed and, now, Loyalists would resort to the methods their enemies had used so ruthlessly and so effectively against them.

Although such well-known individuals as Ian Paisley MP and Peter Robinson MP were present at that important event, they kept a relatively low profile befitting their reduced status in the eyes of the hard men assembled around them. Most of the faces in the hall were unknown and, as a video recording of the meeting shows, those present preferred to keep it that way; they hid their faces from view when the camera came near. The moving spirits behind Ulster Resistance succeeded in remaining anonymous and senior members of the security forces sympathetic to the body's aims, the violent suppression of Ulster's enemies, stayed away from the inaugural meeting so that they would be able to provide more effective assistance in the difficult times that lay ahead.

This new paramilitary organisation was one of the most important of the Loyalist groupings which sprung up in the aftermath of the Thatcher–Fitzgerald accord. Shortly after it was formed, its leaders gave the go-ahead for bank robberies to raise much needed funds to finance the importation of arms. In June 1987, for example, members of three Loyalist paramilitary bodies—Ulster Resistance, the Ulster Defence Association and the Ulster Volunteer Force—robbed a bank in Portadown of £300,000, which was used to buy a huge consignment of weapons from South Africa. These included 200 assault rifles, 90 Browning pistols, 500 grenades, 212 RPG7 rocket launchers and 30,000 rounds of ammunition. The consignment was landed on the County Down coast and transferred to a farmhouse in County Armagh. Ulster Resistance leaders also went on arms-buying expeditions to Israel and continental Europe to ensure that they had all the necessary equipment to achieve their goals.

As the illegal arms imports were stepped up, Loyalist strategists concentrated on the purposes for which they would be used. By the autumn of 1987, just prior to the second anniversary of the signing of the agreement, disillusionment with Britain meant that some Loyalists began to think the unthinkable. Reluctantly, they reached the conclusion that the agreement had ended the union, forcing them to prepare to go it alone, to leave the United Kingdom and create an Independent Ulster. It was an agonising option for a community whose history, religion, culture and identity made them think of themselves as being at least as British as the English or the Scots, and as loyal to the Crown as any people could be. Agonising though the option was, they felt it had been forced upon them by the hated Anglo-Irish Agreement.

So, a small group of Loyalist strategists, made up of businessmen, industrialists, professional people and academics, began to meet in secret to develop their ideas on how to move beyond mere protest and to articulate a coherent vision of life for the province after the British Government had finally disengaged. To avoid creating expectations they could not fulfil, this group—the Ulster Movement for Self-Determination [MSD]—deliberately kept out of the public eye until they had developed a blue-print for the new society they planned to build.

An anonymous member of MSD, described only as an "independence strategist," gave an insight into the group's thinking in an interview granted to local journalist John Coulter in August 1987.[2] Much of the content was predictable, including such policies as the total exclusion of Dublin from the affairs of the province, no role for anyone with Irish Republican beliefs, exclusive control of security by Ulstermen, and the effective sealing of the border, which would be patrolled by a new force of Loyalist volunteers. And what about the half-million Catholics who also lived in Northern Ireland? The MSD made it clear that Catholics had no need to worry, provided they abandoned their aspirations for a united Ireland and accepted that the new Ulster state would have a Protestant ethos. Ulster would be in the future what it had been in the past, a Protestant state for a Protestant people.[3]

If that did not read like a prospectus for a more harmonious future, the MSD strategist's proposals on security were not likely either to win approval from many within the Catholic community. The article continued:

> He warned that the time was fast approaching in the Loyalist community when Unionists would hire paid-for contract killers to assassinate known Republican "trigger men."
> . . . Loyalists would have a "slush fund" to pay such hit men in much the same way as gangland bosses or Mafia chiefs operated.
> More likely the hired assassins would be former SAS person-

nel who had served in Ulster. The Loyalists themselves would compile a dossier on the intended IRA victim and hand it, along with the cash, to the would-be assassin.

The newspaper article was illustrated with a picture of Edward Carson, the Loyalist hero who had defeated Ulster's enemies in London and Dublin earlier in the century, and with a map of the historic province of Ulster—the Six Counties of Northern Ireland and three within the Irish Republic. Coulter explained the significance of the map for the MSD "strategist" as follows:

> While the MSD spokesman outlined that the initial solution to the present Troubles would be found within a Northern Ireland context, he did make a sinister remark about possible encroachments into Éire.
>
> "We want to undo the injustices which were done to our Protestant forefathers when Donegal, Cavan and Monaghan were excluded from the original Northern Ireland settlement. We were robbed of our rightful heritage in the 1920s."

The new Ulster envisaged by the interviewee would certainly be very different from the one that was gradually unfolding in the years immediately after the Anglo-Irish Agreement had been signed. The Loyalist strategist was advocating assassination of IRA men within Northern Ireland and the recapture, presumably by force, of three counties from the Irish Republic to create the dream of a strong, enlarged and independent Ulster State. The MSD's goal was the creation of a sovereign Protestant nation, entirely free of any influence from the Republic of Ireland:

> Our goal . . . must be to bring about a completely new situation in this country.
>
> To create a free Ulster for a free people, no longer at the mercy of either Republican terror gangs or appeasing and treacherous English politicians who do not understand us and do not wish to do so.

Loyalist anger and frustration at Ulster's twin enemies—militant Irish Nationalism and a treacherous British Government—were the central theme of another interview which John Coulter published a month later. Loyalist politician Alan Wright, chairman of the Ulster Clubs movement, was prepared to state publicly much of what the MSD interviewee had preferred to say anonymously. Ulster Protestants, according to Mr. Wright, were no longer prepared to trust or to follow the two Unionist leaders at Westminster, Ian Paisley MP and Jim Molyneaux MP; instead, they were preparing for military confrontation because the time for politics was past.

There are those within Northern Ireland who are preparing and
when the time comes . . . then you will see men and women to the
fore who had this as their philosophy all along . . .

Dominion status would be the one option which the grassroots
would most readily accept now.

It would bring back power to Northern Ireland to enable us to
clean out the cancer of militant nationalism and to bring some
form of stability to the province.

The Ulster Clubs chairman envisaged that the British Government
might try to use force to confront any Loyalist declaration of independence; but he suggested that such a response would be doomed to failure
because of the composition of the security forces within the province.

The majority of the security forces are all good Ulster men and
women . . . they would not stand against those who are fighting
for their civil and religious liberty—they will join us. But to take
such a course requires sound leadership.

Alan Wright told the interviewer that he would prefer leaders such as
Ian Paisley's colleague, Peter Robinson MP or an individual who, in 1987,
was politically unknown in Britain but would later rise rapidly to prominence in the House of Commons, William David Trimble. Until
Ulstermen were in a position where they could rely on the likes of
Robinson and Trimble, said Wright, they would have to continue to make
preparations for an eventual betrayal by London; at that point, he
explained, Ulster Resistance would emerge from the shadows, armed and
ready to fight for Ulster's survival.

[Ulster Resistance] will not be on the streets until it is quite clear
that the Government intends to hand us over to an all-Ireland
state. Ulster Resistance will come to the fore when the type of
work they are preparing for is needed—legitimate force.

They are an army of men—as are other paramilitaries—and
you will not see them until such times as they are absolutely necessary. They are now working behind the scenes preparing for that
day.

John Coulter's articles received little, if any, attention outside Northern
Ireland but, in the light of subsequent events within the province, he
deserves recognition for identifying and reporting on a highly significant
development within the Loyalist community. He had discovered that
Ulster Protestants were secretly preparing themselves for a fight with the
British Government and that they were looking to a new generation of
leaders to guide Ulster to independence outside the United Kingdom, if
that proved to be the only way of protecting their Protestant heritage.

Coulter kept taking the pulse of Loyalist Ulster over the next few years. In a second interview with the MSD, he reported on the growing support for some form of Ulster Independence. The MSD spokesman made it clear that his movement was a nationalist party for Protestants who wished to assert their unique identity as Ulstermen, as opposed to Irishmen or Englishmen, neither of whom were felt to understand or sympathise with Ulster's plight. Ulster Protestant Nationalism was finding a voice and the MSD interviewee gave the name of a potential leader for the emerging independence movement, Presbyterian Minister Hugh Ross; he also mentioned the name of university law lecturer David Trimble, who was said already to have "declared [his] belief that an Independent Dominion of Ulster is now the only solution for us."[4] The MSD spokesman proceeded cautiously to describe the military preparations that were currently underway to enable Ulster to seize control of its destiny.

This was not empty rhetoric. Advocates of independence within MSD knew that the hard men in the shadows, the paramilitaries within Ulster Resistance, had built up an impressive arsenal and were getting ready to use it. They also knew that these hard men would be able to call on the assistance of their allies within the security forces, especially the RUC and UDR. For some members of the security forces had grown frustrated and angry at what they saw as interference by Dublin in the operational role of the police. They believed that Irish civil servants, based at Maryfield outside Belfast, had used the influence given to them under the Anglo-Irish Agreement to prevent Orangemen from marching through Catholic districts as they had done for generations.

There had been ugly confrontations between Orangemen and the police on the streets of Portadown in July 1986 when, in the aftermath of the agreement, Catholics expected the RUC to re-route what they saw as provocative and triumphalist marches away from their areas. In another town, Dungannon, rank and file police officers had rebelled and refused to obey their new instructions, which required them to prevent the Orangemen from marching through Catholic areas. Dungannon RUC officers had been so opposed to Dublin's influence on policing that they had even defied the efforts of their own Chief Constable, Sir John Hermon, who had begged them in vain to obey their new orders. News of this unprecedented rebellion within the RUC was successfully kept out of the media but, as we shall see, it deeply affected some members of the force, including a number of high-ranking officers.

A long-term consequence of the new pressures on the police, which nobody appreciated at the time, was that some senior RUC officers secretly switched their allegiance from serving the British Crown to the cause of Protestant Ulster. They had shown in Dungannon that when the Crown required them, in deference to Dublin, to face down their kith-and-kin, they were not prepared to do so. As Loyalist alienation with Britain deepened in the years after the signing of the Anglo-Irish Agreement, the new groupings—Ulster Resistance, the Movement for Self-Determination, the Ulster Clubs—forged close links with the disgruntled RUC and UDR officers. And once the new groupings decided, as they soon did, that the moment had come to use their newly acquired weapons, they found that there was no shortage of disaffected RUC and UDR officers willing to guide them to their targets.

The first public report of growing dissent within senior ranks of the RUC came, again, from local journalist John Coulter who, after meeting a "fairly senior" RUC officer, revealed in May 1988 that "a doomsday plan to eliminate the IRA is circulating among senior police officers." The plan envisaged a more aggressive, Israeli-style approach towards the IRA, including the introduction of an automatic death penalty for terrorists who kill, an officially sanctioned shoot-to-kill policy, the return of internment, hot pursuit of terrorists across the border and, finally, the internment of all members of Sinn Féin. Rumours also began to circulate, in that year, that the more hawkish and disgruntled RUC officers had formed themselves into a so-called "Inner Circle," which had forged links to Ulster Resistance; but the rumours were officially and repeatedly denied.

The issue of collusion between members of the security forces and Loyalist paramilitaries in the murder of Republicans had been raised periodically throughout the troubles. But the British authorities routinely dismissed such claims as mere Republican propaganda; ministers regularly assured the public, as one had put it, that: "any member of the security forces found to have been helping terrorists . . . will be prosecuted with the full severity of the law." In the face of such categoric statements and in the absence of any hard evidence of collusion—official documents or testimony that would stand up to scrutiny in a court of law—the issue usually faded from the headlines, only to resurface when an IRA terrorist or Catholic civilian was found to have been murdered by Loyalists in circumstances which suggested that the killers had been guided to their target by a sympathetic, if invisible, hand.

In the summer of 1989, it became impossible for the authorities to go on issuing bland assurances that collusion never took place. Two Loyalist terror organisations, the Ulster Defence Association and Ulster Freedom Fighters, admitted on television in Belfast that they had received confidential information on Republicans from members of the security forces. And after Loyalists had murdered a Catholic in Co. Down, a man called Loughlin Maginn, the killers publicly justified the murder by boasting to the media that they had seen the dead man's confidential RUC file which, they claimed, showed he had been a member of the IRA. [The two UDR men who gave the killers this information later received life sentences for their role in the murder.] At the same time, in a move which further embarrassed the British authorities, the Loyalists proved that they enjoyed ready access to sensitive intelligence information by producing photomontages of Republican suspects, documents which they openly admitted they had used to help them identify their targets.

Ulster Resistance also helped to fuel the controversy over collusion that summer when it provided journalist John Coulter with yet another scoop. He published a long interview with the organisation's anonymous Divisional Commander in East Antrim, who explained that he was part of an army-in-waiting, an entirely Ulster Protestant force which would surface to resist any effort to force the province into a united Ireland.[5] "We are totally and completely a military body without interference from politicians of any shade," he told the newspaper. The membership was said to include clergymen from all the main Protestant denominations but it was made clear that nearly all those who had joined were "hand-picked men with military experience of one form or another," organised into cells so that they have good internal and external security. Though the Divisional Commander denied that any serving members of the security forces had been recruited, he let it be known that there were "former members of the security forces in our ranks." He ended the interview with the claim that he knew the identities of all Republicans in his area and with the prediction that Loyalist paramilitaries would soon become "more selective" in their choice of targets.

In an effort to end the growing controversy over collusion and to bolster the reputation of the RUC and UDR as impartial and law-abiding forces, the new Chief Constable Mr. (later, Sir) Hugh Annesley, decided in September 1989 to call in a top English policeman, John Stevens, to hold an independent inquiry into the issue. Mr. Stevens and his team had scarcely begun their investigation when, in October, another local journalist, Terry McLaughlin, published a sensational story which suggested that, if the inquiry were to carry out its task effectively, it would soon discover that the upper echelons of the RUC were staffed by committed Loyalists, senior police officers who routinely assisted those running the Loyalist assassination campaign.[6]

This report in *The Irish News*, the province's leading Irish Nationalist newspaper, revealed the existence of a secret Loyalist cell within the RUC, known as the Inner Circle. An anonymous man claiming to belong to this illegal organisation had turned up on the newspaper's doorstep in Belfast and handed the reporter some of the hard evidence that had, until then, been lacking about the alleged collusion between RUC officers and the Loyalists. The newspaper reported the story as follows:

A secret organisation, comprised of serving and former members of the RUC and pledged to eradicating Republican terrorism, has made available to *The Irish News* sensitive and highly detailed files and documents containing the names of 233 people.

The Inner Circle says it will use the top-level information to remove suspected terrorists in "the battle for the survival of Ulster."

The group has confirmed that the cell of police officers has close links with the Ulster Resistance Movement but declined to say if police officers still played an organisational role in the command of Ulster Resistance.

The highly detailed information on suspected Republican terrorists and political activists is the largest single leak of security force information on alleged Republican activists to the media.

This self-confessed Inner Circle representative proceeded to claim that his organisation had come into existence to fight the Anglo-Irish Agreement and that, by October 1989, it had appointed representatives within every RUC Division and, with only one exception, every RUC sub-division in Northern Ireland, including RUC Headquarters at Knock, near Belfast. The significance of this claim would be hard to exaggerate because, if true, it would have meant that Loyalist death squads could regard RUC stations across the province as friendly institutions that would assist them with their murder campaign.

The disclosure of the existence of this secret Loyalist cell inside the police force gave the Stevens Inquiry added significance. There was enormous interest when, after investigating the RUC for eight months, Mr. Stevens eventually held a press conference at police headquarters to announce his verdict. Rumours had been circulating that he had experienced hostility within the force, as had another English policeman, John Stalker, when he had tried, some years earlier, to probe an alleged RUC "shoot-to-kill" policy run from on high. It was known, for example, that the Stevens team's offices in Carrickfergus had been destroyed by fire; there had been much speculation that it had been started deliberately by disgruntled Loyalists within the force. What, if anything, would Stevens say about this? Would he uphold or repudiate the Nationalist charge that the RUC was riddled with Loyalists who routinely assisted their fathers, brothers and cousins inside the Loyalist paramilitary organisations? In short, would he accuse a significant number of RUC officers of collusion in the Loyalist murder campaign?

Mr. Stevens's verdict was delivered at a crowded press conference at RUC Headquarters in Belfast on May 17th 1990. His conclusion can be informally summarised as: "I found a few bad apples, but the barrel itself is healthy." In Mr. Stevens's words:

I have been able to draw firm conclusions that members of the security forces have passed information to paramilitaries. However, I must make it clear it is restricted to a small number of individuals, who have gravely abused their position of trust. *This abuse is not widespread or institutionalised.* [Stevens's emphasis]

This verdict could hardly have been better for the RUC and for its new Chief Constable. A senior and independent police officer from England had conducted what had been, apparently, a thorough inquiry into both the RUC and the UDR; and he had found no evidence that these two crucially important security organisations had ever been, as their critics frequently charged, systematically involved in the Loyalist murder campaign. Mr. Stevens's verdict had been categoric: there was no evidence of systematic collusion; the reported Inner Circle of Loyalist police officers did not exist; no senior RUC officers were involved with Ulster Resistance; nor was there any evidence that RUC officers had enabled Loyalist death squads to carry out their killings. As for the mysterious fire at his inquiry team's offices in Carrickfergus, Mr. Stevens remained totally silent.

Most of the report dealt with lesser, though important, matters such as the need to tighten up procedures for the control of sensitive documents. A total of fifty-nine people were either charged or reported to the Director of Public Prosecutions for the unlawful possession of documents, for mishandling classified intelligence documents, for communicating their contents to others without authorisation, and similar offences.

By far the most important individual arrested by Stevens was Brian Nelson, a double-agent who had worked both for the terrorist Ulster Defence Association and for British Military Intelligence. As Nelson had been charged with conspiracy to murder, his case was *sub judice;* therefore, it was not discussed at the press conference. Although it would later emerge at Nelson's trial that he, at least, had been passing official intelligence information to Loyalist terrorists, this fact did not alter the overall verdict of the Stevens Inquiry—a verdict which held that, while there had been a few isolated cases of individual corruption, the twelve thousand strong police force was an impartial and professional body. In short, Stevens had given the RUC a clean bill of health.

Naturally, the verdict delighted the RUC's Chief Constable who, standing beside the English investigator he had appointed, added his own message of reassurance to anyone who remained sceptical about the existence of collusion:

> The RUC will not tolerate wrongdoing should it be uncovered within its own ranks or flinch from tackling it in any other branch of the Security Forces, or elsewhere in society. Criminality will be dealt with, without fear or favour.

This statement by the Chief Constable flatly contradicted the claims which various Loyalist leaders, such as the anonymous MSD spokesman, had made to John Coulter and other journalists. Sadly, these Loyalists chose not to react publicly to what Mr. Stevens had found or to comment on what the Chief Constable had said. What they were saying to each other privately can only be guessed at; they may well have felt that, as collusion had been found "officially" not to exist, it was time to swing into action. What we do know for certain is that, shortly after Mr. Stevens exonerated the RUC of "widespread or systematic" collusion, the Loyalists stepped up their assassination campaign. In 1990, as in the year before, they murdered nineteen Catholics, one of them being Denis Carville. In 1991, the number of Catholics murdered was to rise to a record forty-one.

This sharp increase in the number of Loyalist assassinations, in the audacity and efficiency of the killers, and in the vicious, cold-blooded character of the attacks struck widespread fear in the Catholic population of Northern Ireland. Early in 1991, it appeared that the Loyalist death squads could strike anywhere in the province at will and, ominously, escape without detection. Suddenly, it appeared that not only Republicans—IRA terrorists, Sinn Féin councillors, election workers—but entirely innocent and politically uninvolved Catholics like Denis Carville, could fall victim to these Loyalist killers.

Why were these assassinations occurring? Who was behind them? Where did the gunmen get their weapons? Why were they never caught? Could the attacks happen at all, if there was a really serious effort to prevent them? Was it possible that, despite what Mr. Stevens and the Chief Constable had said, the assassinations were indeed due to "widespread or institutionalised" collusion between RUC officers and their Loyalist allies?

These were some of the questions that occurred, at the start of 1991, to another independent English investigator, a young journalist in London working as a researcher in the competitive world of current affairs television. After reading newspaper reports about Loyalist assassinations, the alleged collusion and the Stevens Inquiry, the young researcher was convinced he had found the perfect topic for his next assignment; as he studied the Inquiry's verdict and gazed at the beaming faces of RUC officers photographed with Mr. Stevens at a press conference in Belfast, he was disinclined to believe the comforting message the public had been fed. For, in his short career as a researcher in current affairs television, Ben Hamilton had already taken to heart the journalist's adage: "You only know a story is true once it has been officially denied."

Notes

1   Although Prime Minister Thatcher claimed that the Agreement had not diminished British sovereignty, this was hard to defend in view of the fact that the two governments had been unable to agree on how they would describe each other in the agreement. So the British version reads: "An Agreement between the Government of the United Kingdom and the Government of the Republic of Ireland;" while the Irish version reads: "An Agreement between the Government of Ireland and the Government of Great Britain." This rather basic disagreement between the two governments did little to reassure Ulster Protestants that British sovereignty had not been compromised.

2   John Coulter, *Sunday News*, August 3rd 1987.

3   Ulster Unionist Prime Minister Sir James Craig, later Lord Craigavon, sent out this message when he boasted that the local Parliament devolved from Westminster to Stormont (outside Belfast) was "a Protestant Parliament for a Protestant people." This Stormont Parliament was abolished by a Conservative British Government in 1972.

4   In February 1988, Trimble published a political pamphlet, "What Choice for Ulster?," arguing that the Anglo Irish "dictat" had ended the union with Britain and that Ulster Independence was the best option for the "Ulster British" nation. Trimble's extreme views, which are indistinguishable from those of MSD leader Hugh Ross, will be considered in more detail in Chapter 15. Trimble's pamphlet is noteworthy in view of his election as a Unionist MP in 1990 and, subsequently, to the leadership of the Ulster Unionist Party; his published pro-Independence views suggests an idiosyncratic interpretation of the word "Unionist."

5   John Coulter, *The Antrim Guardian*, June 29th 1989.

6   Terry McLaughlin, *The Irish News*, October 2nd 1989.

Chapter 3

A HIDDEN HAND?

"I'm calling about the research job."

"Oh, I'm sorry. It's gone. You're too late."

"But there's no mention of a closing date in the advertisement."

"Well, maybe. But we've already appointed someone."

"Doesn't seem very logical to me. How will you know you've hired the right person, if you don't agree to see me?"

I will always remember my first conversation with Ben Hamilton, at the time still an Oxford University undergraduate, when he telephoned the Box Productions office one lunch-time in the late summer of 1988. He had just spotted our advertisement for a television researcher to help us make current affairs, science and business programmes. Ben had decided that the job we had advertised was the one for him and, as the above version of our conversation indicates, he was not prepared to let the opportunity pass simply because he had been told the vacancy had already been filled. His refusal to take no for an answer and his cheek in suggesting that we might well be turning down the best candidate, namely himself, appealed to me. For I knew better than he did the attributes that make a good television researcher—persistence, self-confidence, flexibility—and he had just displayed all these qualities to me on the telephone. So I allowed him to invite himself for an interview in London the following day.

Ben had, indeed, phoned too late because my colleague had spent many hours reading application letters and sitting through interviews with bright young hopefuls before, finally, coming up with a short-list of the five best candidates. By the time Ben spoke to me, we had already made our first ever appointment, a candidate who far outshone all the others and who would stay with the company for the next five years.

On paper, Ben Hamilton could not be ignored. He had won a scholarship to the highly regarded Westminster School in London before moving on to Balliol College, Oxford. His examination results were every parent's dream and the subjects he had studied—politics, philosophy, economics— had given him a perfect foundation for the intellectually demanding work involved in researching analytical and investigative television documentaries. But he was also very young, totally inexperienced in journalism, not quite ready to join a team producing factual programmes for nationally networked television. So, as he arrived at our offices in central London in a bid to secure a foothold on the television career ladder, I was subconsciously looking for an excuse to tell him that he ought to gain experience elsewhere and then apply to us again the following year.

We spent an hour or more discussing his undergraduate dissertation in philosophy which, though I did not tell him so, was in the same field I had specialised in as a postgraduate before my own move into television journalism many years before. Although I had not kept up with developments in the subject, the philosophy of science, I had retained sufficient knowledge to ask Ben a series of reasonably informed questions, allowing me to assess his intellectual and argumentative abilities. I was pleasantly surprised by this twenty-one-year-old's rare qualities, a razor-sharp mind and the easy social manner normally found in someone much older. I was so impressed that I decided, on the spot, to offer him a job and I convinced myself that he would be able to help us win sufficient programme commissions to pay an additional salary.

Ben quickly lived up to his promise and researched a number of well-received programmes for Channel 4 and the BBC. He played a key role in exposing the activities of an American entrepreneur, who was living in style in London's Belgravia and planning to boost his already considerable fortune by exporting dangerous toxic waste to a tropical dump site in Benin, West Africa. Ben's research helped to reduce the entrepreneur's army of expensive libel lawyers to silence and, even more gratifyingly, to prevent the illegal export of toxic waste from Europe to Africa. In another documentary, Ben's research helped us place a question mark over the safety of the pioneering "fly-by-wire" computer technology incorporated in the European Airbus A 320 jet airliner. Since that programme was broadcast, the jet has crashed several times with the loss of around two hundred lives.

In his first two years with the company, Ben had gained considerable research experience and had shown the ability to identify suitable topics for future programmes. Box Productions had acquired a reputation for hard-hitting journalism in its documentaries. These included an investigation of the fraudulent takeover of Harrods by three Egyptian brothers and a report on commercial malpractice in the United States by a British-owned waste company, which sported the then Prime Minister's husband, Denis Thatcher, as its public face. Ben had helped to extend our range of programmes by winning a commission from the BBC's science series, *Horizon*, on a breakthrough by British scientists in the search for a cure for AIDS.

At the beginning of 1991, I was immersed in a programme on developments in the Middle East which, in the aftermath of the Gulf War, offered fresh hopes for a settlement of the Palestine-Israeli conflict. We were making a film for Channel 4's current affairs programme *Dispatches* by filming the progress of a former top British diplomat as he shuttled between the Arab capitals and Israel in an effort to assess the prospects for peace. The project had been especially difficult because we had been required to make the programme in just three weeks, an unusually short time even for a current affairs documentary.

While I was immersed in that production, Ben began to take an interest in another long-running and equally intractable conflict, one which had claimed almost three thousand lives during the previous twenty years and, sadly, looked in 1991 like it was set to claim many more. He had been studying media reports on Loyalist terrorism in Northern Ireland and on the sudden upsurge in the assassination of Republicans and Catholics in the province. Although I cannot remember my precise words to Ben when he floated the idea of a programme on this topic, I recall that my immediate and instinctive reaction was not to encourage him to proceed with such a project. But Ben is not, as I have indicated, someone who is easily deflected from a course he has decided to follow. He had dug his way into the subject and suspected, even at that early stage, that official denials of collusion between the Loyalists and the police were at variance with reality. Ben wondered whether a hidden hand might be guiding the Loyalist death squads to their targets.

I remember trying to divert his attention from these matters and interesting him in other potential stories. I warned him that he was proposing to immerse himself in a poisonous conflict which would bring us nothing but grief and unhappiness. I explained that in my fourteen years in the television industry I had deliberately never made a single programme on the issue of the sectarian strife in my native province. My reason was that I had, for years, remained deeply pessimistic about the possibility of political progress through compromise because of the intransigence and prejudice on both sides of the sectarian divide. I also remember telling Ben that there was an infinity of other worthwhile and interesting subjects for us to tackle and that we should leave it to others to make programmes about the sterile and seemingly endless conflict in Northern Ireland. In subsequent years, I have had occasion to ask myself whether I should, perhaps, have been a little more resistant to Ben's proposals but, by then, it was far too late for any regrets.

Ben had become convinced that there was an important story behind the headlines and, as we discussed the subject in February and March 1991, I found myself drawn into what was obviously an increasingly important story. I knew that if we were to find hard evidence of the rumoured collusion, we would probably win a programme commission from Channel 4 and, more importantly, we would be able to show that the official denials—repeatedly and publicly stated—had always been untrue. Such evidence would, I felt, give the Chief Constable an opportunity to deliver what he had promised when, referring to the alleged RUC/Loyalist collusion, he had told reporters at the Stevens Inquiry Press Conference a few months earlier that "criminality (inside the RUC) would be dealt with, without fear or favour."

Suddenly, at the beginning of March 1991, the issue of police collusion became highly topical when it was reported that a gang of Loyalist gunmen had driven into an isolated Catholic area, known to be an IRA stronghold, late on a Sunday night. The gang, armed with machine guns, had sprayed a car as it drove up to a public house on the outskirts of the village of Cappagh in County Tyrone. Three occupants of the car, all Catholics and two of them teenagers, had been shot dead. The gunmen had also managed to kill another Catholic and to wound a number of others, when they had fired shots into the public house itself. After the attack, the Loyalist gang had escaped by driving along the narrow and twisty roads they had used to reach the village, a journey of more than twenty miles in each direction. Local Catholic priests, politicians and community leaders had reacted to the killings in a familiar fashion, alleging collusion and condemning the security forces, the RUC and UDR, for having helped the Loyalists to commit the murders. And the security forces had replied with an equally familiar response, that there was no evidence to justify such claims and that these predictable accusations amounted to nothing more than Republican propaganda.

After I had learned from Ben about what had happened at Cappagh, I took the view that, with a little luck, further research might well pay handsome dividends; we might uncover independent evidence that the killings had resulted from collusion. I remember thinking, at the time, that it was inconceivable that a Loyalist gang would venture into an IRA stronghold in the hours of darkness to carry out assassinations, unless those involved were confident that their escape route would remain open after the shootings. Otherwise the Loyalists would be trapped inside IRA territory. I suspected, therefore, that the gang responsible for the Cappagh attack would probably have had help from the security forces but I also knew that proving my suspicions justified would be an extremely difficult, though not impossible, task. After the Cappagh killings, I began to take more interest in Ben's research and I encouraged him to try to get fresh information about what had happened, new material which would enable us to approach a broadcaster with a proposal for a documentary on this sensitive and important topic.

We decided to pursue the story on our own until we had a much firmer grasp of the background and a clearer idea about what we might achieve if we were to obtain the funds we would need to pay for a short research trip to Northern Ireland. After a short time and having made some progress, we decided we would approach Channel 4, which was the only broadcaster I considered at all likely to show any genuine enthusiasm for such an undertaking. BBC current affairs had long ago been intimidated into self-censorship by the attacks of leading Tory politicians; and its reputation for investigative journalism had hit an all time low, a short time earlier, when *Panorama*—the BBC's current affairs flagship—had given in to right-wing Tory back-bench MPs, who had sued for libel.[1] On Northern Ireland, opinions about BBC coverage will differ but I've always found it significant that British television's celebrated programmes on the notorious miscarriages of justice—the Birmingham Six, the Guildford Four, the Maguire Seven, the SAS killings in Gibraltar—were all produced and screened by the commercial channels and not by the supposed guardian of the public interest, the BBC. Channel 4, which had for years shown a far greater appetite for serious journalism on sensitive topics, seemed to us the obvious place to go.

I had advised Ben, from the outset, to steer well clear of journalists working in Northern Ireland for the mainstream British media. As a young reporter in Belfast in the early seventies, I had observed at close quarters the manner in which both the RUC and British Army had shaped newspaper coverage of the troubles and, in the years that followed, I had found no reason to believe that media manipulation had become any less prevalent. I thought Ben would be unlikely to make much progress if he were to rely on the opinions of the specialist "Ireland Correspondents" who, if they had not already been "captured" by the RUC Press Office, were likely, if he sought their help, to feed him the conventional wisdom. There was also the danger that, if Ben were to make a breakthrough in his research, details of what he had discovered might leak to one or other of the outlets for which these "experts" worked. So, on my advice, Ben deliberately avoided all contact with Belfast based correspondents working for the British press and spoke instead to local journalists known to have good contacts with the Loyalists and to the few reporters who worked in Belfast for the Dublin media.

After Ben had spent two weeks researching this subject in London, we wrote a short programme proposal and sent it to the editor of Channel Four's *Dispatches* programme, David Lloyd. As we were aware that we had nothing new to say, at that stage, about the much discussed issue of collusion, we made no attempt to hide the fact. All we were in a position to offer was a summary of what was already known and an aspiration to find out more about a subject that had, in recent days, become highly topical. I also knew from experience that it would have been foolish to pretend to an expertise we did not possess because, ethical considerations aside, the two editors of *Dispatches*, David Lloyd and Karen Brown, would have seen through any pretence in a matter of minutes. So our immediate goal, during our first approach to Channel 4, was to make a sufficiently good impression to persuade the two editors that we had a chance of coming up with something new, if they would agree to finance the short research visit which Ben proposed to make. After a discussion lasting about an hour, his trip was approved.

At that first meeting, we had all agreed that our enquiries in Northern Ireland would have to be discreet and, further, that we would have to be especially careful to adhere strictly to the professional guidelines for programme production. Discreet because we were proposing to swim in the murky and dangerous waters that lapped around intelligence and terrorism within the province. Professional because we all knew we might, one day, have to face an official or public inquiry into the way we had conducted our investigation. For we knew that if we were lucky enough to find incontrovertible evidence that, as we suspected, members of the security forces were colluding in murder with Loyalist terrorists, we would be unlikely to receive a thank-you note from either the RUC Chief Constable or the British Government.

None of us needed to be reminded of the fate that had befallen Thames Television in 1988 after it had shown *Death on the Rock*, a programme which had documented the unscrupulous methods used by the SAS when they had shot three IRA terrorists dead in Gibraltar. After that programme had been broadcast to millions on the British ITV network, the producers had come under ferocious criticism from the Thatcher Government and its media allies, especially from Rupert Murdoch's *The Sunday Times*. For the Thames reporting team had dared to allow eye-witnesses to the shootings to appear on screen, where they flatly contradicted the official Government account of the incident; the report had left viewers in no doubt that the unarmed IRA members had been executed, riddled with bullets by SAS men as they had tried to flee. Thames Television's reward for its brilliant journalism was delivered a few years later, when it was unceremoniously stripped of its licence to broadcast. So, aware of the hazards we would face if our efforts were at all successful, I handed Ben some relevant reading material for his plane journey to Belfast, a copy of the report of a subsequent semi-official inquiry into how Thames Television's reporters had behaved while making that programme.[2] I wanted to be sure that, if our working methods were ever to come under similar scrutiny, we would be vindicated as fully as were those who had made *Death on the Rock*.

Although Ben based himself in Belfast, he had decided to focus his enquiries thirty miles south of the city, on a part of County Armagh known as "murder triangle." Relations between Catholics and Protestants within this notorious district can be fairly stated as having been, for most of the previous twenty years, somewhere between poor and poisonous. The IRA had murdered dozens of local Protestants belonging to the RUC and UDR, while the Loyalist paramilitaries had tortured and killed many Catholic civilians. The ugly sectarian conflict which, at some time or other, has erupted in most parts of the province, persisted continuously and in a more virulent form in this miserable part of County Armagh, centred on the neighbouring towns of Lurgan and Portadown; many of murder triangle's residents are, as it happens, first and second generation descendants of Belfast slum-dwellers, people who were transferred there during the urban clearances in the 1960s. Optimists had hoped that the migrants, once relocated from grim, inner-city back-to-backs to shiny new housing estates in semi-rural Armagh, would leave their ancient, destructive quarrels behind. But, sadly, the passage of time has shown that the pessimists were correct; thirty years on, the two traditions have continued to distrust each other, trapped and doomed by history and fate.

From the moment they arrived, the Catholics declined even to utter the name of the new town and district to which they had moved, Craigavon, because they saw it as a symbol of their continuing second-class status; Lord Craigavon, the province's first Unionist Prime Minister, is only remembered by Catholics for his message that Northern Ireland was meant to be "a Protestant state for a Protestant people." On the other side of the communal divide, Protestant attitudes were no more generous or forgiving and, each year, thousands of Orangemen continued to insist on trumpeting their supremacy, by holding colourful parades which would, so they claimed, lose their distinctive character and significance if they were prevented from passing through Catholic areas.

Sadly, the "murder triangle" had more than justified its grim reputation in the five years that had passed from the signing of the Anglo-Irish Agreement to the moment when, in 1991, Ben Hamilton arrived there to pursue his research. He would soon receive dramatic confirmation that he had come to the epicentre of Loyalist terrorism and, indeed, to the perfect place to find enlightenment about the rumoured collusion. For, just a few weeks after his arrival in Lurgan, a Loyalist gang launched an attack, which was so savage and cruel that it stunned even those who felt themselves unshockable because of previous barbarities they had witnessed in the locality. This attack became the focus of Ben's research because it had, at once, raised suspicions that a hidden hand was guiding the Loyalists to their targets.

One night towards the end of March, a teenage girl working in a mobile sweet shop parked in the Drumbeg estate in Craigavon (near Portadown), was talking to a girlfriend, aged just seventeen, when a masked gunman walked up to the shop. Without pausing to speak, the gunman immediately shot both girls in the head, killing them instantly. Then, as he was escaping, he happened to see another young person near the van, a man who had chosen the worst possible moment to do his late-night shopping. Though this young man tried to flee, the gunman raced after him and shot him dead also. In less than a minute, a Loyalist assassin had wiped out another three lives within "murder triangle," hatred of Catholics being the only apparent reason for the slaughter. After the killings, local people alleged that this lethal incursion into their estate had been the result of collusion between Loyalists and the police—a claim which the police indignantly denied.

Ten days after these "mobile sweet shop" murders Ben, who was based in Belfast, made one of his many visits to Lurgan. He drove down the motorway from Belfast to the Silverwood Hotel on the outskirts of the town. He was keeping a dinner appointment with a Portadown Loyalist, which had been arranged with the help of a Belfast journalist who had been co-operating with Ben from almost the start of his enquiries, Martin O'Hagan. Ben had first contacted Martin by phone from London after learning about his regular "scoops" on Loyalist paramilitaries, published in the Belfast tabloid newspaper, the *Sunday World*.

Martin had generously offered to put Ben in contact with a few people who he thought might be able to help, one of them being his best Loyalist source within the "murder triangle," someone whom he had first met on the streets of Portadown while reporting on the violent confrontation between Orangemen and the RUC in 1986, shortly after the Anglo-Irish Agreement had been signed. Martin had come to know his Loyalist source well since that time and, despite the differences in their political opinions and religious backgrounds, they had become good friends. Martin and his friend, Jim Sands, spent quite a lot of time in each other's company, visited each other's homes, exchanged Christmas presents each year and, from time to time, laughed together at the consternation they had provoked in Loyalist circles by the publication in the *Sunday World* of exclusive stories about Protestant paramilitaries, which Martin regularly wrote on the basis of confidential information given to him by his well-connected friend.

Sands had offered to talk to Ben on condition that he promise that he would never, under any circumstances, reveal his identity to the authorities. Sands had also insisted that Ben obtain an identical undertaking from anyone else, whether at Box Productions or Channel 4, who might subsequently ask to know his identity. Once Ben had given Sands the undertakings demanded, the Loyalist began to answer the young researcher's questions in what was to be the first of a series of interviews he would give us in the weeks ahead. Sands did not explain, initially, why he had agreed to be interviewed but, as Ben had been introduced by his [Sands's] trusted friend, Martin O'Hagan, he was quite confident that the undertakings he had been given would be honoured. So he raised no objection when Ben switched on his tape-recorder before the first of their interviews got underway.

Having listened to the tape of that first conversation, just a few days after it had been recorded, I had no difficulty in understanding why Sands had insisted on anonymity. For he had calmly, almost casually, admitted in the conversation that he was participating in a murder conspiracy, one which was more organised and more sinister than any of us had ever imagined. He claimed to possess inside knowledge about virtually every single murder the Loyalists had carried out during the previous two years and, most startling of all, he alleged that senior officers in both the RUC and UDR routinely attended meetings of a hitherto unknown organisation which planned and supervised the attacks. After listening to the tape-recording, I knew at once that if what I had just heard was true, this story was one of overwhelming public importance and that its publication would be bound to have profound implications for the RUC; indeed, I felt that the information was of such significance for the police force that publication could even threaten its very existence.

Sands was claiming that the scale of disaffection within the locally recruited security forces was far greater than anyone realised, so great that some police officers were even prepared to collude with the Loyalists in taking innocent Catholic lives, such as had happened in the case of Denis Carville. Contrary to what the RUC, the Stevens Inquiry and the British Government had publicly maintained and continued to assert, collusion in murder between the Loyalists and the police was routine, widespread, institutionalised and provided a frightening explanation for the terrifying and continuing Loyalist assassination campaign.

Sands explained the rationale behind the attacks by describing the anguish and trauma Protestant Ulster had experienced when it had digested the implications of the Anglo-Irish Agreement. It had been a turning point for Ulster Loyalists, the moment when everything they stood for, an exclusively British and Protestant Ulster, had been betrayed by London. When Margaret Thatcher had signed that document with Dublin she had, in Loyalist eyes, effectively ended the union. From that moment on, the Loyalist elite had begun to prepare for the ultimate betrayal of their province, a British disengagement in favour of a united Ireland governed from Dublin. During the period since the agreement had been signed, they had made preparations for the "doomsday situation" they knew to be looming, the day when Britain finally tired of the conflict and announced its complete withdrawal from the province.

Ulstermen and women had, Sands explained, already seized control of their destiny. They had created political and military institutions that would take control of Ulster as soon as the "doomsday situation" arrived.

The most important military institution on the Loyalist side was the body formed to fight the Anglo-Irish Agreement, Ulster Resistance. Although it had faded from the headlines after its inaugural meeting at the Ulster Hall, it had continued to recruit and train the men who would be the soldiers in a future Ulster Army, if and when the British had pulled out.

The most dramatic revelation made by Sands, however, was that Ulster Resistance and all the other main Loyalist paramilitary groups had come together under the control and direction of a new organisation, which had assumed full authority over all Loyalist military and political activity. This hitherto unknown body, the Ulster Loyalist Central Co-ordinating Committee, had—he estimated—between fifty and sixty members, and had been meeting once every six weeks for around two years. The Committee's membership was drawn from all sections of the Ulster Loyalist community, including the business and professional elite.

Sands informed Ben that its chairman, whose identity was a high-level secret, was Ulster Bank executive Billy Abernethy, the man who had chaired the meeting in the Dolphin Bar on the night, the previous September, when the Loyalist conspirators had set in train the events which led to the murder of Denis Carville. Another key figure in this supreme terrorist body—The Committee—was the outwardly respectable Presbyterian Minister who publicly championed the cause of Ulster Independence, "Reverend" Hugh Ross. Sands told Ben that each meeting of the terrorist Committee normally began with Ross leading the entire membership in prayers, daring to call down the Lord's blessing on the proceedings, before the assembled conspirators began the serious business of identifying the individuals whose lives they proposed to end.

The Committee, explained Sands, had quickly demonstrated the efficiency and effectiveness that came from exploiting the intelligence and expertise of its business and professional membership. These elites included a well-known local solicitor, Richard Monteith, and two of the richest businessmen in the province, brothers David and Albert Prentice. Their company, Prentice Garages, was familiar to many people in the province because it possessed the lucrative distributorships for BMW, Mercedes and other prestigious marques of motor car.

Ulster Resistance's leading representative was its chairman, John McCullagh, one of Abernethy's most trusted henchmen. Another Loyalist paramilitary group, the Ulster Volunteer Force, was represented by the Committee's number one hit-man Robin Jackson, known as "The Jackal." It was Jackson who had shot the three young Catholics at the mobile sweet shop in Craigavon and, according to Sands, local members of the RUC Inner Force had organised and supervised the attack. The Protestant Action Force, said Sands, was represented on the Committee by his former school friend Billy Wright, King Rat. And, as we have seen, it was King Rat who had murdered Denis Carville. The other main Loyalist terror groups, the Ulster Defence Association and the Ulster Freedom Fighters, also sent representatives; and as a result, claimed Sands, virtually every Loyalist murder during the previous two years had been sanctioned and organised by the Committee in collusion with disaffected RUC and UDR officers.

Disaffection within the RUC and UDR, Sands explained to Ben at some length, had resulted in the emergence within these two security forces of a secret and illegal third force, known as the "Inner Force." This body was composed of serving police officers within every RUC division in the province and each of these divisions sent representatives, who were said to be the most militant Loyalists within the force, to sit on a so-called RUC Inner Force Ulster Council. The members of this executive elite called themselves by yet another name, the "Inner Circle," and it was this top-level, unofficial police body which supervised the operational assistance given to the Loyalist squads by rank and file RUC officers across the province.[3] Typically, as members of the Inner Force, these regular police officers guided the squads to their targets and, after the killings, ensured that they were escorted safely away from the scene of the crimes.

Sands himself attended meetings of the unofficial RUC Inner Circle and also of the ultimate organisation of Loyalist terror, the Committee. In both cases, he represented the Ulster Independence Committee, the voice of Ulster nationalism that had evolved out of the earlier Movement for Self-Determination.[4] By 1991, supporters of independence had secretly forged an alliance with Ulster Resistance and had—Sands explained—become the equivalent on the Loyalist side of Sinn Féin, the political wing of Republican terror, the Provisional IRA. Indeed, Sands explicitly drew this parallel between the two terrorist movements in Northern Ireland when he told Ben that Loyalists viewed Billy Abernethy as "something like the Loyalist equivalent of Gerry Adams. Nothing happens except it goes through him, militarily or politically, in the whole of Northern Ireland."

By 1991, the shadowy and unknown Ulster Bank executive and former RUC Reserve policeman, Billy Abernethy, had become as important as any IRA figure in determining what was happening on the streets of Northern Ireland. Abernethy's Committee had, according to Sands, already murdered seven people in the month of March and he predicted, correctly, that many more Catholics would die before the year was out.

But could we believe what Sands was telling us? Was he exaggerating or, even worse, was he inventing the entire story? Did he not realise the implications of admitting his involvement in such a murder conspiracy? What, if his story was true, would Abernethy and his friends do to him if they learned he was talking to Channel 4? These were some of the questions in our minds as we decided, at the end of April 1991, to invite Jim Sands to visit us in London.

Notes

1 The BBC paid substantial damages to several Tory MPs in an out-of-court settlement of a libel action over *"Maggie's Militant Tendency,"* a *Panorama* programme on the activities of some of Margaret Thatcher's followers in Parliament. These MPs included Neil Hamilton, who was later disgraced for asking questions in the House of Commons in return for cash payments from corporate clients. Ironically, his downfall resulted from the collapse, in 1996, of another libel action, one which he had brought against *The Guardian* newspaper. By that time, however, the morale of BBC journalists had plummeted and *Panorama* had entered the long decline from which it has yet to recover.

2 *Death on the Rock—Report of Inquiry* by Lord Windlesham and Richard Rampton QC. Faber & Faber, London, 1989.

3 We have already seen that a man, claiming to be an RUC officer from this Inner Circle had visited *The Irish News* in Belfast in October 1989, where he had declared his readiness to murder Republicans in "the battle for the survival of Ulster." [See Chapter 2, pp. 15–16]

4 The President of the Ulster Independence Committee was, as he has remained to date [February 1998], "Reverend" Hugh Ross.

Chapter 4

THE CONSPIRACY

Sands flew into Heathrow airport from Belfast on Friday morning, May 3rd, where Ben was waiting to take him to his hotel in London's West End. At their last meeting in Lurgan, a few days earlier, he had accepted Ben's invitation to come and give us a filmed interview in London. The tape-recording of that conversation, which still exists, reveals that Sands raised the question of payment at an early stage. "Will there be any fee involved?" he had tentatively enquired. Fortunately, in view of accusations that would later be made against us, Ben's reply had been a model of good journalistic practice. His reply, as diplomatic as it was unequivocal, left Sands in no doubt where we stood on the issue. "That's not normally something that we're very happy about," Ben had said, "because, if we pay people to appear, it looks like we're bribing them." Sands was told that he would be paid his expenses and nothing more.

I met Jim Sands for the first time, shortly after he had checked into the modest hotel we had chosen for him. He had arranged with Ben to use the name "Robert McGrath," an alias which amused him because it was, he claimed, a name which Billy Abernethy used on occasions when he thought it wise not to employ his own. So when I arrived at the hotel, near Marble Arch, Ben introduced him to me as "Robert," even though I already knew his true identity. At that stage, Ben and I were the only people involved in the project who possessed this sensitive item of information. In our dealings with Channel 4, we had already begun to refer to him as Source A, the practice we were to follow right up to the transmission of the programme in October and, indeed, for a long time thereafter.

Having listened to the recordings of Sands's conversations with Ben, I was already familiar with his voice and manner. On meeting him, I found his appearance and personality to be, more or less, what I had been led to expect. He was short, somewhat overweight and had the genial appearance of a monk, due to his round, cherubic face and page-boy haircut. He was quietly spoken, obviously uneducated but the occasional flashes of humour showed that, behind the near permanent grin, there was a cunning brain;

and it gradually became clear to me that he was talking about people whom he knew well and whom he revered because of the success of their ongoing assassination campaign. It was still hard to believe, though, that I was talking to a member of the murder conspiracy, someone who had, on his own admission, helped to plan such cruel and heartless deeds as the murder of Denis Carville or the three killings at the mobile sweet shop in Craigavon some weeks earlier.

I was accompanied at that first meeting by _____, an experienced television director who was working with us on a different film and who had kindly agreed, at short notice, to take charge of the technical aspects of the interview with Sands, which we planned to do the following day. The director reassured "Robert" that his features and voice would be altered so dramatically that even his own mother, were she to watch the interview on her television screen, would be quite unable to recognise him. Sands was repeatedly assured that there was no danger of Abernethy or anyone from the RUC knocking on his door, as a result of his being identified in the film. And so, after talking to him for a couple of hours, _____ and I made our way to Channel 4, where we had been summoned to a meeting with Liz Forgan, the network's top editorial executive. Liz was anxious that we fully appreciated the importance of satisfying all legal and regulatory conditions relating to the interview scheduled for the following day, Saturday, May 4th 1991.

I knew that Liz Forgan didn't waste her time on meetings she had no reason to attend. I was wary of her because, on the last occasion I had been summoned to a similar meeting in her office, she had instantly dispatched me to the Caribbean island of Haiti in search of evidence to justify allegations I was proposing to make about a controversial entrepreneur in London; on my return, she allowed our programme to be shown but only after she had been convinced that the evidence would stand up in court.[1] On this occasion, she was equally brisk and decisive. We were, she said, proposing that she agree to transmit a programme in which an anonymous source would accuse the police of collusion in murder. These would be allegations of the utmost gravity and it was, she insisted, imperative that we conduct the interview with this Loyalist in strict conformity with the legal advice the channel had received.

That advice required us to establish, at the outset of the interview, that Sands did not belong to any illegal or proscribed organisation. If, for example, he had admitted to membership of the Ulster Volunteer Force— an infamous Loyalist terror group and a proscribed organisation—we would have had to stop the interview at once. Since the existence of Abernethy's Committee was not publicly known, the organisation had obviously not been proscribed and there was, therefore, no legal impediment to conducting the proposed interview with one of its members. We were also warned about the legal pitfalls of the Prevention of Terrorism Act [PTA] which—we were advised—makes it a criminal offence for an individual to˙acquire information about *future* acts of terrorism in Northern Ireland and fail to pass that information on to the authorities, without reasonable excuse; fortunately, this advice suggested that we were not facing any insuperable problem because, as far as we knew, Sands was not in possession of any such information. So, we noted the importance of focusing our questions on Sands's *past* activities and the meeting ended with Liz Forgan indicating that she was broadly satisfied that we appreciated the delicacy of our assignment.[2]

Next morning, we all gathered at Sands's hotel and set off to a terraced house in Kilburn in north-west London, our production manager's home, where we met the film crew and began preparations for the interview. We had invited Martin O'Hagan over from Belfast because we felt his presence would make Sands feel more at ease. I also wished to be able to tap into Martin's knowledge about Loyalist paramilitaries and about the various attacks they had carried out. Our director took responsibility for altering the appearance of our interviewee, turning his pageboy hair-cut into something more flamboyant, a bouffant which altered the profile of his head. He was also persuaded to wear a leather jacket which we borrowed from a member of the film crew. Sands was placed with his back to a window and filmed against the light so that his face was in shade, making it difficult to perceive any distinguishing features. Sands was reassured once more that the image recorded by the camera would, subsequently, be distorted during the editing process. Once all the relevant technical matters were arranged to everyone's satisfaction the interview got under way.

Ben, who sat just behind the camera, asked all the questions. Throughout the interview, I sat at his elbow and listened intently to every word Sands uttered, intervening as and when I thought it necessary. Liz Forgan was not physically present but she might as well have been. For I was vigilant in ensuring that we all obeyed her instructions, as I did not relish the prospect of appearing in front of her, making excuses for any serious blunder, for having allowed something to happen which might compromise Box Productions or Channel 4. I was keenly aware that the interview with Sands, alias "Robert," alias Source A, was a pivotal event in the production and I was determined that the filming would go as smoothly as we had planned.

We started off by asking Sands to confirm, which he did, that he was not a member of a proscribed organisation. He then proceeded, in a hesitant and painfully slow manner, to give us an unremarkable account of the frustration, anger and disenchantment Ulster Loyalists felt towards Britain as a result of the 1985 signing of the Anglo-Irish Agreement. He became a little more animated and sounded more convincing when he moved on to talk about the conspiracy in which he claimed to be involved; he began by describing the emergence of two secret Loyalist groupings within the RUC, a pressure group called the Inner Force and the more extreme, more Loyalist, Inner Circle.

> So then, it developed within the Inner Force a group known as the Inner Circle, who were more militant, more Loyalist members of the RUC. And gradually, it progressed that the way forward was to take out the terrorists. Shoot, take out known IRA men. Take out people who, from police intelligence sources, from police files, people who were known terrorists. So, then, gradually links were forged with Loyalist paramilitary organisations. That Loyalist paramilitary organisations would carry out the elimination process backed up by good, sound information from RUC files supplied by members of the Inner Circle, who were also members of the Inner Force.

After he had explained that the Inner Force was organised, like the RUC itself, on a divisional basis across the province, with representatives from police stations in each division, he went on to make the startling claim about the scale of the alleged disaffection within the police force.

> Now, within the Inner Force, you have roughly a third of the RUC membership. That includes full-time, part-time and Police Reserve. It's organised on a local police station level. Most of the major police stations have a section of the Inner Force. The smaller outlying police stations would come under the nearest large police station. You have towns like Dungannon, Portadown, Lurgan, which would have ninety per cent Inner Force. You would have other towns, Coleraine, Antrim, Larne, Newtownards, Bangor, which would be between eighty to ninety per cent. You would have places along the border, Enniskillen, Omagh, Castlederg, Bessbrook, Forkhill, Newry would be about sixty to seventy per cent. The men that's on the front line, men that's living in what is seen as terrorist territory.

These were bold assertions which, I thought, might or might not turn out to be true. They would have to be tested in the weeks and months ahead. As the camera rolled, Ben then moved on to ask Sands about the existence of the secret organisation which was said to control and direct the activities of the Loyalist death squads. His reply gives a detailed summary of the composition of the Committee and is an exclusive, insider's account of the mechanics of the alleged murder conspiracy. As we read the transcript of Sands's answer, we should bear in mind the official verdict of the Stevens Inquiry, published just a year earlier, namely that collusion between the Loyalists and the British security forces was not "widespread or institutionalised."

> Operations are all controlled by the Ulster Central Co-ordinating Committee, which is made up of representatives of various groups. The political side is overseen by representatives from the Ulster Independence Party. There's representatives from the Inner Force. There's representatives from Ulster Resistance. There's also representatives from the Ulster Volunteer Force, as well as the Ulster Freedom Fighters. There's also representatives from the Ulster Defence Regiment. It is—the Committee is—it's just a committee bringing together all viewpoints of Ulster Loyalism. All organisations, political, military, paramilitary, all voiced on the Committee. Each Loyalist organisation has representatives able to bring the views of their particular organisation. Normally, for an operation to be carried out, the Inner Force would bring names with files stating that there was certain terrorists which needed to be eliminated. The Committee would discuss this, they would discuss all the implications, the political as well as the military implications. If the Committee so decides that he is to be eliminated, it would then be handed back to the relevant, local Inner Force or Inner Circle squad in conjunction with the local Loyalist hit squad. And then they will plan and organise the elimination. And it will be then left to the Inner Force to organise and to pick the date and pick the time when an action is carried out. It would be totally in the hands of the Inner Circle, the Inner Force to organise and to direct the Loyalist squad.

The Committee, he revealed, had been in existence since the middle of 1986 but it had been "organised effectively in operation" for less than a year, since the summer of 1990. This meant that the conspiracy had been running for more than four years without any hint of its existence coming publicly to light. Sands also revealed precise details of the composition of the Committee's membership, giving us an insight into the importance of the Ulster Independence Party, which provided more than a third of the members—a total of twenty-two representatives led by Presbyterian Minister Hugh Ross and which included Sands himself. The Committee's second largest grouping was the unofficial RUC Inner Circle and Inner Force contingent—a total of eighteen members; all of them were said to be or to have been senior figures in the RUC, the two most important being ex-Head of Special Branch Trevor Forbes and a serving, though unnamed, Assistant Chief Constable. Sands had previously told Ben that Forbes, also a former Assistant Chief Constable, was a key figure in the conspiracy and that he had regularly passed RUC files on Republicans to the Committee, handing them to well-known Loyalist politician and Ulster Unionist Party member, Frazer Agnew.[3] The rest of the membership, a further twenty individuals, were said to have been drawn from all classes in the Protestant community and especially from the main Loyalist paramilitary organisations; these people, Sands said, included "prominent individual people . . . such as solicitors, accountants, people with knowledge of banks, as well as prominent businessmen."

As the interview progressed, Sands began to talk more freely and he appeared to enjoy the experience of being at the centre of so much attention. He had no evident difficulty in recalling such details as, for example, the names of the various towns where the Committee had met. And when Ben asked him to identify precisely the locations for these meetings, he was able to list them, one after another, without any tell-tale sign of hesitation or uncertainty. As I listened to his replies, on my guard for any sign or clue that he was not what he was claiming to be, I gradually became convinced that I was listening to someone who was talking about his personal experiences, meetings he had attended and discussions he had witnessed. I believed he was telling the truth.

> The meetings have taken place in Armagh Orange Hall, in Killicomaine Community Centre, the Seagoe Hotel in Portadown, Mourneview Community Centre in Lurgan, Banbridge Orange Hall, Newcastle Orange Hall, the Slievedonard Hotel in Newcastle, Portrush Presbyterian Church Hall.

The Committee's two previous monthly meetings, in March and April 1991, had been held at the Magherabuoy House Hotel in Portrush and at the Inn on the Park Hotel in Dungannon, the latter owned by the [Loyalist] Orange Order—dates which we had already learned from an earlier, tape-recorded conversation between Sands and Ben. So, within half an hour of the start of the filmed interview in London, we had obtained a detailed account of the alleged Committee's composition and past meetings; we had learned that most of its meetings had taken place in the east and south-east of the province—many within the notorious "murder triangle"—where Loyalist representation is strongest and, as we've seen, the sectarian conflict is most naked and raw.

One of Sands's central themes, repeated several times in the filmed interview, was that the recruitment of middle-class professionals had resulted in a more united, more integrated effort. By bringing all the various Loyalist factions together in one umbrella organisation—the Committee—these professionals had created a uniquely efficient body; it was not run as a political party, nor even as another, more powerful paramilitary organisation. "It's run as a business, with business expertise being given by experienced people . . . Nothing happens now without actually getting the go-ahead from the central Committee." This "business," which was pledged to the elimination of the Republican menace, was—Sands revealed—managed as a joint venture between the professionals and senior police officers belonging to the RUC Inner Force. "The Loyalists will not move without the Inner Force giving the okay."

> The Inner Force is organised on an all Ulster basis. Therefore, they're able to move throughout Ulster. They can move anywhere at will. People from within the Inner Force boast that no terrorist is safe, no Republican is safe in Ulster. The terrorists can be removed at will, if and when the Inner Force decide.

As the interview progressed, I wondered whether Sands realised the significance of what he was telling us, knowing that we intended to publish his revelations in a nationally networked documentary on Channel 4. Already, less than an hour into the interview, he had claimed that, contrary to the repeated assurances of the British Government, the two most important security forces in the province, the RUC and UDR, were effectively at the disposal of the Loyalists, giving this unknown terrorist Committee the ability to eliminate anyone it wished within Northern Ireland. As I listened to him calmly unveiling the facts about the murder conspiracy, I felt that if what Sands was telling us turned out to be true and we were ever to be able to prove that it was true, the RUC Chief Constable would soon find himself in an untenable position. Sir Hugh Annesley could be out of a job and the British Government would have little choice but to start afresh by creating a new and genuinely impartial police force for Northern Ireland.

As we were all well aware of the British Government's repeated denials of the existence of collusion, we asked Sands to explain how the Committee had managed to run such an elaborate murder conspiracy, without any hint of its existence and composition ever having reached the ears of the Stevens Inquiry. Sands appeared to relish our question and to take particular pleasure in revealing information about how the efforts of Mr. Stevens and his team had been sabotaged by senior officers within the RUC Inner Force. The Committee, we were told, had been able to monitor the Inquiry's progress at every stage and had regularly tipped off Inner Force officers in advance, warning them that investigators would soon be arriving at their RUC stations.

> . . . the Inner Force were able to report back to the Ulster Central Co-ordinating Committee the movements, what was actually going on with the Stevens team. You actually had a situation where drivers from the RUC were appointed to drive the team about Northern Ireland, by members of the Inner Force. That's

why the Inner Force were able to report back to the Central Co-ordinating Committee where the Stevens Inquiry team were planning to go. Normally, they had like a week's plan, a week in advance, so really the Loyalists knew where Stevens was going a week before he went . . . they were able to give a week's notice so that their tracks could be covered.

Sands went on to make an even more startling revelation about the Inner Force's alleged sabotage of the Stevens team's efforts; he described how the Committee had invited a number of RUC officers to one of its meetings, following the outbreak of a fire at the Stevens team's offices in Carrickfergus, County Antrim.

They also brought the people from the Inner Force who had set the fire in the office, because to the Loyalists, it was a great joke. To the Loyalists it was something to laugh about, as the whole inquiry was seen as a joke among the Loyalists . . . The official line was that it was a member of the Inquiry team that had accidentally thrown a cigarette into a waste paper basket, which had started the fire, that was the official line. But the fire was actually started a number of hours after the last member of the Inquiry team had left the building. You had a situation where members of the Inquiry team came into the canteen [in RUC Headquarters] and you had members of the RUC, the Inner Force, sitting in the canteen who broke into song, "We did not start the fire." The Inquiry team was seen as a joke. It was seen as something that was coming into Ulster to sort of lighten up the lives of the Ulster people.

Such was the contempt for the Stevens Inquiry within the RUC, said Sands, that disaffected officers even went so far as to suggest that collusion, the subject under investigation by the English policeman, could be traced to the very top of the RUC. The officers had pinned a notice on the door of the Chief Constable himself; and the words on the notice, said Sands, had been: "Head of RUC Inner Force."[4]

Once we had recorded a full account of what we might call the Committee's standard operating procedure, we moved on to ask Sands about five different attacks, sanctioned and organised by the Committee, in which a total of ten people had been murdered by Loyalist squads. In all five cases, Sands had been present at Committee meetings which had either discussed and approved the attack or, as in the case of Denis Carville, assessed the manner in which the assassination had been carried out.[5] He was able, therefore, to give reliable first-hand testimony about the Committee meetings where RUC Inner Force members colluded with fellow Loyalists on the overall strategy of the ongoing assassination campaign. Sands did not participate directly in any of the attacks but he wit-

nessed and participated in lengthy discussions when the assassins reported back to the Committee on how the actual operations had been carried
out. One such operation was the murder of Denis Carville.

The revelations about Denis's murder, laid out at the beginning of this
book, were made to us by Sands on four separate occasions, twice in his
tape-recorded conversations with Ben in Lurgan, once in his filmed interview in London and, finally, in conversation over dinner after we had completed filming on Saturday, May 4th 1991.[6] Sands appeared to appreciate
that the Committee's individual members were especially vulnerable over
this killing because they knew that the dead youth had been an entirely
innocent Catholic, murdered simply because of his religion, someone
whose death could not be justified by an appeal to his or to his family's presumed political sympathies. Sands knew, as we did, that Denis's murder
had been especially shocking because it had been a naked sectarian killing.
So Ben and I were particularly keen to obtain from Sands a precise
account of how the murder had been arranged. Ben began the questioning, speaking quietly and with a simple question: "How did it come about
that Denis Carville was shot by the King Rat?" What follows below is the
complete, unedited transcript of what Sands replied about how this murder had taken place.[7]

> Previous there was a young UDR man called Colin McCullough
> [who] was shot just more or less [at] the same spot and so, that
> the IRA would know that there was going to be direct retaliation,
> they wanted someone who was in the same situation, a young man
> sitting with his girlfriend in the car, so that the message would go
> to the IRA that we will have direct retaliation. So the Inner Force,
> they met with King Rat, some of his squad, to plan and set up the
> operation. They then, on the night, [the] Inner Force car went
> round the car park at Lough Neagh where Colin McCullough had
> been killed, and they were just checking on cars, checking on doc-
> uments of cars, just to pick out somebody who was in a similar
> situation as Colin McCullough. And they checked a few cars.
> They then decided that there was a car that was very similar to
> Colin McCullough and, just by luck or bad luck, Denis Carville
> was picked. The number was radioed through to Lurgan police
> station. It was confirmed that the car came from a Roman
> Catholic area, therefore it was a Roman Catholic car. The Inner
> Force then went to pick up King Rat, who was sitting in his car in
> the car park of the Silverwood Hotel in Lurgan. They then
> brought him in, pointed out the target. King Rat walked up to the
> car, and as the RUC had been or the Inner Force had been previ-
> ously looking, checking on people's identification, King Rat asked
> for identification. While Denis Carville was looking for his iden-
> tification, his driving licence, King Rat shot him. King Rat then

got into his car and was carried out of the area by the Inner Force car and, seeing that he was safely home, they went back to duty.

Q: So it was an on-duty police car?

A: Yes.

Q: And whose idea was it to show direct retaliation for murders that the IRA made?

A: Just previous to that there was a statement went out from the Loyalists saying that there would be retaliation, there would be retaliation for any crimes committed by the Provisional IRA and, Colin McCullough from Lurgan, they wanted to show that— because previously people within Ulster had bluffed and had talked about what they would do. They wanted to show the Provisional IRA that we will carry out direct retaliation. Then, when it was reported back to the meeting, everyone was very well pleased that that had been carried out completely successful. And again, it showed very good co-operation between the Inner Force and the Loyalist squads.

Q: Were you saying that the RUC set up Denis Carville to be hit by the King Rat because he was a Roman Catholic?

A: There really wasn't time to plan to have a Republican sitting at Lough [Neagh] car park with his girlfriend. It wasn't something that could be set up. It wasn't something that would maybe be able to be arranged, but something was needed to be done quick. And so that the IRA would know that the Loyalists would not just bluff. That when they said direct retaliation, there will be direct retaliation.[8]

Q: Do you think it's acceptable to have innocent casualties?

A: In war situations, the way the Ulster people look, the Ulster Loyalist Committee look on [it], in a war situation, is there any innocent?

Q: Are you saying that the RUC singled out Denis Carville for retaliation because if you did not have a Republican, a Roman Catholic would do?

A: The Inner Force went in, first of all, to pick out a target to hit, that would be somebody in a similar situation as Colin McCullough. If, by some chance, there was a known Republican sitting there with his girlfriend, he would have been the obvious target. But that wasn't the case. Never come across a known Republican. And they wanted it done that night so that in a short space of time, that there would be no mistake that the Provos were getting the message that this is in direct retaliation for Colin McCullough. So the person that the Inner Force picked out for King Rat to kill was Denis Carville.

Now, when it was discussed at the Central Co-ordinating Committee after the event, there was a file that had come from the Inner Force in Lurgan stating that Denis Carville had sympathies towards the Republican movement. Now, if that had not have been there, there would maybe have been questions asked at the Central Co-ordinating Committee why an innocent Catholic was targeted and why not just abort the operation? But because the file showed that he had Republican sympathies, that they felt there was nothing wrong with the operation. But, actually at the time when they pointed Denis Carville out, they didn't know if there was any Republican sympathies within his family or within himself. They didn't know that at the time. He was just picked out because he was a Roman Catholic in a similar situation as Colin McCullough.

Denis's murder was condemned in the most forthright terms by both Catholic and Protestant leaders in Northern Ireland. "A disgrace to Protestants" was the verdict of the Church of Ireland's leader, Dr. Robin (now Lord) Eames. "Ruthless and beyond comprehension" were the words used by Monsignor Christopher Murray at the funeral Mass. Civic leaders also expressed their outrage. "The people responsible for this murder," declared Alderman James McCammick, Mayor of Craigavon, "have no place in our society."

Denis's representative in the House of Commons, recently elected in a by-election and a future leader of the Ulster Unionist Party, David Trimble MP, was quoted by the local newspaper as saying that it was sad that "some idiots have gone and taken the law into their own hands." The newspaper report did not expand on this bizarre comment, nor did it identify either the law the idiots were supposed to have been enforcing or the one Denis was being presumed to have broken.[9] Trimble subsequently paid a brief visit to the Carville home but the dead youth's parents, though unaware of their MP's association with members of the Committee, declined to talk to him.

All these public reactions, Trimble's aside, were in sharp contrast to the opinions expressed within the Committee when, shortly after the funeral, the conspirators met to discuss the killing and its consequences. All the members were, according to Sands "very well pleased" at what had been a "completely successful" operation. Denis's murder, they felt, was evidence of "very good co-operation" between the RUC Inner Force and the Loyalist squads.

In its front-page report on the funeral, the Dublin newspaper *Sunday World* carried an intriguing story, given that the identity of the killer was publicly unknown:

> The cold-blooded Loyalist killer of 19-year-old Lurgan youth Denis Carville turned up at the young man's funeral on Tuesday dressed as a mourner. The murderer was spotted standing at the top of the town's Francis Street, next to the dead man's home in Parkside Street. The killer was wearing a neatly-cut suit and a black tie. He was accompanied by another man and they were

later joined by a third known Protestant paramilitary . . . Then the killer, along with his two cronies, walked along Edward Street where one of them had parked a car . . . Loyalist sources claim the mid-Ulster UVF intends to kill a Catholic for every Protestant member of the security forces murdered by the [IRA] Provos—using the new hit-man who likes to watch his victims being buried.

This report was written by Lurgan journalist Martin O'Hagan on the basis of information provided by one of the "cronies," Martin's friend, Jim Sands. Martin was told by Sands that it was he who had been standing near the chapel, watching silently as the hearse made its way to the graveyard. At that moment, the killer, Billy Wright, alias King Rat, had walked up to Sands, had stood beside him and then spoke the following words to his friend in a quiet voice: "I just came to make sure he was dead."

It is fitting that the last word on this terrible crime should be given to Denis's mother, Jean, for whom the memory of that night is as vivid now as it was at the time. Her Catholic faith assures her that justice will eventually be done, if not in this world, then certainly in the world to come. Her only public comment about her son's murder was made just after the funeral: "I would rather be in Denis's place tonight than in the place of the man who pulled the trigger."

To this day, nobody has been arrested or charged with the murder of Denis Carville.

****

Seven months before the murder of Denis Carville, another Lurgan Catholic was also shot dead by a Loyalist squad. In this case, the Catholic population of the town mourned the dead man on its own. There were no similar expressions of regret, condemnation or outrage from the Protestant community. For the murder victim, thirty-one-year-old Sam Marshall, had not only proclaimed his Republican sympathies and campaigned on behalf of Sinn Féin, the IRA's political wing, he had served a six-year prison sentence for a terrorist offence and was facing another terrorist charge at the time of his death. The controversy, which erupted immediately after this killing, served only to deepen the divisions in the town because the Catholics alleged that he had been a victim of collusion between the police and the Loyalists; the Protestants, in so far as they were aware of the dead man's Republican activities, would undoubtedly have sided with the RUC. By early 1991, when we had begun our research in the area, Sam Marshall's death had become a focus for Catholic suspicions about collusion but, in the absence of irrefutable evidence about any RUC role in his death, the police were able confidently to dismiss the allegations as malicious Republican propaganda.

Catholics suspected collusion in this case because of the circumstances surrounding the murder. The attack had occurred in darkness, on the night of Wednesday, March 7th 1990, shortly after Sam Marshall and two Republican friends—Colin Duffy and Tony McCaughey—had left Lurgan's RUC station, where they had just signed their names in the police register as part of their bail conditions. All three had been arrested in January 1990 and charged with the possession of ammunition; the police had found ten bullets in a raid on McCaughey's home, where Duffy and Marshall were visiting at the time. When the three were later released on bail, they were required to report twice a week to Lurgan RUC station. Information about the dates and times of their obligatory visits to the police station was, at that time, highly sensitive because, as three well-known Republicans, they were all potential targets for Loyalist terrorists; so only a few people—their solicitor, the RUC officers based in Lurgan police station and, naturally, the three men themselves—were allowed to have this information, which they were supposed to keep to themselves.

On the night in question, however, it appeared that others had managed to find out the precise time that the three Republicans would be making their way from their homes to the RUC station in Lurgan's town centre. For, as the three Republicans walked towards the police station, they noticed that they were being tailed by the occupants of a red Maestro car—registration number KJI 1486—which was driven past them a number of times. Their suspicions deepened when, as they came out of the RUC station, they also noticed that two men were standing inside the security post just outside the station, an unusual occurrence because they knew that this post was never manned at night, for security reasons; as the post was slightly above head level, the three men were unable to see whether the two occupants were wearing RUC uniforms but they did establish that the two were not wearing RUC caps. Suspecting that the two post occupants were there so that they could radio a surveillance message to their colleagues in police cars, the three Republicans decided they would proceed directly in the direction of their homes. Almost immediately, they again spotted the red Maestro and, having done so, they waved to the driver to signal that they were aware they were being followed.

When they had walked about a third of the distance back to their homes, the three noticed another car, a red Rover, as it drove past them travelling towards the town centre; and they saw that it contained three men. A few minutes later, the Rover passed them a second time, now travelling away from town in the same direction as they were walking. By now, the three friends realised that they were in danger and Sam Marshall commented anxiously: "We were let out to be set up." These proved to be the last words he would ever speak because the Rover stopped abruptly in front of him and his friends; the car doors opened and two men, armed with rifles, jumped out and started firing. Sam Marshall fell to the ground, wounded in the legs and unable to move. His two friends, who had escaped serious injury, managed to flee. Sam Marshall's short life was now almost over. For, as he lay bleeding on the road, one of the two gunmen ran towards him, pointed the rifle at his head and fired two shots, killing him instantly.

After the murder, the gunmen climbed back into their car but, according to eye-witnesses, they displayed no concern about making a quick getaway. They continued shooting, firing their weapons into the air and, for some minutes, drove around a nearby Catholic housing estate, as if looking to find the two survivors who had raced down an alleyway into the estate. Local residents, alerted by the gunfire, spotted both cars in the estate and they later testified that one of them, the red Maestro, had been parked inside the estate at the exact moment of the shooting. The gunmen's apparent lack of concern about being intercepted by an RUC or British Army patrol led many in the Catholic community to allege that there must have been some form of collusion between the Loyalists and the security forces. Although the attack had happened within hearing distance of Lurgan's RUC station, a mere six hundred yards away, the Loyalist assassins seemed to know they had nothing to fear. That, at least, is what Lurgan Catholics believed at the time and it is the reason they later organised a protest march in the town, on the first anniversary of Sam Marshall's murder.

These allegations of collusion had spread throughout the town's Catholic community within days of the killing. In supporting the allegations, the Marshall family pointed out that only the police, the three men themselves and their solicitor were supposed to have known the date and time set for the bail signing; the family accused the police of having leaked this crucially sensitive information to the Loyalist squad. The Marshall family also wrote to the RUC Chief Constable, asking him to state whether the red Maestro, with the registration number KJI 1486 noted by the eye witnesses, had been an RUC surveillance vehicle.

Subsequently, the Chief Constable replied to the collusion allegations, indicating that the red Maestro had been "eliminated from police enquiries" but carefully refraining from giving a categoric answer as to whether the red Maestro had or had not belonged to the RUC or to any other branch of the security forces. The RUC Press Office told reporters that the Marshall murder had been a "foul, evil crime and it will be investigated as painstakingly, thoroughly and impartially as any other murder." But this reassuring message from RUC Headquarters in Belfast failed totally to convince Lurgan's Catholics that the RUC had not, in some shape or form, been implicated in the Marshall murder. Before long, graffiti began to appear on walls in the town, accusing the RUC in general and, in particular, the police officer who had been in charge of the three men's bail conditions, Inspector Alan Clegg. Some months after the murder Mr. Clegg produced the RUC's official report on the crime and concluded that the allegations of collusion, including those directed against him, were without foundation:

> The investigation uncovered no evidence of any nature to confirm the suggestions of police collusion with any organisation in carrying out the attack.

His report also noted that the red Rover, which had been stolen some time before the attack, had been found burnt-out some time after the murder, around forty-five miles away from Lurgan. But he made no reference at all to the car which had aroused so much suspicion among Lurgan Catholics about police collusion in the crime, the red Maestro, registration number KJI 1486.

Before our introduction to Jim Sands and our subsequent discovery of the existence of the Committee, we had investigated the background to the murder of Sam Marshall in an attempt to establish whether the collusion allegations were justified. Although we concluded that the circumstantial evidence—the surveillance cars, the mysterious occupants of the external security post, the apparent leak of the sensitive information about the timing of the bail signings, the gang's seeming indifference to their possible apprehension—strongly suggested that the Loyalists had been helped, we also knew that we had found nothing conclusive, no irrefutable evidence that would have stood up to rigorous examination in a court of law. Still, we felt that the Marshall case was well worth further investigation because we had no doubt that the RUC was being less than frank about many aspects of the attack; there was, we thought, a possibility that we might eventually find out the full story about Sam Marshall's murder.

Before Sands came over to be interviewed in London, I had already listened to what he had told Ben about this murder; their tape-recorded conversations were full of details on the killing. For example, he had already told us that the killing had been carried out by the Committee's most experienced assassin, Robin Jackson, The Jackal. Sands had been so forthcoming about the RUC's role in this murder that we had decided that, once the London interview was under way, we would ask him to describe the background at some length. How had it come about, we asked, that Sam Marshall had been shot?

> The Inner Force saw it as a good opportunity not only to remove Sam Marshall but to remove two other known Republicans from

Lurgan. He was attending Lurgan police station as part of a condition of bail. They seen that just as an opportunity that could not be missed, to remove three known Republicans. The operation was discussed. It was decided that it would be left in, as usual, in the hands of the Inner Force to organise. The Jackal and his squad were picked to carry out the operation. They were then briefed by the Inner Force, they were taken and shown the route that was in all probability would be taken by the Republicans going to Lurgan police station. They were briefed on who the people were. They were briefed on their connections to the Republican movement. Then they come to the actual day of the operation they were told approximately when he would be attending the police station.

It was arranged that there would be two cars. That one car would follow when they were coming from Kilwilkie in Lurgan, in the car there would be a driver, there would be a member of the Inner Force plus a gunman, and whenever they felt that an opportunity arises to carry out the operation that the operation would be carried out. But on the walk up from the estate to the police station there was no opportunity arose to carry out the operation. So then the second car, again with a driver a member of the Inner Force, the second car, the gunman was The Jackal himself and they had to just sit and wait for the three Republicans coming out of Lurgan police station. Again they were briefed that they would follow the three men on their way back to the Kilwilkie estate and with the opportunity that they would be able to carry out the operation. When the three men came out of the police station on their way home, the opportunity arose where The Jackal thought he could do the job, so he just riddled the street, shot everywhere. After the event, he said that he was surprised that he only hit Sam Marshall. But the occupants of the first car had went into the pillar box of the police station, for whatever reason was never made clear, but that's where they went, probably to keep out of sight in case they were seen by passers-by, so that there'd be no witnesses.

After the operation, the Inner Force as usual gave The Jackal and his squad a safe passage back to their homes. Again, it was reported back to the Central Co-ordinating Committee that the operation had been successful, but disappointment that there was only one casualty. But overall they felt that, felt it had been a success and that, again, the Republican movement would know that the Loyalists are not, not bluffing.

Q: And there were police officers in both cars?

A: Yes. They like to pinpoint the people. The Inner Force like to be there, so they can oversee the operations, that they can see the operations are done professionally. They bring their sort of RUC training, and a lot of people say, to good use.

Q: When Sam Marshall and his friends were signing on their bail at Lurgan police station, did the police officers who were meeting them there, did they know that they were about to be killed?

A: Lurgan police station, being ninety per cent Inner Force, I'd be very surprised they didn't, because probably it would have been discussed at local level. It would have been discussed at the local Lurgan police station level and then, probably, would have been discussed at divisional level before actually going into operation.

Sands had discussed the Marshall killing with Ben, almost a month before the London interview, when they had met in Lurgan on April 8th 1991. On that occasion, he had explained that two off-duty policemen from the Inner Force in Lurgan's RUC station, one in each car, had participated in the murder. Now, in his filmed interview, Sands confirmed this but he also provided two additional and significant revelations: namely that the three men in the red Maestro would have killed Sam Marshall and his two comrades before they reached the police station, if an opportunity to attack them had arisen; and that two of the red Maestro's three occupants had moved into the RUC's external security post when the three Republicans were signing on for bail inside the police station. The attack had gone so smoothly, according to Sands's original account, because the man in charge of Lurgan RUC station, Inspector Alan Clegg, was a member of the Inner Force; and it was in that capacity that he had leaked to the Loyalists the highly sensitive information about the dates and times Sam Marshall and his two friends would be visiting his police station.

Two years after Sam Marshall's murder, in June 1992, a Loyalist UVF member, Victor Graham, was put on trial for many terrorist crimes; he confessed to having helped with the hijacking of the red Rover car used in the Marshall murder and received a life sentence. But Graham did not mention the role played by the Committee, nor did he reveal any information about his accomplices.

To this day, none of those directly involved in the killing have been arrested or charged with the murder of Sam Marshall.

****

Before his visit to London, Sands had told Ben that Robin Jackson was also responsible for the atrocity that had occurred in Craigavon (near Portadown) two months earlier, March 1991. The Jackal had been the leader of a six-man squad which had attacked the mobile sweet shop in the belief, which turned out to be mistaken, that they would be able to kill its owner, a Republican called John Jenkinson. Sands had already told Ben that the Committee had sanctioned this attack and that it had been organised by serving officers within the RUC Inner Force. So, during the filmed interview, we invited him to expand on his earlier account, asking him to take us through the various steps leading up to the murders of seventeen-year-old Katrina Rennie, nineteen-year-old Eileen Duffy and twenty-nine-year-old Brian Frizzell, a triple murder about which the RUC Chief Constable Sir Hugh Annesley would later comment: "Even by Northern Ireland standards, the killings hit an all-time low." What would Chief Constable Annesley say, I wondered, when our television programme revealed that these three murders would, almost certainly, never have occurred but for collusion between his own officers and Robin Jackson's squad of fanatical Loyalists? How would the Chief Constable react to our source's detailed account of how the RUC Inner Force had helped The Jackal to murder three entirely innocent young Catholics? This is what Sands said:

> Well, the owner of the sweet shop was, files came into the hands of the Ulster Co-ordinating Committee showing that he was very prominent in the Provisional IRA . . . that [file] had been compiled over a number of years by British intelligence showing that he was very prominent, giving dates of operations that he'd been involved in, giving dates when he'd met certain people that were known Republicans . . . for whatever reason British Intelligence wanted him removed, they handed the file so that there could be evidence to show that he was a legitimate target. So, when this file come into the Loyalists' hands, it was passed then to the Inner Force, who done their own investigation and come and got photographs of files, also showing that he had connections with the Provisional IRA. So, after a series of meetings to discuss it, to discuss the implications of working with British Intelligence, that there is a fear within the Ulster Co-ordinating Committee that British Intelligence will come in and use the Loyalists the way they'd been used in the early '70s. So there's a lot of people very wary of any involvement with British Intelligence.[10]
>
> So, after meetings and after things were discussed and things . . . they decided that the operation be set up. So, again, it was left to the hands of the Inner Force to organise and to plan. They watched the movements of the sweet shop. They took The Jackal, who was given the job of eliminating the owner, and they worked in conjunction, planning and organising over a matter of months, weeks. And on the night, Inner Force came, picked up the squad that was to carry out the operation, got them in, gave them a safe road in, as was usual. They left a car and a van which The Jackal's squad were using for the operation on a lane just behind Lurgan town cemetery.
>
> The Inner Force car then went a mile or so to the Drumbeg estate. They drove around looking, checking everything was all right

for the operation to be completed. Then drove out of the estate, a few minutes later drove back in again. There was a man then walking across from the opposite side of the road towards the sweet shop, who answered the description of the owner of the sweet shop. On seeing him going across towards the sweet shop, the Inner Force car then went to where the van and the car were sitting with The Jackal's gang. They then led them in to the entrance of the Drumbeg estate. The van drove in to the estate and the car sat at the entrance, just as a back-up. There was a driver and two men in the van.

The Jackal went into the sweet shop, the owner wasn't there, there was two girl assistants. But then The Jackal decided he wasn't going to go away empty handed, so he shot the two girls, and coming out he then shot a man who was coming across as a customer to the sweet shop. Shot him and got into the van and away. They met up with the car at the entrance to the estate, they in turn then met up with the Inner Force car, who then led them safely back to their houses.

Q: Fine, thank you. What happened at the report back to the Central Committee?

A: They felt that it had been a good operation, that it went according to plan except that the owner was missed. But the, organisation wise, they felt that it went very well. They felt they had, The Jackal's gang and the Inner Force had co-operated very well, got on well together. Everything had went timewise according to plan. It was just a pity the owner wasn't there at the time, but as was pointed out at the meeting, there will always be a next time. And that that [had] put the wind up them.

And the Inner Force then brought files showing that one of the girls was from a Republican sympathising family, as was the man customer. Files, they had photocopies on file they had got from Lurgan police station. Because the Inner Force always liked to come to the meeting with proof. That they're not, there's not innocent people being killed. Because it's, the Ulster Co-ordinating Committee's not at war against the Catholics. But they are at war against Republicans. And Republican sympathisers. So the Inner Force always like to have files on hand that they can show to the Committee, that there is legitimate targets being taken out . . .

Q: When The Jackal killed the two teenagers and the young man, he knew nothing about them. Why did he kill them? Did he know anything about them, and why did he kill them?

A: He went in to get the owner of the sweet shop. When he went in, he was going on information from the Inner Force that this, the owner, was on his way to the sweet shop. He went in expecting to find the man in the van. He went in, the man wasn't there, there was just the two girl assistants. And it would [have been] uncharacteristic of The Jackal if he turned around and left. When he has a gun in his hand he's gonna shoot somebody. Now, he didn't ask them, stop and ask are you Republican sympathisers, he didn't stop and ask them are you a member of the Provisional IRA, he just shot them. The same with the man outside. He didn't stop to ask him did he vote Sinn Féin. He just shot him. Then, it's up then to the Inner Force then to get the files if there is files on the people or the families, so that they can go back to the Committee and say well, we didn't get the person we wanted but er, according to the files in the police station, they are Republican sympathisers, all have connections with the Republican movement.

Sands had admitted, as we can see in the above extracts from his interview, that he had known of the arrangements reached between the RUC Inner Force and the Loyalists to murder the sweet shop owner and that he had attended the Committee meeting which had reviewed the operation, judging it to have been a satisfactory, if not perfect, outcome. Although Sands was quite open about his role and responsibility as a Committee member, he had been even more indiscreet about this atrocity when he had discussed these three murders with Ben, some days earlier, during one of their dinner conversations at the Silverwood Hotel in Lurgan. For he had, on that occasion, revealed that an RUC Special Branch agent "Bertie"—the agent's surname was not made clear to us—was the person who had briefed Robin Jackson on the proposed target and who had helped the RUC Inner Force to oversee the attack.

> He works for [RUC] Special Branch. But he's British Intelligence, he's the man that gives the Loyalists, works with the Loyalists through British Intelligence. So if you'll scratch my back I'll scratch yours.
> [BH: And what exactly has he been involved in?]
> He's been, a lot of it's with giving information on Republicans . . . that Special Branch would want removed or British Intelligence want removed. And he has passed information on.
> [BH: Have any of the people who've been removed recently fallen into that category?]
> He was the man that, he tipped him [Robin Jackson] off about John Jenkins[on] that owned the mobile shop. He met Robin Jackson twice to discuss that. He brought files that were supposed to have been got from John Jenkinson's house, showing that he was the treasurer of the Provisional IRA in Lurgan. They were supposed to be from his house in a [police] raid and had John Jenkinson's signature on it. He give them till [to] Robin, they actually met here [in the Silverwood Hotel.]

Sands also explained that, in an effort to persuade the Catholic community that the RUC was taking effective action over the killings, two men—neither of them members of Jackson's gang—had been arrested in connection with this particular incident. These two Loyalists had simply been told by other unnamed individuals to go out and hijack a vehicle but, according to Sands, they had not known the purpose for which it was to be used. [Both would later receive prison terms for their role in the attack.] The RUC would, therefore, certainly have known that neither of these men had been guilty of the three horrific murders, just as they would have also known about Robin Jackson's role. We asked Sands if it would be correct to say that:

> Yes. Within an hour of the killing, the majority of policemen in Northern Ireland well knew who'd done it. They know the names of the people, they know the names of the squad. Not just Inner Force members, but RUC men outside the Inner Force know who the people are.

Sands had, at this stage of the London interview, confirmed most of what he had already told Ben about the mobile sweet shop murders. His accounts of the attack had been consistent, convincing and strikingly different from anything that had been written or spoken about these events in the newspapers. There had been rumours about collusion and witnesses living in the Drumbeg estate had even voiced their suspicions to the media in the immediate aftermath of the killings. Yet nobody had ever suspected that the entire operation had been meticulously planned in advance on behalf of a Committee composed of some of the most respectable, or seemingly respectable, citizens in the province. Perhaps the most chilling aspect of Sands's account was his revelation that, despite the outcry over the slaughter of two innocent teenage girls and an equally innocent young man, the Committee's collective membership—those listed in Appendix One of this book—had voiced no disquiet about Jackson's on-the-spot decision to kill all three Catholics, a decision taken when he realised that the RUC Inner Force had misled him about the presence of the man he had originally intended to murder.

Exactly four years after the murders, in March 1995, a Portadown Loyalist confessed to having been a member of the gang responsible for these crimes. He was sentenced to life imprisonment by the Lord Chief Justice of Northern Ireland, Sir Brian Hutton. Yet, at his trial in Belfast, there was no mention of the RUC Inner Circle, RUC Inner Force, RUC Special Branch agent "Bertie" or of the death squad's leader, Robin Jackson, The Jackal. Sir Brian was quoted as saying, as he passed sentence, that it was "unfortunate" that the rest of those involved had not been brought to justice for this "appalling act of savagery and brutality." I assume that when Sir Brian made this comment he would not have known that he was, in fact, referring to around sixty eminent citizens living in the province, including such distinguished figures as Trevor Forbes OBE and "Reverend" Hugh Ross.

To this day, none of those *directly* implicated by Sands in the murders—neither Robin Jackson, nor "Bertie", nor the RUC Inner Force officers involved, nor the Committee members who sanctioned and organised the attack—has been arrested or charged with any of the three mobile sweet shop murders.

****

Cappagh, a small village in County Tyrone, has given its name to another Loyalist atrocity, the murder of four Catholics—including two IRA members and a seventeen-year-old boy—at a public house late one Sunday night at the beginning of March 1991. Until we met Sands, we knew no more about this attack than anyone else, which is to say, simply, that collusion was suspected but unproven; it was widely believed that an IRA meeting had been in progress at the public house, Boyle's Bar, and that the Loyalists had, somehow, learned about it in advance. When the Loyalist squad reached the village, they arrived just as a car containing three young people—the two IRA members and the boy—approached the public house. The Loyalists immediately sprayed the car with automatic fire, killing all three occupants; one of the gang then ran to the pub and, after poking his weapon through a toilet window, fired several shots, one of which killed an entirely innocent Catholic who happened to be in the toilets at the time. After the attack, the gang escaped along the narrow, twisting roads which lead from the village, eventually joining the motorway near the town of Dungannon.

Before coming to London, Sands had given us new information about the Cappagh attack. He told us that a gang of nine or ten Loyalists, Billy Wright—King Rat—and his "rat pack," had driven to the village in three cars. A fourth, unmarked police car, containing two on-duty, uniformed members of the RUC Inner Force, had led the way and had guided the gang through two police checkpoints, one outside the town of Pomeroy, the other outside Dungannon on the way to the M1 motorway. After the attack, the RUC car had guided the squad safely back to the motorway.

During the filmed interview in London, Sands told us that he was uncertain about the day on which the Cappagh attack occurred. He thought, wrongly, that it had taken place on a Wednesday when, in fact, it had occurred on a Sunday night. However, Sands was not troubled by his mistake and assured us that he was confident about the accuracy of the rest of his account. For he had, unusually, attended the morning meeting of the Committee which had authorised the Cappagh operation; it had then been carried out later on that same day.

Q: Are you confident that the meeting for the Cappagh operation
was the day you said it was? (Wednesday)

A: Because the operation was so hastily arranged, I couldn't
be one hundred per cent sure, but it was—the details are right, the
details are, but I'm not a hundred per cent sure of the day because
it was so hastily arranged, because nobody was expecting the SAS
to be moved out and the police patrols to be removed. And it was
the night before [the attack] the decision was given, so it was
phone calls made mostly in the middle of the night to people on
the Committee to attend the meeting in the Seagoe Hotel
[Portadown] the next morning. So I couldn't be a hundred per
cent sure actually of the day, cos the meeting was the morning of
the shooting.

Sands began by explaining that the Inner Force had learned that a
meeting of the East Tyrone Brigade of the Provisional IRA was going to
hold a meeting at Boyle's Bar in Cappagh. The pub had been under constant surveillance by the SAS for weeks but, suddenly and inexplicably, a
decision had been taken to withdraw the SAS and, apparently, the IRA
meeting was to be allowed to proceed. The prospect of killing the East
Tyrone Brigade at their meeting was, said Sands,

. . . an opportunity that the Inner Force felt they could not let go
. . . They felt that there was, because a lot of the members of the
RUC in that area were members of the Inner Force, they felt that
they could carry out a good, successful operation . . . there was a
meeting called of the Central Co-ordinating Committee which
gave the go-ahead for the operation to take place. The Inner Force
met, the Inner Force from Dungannon and from Portadown, met
with King Rat and his squad, who discussed the operation to plan
and to just generally . . . the operation went well. So the Inner
Force, then, that night, took, an Inner Force car from Portadown
took King Rat and his squad, actually they went in three cars for
the squad, and one car for the Inner Force went in front, making
sure there would be a clear run . . .

So the Portadown car took King Rat and the squad up to the
roundabout, the roundabout up to Dungannon. They then met,
then, an Inner Force car from Dungannon who then took the
squad up to Cappagh. Upon arriving at Cappagh, they didn't
know what would happen. They had, there was King Rat and
eight others in the squad. King Rat went in the first car. Just as
they were coming up, there was a car coming into the car park,
which was men going to the meeting and they fired at those men
in the car. They then fired through a window. They tried the door
of the pub but it was closed. Later, King Rat said that it was barricaded, he couldn't get in. He then turned his guns again on to

the car but the Inner Force felt that they were not enough there, that they needed to get out of the area.

They actually had to pull King Rat into the car. He, they had to put King Rat into the car because he wouldn't go. He said he wanted to make sure that the Fenians were dead. He then, the Inner Force car then, led the cars from the Loyalist squad out of Cappagh into Dungannon, back to the motorway where they met up with the car from Portadown who led them back into Portadown again.

The Cappagh attack was discussed in detail at the next meeting of the Committee and some members were critical of the failure to kill more people.

The Jackal thought that the door should have been smashed down and that they should have wiped the pub out. That there was enough men there to do the job and it wasn't much point sending a big squad in if they weren't going to do the job. But the Inner Force, they like to, the Inner Force like to go in, do the job quickly and get out again. They don't like hanging about, they say that if you hang about too long it increases the chances of witnesses and that they don't like hanging about too long. They want to go in and get the job done, if it's successful, it's successful. If it fails, it fails, but they go in very quickly.

Reaction to the murders provided eloquent testimony on how Catholics and Protestants differ over allegations of collusion, as they do on many other important matters in Northern Ireland. A typical Catholic comment came from a local councillor, who felt it was "damn suspicious" that a Loyalist gang could "operate in an area in which there is such a high level of security." Such remarks were, in the words of Free Presbyterian Minister and, at the time, Democratic Unionist MP William McCrea, "blatant, unfounded propaganda by Nationalist politicians." The war of words continued long after the funerals of Thomas Armstrong (52), Dwayne O'Donnell (17) and the two IRA members John Quinn (21) and Malcolm Nugent (21).

Eight months later, in November 1991, Billy Wright gave a newspaper interview in which he boasted that the Cappagh attack had been a "gem," a perfect military strike against the IRA. King Rat flatly denied that there had been any security force collusion in the Cappagh attack.

Republicans always claim that there is security force collusion after something like Cappagh yet per ratio, the RUC have brought to book more Loyalists than Republicans. The Loyalists have paid dear at the hands of the security forces. There is not one shred of evidence of collusion. We have aborted three out of every four operations because of security force activities.[11]

Billy Wright's denial would, I believe, not have been believed by many who read those words in November 1991, especially if they had known what we had learned—namely that the individual, who had given the inside story on the Cappagh attack to Channel 4 a month earlier, was one of King Rat's old school friends from Portadown, Jim Sands.

To this day, nobody has been arrested or charged with the murder of Dwayne O'Donnell, John Quinn, Malcolm Nugent or Thomas Armstrong.

****

Patrick Finucane, a prominent Belfast solicitor, was shot dead in front of his wife and children when three masked Loyalists burst into the dining room of their home on a Sunday evening, February 12th 1989. Two masked gunmen riddled him with bullets, shot his wife in the leg and managed to escape undetected before the alarm was raised. From that day until now—exactly nine years later—the identity of the killers has remained a mystery, known only to a handful of people; nobody has been arrested or charged and, officially, the RUC's file on the murder remains open. Repeated denials of collusion have not prevented the Catholic population of Northern Ireland and others elsewhere from suspecting that Patrick Finucane was, like many others, targeted by Loyalists working in close collaboration with unknown members of the local security forces. There were good reasons for the suspicion. For example, several of Mr. Finucane's Republican clients, having been interrogated by RUC officers at the infamous Castlereagh Detention Centre in Belfast, had been told that their high-profile solicitor would be "removed" before long. Another reason was that, on the day of the murder, RUC road blocks—which had been in operation near the Finucane home throughout the Sunday afternoon—were suddenly and inexplicably removed about one hour before the assassins struck.

Patrick Finucane had been a particularly outspoken critic of human rights abuses by the RUC and had taken the British Government to the European Court over the alleged misconduct of the security forces. At the time of his death, he was still acting for the families of three Republicans who, in 1982, had been shot dead in Co. Armagh by police officers in circumstances which suggested the RUC was operating a "shoot-to-kill" policy. The resulting controversy had forced the British Government to initiate an official "shoot-to-kill" inquiry under an English detective, John Stalker. And it is John Stalker who provides the best insight into the hostility, indeed downright hatred, which RUC officers felt towards Mr. Finucane. In his book, *Stalker*, the English detective describes an incident at the Crumlin Road Crown Court in Belfast when, after talking briefly with Patrick Finucane, he was approached by an RUC officer. Stalker wrote:

> The sergeant came up to me and said, 'May I speak to you, Mr. Stalker? Do you know who that was you were speaking to?' I replied, 'Yes it was Martin McCauley and his solicitor. The sergeant said, 'The solicitor is an IRA man—any man who represents IRA men is worse than an IRA man. His brother is an IRA man also and I have to say that I believe a senior policeman of your rank should not be seen speaking to the likes of either of them. My colleagues have asked me to tell you that you embarrassed all of us in doing that. I will be reporting this conversation and what you have done to my superiors."
>
> I was surprised at his studied vehemence, although I recognised his comment for the honest bigotry it clearly was, and I let the matter go. But what he had starkly illustrated to me was the bitter depths of hatred even among professionals . . .

In the years that followed that incident, Patrick Finucane had scored many further victories for his clients and it was unlikely, therefore, that RUC officers would have become any more favourably disposed towards him. Indeed, such attitudes were likely to have been strengthened by the later comments from a Conservative minister in the House of Commons, who suggested that some solicitors in Northern Ireland were, in effect, IRA supporters. Home Office junior minister Douglas Hogg MP provoked uproar when he stated that "there are, in the Province, a number of solicitors who are unduly sympathetic to the cause of the IRA." During the debate that followed that comment, one MP castigated him and all too accurately predicted that such a remark might cost someone's life in Northern Ireland, "if the assassin's bullet decides to do, by lead, what this minister has done by word." A month after Hogg's comment, which he pointedly refused to withdraw, a Loyalist squad had made the prediction come true.

Although the controversy over Patrick Finucane's death continues to the present day, the only new evidence relating to the murder had, by 1991, come from Jim Sands, who first told us in April that year what he knew about the crime. He repeated his story during the subsequent filmed interview in London.

> Representatives from the Inner Force [who] advised that maybe the time was right to remove Pat Finucane who, according to files that had come from Knock Headquarters, that Pat Finucane was very prominent within the Provisional IRA. They felt that the time was right now to remove him, even though he was a solicitor, he was still very much like with the Provisional IRA and they felt that the time was right to remove him.

Sands explained that the Committee had also obtained documents which had come from Brian Nelson, a double-agent who had been working for British Military Intelligence as well as the Loyalists.

> From the British Intelligence files, I seen those files, it stated his connections through his relatives, that he was involved with the Provisional IRA. It gives dates of meetings that he'd had with prominent people within the Provisionals. It gave meeting places where he had met them. It gave details of his movements. It gave details of trips to Dublin where he had met with the Provisional Army Council. There was also copies of the Gardaí, Republic of Ireland Special Branch leaflets, which must have been passed from the Republic of Ireland to the British, including his movements in Dublin, people who he had met in Dublin who were known members of the Provisional IRA. And everything pointed to him being very prominent within the organisation of the Provisional IRA.

After considering the documents and the RUC Inner Force's proposal that the solicitor should be "removed" the Committee decided, at a well-attended meeting held in Finaghy Orange Hall at the end of January 1989, to agree that it was now "an appropriate moment" to end Mr. Finucane's life. Sands was one of those who consented to the Inner Force's proposal.

> Q: So who was it who actually killed Pat Finucane?
> A: The actual job was carried out by people connected with the Ulster Resistance, with help from Brian Nelson and the Inner Force.

I have no reason to doubt that Jim Sands told us the truth in 1991 about how the Committee had sanctioned Patrick Finucane's murder. However, Sands was unable to tell us the *full* truth about this crime and did not, for example, give us the names of the gunmen who had committed the murder. So when, in 1996, I managed to meet a second member of the Committee, Ken Kerr, I naturally asked him to tell me everything he knew about this killing. We will see that Kerr felt able to supplement the account provided by Sands and that, when pressed to do so, produced what initially seemed to be incontrovertible evidence about those responsible for the murder. He handed over a tape-recording which, had it been authentic, would possibly have led to life sentences for the five Committee members whose voices had, supposedly, been secretly recorded on the morning they had met to finalise the logistical details for the killing. In fact, as we shall see, the tape-recording was a fake and Kerr's "revelations" were designed to distract me from the account already given by Sands back in 1991.

To this day, no-one has been arrested or charged with the murder of Patrick Finucane.

****

Denis Carville; Sam Marshall; the three victims at the Craigavon mobile sweet shop; the four victims at Cappagh; Patrick Finucane. Jim Sands had told us, in front of the television camera, what he knew about how these ten people had come to be murdered in five separate Loyalist attacks, carried out between February 1989 and March 1991. He had claimed first-hand knowledge of the murder conspiracy by virtue of his participation in the regular meetings of the Committee. He frankly admitted that he had never taken part directly in any of the attacks and that his knowledge about actual operations had been based mainly upon reports presented to the Committee after the killings or upon conversations with the gunmen, friends such as Billy Wright. In short, he had given us first-hand testimony about the general murder conspiracy, second-hand testimony about the actual murders themselves.

Sands had been more reserved in his filmed interview than in his earlier tape-recorded conversations with Ben. When invited, for example, to give us the names of Committee members he identified only seven of the conspirators, although he had been willing to name many more in earlier conversations. We ended the interview by asking him to explain something which had puzzled me when I had first learned of his existence and of his willingness to talk about the murder conspiracy. Why, we asked him, had he decided to go public and why should we believe what he was saying?

> Well, personally, I have nothing to gain and really it makes no difference to the situation in Ulster because past history has shown that no matter how many programmes are made about the situation in Ulster, that the people in Britain just don't, do not care, the British authorities just do not care. The RUC know who the death squads are and a programme like this is gonna make no difference. They are not going to pull them in . . .
>
> . . . there's thinking within the Ulster Central Co-ordinating Committee that the time is now right for to go public or to let people know that there is someone in Ulster who is fighting for the Ulster cause . . . that Ulster is seeking independence, Ulster is seeking the removal of the British from Ulster and that both sections can come together to live together as one.

As I listened in silence to Sands's rationale for speaking to us about the murder conspiracy, I believed that he was seriously underestimating the impact his revelations would have, possibly for himself and probably for the RUC. Yet even though I expected his remarks to make headlines once they were broadcast on Channel 4, I did not myself appreciate, on that Saturday afternoon in May 1991, that seven years later I would still be living with the consequences of the documentary we were then making. Nor did I realise how exceedingly difficult it would be to uncover the truth about collusion or to get the story published. I certainly did not anticipate that the enterprise on which we had embarked in 1991 would be satisfactorily completed only with the publication of this book in the United States in 1998.

****

Our interview with Sands lasted from late morning until early evening. By the time he had answered all our questions, we had recorded seven half-hour video tapes and obtained a unique account of a secret and continuing murder conspiracy, involving a sizeable if indeterminate proportion of the locally recruited security forces in Northern Ireland. If what he had admitted could be shown to be true, the consequences were as frightening as they were profound. Frightening because any Catholic in the province could, potentially, share the same fate as Denis Carville; Sands had admitted as much when he conceded that Denis had been selected because no known Republican could be found. Profound because a secret and illegal organisation within the RUC and the UDR was facilitating the Loyalist assassination campaign; there was little doubt that the Committee would kill more Catholics in the months ahead.[12]

Our next task would be to test the truth of his claims by comparing his account of the various incidents with all the available evidence. I knew it was unlikely that any other member of the Committee would step forward and that it would be foolish, even dangerous, for us to confront any of the conspirators with what we had been told. Still, we had achieved our immediate goal and we could leave those problems for another day. After the film crew had left, we drove back to Channel 4 to make sure that the video tapes were securely under lock and key. Then, it was time for dinner and many more hours of discussion with "Robert," our unique Loyalist source. I sat directly across the dinner table from him, listening carefully as he spoke, ever more freely, about the murders the Committee had organised. When Sands tried to convince me that the conspirators were purely political and non-sectarian, that only Republicans rather than Catholics were being targeted, I pressed him to justify the murder of Denis Carville. Eventually, forced to concede that Denis had been an entirely innocent victim, Sands shrugged his shoulders and grinned, "Och, sure he was only a Fenian."

Notes

1   *The Harrods Sale*, Channel 4, 1988.
2   We would later learn that the PTA applies not merely to *future* acts of terrorism in the province; it also imposes a "duty to inform" on anyone who learns information about *past* acts of terrorism. In short, we were proceed-

ing with the production on the basis of an exceedingly liberal reading of the PTA, one which, in the light of subsequent events, Channel 4 would be unlikely to receive in similar circumstances today.

3   Sands had given Ben this information during a tape-recorded interview over dinner at the Silverwood Hotel in Lurgan in April 1991. These recordings, which taped conversations lasting for around three hours, still exist.

4   We have already seen that such an accusation is inaccurate and unfair because the real head of the illegal RUC Inner Force was RUC Assistant Chief Constable Trevor Forbes. Sands did not tell us whether RUC Chief Constable Sir Hugh Annesley was ever made aware of the notice pinned to his door; nor did he indicate what response, if any, Annesley may have made.

5   Sands claimed to know which Committee members were present in the Dolphin Bar, along with Billy Abernethy and Billy Wright, when they hatched the plot that led to the murder of Denis Carville.

6   Another self-confessed Committee member, Ken Kerr, told me that he had also been present in the Dolphin Bar when the murder was planned. However, as I believe Kerr was deceiving me about the conspiracy, I have suspended judgement on any role he may have had in this murder. [See Chapter 14]

7   Copies of the unedited video recording tapes of Sands's London interviews still exist. Only brief extracts from these tapes were included in the broadcast programme. I am confident that anyone able to view the tapes in their entirety would be satisfied that Sands was, as he claimed, a key member of the murder conspiracy. Hopefully, these tapes will become widely available one day.

8   At the inquest a year later, Denis Carville's girlfriend Lynn Hughes told the court that the gunman had asked Denis only about his religion, the chapel he attended, the name of his priest and whether he was wearing a St. Christopher medal. She told the court that, after Denis replied that he was wearing a Celtic Cross, the gunman shot him twice.

9   David Trimble MP, quoted in the *Lurgan Mail*, October 12th 1990.

10   The possible role of British Intelligence in the Committee's activities will be discussed in Chapter 14, where we shall see that Committee member Ken Kerr sought, in 1996, to persuade me that British Intelligence enthusiastically endorsed the Loyalist assassination campaign—a claim that deserves to be treated with a degree of scepticism, in view of my later discovery that Kerr is an accomplished liar.

11   *Sunday Tribune*, Dublin, November 24th 1991.

12   See Chapter 14.

Chapter 5

THE INVESTIGATION

Ben Hamilton's curiosity, David Lloyd's judgement and Channel 4's money had, in a very short time, taken us much further than any of us had dared to hope. If Sands was telling the truth, collusion—so vehemently and repeatedly denied by the RUC and the British Government—was deeply embedded and pervasive within the province's security system, so much so that the Loyalist death squads could strike anywhere, at any time, with impunity. But could we be absolutely sure that Sands was telling the truth? That was the question we had all asked ourselves, after first hearing about his existence and his allegations. And it was a question we would go on asking ourselves for some time to come.

At an early stage, I had emphasised to Ben that we had to guard our company's reputation against the possibility that this man, plausible and convincing though he appeared, might be mentally unbalanced or pursuing an illegitimate agenda of his own. I speculated that he might—possibly, though unlikely—turn out to be a fantasist who had invented a wholly fictitious scenario in order to glorify himself, to blacken the name of the RUC or for some reason that we could not begin to fathom. He might even be attempting to discredit us or Channel 4 by "planting" a story that would subsequently turn out to be a "hoax," an utterly false series of allegations that would ruin our reputation and destroy our livelihood.

Like every other reporter in Britain, I had enjoyed that spectacle of hubris and nemesis, the hilarious fiasco over the "Hitler Diaries" when Rupert Murdoch's flagship newspaper *The Sunday Times* discovered, too late, that its scoop of the century was a hoax to rival any in the colourful history of journalism. I reminded myself of the role the episode had played in the demise of that newspaper's credibility and status. We were determined to avoid becoming embroiled in a similar farce, where the desire for a "scoop" induces a credulity about the facts and a lack of critical scrutiny. Everyone involved in the project, both at Channel 4 and Box Productions, was agreed that everything Sands had told us would be subjected to the most stringent examination so that we could avoid a repetition of the ridiculous situation into which *The Sunday Times* had been led by the fraudulent "Hitler Diaries."

Shortly after we had recorded the interview in London, an experienced film director, Nick Read, joined the production team. Nick was well known to David Lloyd as someone with the many attributes essential to his role on the project, especially a cool head and the ability to keep a secret, as well as the required technical skills in filming, editing and producing a finished programme. Nick proved to be an ideal choice and we were to work in harmony with him for the next five months, right up to the day of transmission in October 1991. After a number of lengthy editorial discussions at Channel 4, Nick and Ben flew back to Belfast to begin the formidable task of finding evidence to enable us to assess what credence we could give to Sands. I supervised the project from London and reported regularly to David Lloyd or Karen Brown at Channel 4.

Our research focused mainly on the five incidents which we had explored in detail with Sands. The Carville family, though they had been visited by dozens of journalists in the few months since their tragedy, always made time to answer our questions. Although we were careful not to add to the family's distress by telling them any of the details we had learned about those allegedly responsible for their son's death, we did indicate that the full story, when it became known, would generate fresh publicity over the killing. After meeting the grief-stricken family and hearing from the dead youth's father how, after the murder, he had been taunted at a checkpoint by UDR soldiers rejoicing at his loss, I resolved that I would do all in my power to ensure that the full story about this barbaric act was brought to public attention. For, when I left the Carville home, I had no doubt that Denis had been an entirely innocent young man, murdered by Billy Wright [King Rat] with the help of his RUC collaborators and on behalf of Abernethy's Committee.

The case of Sam Marshall was very different. He had been a Republican, a Sinn Féin activist with a terrorist conviction and, at the time of his arrest, had been at the home of his brother-in-law, who was trying to flush bullets down a toilet as an RUC patrol was racing up the stairs. Still, none of the above were capital offences and, if Sands's allegations could be believed, Sam Marshall had also been murdered as a result of collusion between the Loyalists and the police. Nick and Ben began to check out Sands's version of events by interviewing members of the Marshall family and witnesses to the attack. The information they gathered, while falling far short of proof, certainly gave rise to justified suspicions about security force involvement in the killing. For example, the dead man's sister, Frances, told us in a filmed interview that she had three reasons for believing the police were involved in her brother's murder.

Sam was always afraid for his life because he had been threatened in Gough barracks that he was going to be killed. And actually the last time he was interrogated in Gough barracks, he was told that the next time he will be seen will be in a brown box. Also, because of the cars that had been following him prior to his death. As he said, they were known [RUC] Special Branch that had been in these cars, that had actually questioned him . . . One of my main reasons why I think it was police collusion was because the three boys had to sign on bail at Lurgan police station on Wednesday evening at 7:30 pm. The only ones to know this was the solicitor, the inspector in charge of the case and the three boys themselves.

It would appear that the police's loathing for Sam Marshall continued even after his death, as his sister also explained.

Even after Sam had died, police had been in the graveyard looking to know where he was going to be buried, would it be in a Republican plot or where? Why did they want to know this? On the morning of his funeral we received a letter saying that Sam is getting buried beside his wee daddy. How would a Loyalist know that? I mean, Loyalists are never seen in a graveyard, and I don't think on that occasion there would be anybody around the graveyard at that time. So I think the police had been in at that time. They had been in looking to know where Sam would be buried. So we think the letter came from them.

The evidence we gathered from the witnesses to the murder was entirely consistent with and, indeed, reinforced what Sands had told us. Nothing we learned about the events leading up to the attack contradicted his account or challenged his veracity in any significant way. We concluded, on the basis of all the available evidence, that his account of the murder was true.

Detailed enquiries into the other murders—the four men at Cappagh, the three at the Craigavon sweet shop and Patrick Finucane in Belfast—all led us to the same conclusion. None of the information gathered conflicted in any significant way with what Sands had told us; much of it corroborated the account he had given. However, the most compelling corroboration of what he had claimed came from an incident which occurred, quite by chance, in the middle of the summer, a short time after Nick and Ben had started filming. This incident convinced us that Sands was exactly what he claimed to be, a man who sat at the Committee's top table, alongside Ulster Bank manager Billy Abernethy and Presbyterian Minister Hugh Ross, facing the rest of the conspirators when they met to decide whose name would be next on the assassin's list.

Ben had been in his hotel room in Belfast when the receptionist rang to say that a man was waiting to see him in the lobby. When Ben went downstairs, he found a tall, slim middle-aged man with receding hair, a thin black moustache and wearing glasses. The man, a quietly-spoken individual, said that he had come to drive the young researcher to a meeting with a representative of Ulster Resistance, an appointment Ben had been trying to arrange ever since he had arrived in Belfast. Ben knew that he was, potentially, walking into a dangerous situation because this secret organisation, though not illegal, was effectively the Loyalist equivalent of the IRA and, as Sands had told us, deeply implicated in the Committee's murder campaign. Ben later told me that, far from being worried, he was thrilled that his efforts appeared, at last, to have been rewarded. As the driver led him to his car, Ben was preparing his thoughts for the meeting and taking care not to give his driver any indication that he already knew some of Ulster Resistance's supposedly best kept secrets. Ben was aware that the individual he was being taken to meet would, most probably, be a member of the Committee.

The driver made his way through the Belfast traffic and on to the M1 motorway, which leads to the south of the province, including Armagh and the area known as "murder triangle." As they drove along, the driver talked freely with his passenger and Ben, listening attentively, grew ever more confident that he would eventually obtain sufficient evidence to corroborate Sands's story. After an hour or more, the driver pulled into the side of the road, stopped the car and waited until another man, dressed in a tracksuit, climbed into the back of the car. This third man was introduced by the driver as the Armagh Commander of Ulster Resistance but Ben was not given his name. In reply, Ben resorted to his "cover story," explaining that he was researching a television documentary on the Ulster Independence movement, Loyalist disenchantment with Britain and the prospects for a negotiated settlement to the troubles in Northern Ireland.

This cover story had been agreed with David Lloyd because we all felt that it would be the height of folly to give any of the Loyalist paramilitaries even a hint of what we had discovered about the Committee and its activities. So the three men sat in the car for a couple of hours, discussing the political and military aspects of the conflict, with Ben listening carefully for any sign that his two companions knew any of the secrets Sands had divulged about what was really going on. Eventually, the meeting ended and the unidentified Ulster Resistance "commander" departed, leaving the driver to begin the return journey to Belfast. The rest of the trip was uneventful and the driver, also unidentified, dropped Ben off at his hotel.

A few days later, Ben had a routine, necessarily discreet, meeting with his secret source. Sands opened the conversation, saying: "I hear you met the Chairman." Ben, somewhat puzzled, shook his head and replied: "No, I haven't. At least I don't think so." Sands smiled knowingly: "Oh yes, you have. He was your driver." Ben was clearly astonished by this revelation because Sands immediately felt it necessary to assure him all was well. "He liked you," he added, before going on to demonstrate that he knew what had transpired in the car. This unexpected revelation about the driver and the accurate account of the conversation the three men had held convinced Ben, as it later impressed David Lloyd, Karen Brown and me, that Sands was exactly what he claimed to be, a well-placed and well-informed member of the Committee. There remained, of course, the possibility that Sands had learned of Ben's journey from someone else and was now falsely claiming to have heard the details directly from Abernethy. This seemed extremely unlikely and, a few days later, events unfolded which enabled us to dismiss this possibility altogether.

Shortly before that encounter with Sands, Ben had arranged to interview one of the alleged Committee members, Reverend Hugh Ross, in his capacity as leader of the Ulster Independence movement. Ross had emerged, in the years since the signing of the Anglo-Irish Agreement, as the most visible champion of Ulster nationalism and had stood, unsuccessfully, as a candidate in a Parliamentary by-election in the constituency of Upper Bann the year before.[1] We decided to approach him for an exclusively political interview, as we thought it would be naive, as well as dangerous, to pose any questions to him about the murders he had sanctioned and helped to organise. Ross had accepted our invitation.

Nick, Ben and the camera crew turned up early for the interview, arriving at Ross's house just as he opened his front door to allow a visitor to leave. Ross greeted Ben, who was taken aback to discover that the visitor was none other than the man who had, a few days earlier, collected him from his hotel in Belfast and driven him to meet the Ulster Resistance "commander" in Armagh. "Mr. Hamilton," said Ross, "let me introduce you to my very good friend, Billy Abernethy." The Committee chairman, who had tried unsuccessfully to signal to Ross to keep quiet, smiled at Ben as he realised the researcher now knew the identity of his "driver." Ben also smiled, as he explained diplomatically to Ross that he and his "very good friend" had already met. Ben made light of the incident and proceeded, without further comment, to film the planned interview with Ross.

The significance of this incident was, for all of us, considerable. Sands had told us that Ross and Abernethy were friends, a fact which had now been confirmed. Sands had earlier surprised Ben when he had told him that his "driver" had, in fact, been the Committee's chairman, Billy Abernethy; now this, too, had been confirmed, albeit inadvertently, by Ross. We had, unexpectedly, acquired confirmation of the accuracy of Sands's information, proof that he had inside knowledge about what Abernethy was doing. This did not, of course, prove that all of Sands's allegations about the Committee were true, but it strengthened our confidence in him and, especially, in what he had told us about the roles Abernethy and Ross were playing in the murder conspiracy.

Later, Ben reflected on the real identity of the "driver" and saw how unlikely it was, in retrospect, that this man could have been a mere chauffeur. For as their car journey into Armagh had progressed, the "driver" had displayed a deep and wide knowledge of local politics, paramilitary activity and the Loyalist agenda for the future of the province. He had told Ben, with evident pride, that he had been a member of the RUC Reserve and he had produced a police medallion and revolver to prove it; and when an RUC patrol had stopped them at a checkpoint on the motorway, Ben had noticed how one of the police officers had recognised and deferred to his "driver."

Another aspect of the journey which, also in retrospect, indicated the driver's special status was the sudden appearance of a number of other cars, forming a convoy. The driver, clearly amused, had told Ben to look in his mirror where he would see that they had acquired some company. As Ben had obviously been impressed, the driver felt able to remark: "Makes you wonder who runs this place, doesn't it?" And it was only after we had learned the true identity of Ben's driver that we were able to appreciate the significance of his parting remark, as he dropped the researcher at his hotel in Belfast. "Be careful what you write, Ben Hamilton," the driver had warned, "you'd be an easy man to find."

Throughout the summer of 1991, Nick and Ben commuted on a regular basis, every few weeks, between Belfast and London. Everything they learned was fed back to me in London and shared at once with the commissioning editors at Channel 4. Slowly, gradually, as the research effort continued, our confidence in the story grew and by July we were convinced that, though Sands had not personally participated in any of the attacks and though he might be exaggerating certain aspects of his story, his principal allegations were, almost certainly, true. An unprecedented Loyalist coalition had formed a secret Committee; this Committee controlled the death squads; a sizeable part of the RUC, possibly as much as a third, was controlled by the Loyalist Inner Force; collusion between the police and the Loyalists was highly organised; and our secret source, Jim Sands, had been a first-hand witness to the murder conspiracy from the Committee's earliest days. These would be the revelations which, we hoped, would form the centrepiece of the proposed documentary; and as the research continued, through the summer of 1991, we did all in our power to ensure that we would have completed the programme in time for the launch of the *Dispatches* series at the beginning of October.

We were fortunate in being able to find an experienced camera crew, a team which enabled us to work effectively but without raising any suspicions about what we were actually doing. Throughout the long history of the troubles, so many television crews had come and gone that, despite the immensely sensitive questions we were asking, no-one seemed to be paying any undue attention to our activities. Obviously, we could not reveal to anyone outside the production team that we were making a programme about this unknown Committee and its ongoing campaign of political assassination. So we stuck to our agreed cover story, namely that we were making a programme about the rise of Ulster nationalism in the wake of the Anglo-Irish Agreement—a cover story which was true as far as it went, though far from being the whole truth. Disclosing the whole truth about our intentions would, as I have already said, have been exceedingly unwise; most probably, it would have caused an acute threat to the crew's security and thereby brought the entire project to a swift conclusion.

Our interview with Hugh Ross, which necessarily steered clear of his secret paramilitary activities, focused on his Movement for Self-Determination which, by 1991, had evolved into an explicit Ulster Independence movement. Nick and Ben explored his views on a range of subjects but gave no indication that they already knew from Sands that this Presbyterian Minister was a moving spirit behind the Committee, a ruthless fanatic pledged to the elimination of those whom he deemed the enemies of Ulster, especially but not exclusively members of the Provisional IRA. Ross sought to present himself as a respectable, law-abiding politician who had set up the Ulster Independence Committee in 1988 to further the aim of creating, through purely peaceful means, a sovereign, independent state, which would be known as Ulster. So, once the filmed interview was under way, we asked him to tell us more about the relationship between his "peaceful" Ulster Independence movement and the openly violent Loyalist paramilitaries. In reading his reply, we should bear in mind Sands's testimony that all Committee meetings began with this Presbyterian Minister calling down the Lord's blessing on the deliberations of those present, those who had freely assembled to sanction and plan murder.

> Within the colony of Northern Ireland, there are paramilitary groups who have pledged support for Independence. One such grouping would be known as Ulster Resistance, which originally was started in the Ulster Hall and had the political backing of Dr. Ian Paisley and also Mr. Peter Robinson of the Democratic Unionist Party. And in those heady days, they had several demonstrations in various centres of population, and then suddenly, political backing was withdrawn because they realised that there could be a certain amount of weaponry in and around Ulster. Now, Ulster Resistance—*as far as I am led to believe*—has continued, which is open knowledge or common knowledge to most people within the colony of Northern Ireland, or of Ulster.

> They, I know, pledged their support for independence but, at this moment in time, they are *totally separate* from the Ulster Independence Committee . . . we are totally separate from all paramilitary groups within Ulster. [my emphasis]

But could he envisage a scenario in the future where he might solicit the support of the Loyalist paramilitary groups?

> One cannot predict the future in relationship to England absolutely refusing to negotiate independence or, for that matter, the world of international opinion going against the concept of Ulster Independence. I, of course, cannot envisage such a time coming, because I believe it's very logical, it's an honourable way out for all concerned, and therefore I cannot envisage a scenario where negotiated independence would be refused. *But let it be said that in every instance throughout the world, where reasonable terms have been refused, then people have the right to self-determination and the people have the right to ultimately stand up and be counted, and to resist the foreign powers that are enslaving them, such as the enslavement of the Anglo-Irish Agreement or any replacement agreement will be the same thing, and they have a right to fight against tyrannical and arbitrary power.* [my emphasis]

Ross's mask had slipped and he had begun to sound very much like a Loyalist version of Sinn Féin's Gerry Adams. Like Gerry Adams and the IRA, who have used terrorist violence to try to force a million Protestants into a united Ireland, Ross readily entertains the prospect of forcing Northern Ireland's half-million Catholics to acquiesce in the creation of an independent Protestant Ulster. Ross's mask slipped further when he proceeded to admit that there were good reasons for his pretence that Ulster Independence and Ulster Resistance were entirely separate organisations; he indicated that he was aware that his apparently respectable and peaceful crusade for Ulster Independence would be damaged if, as with Gerry Adams and Sinn Féin, people knew that he, too, was closely associated with a terrorist organisation. He seemed to think it would be damaging if he was known to keep a gun under the table when he talked about negotiating an Independent Ulster. So we asked Ross to explain why those committed to Ulster Independence preferred not to adopt a higher public profile.

> Those who have committed themselves to an independent Ulster as their first ideal, and first option, and only alternative, come from the world of banking, education, civil service and they are those who are in various organisations such as the Orange Order, the Apprentice Boys, the Royal Black Institution and, of course, there are others within the midst of the Roman Catholic people

who have pledged themselves to independence also . . . so, from virtually every section of the community, I could produce those who give their full allegiance to the concept and ideal of an Independent Ulster.

If we had been making a political documentary about Ulster Independence, we would have replied to Ross's rhetoric with some tough questions, such as how the Anglo-Irish agreement had "*enslaved*" the people of Northern Ireland, or what he planned to do to compel the Catholics to abandon their Irish nationalism and accept the proposed Protestant Ulster? But, as our real purpose was an investigation of RUC/Loyalist collusion, we merely recorded Ross's opinions, thanked him for his contribution and took our cameras elsewhere. It was a shame, though, that we could not risk confronting him directly with what we had learned about the Committee's activities, especially its financing of arms deals through a highly profitable trade in drugs and pornography, imported from Continental Europe and sold at great profit south of the border, inside the Irish Republic. How, I wondered, would Ross's involvement in such activities go down with his Presbyterian congregation in County Tyrone?

Our next step, in attempting to corroborate what Sands had told us, was to arrange an interview with another member of the Committee— someone who, like Ross, also could not afford to be totally frank about the extent of his illegal activities. Sands had explained that Billy Wright [King Rat] had been responsible for some of the worst atrocities inside "murder triangle," that he was "a good seasoned terrorist" who had "committed his first murder at the age of nineteen."[2] So, it came as a surprise to find that King Rat was at least as articulate as Ross, able to provide a coherent, if frightening, rationale for Loyalist violence against Catholics. For example, we asked him how he could justify the Loyalists' policy of killing Catholics in retaliation for IRA murders.

> Retaliation is, unfortunately, a natural reaction. I mean it's very difficult for Protestants to sit back and allow their community just to be wiped out, and I don't believe that there's another community either in England, Scotland or Wales that would accept the elimination of the ordinary folk within their community without reacting to it. Sometimes the Catholic community seems to take the killing of Protestants with um absolute, it's got nothing to do with us. They don't actually seem to be able to feel the pain that the Protestant community are feeling and the attitude to retaliatory strikes are that the Catholic community then feels the pain that they've inflicted on the Protestant community, and hopefully the desired effect will be that both communities realise the futility of the assassination campaigns. I believe that that happened within Lurgan, in the Lurgan area. I believe that when the IRA

started their campaign off there was no peace movement. There was no cries for peace whenever the IRA were shooting the people coming out of church . . . however, when Protestants took the law into their own hands and shot IRA men *and shot Nationalists in retaliation*, I believe that peace movements sprung forth from because there was a feeling within the Catholic community, this is silly, it's futile, let's stop it. [my emphasis]

Billy Wright's argument that the IRA's terrorist campaign inflicted great pain and anguish on working-class Protestants cannot be denied. Though the IRA will claim that their real enemy was the British Government, the victims of their terrorist violence were overwhelmingly Ulster Protestants. So it was understandable that Billy Wright chose, in his filmed interview, to view IRA murders as an out-and-out sectarian attack on the Protestant community. This provided him with what he considered ample justification for vengeance, retaliation in kind—not just against IRA activists—but against the general Catholic population. He had told us explicitly that he considered it morally acceptable to shoot Nationalists, meaning Catholics, in retaliation for the murder of Protestant soldiers by the IRA; implicitly, his answer had justified the murder of Denis Carville in retaliation for the IRA's murder of the young UDR soldier, Colin McCullough.[3]

Morally justifiable though King Rat's policy appeared to him, he also knew that those who implemented such a policy were committing murder under British law. So when, during filming, we asked King Rat directly whether he had murdered Denis Carville, he knew what the law obliged him to say; yet, as was clear from the excerpt we included in *The Committee*, he had been shocked by Ben's question which, in its simplicity and directness, had left him struggling for words.

> Q: In the case of . . . Denis Carville, locals believe that Billy Wright from Portadown pulled the trigger. Was that you and would you like to comment?
> A: It most definitely wasn't me. The Denis Carville murder I have never been accused of. I know nothing about it, absolutely nothing about it. I've never been arrested for it, I have never been questioned for it, I was arrested and questioned in reference to Cappagh. The RUC were absolutely satisfied that Billy Wright from Portadown had nothing to do with Cappagh. Indeed it was impossible, because the movements of Billy Wright were well known to the security forces at the time of Cappagh, and the police are well aware that Billy Wright is completely innocent of these charges that have been laid against him, and laid against him by left wing and Republican media. So I can assure you that it wasn't me.

Billy Wright's assurance that he did not murder Denis Carville, coming as it did after his exposition of the Loyalist rationale for killing

Catholics in retaliation for IRA murders of Protestants, was not credible. His agitated, strident tone made him sound totally unconvincing, as he sought to transfer the blame for the crime to the IRA. The way Billy Wright viewed the killing was that whoever had pulled the trigger on Colin McCullough had also imposed a death sentence on Denis Carville.

> The men that one can blame are running round Kilwilkie [Catholic housing estate] with their chests out, well known to the security forces, well known to the Catholic community, and that the death for Colin or for Denis Carville can be blamed on the men that killed Colin McCullough, who are known probably to Mrs. Carville and Mr. Carville. They are the people to blame for the death of Catholics that would lose their lives. These heroes within the Nationalist community, thugs and gangsters.

When we asked him about the Cappagh murders, he also denied any involvement while saluting those who had carried them out. Proof of his innocence, he suggested, lay in the fact that the RUC had picked him up for questioning shortly after the incident, only to release him when satisfied that he had not been involved. And he claimed that his police interrogators had not, in any event, been greatly bothered by the killings because they believed that all four victims had been dedicated Republicans or worse, IRA terrorists. We did not feel it appropriate to challenge King Rat about his role at Cappagh, any more than we felt able to enquire whether the RUC men who questioned him after the attack were the same Inner Force officers who had guided his squad into the village and out again, once it had completed the assignment commissioned by Abernethy's Committee.

Our interview with Billy Wright strengthened our conviction that what we had learned from Sands was, in all essentials, correct. Although his fervent denials of any involvement in specific incidents were totally unconvincing, his overall performance gave us a valuable insight into the mind of the Loyalist terrorist; he displayed an understandable hatred of the IRA and its irrational campaign of murdering Ulster Protestants in the pursuit of Irish unity; he expressed a heart-felt sense of betrayal by Britain for having rewarded the IRA with the Anglo-Irish Agreement; and he declared that he would rather die fighting Republicans than allow them to achieve their goal. King Rat's interview left us with few doubts that, despite his denials of responsibility for past murders, he would be receiving fresh commissions from the Committee before long.

By the middle of the summer we had completed most of our filming and had recorded numerous interviews with a wide range of individuals, including witnesses to the attacks, friends and relatives of the victims, Loyalist paramilitaries, politicians from both sides of the sectarian divide and a wide range of pundits and commentators. Although we had not found a second Committee member to corroborate Sands's confessions, we did manage to record two further interviews with two very different individuals, both of whom provided a degree of support for the programme's central theme, official collusion in the Loyalist murder campaign.

One of these interviewees was a man who, we knew at an early stage, would present problems if we included any of his comments in the broadcast programme.[4] Ben had met him when he stopped his car, on the spur of the moment, to give a lift to a hitch-hiker. In the course of the conversation which ensued, the hitch-hiker had gradually revealed details of his life, that he was a Scotsman who had lived in the province for years, that he had a son in the RUC, that he had been baptised a Catholic but had lost his faith. And once the hitch-hiker, Edward Quinn, had learned the nature of the television researcher's assignment, he had surprised Ben by revealing that his criminal past meant that he would be able to help us with our programme. Quinn told Ben that, some years earlier, he had participated in a Loyalist murder of a Republican, which had been carried out in collusion with the police; and he provided a fascinating detail, namely that members of what he called a police Inner Circle had been involved. A chance encounter had presented us with an extraordinary result, a second person who would provide personal testimony that police officers were colluding with Loyalists in the murder of Republicans.

It would, naturally, have been preferable to have discovered Quinn through orthodox research methods but, given that we had come across him and that his story sounded plausible, the question arose whether we should include any part of his testimony in the programme. We anticipated, correctly as it turned out, that the RUC would pounce on the circumstances of our initial meeting with him and seek to use it to discredit both his contribution and the overall programme. After discussing this possibility and other potential problems, such as Quinn's lack of verbal skills and his fondness for the bottle, we finally decided that the element of limited corroboration he was able to provide outweighed these potentially embarrassing factors and we opted to insert part of his interview in the programme.

> I'm a kind of liaison officer. I pass information back and forward, ok?. . .I get tips now and again, right, and they're checking me and they ask me to find out things for them. And I take a few sightings here and there and follow people's movements for a hit . . . Alright. Me and this UVF fellow, alright, we were called to Belfast. We went to, well I'll not be meeting, don't get me wrong, I was not involved in the meeting, but we stay in a hotel waiting, I was told the Inner Circle was meeting, a wee meeting right. And me and this fella, well the UVF fella, we sat in the hotel and waited for instructions. And I've seen the envelope getting passed over.

And in the envelope, I don't know how much money was in it, I'd no idea, but there was a name on it . . .

. . . Q: And how was this information used?

A . . . I'm goin to tell you the whole truth. We was told, right, we was told we'd fifteen minutes clear after the "hit," and the road would be cleared, there wouldn't be police in sight. That's true, now. We were guaranteed fifteen minutes after the phone call was made, after that. That gave us what twenty, twenty-five minutes to get away.

Edward Quinn had confessed, on camera, to his involvement in murder, a crime which in Northern Ireland, as in the rest of the United Kingdom, carries a mandatory life sentence. His offer of a filmed interview had been conditional on our agreeing to provide him with an identical undertaking to the one we had already given to Sands, namely an assurance that we would not, in any circumstances, reveal his identity to anyone; and all involved in the project, at both Channel 4 and Box Productions, had agreed to abide by Quinn's condition because we felt strongly that the public ought to know what we had discovered.

The other interviewee, whose contribution also corroborated part of Sands's testimony, was John Coulter, the local journalist with first-class contacts inside the RUC Inner Circle and among the Loyalist paramilitaries. As we have seen, in the years that followed the signing of the Anglo-Irish Agreement he had led the way in documenting the rise in support for Ulster Independence and in revealing the existence of a body of disgruntled Loyalists within the RUC, the Inner Circle. We asked John Coulter to help us explore further the Inner Circle's current attitudes, in a period when the Loyalists were killing more people than the IRA. We commissioned him to put a series of questions to his unidentified high-level RUC contact, starting with the Inner Circle's attitude to the British Government's search for a negotiated settlement.[5] This is what his secret RUC source said:

The Foreign Office people at Whitehall and the English civil servants in the Northern Ireland Office desperately want to bring the doves of Sinn Féin to the negotiating table . . . but the English military people want a three to four week campaign spearheaded by the SAS to take out at least one hundred and twenty people on both sides, including politicians, which would be Sinn Féin councillors. This would free the constitutional politicians on both sides to get on with the "wheeling and dealing," that is the talks process. Martin McGuinness and Alex Maskey are regarded as hawks in the Republican movement and they would be two politicians from Sinn Féin who would be eliminated. The SAS had already drawn up this plan three or four years ago.

This was a senior RUC officer's frank assessment of two different strands of thinking within the British political and security establishment. Anonymity had allowed him to discuss freely the prospect of hawkish Republicans being "eliminated," sentiments which echoed the much less fluent account already given to us by Sands.

> The objective of the Inner Circle will be, basically, to ensure that the hawks in the Republican movement are killed and this will leave the talkers . . . All the hits that are being carried out at the moment are against the hawk wing of the Republican movement . . . Gerry Adams would go totally political and I think he would be spared. McGuinness is a hawk and he would have to go.
>
> Q: How will the Inner Circle implement this strategy?
>
> A: The hawks have to be made ineffective. They must be discredited in the hope that their own people would do them in anyway. There was an initiative floated by the doves in response to political statements made by Brooke [Sir Peter Brooke, UK Secretary of State for Northern Ireland], but this was stifled by McGuinness. You could see a terrorist campaign to take out the hawks, or you could get an IRA feud going. The Roman Catholic people as a whole are fed up with the terrorists because they've suffered a lot from random killings. There has also been the random killings of Roman Catholics to let the IRA know that Protestants can kill Roman Catholics too. Pressure is being brought to bear on the IRA, and the Roman Catholic people are saying to their priests—"My husband would not have been killed if the IRA hadn't killed that Protestant businessman."

"Kill the fish, poison the water." The Inner Circle's two-pronged strategy for defeating the IRA involved the elimination of the hawks in the Republican movement, and allowing the Loyalists to retaliate against the general Catholic population so that it would recoil, eventually, from giving succour to the IRA. Although the language used by the Inner Circle's representative was more moderate than King Rat's, the sentiment was the same. The IRA would not stop, the RUC Inner Circle representative told John Coulter, until the pain and anguish inflicted by Loyalists on the wider Catholic population had become unbearable.

> Q: Is the Inner Circle killing people?
>
> A: It has taken the Protestant paramilitaries twenty years to reach the situation that the IRA were at in the early Seventies— Cappagh, Buncrana [where Sinn Féin councillor Eddie Fullerton was murdered by Loyalists in May, 1991], and several other incidents, including the lawyer Finucane. He was one of the [IRA] Provos' out-and-out spokesmen to the extreme. Whoever did him, did society a favour . . .

Q: How do the security forces' commanders view the present killings being claimed by the Loyalists?

A: I am sure the higher echelons of the RUC and Army see the Protestant attacks on Sinn Féiners as serving a purpose. The Protestant gunmen are now trained to a higher level. As for Coagh, Loughgall and Strabane [*where IRA men were shot dead*] these were hard gunmen to locate, so the security forces did them themselves. [my additions in italics]

So, John Coulter's anonymous source within the RUC Inner Circle explicitly welcomed the murder of Belfast solicitor Patrick Finucane and implicitly supported the Loyalist strategy of murdering innocent Catholics to pressurise the IRA into calling off its campaign. The interview ended with the officer saying that his organisation was "dormant at the moment because the Loyalist paramilitaries are becoming more active;" but he then went on to explain how the RUC could assist the Loyalists.

The Inner Circle could certainly aid a Loyalist campaign by feeding information and intelligence [to the Loyalists]. The Inner Circle could, in fact, pass on details of target movements; they could also cover the tracks of those involved in the assassinations, and could assist in training. But again, I stress, the recent killings are because of a growing professionalism within the Loyalist paramilitaries in recent years. Since the death of a Protestant businessman in Belfast, the business community is contributing funds to pay for the hitmen . . . They [the businessmen] are also anxious because it doesn't seem to them that the security forces can do the job, so that someone has to be brought in to take out the terrorists.

As I read the transcript of John Coulter's lengthy interview, I suspected that the RUC officer was taking great care about what he did and did not reveal. Although he had drawn attention to the growing professionalism of the Loyalists and to the involvement of business people in their murder campaign, he had not made any explicit reference to the Committee. This caused me no surprise because I felt that such an intelligent and politically shrewd individual would not have wished to compromise the Committee's aims by revealing its existence, even anonymously, to Channel 4. I reminded myself of Sands's claim that precisely eighteen members of the RUC Inner Circle attended regular meetings of the Committee and I found no great difficult in persuading myself that John Coulter's interviewee, whoever he might have been, was possibly one of them.

Overall, the Coulter interview underpinned the central allegations made by Sands and left me convinced that the truth about collusion had, unquestionably, eluded the best efforts of the Stevens Inquiry. Its verdict,

I felt, would possibly have been rather different if the English policeman had employed the services of the likes of John Coulter and persuaded an RUC Inner Circle representative to speak as freely to his Inquiry team as he had done to Channel 4.

By the middle of July 1991, we knew what the programme was going to say about the nature and scale of the collusion involved in the Loyalist murder campaign. We had filmed most of our interviews and were far advanced with the editing of the film. We had kept Channel 4 fully briefed and followed to the letter the legal advice the Channel had obtained. We knew that our programme, when broadcast, would be likely to generate great controversy. But our main concern, at that time, was to preserve our secrecy, so that the British authorities would not be able to prevent transmission. We had managed to keep a low profile during filming but, given the sensitivity of what we were doing, we worried constantly that the Committee might have discovered our true purpose; we had, after all, filmed interviews with Billy Wright, Hugh Ross, Nelson McCausland—a Belfast City Councillor—and other murder conspirators. All of this had imposed a strain and, with two months still to go to the likely date of the broadcast, I knew that those tensions were going to remain.

Fortunately, Sands continued to maintain discreet contact with Ben and had kept us abreast of developments within the Committee. He had, for example, told Ben in the early summer that Billy Abernethy had done some research of his own, making the effort during a business trip to England to carry out reconnaissance on Ben's home and on mine. Sands, who had never visited nor been told anything about my home, a remote farmhouse in Oxfordshire, had been able to give Ben an accurate description of its location, setting and architectural features, details which he claimed had been reported back to him by Abernethy. Although Sands had also told us there was no cause for alarm, I confess I was unsettled by the news that the chief conspirator himself had taken the trouble to locate and drive to my home. And I was even more unsettled when Ben passed on, via Sands, Abernethy's favourable verdict on the property: "The wee Fenian has done very well for himself since he left Ulster in 1969." This comment, laced with the all-too-familiar bigotry and, no doubt, reflecting Abernethy's access to the official RUC file on my student activities in Belfast, sounded authentic.[6] It left me feeling again that I should, perhaps, have resisted Ben Hamilton a little more firmly when, back in February, he had proposed that we immerse ourselves in the troubled affairs of my native province.

Tension rose further towards the end of July as a result of an incident involving our film editor, Keith Wilkinson, who was by then far advanced with the assembly of the finished programme. Keith was returning to work when he stumbled across two tall, fair-skinned men attempting to break into his car, which was parked in the street in Covent Garden in London. One of the men had a large bunch of keys and was testing them, one by one, attempting to open the car's front door. Keith immediately raced towards the two men, shouting that they were thieves and hoping that someone would come to his aid. The two would-be-thieves responded calmly, virtually ignored Keith's shouting and merely signalled to each other that the time had come for them to disappear. They walked quickly and silently down the street, doing so in a manner which suggested to Keith that they were not ordinary car thieves. More likely, he thought, they were plain clothes police or intelligence personnel, intent on seizing video tapes relating to the programme. Whoever they were, the incident intensified our concerns.

A second incident at the editing rooms was even more disturbing, for it led us to fear that somebody with impressive lock-picking skills was taking an interest in our project. One Sunday night in July, a mysterious burglary occurred in which a large, heavy safe was removed; the safe was such that it must have taken three or four strong men to lift it and carry it outside, presumably to a waiting vehicle. Strangely, the thieves had shown no interest in any of the company's video editing and audio equipment, which was worth many thousands of pounds. What most shocked the safe's owners, however, was the fact that the office's sophisticated, electronic alarm system had not been activated. The facility house managers, shaken by what had occurred, told us bluntly that they thought the break-in must have been connected to our sensitive Irish project. True or false, we had little choice but to move and, within hours, a decision was taken to transfer the entire production to more secure offices, which were located within Channel 4 itself. Our very last task, therefore, before we all set off for a much needed holiday, was to gather together all materials already generated during the production—including video tapes and the half-finished programme—and take them to Channel 4, where they were safely held until our return to work in the middle of August.

Ten days in the sun with my family helped me to relax and, for a time, to put aside the concerns that had kept us all under pressure for months, concerns which would undoubtedly return in the weeks leading up to transmission. In fact, they returned virtually from the moment I arrived back home from the airport. A mere two or three hours after I had unpacked my suitcase, Ben phoned me at home to say that he needed to meet me as soon as possible. So, next morning, he drove to my house together with an individual I had not met before but who was introduced to me as "Neil" and described as "a security consultant hired by Channel 4." The happy memories of my foreign holiday began quickly to fade as

Ben delivered the latest news from inside "murder triangle," where Sands had been keeping his finger on the pulse of Loyalist paramilitary activity and, especially, on the Committee's plans for the rest of the summer. I was told that he had contacted Ben with an urgent warning about a threat to our safety; he reported that four members of the Committee, led by Abernethy, were due to visit Ben and me at our homes in England over the coming weekend. This had been reported to Channel 4, which had hired the security consultant, "Neil," and asked him to decide quickly whether our homes had adequate security or whether we ought to move. It didn't take "Neil" very long to decide that my remote farmhouse was totally exposed and vulnerable. Within minutes, he indicated that I ought to give my family another short holiday, a weekend break far away from my home and in a place where Abernethy and company would not think of looking.

Sands had named two of Abernethy's proposed travelling companions. One of them, Graham Long, was said to be an explosive expert and a former member of the SAS.[7] The other was John McCullagh, the Ulster Resistance leader who would, we understood from Sands, head the Ulster Army after any Declaration of Independence. All I knew about him was that he had featured in an anecdote about Ian Paisley MP, which Sands had told to Ben. Sands had revealed that, during the summer, McCullagh and Abernethy had held a meeting with Paisley; after a time, McCullagh had placed a revolver on the table and told the shaken MP that one of the bullets would be reserved for him if he made any concessions to Dublin in the political negotiations which the British Government was trying to initiate at that time.

So, it was not surprising that Channel 4's Chief Executive Michael Grade, when informed about all these matters and told of the impending arrival of Abernethy, Long and McCullagh, had decided to call in the police. He arranged, at short notice, a visit to Scotland Yard where he briefed the commander of Special Branch on the security threat that had arisen for those involved in making the programme. The following day, two Metropolitan Police officers came to Channel 4, where they advised us on how to enhance our security, by varying our movements, routinely checking under our cars for explosive devices and so on. We were also told that Special Branch had alerted officers at Heathrow and Gatwick airports, so that they would be able to intercept the four Loyalists, as soon as they arrived in England.

Once the weekend had passed, without incident, we returned to our homes and carried on with the project. For the next two months, we worked flat out to complete the documentary and to ensure that it met the stringent legal and editorial standards governing Channel 4's factual programmes. Towards the end of September Liz Forgan, the Channel's director of programmes, decided that the programme would, as we had hoped, open the *Dispatches* autumn season. It was given a peak-time slot, scheduled for 9 pm on Wednesday, October 2nd 1991.

A few days before the broadcast, I called the RUC's Press Office at Knock Headquarters in Belfast and spoke to its chief press officer, Bill McGuckian. There was, if I recall correctly, what might be described as a stunned silence when I told him the central allegation of the *Dispatches* programme—that disaffected police officers within an RUC Inner Circle were colluding with Loyalist death squads in the murder of civilians. Our request for a filmed interview with the Chief Constable was, predictably, refused and our allegations about collusion elicited only a brief response, one which was faxed to Channel 4 on the day before the broadcast and shown to the *Dispatches* audience immediately after the programme had been screened. It read:

> Allegations of collusion between members of the Security Forces and Loyalist paramilitaries were fully investigated by Deputy Chief Constable John Stevens of Cambridgeshire. As a result, twenty-six persons have been convicted and fifteen persons are awaiting trial. No police officers were charged because no evidence was found to substantiate charges. Specifically, the allegation of a so-called Inner Circle in the RUC was thoroughly investigated by Mr. Stevens but no evidence was found to support the allegation.
>
> If any persons, including the makers of this programme, have any evidence regarding the commission of a crime they should make such evidence available to the police.

Over one million Channel 4 viewers had watched the specially extended edition of *Dispatches*, partly due to the publicity arising from a well-attended press screening of the film, *The Committee*, held at Channel 4's offices the day before. The first half of the forty-eight minute programme gave an overview of events since 1985, the rise of Ulster nationalism, the growth in Loyalist terrorism, disaffection within the police, the emergence of the Inner Force, the Inner Circle and the Committee; the second half gave details of four attacks—Cappagh, Sam Marshall, Patrick Finucane and Denis Carville—to demonstrate how collusion had become an integral part of the murder conspiracy run by the Committee. Unfortunately, we were obliged, for legal reasons, to drop all reference to the three mobile sweet shop murders; as two men had been charged with offences relating to the supply of the car used in the attack, coverage of the incident in our programme might have led us to commit a contempt of court.

The RUC's terse statement was, we felt, a totally inadequate response to the extremely serious allegations contained in a nationally networked, high-profile investigative documentary. And it was, we also thought, a public relations blunder of the first magnitude because it had failed to challenge directly the first-hand testimony about collusion of a self-confessed, albeit anonymous, conspirator to murder. Viewers were left to conclude that the RUC Chief Constable had failed to appear because he had had no answer to the detailed revelations contained in the programme.

Those who called Channel 4 after the broadcast were divided in entirely predictable ways. Most callers were from Northern Ireland itself, with Protestants expressing anger and dismay, Catholics voicing approval that their suspicions had been confirmed. As the calls came in, everyone involved in the production at Channel 4 and Box Productions—television executives, lawyers, journalists, technicians and production personnel—were already celebrating the fact that, after seven long and difficult months, they had finally managed to get the programme on air. The champagne flowed, glasses were raised, toasts were proposed and all were agreed that, no matter what the RUC's final reaction might turn out to be, we had achieved something special—we had shown, for the first time, that a British police force was colluding with death squads in a part of the United Kingdom.

And, since nobody present doubted the truth of the programme's allegations, it was naturally assumed that Channel 4 would stand by them to the end. Subsequent events have shown that this assumption was wrong.

Notes

1 This was the by-election which allowed David Trimble to enter the House of Commons for the first time. Although Trimble was elected as an Ulster Unionist, his 1988 pamphlet—*What Future for Ulster?*—showed that he and Ross held similar, pro-Independence views.

2 I later learned that Sands was referring to the murder of a twenty-year-old Catholic, Peadar Feagan, who was shot by Billy Wright in Lurgan in November 1981.

3 Billy Wright's short and violent life was accurately described by *The Times*, following his death in December 1997. "Billy Wright took the old Loyalist dictum—'Any Teague (Catholic) will do'—to new depths." *The Times*, December 29th 1997.

4 Our fears proved to be well-founded, as will become evident when we examine the RUC's response to the programme. [See Chapter 9]

5 John Coulter told us that, though he did not know the name of his high-level RUC contact, he was satisfied that his informant was a senior member of the force. Mr. Coulter also gave us a transcript of his RUC Inner Circle

interview, which he signed to confirm that it was authentic. Later, after the Channel 4 broadcast, Mr. Coulter came under enormous pressure from the RUC to retract the statement; but he has never challenged its authenticity, although he objected vehemently to the use we had made of it. [See Appendix 4]

6   In my student days at Queen's University, Belfast I had played a modest role in the emerging civil rights movement and had joined the student protests against religious discrimination by the Ulster Unionist Government at Stormont.

7   Sands would later reveal that Graham Long had been the unidentified individual whom Abernethy had introduced to Ben, after he had collected him from his hotel in Belfast and acted as his "driver."

Chapter 6

SHOOT THE MESSENGER

Our story had been published; a million television viewers had been told that members of a police force in the United Kingdom were running death squads; one of the conspirators had confessed, albeit anonymously, on screen; another had been identified as Denis Carville's assassin; Channel 4 had put its reputation as a national broadcaster on the line; whatever might happen next, our discoveries and allegations had entered the public domain and had stained the already tarnished reputation of the RUC. We had produced compelling evidence that the RUC had become, in part, a terrorist organisation employing the exact same methods as the terrorists in the Provisional IRA.

The outcome might have been otherwise. As we had discussed our plans among ourselves, in the days leading up to the broadcast, we worried that for one reason or another the programme would never reach the screen. The police might decide to seek an injunction which, if granted, would mean that a judge, not Liz Forgan, would decide the programme's fate—a prospect that did not fill any of us with confidence. Another possible outcome, which we also feared, was that the police would come knocking on our door, armed with a search warrant or a court order granting them the power to seize our materials, including the completed film. If that turned out to be the main result of my phone call to the RUC Press Office, the programme might never have been shown at all. And there was a further possibility, which none of us could safely dismiss from our minds, that the shadowy forces that had already taken a malign interest in our work might decide to stage a second burglary, to seize our materials and thereby suppress the story.

All these concerns were debated at length with Channel 4 and, eventually, we all agreed that the wisest course, given the possibility of legal or illegal intervention by forces of the State, was to gather together the most sensitive materials—documents, tapes, notebooks, recordings—and immediately send them abroad, out of the jurisdiction of British courts, so that we could retain control over all materials essential for the defence of the programme and ourselves. So, on the day I called the RUC Press Office to divulge what we had discovered, a student friend of Ben Hamilton flew from London to Paris with a suitcase containing various items which Ben had judged to be of particular importance. Once we had received confirmation that our courier had completed his assignment and that the materials were securely stored in France, we felt able to relax in the knowledge that, whatever action the RUC might take against us, we would have powerful ammunition which we could deploy in our defence.

Immediately after the programme had been broadcast, Channel 4 had told its viewers that all information obtained by the programme makers, except that which would identify sources, would be given to the British authorities. This was contained in a dossier which had been compiled just before transmission and which included virtually everything we had discovered during the previous seven months. It contained a transcript of our filmed interview with Sands, lightly edited to protect his identity; it gave names and details of nineteen individuals whom he had identified as Committee members; and a separate list itemised sixteen assassinations that the Committee had sanctioned and supervised between 1989 and 1991.[1] We had no doubt that our dossier would be of enormous benefit to anyone genuinely trying to identify and arrest the Loyalist killers. I also believed that an experienced investigator would be able, working from the information in the dossier, to track down other, unidentified members of the Committee, including Sands himself;[2] this possibility, that Sands could be tracked down by skilled detective work, caused me no concern whatsoever. For our undertaking to Sands, that we would protect his identity, did not mean we had any desire to help him escape responsibility for the crimes he had committed before we had first encountered him.

While our dossier contained sufficient incriminating information to land the conspirators in deep trouble—arrest, interrogation, murder charges—we all knew we could not seriously expect any such developments from the RUC. And, therefore, we were not at all surprised when, on the day after the broadcast, RUC Chief Constable Hugh Annesley angrily attacked the programme and dismissed its allegations as totally lacking in foundation. We were, however, taken aback when he then proceeded, without any trace of embarrassment over his manifest deficiency in logic, to announce that he was setting up an internal police inquiry into the programme—an inquiry which, presumably, was expected to find out whether our allegations were, despite his public verdict, actually *true*. This unsatisfactory exercise, the RUC investigating itself, was not even addressed by the Chief Constable and he seemed not to appreciate the general scepticism that his inquiry would eventually deliver a verdict contrary to his own.

Though a weary cynicism was the natural reaction to his predictably inadequate comments, we knew we had to follow our legal advice to the letter and co-operate with the RUC to the fullest possible extent. This meant that, a few days after transmission, David Lloyd hosted a rather brief and somewhat tense meeting at Channel 4 with two of the Chief Constable's most senior colleagues, Detective Chief Superintendent Jimmy Nesbitt, who had been appointed to lead the inquiry, and his assistant, Detective Inspector Chris Webster. David handed over the dossier and explained that, for reasons that had already been made clear in the broadcast, we were not prepared, under any circumstances, to disclose the identity of our anonymous source. For, having discussed the issues again with our lawyers, we still believed that we must continue to honour the undertaking we had given to Sands.

Throughout this period and beyond, we managed to keep in touch with Sands who let us know, through Martin O'Hagan, that he had greatly enjoyed the programme and had been impressed by the alterations we had made to his appearance and by the effectiveness of his overall disguise. He assured us that he was totally confident that neither the police nor other members of the Committee would succeed in identifying him as the suspect or "the traitor," as the Loyalists were then describing Channel 4's anonymous interviewee. And he also let us know that he did not doubt that we would keep our word, that we would resist all pressure to hand over his name. Though the broadcast had sparked off a frantic search within "murder triangle" for "the traitor's" identity, the messages we regularly received from Sands at that time were to the effect that he was confident the finger of suspicion would not fall on him.

I recall wondering to myself whether Sands might not be tempting fate in adopting such an insouciant attitude to the hunt then under way in Lurgan and Portadown. We had, after all, given the police the names and details of nineteen individuals whom Sands had identified as his fellow members of the Committee. One of the nineteen, Hugh Ross, was a man for whom Sands had expressed great admiration and with whom he had worked closely for some years. We all feared that, as Ross's acolyte, Sands might come under suspicion. Yet we also knew that we had no choice but to trust his ability to judge the dangers he faced, to leave him alone and hope that he would not do anything to draw attention to himself as the one who had compromised all the conspirators by sharing their secrets with Channel 4.

Some weeks after the RUC detectives had collected the dossier, we received an update from Sands, via Martin O'Hagan, on what was going on in the now intensely suspicious and jumpy Loyalist community within "murder triangle." We learned that Nesbitt, Webster and their colleagues had followed up at least some of the leads in the dossier. All those named as Committee members, we were told, had been visited and questioned by the police but, when they had denied any knowledge about the Committee and had expressed surprise at the allegations made against them, the investigating officers had been perfectly content to take them at their word and leave it at that. These reports confirmed our strong convictions that there had never been any serious prospect of any of the conspirators being arrested, much less charged with murder or subversion.

Nevertheless, according to Sands, the broadcast had made a big impact within "murder triangle." Everyone involved was said to have been traumatised by the programme's accuracy; and they were reportedly frightened about what else might yet emerge about their past activities. Sands, who had displayed a sharp, if twisted, sense of humour during his trip to London, sent me a personal message following a routine visit he had received from one of the Chief Constable's investigators. Detective Inspector Webster had come to question Sands about any possible contact he might have had with Channel 4 and, we were told, had been easily persuaded that whoever the culprit might be, it had definitely not been Jim Sands. As their brief encounter ended, Webster indicated to Sands that his hostility was not, as one might perhaps expect, directed at those responsible for the assassination campaign but was reserved instead for Channel 4's production team and, most especially, for me. "It's a wonder," Sands reported Webster as commenting, "that one of you wouldn't rub out that wee Fenian over in London." Once I had heard this revealing remark, I knew for certain that, as far as the RUC was concerned, Abernethy, Ross, Monteith and all the other conspirators had nothing to worry about. We could safely predict the outcome of the "inquiry" that had just begun.

David Lloyd had assured his two RUC visitors that if, when they had read the dossier, they wished to ask any further questions he would do his best to answer them, subject only to the proviso that he would not compromise our sources. As time passed, it gradually became clear that the two detectives were less than enthusiastic about following this course and indeed, throughout the rest of October, the RUC made no attempt to contact either Channel 4 or Box Productions. Their only public response was a stream of press stories suggesting that the dossier, like the programme itself, had been—as one unidentified RUC officer reportedly put it—"a pack of lies." Then, as the month neared its end and as we had just begun to recover from our long ordeal, the RUC suddenly made its move. The Chief Constable's inquiry team had decided that, as we would not volunteer the name of our source, we would have to be compelled to do so; and, if necessary, we would be made to do so under the threat of imprisonment.

The move came on the morning of Thursday, October 31st, when three

Metropolitan Police officers from Scotland Yard arrived at Middlesex Crown Court in Parliament Square, just opposite the House of Commons. The three officers, acting on behalf of the RUC, told a judge in chambers that a terrorist investigation was under way in Northern Ireland, as a result of a Channel 4 programme; an anonymous source had appeared in the film and testified about his involvement in terrorism and murder; it was clearly of vital importance that this person be apprehended and interrogated at once, so that the police could prevent further crime; since those who had made and broadcast the programme were refusing to co-operate, the RUC was seeking Production Orders under the Prevention of Terrorism Act against both Channel 4 and Box Productions. The judge readily granted the order and, a short time later, the three detectives made their way across London to my office in Soho. When they had come in and sat down, they produced the court order, which I was asked to sign. They then handed me a duplicate copy of the order.

Although a visit from the police had been half-expected, it still came as a shock to have three Scotland Yard detectives sitting in my office, warning me of what would happen if I were to disobey the order. One of them pointed to the small print on the back of the document, which highlighted the severe penalty—up to five years in prison—that could be imposed on anyone who deliberately destroyed or concealed materials covered by the Production Order, or who might compromise the investigation by divulging the fact that it was under way. As he spoke, I recalled that Channel 4's lawyer, Jan Tomalin, had impressed upon us all the importance of remaining silent in the event that a police officer were to turn up on our doorstep. So I waited patiently until the Scotland Yard officers had delivered their message and then, as politely as I could manage, I showed them to the door. As they made their way down the stairs, I rushed back to my office and phoned our solicitor, Brian Raymond, who seemed pleased that the waiting was over and that the long anticipated legal battle over the programme had begun.

Jan had introduced me to Brian at Channel 4, at the press screening of the programme on the day before the broadcast. She had chosen him to represent Box Productions because he was widely acknowledged to be an indefatigable and imaginative champion of civil liberties and human rights. His numerous court room triumphs had included, for example, the sensational acquittal of Clive Ponting, the civil servant who had leaked embarrassing secrets from the Ministry of Defence about the sinking of the battleship *General Belgrano* in the Falklands War. Such high-profile successes had won Brian recognition as one of Britain's leading media lawyers and I soon realised how fortunate we were to have him masterminding our legal defence.

Brian told us bluntly that we faced an uphill task in seeking to persuade the judge to rescind the Production Orders because the police, he said, would be able to say that the material being sought would be of vital importance to them in their ongoing terrorist investigation. Our best strategy, Brian suggested, would be to try to persuade the judge that lives would be lost if he did not cancel the Production Orders; we should argue in court that handing the names of our sources to the RUC was tantamount to writing them down and posting them to Billy Abernethy; since eighteen RUC Inner Circle officers sat on the Committee, it would only be a matter of time before the conspirators learned that it had been Ross's acolyte, Jim Sands, who had compromised them all, by appearing on Channel 4. Our best hope, therefore, was to invite the judge to accept that his Production Orders, if obeyed as the law required, would create a grave risk that Sands's name would leak from the RUC to the Committee, with potentially fatal consequences.

Brian further advised that we might also be able to persuade the judge that the lives of the programme makers could be similarly threatened because the Committee might be able to learn our personal details, including the addresses of our temporary "safe houses," again through a leakage of information from members of the RUC Inner Circle; we could try to persuade the judge that this risk to the production team was real because, since the broadcast, we had received a number of written death threats containing sensitive and unpublished information, which suggested that they had been written by someone close to or on the Committee. In summary, we were advised that our chances of overturning the Production Orders were slim and that our hopes rested on the exceptional circumstances of our case—the alleged corruption of the RUC and the consequential security threat to our source and to ourselves.

We arrived at Middlesex Crown Court on the morning of November 15th to plead our case in front of His Honour Judge Derek Clarkson QC, the man who had granted the original Production Orders to the RUC just over two weeks earlier. Jonathan Caplan QC, representing both Channel 4 and Box Productions, opened the proceedings—which were held *in camera*—by giving a brief summary of what the programme had alleged and an account of the security threats that had arisen during the production, describing how four of the programme-makers and their families had been rehoused in safe accommodation at Channel 4's expense.[3] He then developed his case by reading to the court an extract from a letter Channel 4's Chief Executive, Michael Grade, had written to the Metropolitan Police in an effort to persuade them not to proceed with the Production Orders.

> The programme makes serious allegations about the involvement of the RUC in the activities of the Committee and there is, there-

fore, a real concern that information in the hands of the RUC could find its way into the hands of Loyalist paramilitaries. If the material sought from Box and Channel 4 is disclosed, as the Production Orders require it to be, and the investigation remains under the control of the RUC, the new home addresses of the production team and the other information about their activities in making the programme will be revealed. This information, in the hands of members of the Committee (upon which senior serving members of the RUC are to be found) would place the programme makers in danger. This danger will continue until such time as the investigation into the allegations made by the programme is conducted by an outside force.

Further, this programme was made possible by the cooperation of sources without whom it would not have been possible to make these serious allegations public. This cooperation was gained by giving undertakings to respect the confidentiality of those sources. We are confident that if the identity of those sources became known to the Committee, their lives would be at risk.

After our barrister had outlined the basis of our case, Judge Clarkson intervened with a few observations, which showed that he had clearly grasped our argument but, to our dismay, also showed his instinctive and apparently uncritical support for the police force in question, that "highly reputable concern," the RUC.

You say if we reveal all, in particular to that highly reputable concern, the RUC, ex-hypothesi on the basis of what the programme shows, we are doing two things. We are revealing information to a body which is already—and I must be careful in my choice of words—corrupted to some extent, and there would be a probable risk of the material reaching hands it should not reach and of untold damage being done, not only with the consequence of further, and possibly furthering, the knowledge that the so-called Committee already possesses, but putting in jeopardy the lives and welfare of a large number of people connected with the programme, as well as primary and secondary and other sources.

At this point I felt that, whatever decision Judge Clarkson might ultimately reach, we could not reasonably say he did not understand our position. Our mood had grown lighter as the morning wore on and the judge had appeared to be sympathetic to Mr. Caplan's developing argument. Our spirits rose further when, having been told by Mr. Caplan about the Chief Constable's precipitate reaction to the broadcast, Judge Clarkson intervened again and said, disapprovingly: "That is rather like the judge who announces his decision before he tries the case . . . I suppose it may be said that Chief Constables do not have to be as judicial as judges do."

Such remarks led those of us sitting silently on the court benches to consider whether, despite what we had been led to believe, the Production Orders might yet be overturned. And as we stood up to wait for the judge to leave for lunch, I looked across at the glum face of the RUC's Detective Chief Superintendent Nesbitt and wondered to myself whether he was as pessimistic as he looked. I allowed myself the luxury of imagining him on his plane back to Belfast that night, his afternoon having been even less enjoyable than his morning. However, I soon banished this thought from my mind, for I knew that the Crown had not yet presented its case and that it had powerful arguments on its side.

Our optimism was tempered with scepticism because we all knew that any judge was bound to be favourably disposed to a police request for his help in the fight against terrorism. We also knew that the emergency legislation, the PTA, embodied in law the British public's revulsion at IRA atrocities and had been rushed on to the statute book in the emotional aftermath of the slaughter of innocent civilians in Birmingham in 1974. Parliament had deliberately and decisively tilted the balance in the law in favour of the police, brushing aside the traditional rights and liberties of the subject, with a series of draconian "temporary provisions" which applied to everyone, journalists included. The harshest measure in this coercive legislation was and remains Section 18, which imposes on everyone—again, journalists included—a duty to pass on to the police any information obtained about terrorism, whether in the past, the present or planned for the future. Section 18 provides that:

> (1) *a person is guilty of an offence if s/he has information which he knows or believes might be of material assistance—*
> *(a) in preventing the commission by any other person of an act of terrorism connected with the affairs of Northern Ireland; or*
> *(b) in securing the apprehension, prosecution or conviction of any other person for an offence involving the commission, preparation or instigation of such an act,*
> *and fails, without reasonable excuse, to disclose that information as soon as reasonably practicable . . . to a constable . . .*

Although no journalist has ever been prosecuted under Section 18, its provisions had long overshadowed the work of the investigative journalist in Northern Ireland. Arguably, virtually everything we had discovered about collusion between Loyalists and the RUC Inner Circle, was covered by Section 18 and required us to report our findings to the very same police force we had found to be riddled with corruption. Sadly, the PTA made and makes no allowance for what we had discovered—that the authorities, the "constable" referred to above, might be disaffected members of the RUC Inner Force or Inner Circle, wearing the uniform of the

Crown but secretly colluding with one form of terrorist, Ulster Protestant/Loyalist, against another, Irish Catholic/Republican, in what many view as a civil war between two rival ethnic communities. Those who rushed the PTA into law made no provision for such an eventuality, the fact that a large part of a British police force was actively engaged in the promotion, rather than the prevention, of terrorism. We had not merely discovered an unprecedented murder conspiracy when we stumbled across the Committee; we had also found a constitutional impossibility, a "blind spot" in Britain's anti-terrorist legislation, which could not allow for the remarkable fact that a significant part of the RUC had become a terrorist organisation.

Brian Raymond would later write that the existence of Section 18 was incompatible with a liberal democratic society and that it created a "no-go" area for journalists. Any researcher who proposed, as Ben Hamilton had done at the beginning of 1991, to uncover secret information about collusion was running the risk of breaching Section 18. Brian argued that the public interest required that this part of the PTA should be abolished:

> From the specific viewpoint of the broadcaster, however, Section 18 negates the acknowledged function of the journalist as a source of information independent of the State. If the journalist is forced to hand all his or her information to the authorities as soon as it is acquired, then the government has an effective monopoly over all information in this sphere of activity, including, most significantly, information about its own wrongdoing, if that were to occur. Furthermore, the Section has no limits of time within it—even an investigation into the false convictions of the Birmingham Six or into IRA activity in the 1920s would be caught by its provisions. A statute which can only be enforced sensibly by a highly selective application of its provisions only serves to bring the law generally into disrepute while remaining a potent and unpredictable threat to those involved in otherwise perfectly legitimate and lawful activity.[4]

Fortunately, the RUC had not chosen to deploy Section 18 against us, perhaps anticipating—correctly, I believe—that publicity over a television journalist going to prison for exposing RUC collusion with Loyalist death squads would not enhance the force's already tarnished image around the world. Nor had the police chosen to use against us other *coercive* sections of the PTA, such as Schedule 7, Paragraph 6, which gives a judge the power to order any person against whom a Production Order has been made to give an explanation of "any material seized"—an order, for example, to identify the "Source A" referred to in the dossier we had handed over. Indeed, the RUC had chosen not to use the PTA against any individual, choosing instead to act only against the two companies involved, Channel 4 and Box Productions. We speculated on their reasons for pursuing this course and concluded that it may have been taken for the reason that companies cannot be sent to prison for disobeying court orders, while journalists might welcome the publicity such a fate would bring.

As we ate our lunch and discussed what had transpired in Judge Clarkson's court room that morning, we were well aware of the nature of the legal weapons the PTA had placed in the RUC's arsenal and we knew that they would not hesitate to use them against us. For the programme's allegations were, we believed, so grave that it was imperative that they be discredited; if they were not totally undermined and, as a result, were to become generally accepted as the truth—namely that a large part of the RUC was at the disposal of the Loyalist death squads—then the force would be unlikely to survive in its present form. The legal proceedings that had got under way that morning were, I firmly believed, the first step in a strategy designed to suppress the scandal and to enable the "investigators" to deliver the verdict the Chief Constable had announced when he had stated: "I utterly reject last night's television programme as an unjust and unsubstantiated slur on the good name of this Force." The RUC's overall strategy would not become clear for some time but, as we will see, the "investigators" had laid plans for discrediting the programme, whether they succeeded in identifying our source or not.

After lunch, the Crown's barrister, Mr. David Calvert-Smith, opened his case by recognising that the PTA was a desperate measure, a response to the desperate situation in Northern Ireland.

> It contains provisions which to the common lawyer—if I can, without disrespect to your Honour or my learned friend, class the three of us—are quite repugnant to our normal concept of the way in which the criminal process is conducted. Parliament has seen fit to pass it and it is for us at the Bar and for your Honour on the Bench, we would respectfully submit, to apply it. The clear intention of the Act is to override, and in some cases create new offences for failing to override, the normal course of the criminal law.

Before dealing with the court's immediate concern—whether or not the Production Orders should stand—Mr. Calvert-Smith fired a shot across our bows by suggesting that we may well have violated the most serious of the act's "repugnant" provisions, Section 18; he preferred not to comment further on that point "*at this stage.*" But he clearly envisaged the possibility that we might be compelled to return to court, at some future date, to face a prosecution for failing to inform the authorities, the RUC, about what we had uncovered about terrorism in the province. Having indicated the Crown's readiness to use the PTA's entire arsenal of "repugnant" provisions against us, he then turned to the dispute over the Production Orders and explained to the court that Schedule 7 of the PTA required the judge to override the normal legal protection offered to journalistic material which may be held in confidence. Such material, he explained, is normally protected as "excluded material" under the Police and Criminal Evidence Act 1984—which means that a police officer cannot, for example, seize a journalist's confidential notebooks without first obtaining a judge's permission. He spelled out the PTA's provisions on such protected or "excluded" journalistic material.

> The whole point of Schedule 7 is to override the normal application of the criminal law in the Police and Criminal Evidence Act . . . The whole point of Schedule 7 is that it [the material sought] has to contain excluded material. You cannot make the order unless you are satisfied that it does contain such material.

So the argument that the programme's sources had given their information in confidence and that the journalists were bound to respect that confidence, said Mr. Calvert-Smith, "simply flew out the window." The PTA has no truck with journalistic confidentiality, he suggested, with the result that Channel 4 and Box Productions had a legal duty to hand over all materials, including any that had been acquired in confidence. "I suppose," he added, "if I may be forgiven for being oversimplistic, what I am saying, in essence, to you is that Parliament has given the police a thirty-love start, if we are talking of a game of tennis, by overriding . . . the normal protections that apply in the normal field of criminal law."

Having effectively demolished the admittedly remote prospect that the judge would be swayed by the fact that we had obtained information in confidence, Mr. Calvert-Smith proceeded to attack our only remaining hope of success, namely the risk to life that might result from our obeying the Production Orders. Before doing so, however, he assured the court that the RUC was determined to establish the truth of the televised allegations and that it was, therefore, vital that the police obtain the identity of Source A, as soon as possible. The judge must ask himself: "What is the public interest in finding out if this ring [Inner Circle] exists; if it does, who is in it and can we not root them out?. . .How can the allegation really be pursued unless they know the source from which the allegations have come?" He then proceeded quickly to demolish our second argument— that the material sought might identify our new home addresses, thereby creating a security threat—by telling the judge that the RUC investigators had no interest in obtaining such information. "There would be no objection from our side if those pieces of information were withheld."

This concession meant that our only remaining hope of persuading Judge Clarkson to rescind the Production Orders was to persuade him that our key source on the Committee—Source A—would be killed if his name was given to the RUC and, from there, it then made its way to Abernethy and company. And on this point, at least, we seemed to have made progress. For the judge indicated that he accepted our argument that, if the material were to be handed over, Source A's days could be numbered.

> The fact is that your supergrasses and others are protected far more than most cabinet ministers, are they not, when they are giving evidence. It is not because somebody is going, to use a modern phrase, to "rough them up." They are going to be killed. I have lived long enough to know, many years ago, when murder was exceptional. Now homicide is general . . . There is a real risk in this case that Source A will be killed. Is that accepted?

Mr. Calvert-Smith replied that, while he did not accept that, he believed Channel 4 to be genuinely concerned about the risk to the life of its source. "Whether there is [a risk], with the greatest of respect, depends on whether these allegations are worth tuppence." He added that we would never know the truth, if the judge failed to uphold the Production Orders. "Unless the police are able to make the enquiries into whether there is such a ring, who are members of it and bring them to justice, we shall never know."

The Crown then called RUC Detective Chief Inspector Samuel Ronald Mack, who testified on oath that the investigation was genuine, a serious attempt to establish the truth about the programme. It was, he said, obviously important to discover the identity of Source A. Chief Inspector Mack told the court:

> We may think this [programme] is a tissue of lies. It may turn out to be a tissue of lies; it may turn out to be a very important issue in the investigation of the killings of these seven people who have been killed. I make the point that others have been killed since the programme and will still be killed and continue to be killed.[5] If this source exists, and is a member of this Committee and knows about these murders which are under investigation, we want to certainly assess that. At the same time, if the allegation is true that there are members within the police force who are in collusion, we want to thoroughly investigate every aspect of it. No stone will be left unturned on this aspect. It has been given a very high priority.

After this testimony, the judge commented that his lay friends would say that allowing Source A to be interrogated by the RUC—"the very force he is attacking"—is "a strange way of doing things." When Mr. Mack assured him that the source would be "handled professionally and very carefully," Mr. Calvert-Smith explored the possibility that Source A might turn out to be a defendant, rather than a witness, as he had confessed to participating in a murder conspiracy.

Mack: That is depicted on the programme and reading the transcript, yes.

Calvert-Smith: He allegedly puts forward his motives for coming forward in the way he has to television as being to "reassure" the Loyalist community that people are fighting for them and taking steps to eradicate Republicans who the "police" have failed to remove from the community. That is the justification that we see in the transcript for his behaving as he did.

Mack: Yes.

Calvert-Smith: Therefore, as you said to his Honour, you would want to get from him any information, and particular evidence to substantiate that information, which may give evidence with a view, either perhaps to calling him as a witness or to prosecuting him on his own or with others?

Mack: I take those points, yes, and the degree of enquiry and collusion that would be required, taken that these allegations are, in actual fact true and the degree of collusion is mammoth, one must look at that. If the allegations are correct, the degree of collusion spreads right through the British Army here on the street, and in areas where there is the Ulster Defence Regiment, and the police, so it is to be a collusion, if these allegations are correct, of all those particular organisations.

The detective had testified on oath that, if the RUC found Source A and discovered he was telling the truth, he and his co-conspirators could go on trial for murder. What's more, he conceded—again, on the assumption that Source A was telling the truth—that the degree of collusion, involving the British Army, RUC and UDR, could, possibly, be seen to have been "mammoth." Unfortunately, no-one in the court room asked Mr. Mack whether it was at all likely that the RUC could tolerate a genuinely independent investigation and allow it to arrive at such an unpalatable conclusion, namely that much of the force was actively involved in promoting terrorism.

We already knew from Sands, after all, that the RUC inquiry was completely bogus and that—despite Mr. Mack's sworn testimony—there was no prospect whatever of it delivering a truthful verdict.[6] So, when Mr. Caplan rose to begin his cross-examination and to try to obtain for the court a sense of the thoroughness of the RUC's internal inquiry, he asked the detective to tell us what he knew about the Committee's alleged chairman, Billy Abernethy. We should remember that these proceedings were taking place six weeks after the programme had alleged that a campaign of political assassination, which was still ongoing, was being run by an Ulster

Bank manager and part-time member or former member of the RUC Reserve.

Caplan: Is it right that Mr. Abernethy, the name that I mentioned this morning, was a former member of the RUC?

Mack: I know Mr. Abernethy as a Bank Manager in the Ulster Bank. I believe it is in Tandragee, Co. Armagh. I have no knowledge of Mr. Abernethy being a member of the RUC.

Caplan: Have you looked at his files?

Mack: Not personally.

Caplan: It was said a moment ago that there was a need to discover the identity of Source A, so that the allegations in the programme could be verified. Do you remember saying that?

Mack: That is quite right.

Caplan: There are nineteen names in the folder which you, or your superiors, have as being alleged members of the Committee in question.

Mack: There are nineteen names.

Caplan: I do not want to know what you have done, or what you are doing, but it is feasible, is it not, for those nineteen individuals to be checked either by means of surveillance or by some other form of investigation?

Mack: That is quite correct. If we can establish who the nineteen people are. I have said, and I say again, they do not all exist.

Judge Clarkson: Some of them do?

Mack: Some do and some do not.

Caplan: There are other names in the dossier, and it is perfectly possible for you to speak as you already have done to some of those people?

Mack: Yes.

Caplan: There are details of where it is said the Committee held meetings throughout the province. Is that not right?

Mack: That is correct. Those have been looked at and are presently under investigation. Again, I say without revealing anything too much of the inquiry, that some of these places do not exist and no meetings took place.

Those of us sitting in court, who had been involved in the programme for the past ten months, were astounded by the detective's performance. He was testifying, on oath, just six weeks after Channel 4 had handed his colleagues an eighty-seven-page dossier containing details on sixteen political assassinations which had, allegedly, taken place during the previous three years; killings sanctioned and organised by a secret Committee; whose chairman was, of all things, an *ex-policeman*—a former member of the RUC Reserve. Yet the detective was now asking the court to believe that, in the course of the investigation set up six weeks earlier by the Chief Constable himself, he had not yet managed to establish, one way or the other, whether the alleged chief conspirator was or was not a member of Her Majesty's one and only police force in the whole of Northern Ireland.

The detective was also decidedly unenthusiastic about the other information contained in the dossier: the other eighteen alleged Committee members?—"They do not all exist;" the locations where they were said to have met?—"Some of these places do not exist and no meetings took place;" have you looked at Abernethy's file?—"Not personally." Chief Inspector Mack's cross-examination had been brief and Mr. Caplan had, necessarily, been circumspect with his questions. Yet the message from the witness box had come over loud and clear; yet again, what we had heard privately from Sands turned out to be totally correct. We had heard nothing from this RUC "investigator" to challenge our belief that the ultimate verdict of the inquiry would, when it came, completely exonerate the entire force.

Although the two barristers debated the issues until late into the afternoon, the wide gulf that separated them did not shrink. Mr. Calvert-Smith maintained that the RUC's investigation would get nowhere without the name of Source A and, he added, the spirit of the PTA required the judge to uphold his original Production Orders. Mr. Caplan argued that "if eighteen representatives of the RUC in an Inner Force sit on the Committee . . . then . . . the risk of that material [Source A's name] finding its way to the Committee is a risk . . . that amounts to a threat to life." Each side had vigorously argued the merits of its case and pinpointed the weaknesses of its opponent. The arguments had been presented so clearly and forcefully that Judge Clarkson confessed, as he began to deliver his ruling, that he had, throughout the day, found himself torn one way and then the other, before finally coming to his judgement.

He began by saying that the programme had raised matters of "immense public concern," which were now being investigated by the RUC. This was not an ideal state of affairs because the two companies were being asked to hand over material to "the very body that may profit from it, and profit from it in the most evil way." It would have been "very desirable" to have had the investigation under the control of a "manifestly independent body." This, however, was a matter for the executive, not the judiciary; so the question for the court was whether the material should be handed to the RUC?

> What is in question is whether it is in the public interest to compel this revelation, having regard to the possible or even likely consequences. What is said at once, is that so far as the material that reveals the identification of Source A and other individual sources

who were material in the programme, as far as that revelation is concerned, it will almost inevitably put them at risk; a number of individuals who are at present not at risk of this kind, will become vulnerable to attack, almost certainly involving the infliction of fatal injury . . .

. . . my first reaction was to think straight away, it cannot really be my duty to compel disclosure of information that may lead to any appreciable risk that an individual may be set upon or even killed as a result of an order that I make. I do find, as a fact, on the material that has been placed before me—and the arguments that have been so well conducted from both sides—that to compel the two respondent companies to impart that information that relates to Source A and possibly other individuals, will almost inevitably expose those individuals to risk of death . . .

The question, therefore, is: Is the court to make an order in these circumstances? Having reflected carefully on the position, because it is an enormous responsibility, it seems to me that there are circumstances in which the court's duty does so compel . . . I come, with some reluctance I must admit, to the conclusion that the public interest does demand in this particular sphere there should be the fullest cooperation between those who have the information and material to hand, and those who can and will make use of it . . . they must hand material over to the Royal Ulster Constabulary so matters can be further investigated . . . I am not prepared to hold that nothing will be achieved by way of benefit . . . I have no doubt at all that I have reasonable grounds . . . for believing that it is in the public interest to hand them over . . . I decide, as I say not without hesitation and not without some regret, that the objection to my order is not one I can uphold.

The only qualification he allowed was to permit us to retain any document which might lead to the identification of the home addresses of the journalists involved. On the main issue, whether we should hand over to the RUC all material in our possession, we had lost. The Production Orders had been upheld and both Channel 4 and Box Productions were given a further seven days to comply. Now, the glum faces were on our side of the court room and it was the turn of the police to show their satisfaction with the outcome. As we gathered our papers and shuffled out into the street, downcast but still determined to protect our sources, we wondered what would happen next.

His Honour Judge Clarkson had been surprisingly candid in his admission that he had felt himself pulled in both directions, inclining initially to our point of view, subsequently leaning in favour of the police and, finally, reaching a decision that the public interest lay in handing over all our material to the properly constituted authority, the RUC. As I listened to his exposition of the arguments that had guided him to his decision, I wondered what he would say when he discovered that he need not have been so troubled. For none of us had ever been prepared, regardless of any judgement he might have reached, to breach our undertaking to Sands.

Prior to transmission, we had all believed that the public interest required us to do everything in our power to expose the murder conspiracy and the collusion that had enabled the Committee to end so many lives; and once the programme had been broadcast, we felt equally strongly that we could not honourably go back on our word and betray Sands to the police. Quite apart from any consideration of the consequences of such a betrayal, we felt that there was an important principle at stake. If we were to breach the undertaking we had given, it would reduce the likelihood that, in similar circumstances, another journalist would persuade a potential source to testify about official wrongdoing in return for a promise of protected anonymity. We had long known that in giving the undertaking to Sands we were, potentially, on a collision course with the law; and once Judge Clarkson had made his ruling, that potential conflict had become all too real.

The entire proceedings in the Middlesex Crown Court had been held in secret. Our lawyers had stressed repeatedly to us the importance of maintaining a strict silence about what was going on, a demand that required constant vigilance in the gossipy media world in which we lived. With all our existing problems, we had no wish to place ourselves in contempt of court for having divulged what had taken place in front of Judge Clarkson. Yet such fears appear not to have weighed so heavily on the minds of those who had brought the proceedings, the RUC and Scotland Yard officers who had sat opposite us in the court room throughout the hearings. For, just ten days after the hearing, two newspapers—the London-based *Sunday Telegraph* and the Belfast-based *Sunday News*—published accurate and detailed accounts of what had transpired in Judge Clarkson's court room.

The *Sunday Telegraph* story, under the headline "TV team ordered to name hit squad sources," told its readers that "RUC headquarters in Belfast will make no comment on the progress of the investigation," a reticence which clearly did not prevent someone who had been present in court from divulging what had gone on. The *Sunday News* story, under the headline "RUC SCORNS C4 DOSSIER," openly admitted that the newspaper had been briefed by RUC detectives appointed by the Chief Constable to investigate the programme's allegations. The story began with these words: "Detectives probing allegations of a secret RUC Inner Circle believe they are close to exposing it as 'a pack of lies'." The newspaper then proceeded to report comments, attributed to unnamed RUC sources, which bore a remarkably similar resemblance to the sworn testimony RUC Detective Chief Inspector Mack had given in the *in camera* proceedings in London.

> "It is becoming more and more likely that Channel 4 were led a merry dance," said an RUC source.
>
> Sources also said that the two names of RUC officers contained in a dossier handed over to C12 [the RUC's Serious Crime Squad] *don't exist*.
>
> Files on all former and serving RUC officers have been checked and they are not listed.
>
> Even the names of businessmen, solicitors and bankers named in the dossier are a joke.
>
> "A child could have told Channel 4 they were not involved in anything," the source claimed. [my emphasis]

As we were legally prohibited from countering these RUC-inspired newspaper reports, we could do nothing to counter the impression forming in the public mind that the *Dispatches* programme had been factually inaccurate and, quite possibly, "a joke," "a merry dance," "a pack of lies"—a hoax. We will see later that these newspaper reports were merely the first skirmish in a long propaganda war which the RUC would wage against Channel 4 and Box Productions over the programme.

A week after the court hearing, our solicitor Brian Raymond wrote to the Crown Prosecution Service [CPS] to say that a pile of documents had been prepared for collection in obedience to the judge's order. He then turned to the more delicate task of informing the Crown that other documents, which until now nobody had referred to, had been sent abroad and that we did not propose to bring them back into the court's jurisdiction, regardless of the judge's order.

> It is true that during the production of the programme a great deal of material, including for example, taped conversations with Source A, came into existence. By its very nature, such material was extremely sensitive and required the most careful security measures to prevent it falling into the wrong hands. Such material was, as a consequence, kept to an absolute minimum and when no longer required was destroyed. Advice was taken from Leading Counsel (Mr. Gareth Williams QC) who advised, in the context of Section 18 and Schedule 7 of the Prevention of Terrorism Act, on what measures could properly be taken in relation to material which had been gathered.
>
> At the end of the production process but before transmission, such material as had not been destroyed was collected together and, on legal advice to Channel 4, sent out of the jurisdiction of the Court, again for security purposes and to avoid any improper seizure.

Channel 4's letter to the CPS, which also contained the above two paragraphs, added another significant passage:

> Indeed, the only person within either of the respondent companies who knows the precise whereabouts of this material is an employee of Box Productions who is currently out of the jurisdiction and not likely to return in the near future since he is in fear of his own safety. We would refer you to the judge's ruling if you are in doubt as to whether such fear is well founded.
>
> No individual within our client company knows of the precise whereabouts of this material but it is certainly not within our client's possession.

The employee referred to was Ben Hamilton, who had flown to South Africa for a well earned holiday and to place himself far away from anyone planning retaliation against him for his role in getting the programme on to the screen. Ben had been identified as a possible target by the author of several anonymous threatening letters we received shortly after the broadcast. His absence meant that the material the RUC was seeking and which the judge had ordered to be handed over was inaccessible to both Channel 4 and Box Productions, as only Ben knew where it was actually stored. However, I felt at the time that Channel 4's claim not to have "possession" of the material was bound to be challenged by the CPS, as was the cheeky assertion by the solicitors for both companies that "our clients have, therefore, complied with the order." So it did not come as a surprise when, just before Christmas 1991, the CPS wrote to tell us that it did not share this assessment and that it had, therefore, relisted the case for another hearing by Judge Clarkson. We were required, as we had anticipated, to appear again in his court room in the New Year, on January 9th 1992.

And so, just under two months after Judge Clarkson had upheld his original Production Orders, we found ourselves back in his court room, with our lawyers doing their utmost to avoid a situation in which we would be legally compelled to hand over documents containing the identity of our source. The Crown's barrister, Mr. Calvert-Smith, began by telling the court that the previous hearing had been conducted on "what can only be described as an entirely false basis." He suggested that Judge Clarkson had been forced to agonise, quite unnecessarily, over the possibility that his orders would pose a threat to the life of Source A—when there had never been any such risk at all, due to the fact that all sensitive programme materials had been sent abroad. The two letters from the solicitors acting for Channel 4 and Box Productions were, maintained Mr. Calvert-Smith, "really not good enough;" and he claimed that it was now quite obvious that the court's orders had not been complied with. He then invited Detective Chief Superintendent Jimmy Nesbitt, who was leading the

RUC's "investigation" into the programme, to testify on oath about the importance of getting full compliance by both companies with the Production Orders.

> *Calvert-Smith*: What about Source A and his importance or otherwise to the investigation?
> *Nesbitt*: Source A is crucial to the investigation, your Honour.
> *Calvert-Smith*: Because?
> *Nesbitt*: Because, your Honour, he alleges that he had knowledge of and took part in the planning of acts of murder and other terrorist crimes; that he had knowledge of other persons who had taken part in these crimes and of members of the Royal Ulster Constabulary who were also accomplices in these matters.

Mr. Calvert-Smith had, in his opening remarks, told the court that the RUC had raised another, quite different, concern as a result of studying the documents that had been handed over. Though they had made no progress in their effort to identify Source A, it appeared that there was an £80,000 hole in the accounts, an unexplained difference between what Channel 4 had paid Box Productions and what the company's records showed to have been spent. The Crown now put this matter to the RUC:

> *Calvert-Smith*: Why is it that the RUC are anxious to know whether another £80,000 was in fact disbursed by Box, and if so what is the relevance of it to your investigation?
> *Nesbitt*: The relevance is, your Honour, that we have discovered that some money was paid over to persons in Northern Ireland who helped out the Box Productions team. If they have interviewed members of the paramilitary organisations in connection with the programme, there is a possibility that some of that money could have gone to fund some of these organisations, Sir.

After the detective had left the stand, Mr. Calvert-Smith proceeded to draw attention to the fact that Channel 4 executives had explicitly stated in television interviews that they had satisfied themselves of the truth of the allegations made in the programme. He suggested that it was, therefore, obvious that the broadcaster must have had access to documents which had led the television executives to the judgements they had reached about the truth and accuracy of the broadcast. So the Crown was telling the court that it had expected to receive many more documents relating to the programme, not just from the production company but from the broadcaster as well:

> In general, senior officials, directors of programmes and the deputy commissioning editor are saying that it is not simply Box Productions who effectively had the evidence: "But we, as the responsible broadcasters, satisfied ourselves, no doubt through

documentation and so on, that it was a fair and accurate report that we put out in the *Dispatches* series."

Our lawyers had been left in no doubt about our determination to protect our sources and they knew that we would not, under any circumstances, betray Source A to the RUC. So when our barrister, Mr. Caplan QC, rose to answer the Crown's opening statement, he was well aware of the tricky position we now found ourselves in and he sought to defuse the judge's apparent irritation by explaining why, back in November, we had not revealed the fact that our most sensitive materials had been sent out of the court's jurisdiction before the programme had been broadcast and long before the Production Orders had been issued.

Your Honour, in relation to Source A, what we were doing on November 15th was challenging the public interest of such an order being in existence at all . . . those whom I represent were entitled, raising the ground that they had, to say that we wished to challenge the entirety of the order. And once the order had been confirmed, to volunteer, as they were obliged to do, what was not in their possession, and why not. But Your Honour, the other way round, in a case such as this, would have meant disclosing information which was not the kind of information that they wished to disclose.

Unfortunately, this elegant formulation did not dispel the judge's irritation and instead provoked him into the first of a number of outbursts, which quickly plunged us into gloom about what the eventual outcome of the day's proceedings would be. Judge Clarkson replied to the above as follows:

This becomes the most elliptical exercise or argument I have heard in a long time. I am going to say quite categorically now that I am beginning to be very disturbed indeed by all this. This programme was put out, I imagine, for two reasons. First of all because it is the concern of Channel 4 and Box to entertain the public, and they can entertain the public with lies, half lies or the truth.
Caplan: Your Honour, I interrupt to say I think the concern would be to inform the public.
Judge Clarkson: Yes, but you know what I mean . . . This was entertainment, but it also secondarily had another purpose surely, which was to provoke interest in the very grievous thing that is going on in Northern Ireland, namely terrorism by and on behalf of the Loyalist cause . . .
We spent a great deal of time, as I recall, going into what might happen and, if it is right, what the effect of an order would be. It would reveal to the RUC, some of whose members were suspect,

material that could lead to even further trouble . . . I well understand the tradition and practice of the journalist . . . they do endeavour to protect sources in general, and that is fair. They do not want to disclose things without orders of the court.

But once the process begins and the courts get involved, it seems to me that there should not be any kind of shadow-boxing, should there, Mr. Caplan? The judges do deserve a little more respect than that. And I was not told last time at all, was I, anything that led me to think that as a result of my order Source A was not to be revealed. If you asked me what I thought was to happen last time, it was that Source A, the identity and possibly the whereabouts of Source A would, most regrettably, be revealed. And I went away troubled about this, I may say partly because I have a personal concern, not just a judicial concern. And I went away sorely troubled by the thought that, as a result of what I had ordered or confirmed, I might be consigning somebody to a very unpleasant fate. And I felt concerned by this . . . You spent a good part of the day convincing me of how wrong it would be and how unwise it would be, and inhuman perhaps, to confirm my order, you see.

I am puzzled now why it is that, on 22nd November, the letter was being written [from Channel 4 and Box Productions] saying in effect: "We just cannot give you any information. We have out it, [*sic*] on legal advice really, [it's] out of our power to give you any information." Is not that the effect of the paragraph?

Mr. Caplan did his best to cope with Judge Clarkson's growing irritation at our failure to comply with his order. He was cut short by the judge when he began to repeat his argument that, at the last hearing, we were challenging the order in its entirety and that we did not, at that stage, feel any obligation to divulge the fact that the most sensitive programme materials were no longer within the court's jurisdiction. As soon as Judge Clarkson had shown his lack of sympathy for this line of defence, Mr. Caplan switched the discussion to the question whether it could be said that the documents, which had been sent abroad, could be said to be in the possession of Box Productions, especially in the light of a signed contract that had vested ownership with Channel 4.

> *Caplan*: My only caveat—and I am thinking aloud if I may for a moment—is whether it can be said that those documents abroad are actually within the possession of Channel 4 or Box. And, if not, whether under [PTA] Schedule 7 they can be ordered to require somebody who has immediate possession and control of them to return them, under the powers of Schedule 7. I just think aloud when I say that.
>
> *Judge Clarkson*: I think aloud: if I make an order I do not expect people to put all kind of obstacles in the way.

Judge Clarkson brushed aside all legal technicalities about ownership, possession and control. As far as he was concerned, he had made an order and he expected it to be obeyed. The time had come for Mr. Caplan to recognise, on behalf of his clients, that the court would not tolerate any further complications or delay. Looking down from the bench, His Honour's tone grew distinctly menacing, although he quickly reverted to the more benign humour which we had seen earlier in the day.

> *Judge Clarkson*: As I say, I hope I am not being trifled with, Mr. Caplan, in these proceedings, because if I get that impression I shall be very robust, I can assure you.
>
> *Caplan*: Your Honour is in no sense being trifled with.
>
> *Judge Clarkson*: I did not think so . . . My concern is to see that this order is complied with and in relation to that particular material [which was sent abroad].

While Judge Clarkson refused to accept the Crown's view that we had placed an "unreasonable obstruction" to the implementation of the Production Orders, it was clear that he expected us to cooperate fully with the RUC. And, addressing Mr. Calvert-Smith, he again stated his reservations about requiring us to facilitate the very same police force against which such grave allegations had been made.

> *Judge Clarkson*: You remember how, at first, when you were addressing me (and, I think, Mr. Caplan was persuading me) I was very troubled by the thought that what was really being asked for was the surrender to the Royal Ulster Constabulary . . .
>
> *Calvert-Smith*: Precisely.
>
> *Judge Clarkson*: . . . of material, in circumstances where it seemed a little strange, if I say Irish, I hope I shall not be . . .
>
> *Calvert-Smith*: I am afraid Your Honour may.
>
> *Judge Clarkson*: Right, yes, but you know what I mean. It is a little ironic that we were being asked to hand over material to the very organisation which itself was being criticized on the programme. And I saw, at once, you remember, you had a bit of an uphill struggle. Then it occurred to me, and so I held, that this was not really for me to decide. It had been decided, already, by the Secretary of State for Ireland [*sic*] and others who should conduct this investigation. It is not for me to say that it should be conducted by someone else. And, that being so, I thought it right, and you persuaded me that under the Statute it was right, that this material should be disclosed . . . I do hope, now, that the effect of the order will be that any material, such as is referred to, will now be disclosed.

As the day's hearing came to an end, Judge Clarkson's mood appeared to lighten and he seemed to believe he had resolved all outstanding difficulties; the missing materials would be brought back from France and immediately handed over to the RUC; though the fact that the RUC was investigating itself was "rather Irish"—by which he presumably meant it was unsatisfactory, not quite up to English judicial standards—this aspect of the affair was not his concern; still, now that he had made his decision, the RUC could proceed with its investigation. So, before bringing the day's business to an end, His Honour felt able to declare that he was "beginning rather to enjoy these proceedings," that he would "be sorry when they came to an end" and that he had been treated "with very great consideration by all." As I watched the learned judge retire contentedly to his chambers, I wondered how he would react when he discovered that the two companies had decided, after the most careful consideration of the consequences and with the very greatest respect to His Honour, that they would *not* hand over the outstanding materials, regardless of the consequences. I surmised that His Honour would be inclined, in his own words, "to be very robust" and that we would not have to wait very long before discovering what exactly he meant by those ominous words.

After the hearing, our solicitors quickly prepared a joint letter informing the Crown Prosecution Service that the two companies felt unable to comply with Judge Clarkson's orders. With all due respect to the court, our solicitors wrote, the sensitive materials—those which would undoubtedly enable the RUC to unmask Source A—would remain securely stored in France, beyond the jurisdiction of the court. And so, shortly after this letter had been sent, we were informed by the CPS that we should present ourselves for a further, third hearing in front of Judge Clarkson on the morning of Wednesday, January 22nd 1992. It was an appointment all of us would have preferred to avoid but one which we knew we had no option but to keep. None of us relished this prospect less than did our barrister, Mr. Jonathan Caplan QC. To him fell the unenviable task of explaining to Judge Clarkson why, despite the court's awesome powers, we felt obliged to disobey his orders.

Once the court was in session, Mr. Caplan began by quoting from the letter Channel 4's solicitors had sent to the CPS and which referred to two sets of documents which—despite the judge's orders—we were refusing to give to the RUC.

> *Caplan*: 3) Documents taken out of the jurisdiction by Ben Hamilton on the instructions of Channel 4 and Box.
>
> 4) Documents which might reveal the identity of the researcher (and inevitably his whereabouts). He was not among those individuals who was re-located and is therefore particularly at risk.[7]
>
> Your Honour, without going into detail, I think what matters is obviously the next paragraph.
>
> "Our client"—that is Channel 4—"having considered the

matter carefully in the face of clear legal advice and its consequences, has resolved by unanimous decision of its Board that it
is unable to complete its compliance with the Production Order
by producing material within (3) and (4) above. Our client recognises that it is thereby in breach of the order but it feels unable
to expose either Source A or the researcher to such grave personal risk. This decision is based not simply on what may be
described as 'journalistic' reasons relating to the protection of
such sources but because it genuinely believes that the risk of
death to the individuals must outweigh, in its own conscience,
any other consideration.

"It follows that since our client is unwilling to give access to
documents which may lead to the identity of the researcher or
Source A, it would feel equally unable to comply with any order
it obtained under Schedule 7 of Paragraph 6 of the 1989 Act.

"Our client is aware of the consequences which could follow
this letter and we are therefore arranging for the matter to be relisted so that our client can explain its position to the judge for
him to determine what course should now be taken."

Your Honour, a similar letter, in identical terms, was delivered
to the Crown Prosecution Service at this court by hand on behalf
of Box Productions.

Mr. Caplan made no attempt to disguise the fact that his two clients,
Channel 4 and Box Productions, now found themselves in breach of the
judge's orders. He conceded that the companies were, therefore, in contempt of court and would have to pay an appropriate penalty. After this
frank admission, he then sought to persuade the judge that the proper procedure, on the basis of legal precedent, was to refer the matter to the
Attorney-General who would, in due course, begin proceedings in the
Divisional Court. "The reason," he argued (quoting a former master of
the Rolls), "is that the judge should not appear to be both prosecutor and
judge: for that is a role which does not become him well." In legal terms,
Mr. Caplan argued, a contempt would only be urgent and imperative if
immediate action was called for, such as when a witness is threatened during a trial or court proceedings are disrupted by violent action.

The Crown's barrister, Mr. William Boyce (who had replaced Mr.
Calvert-Smith), objected to the proposal for a reference to the Attorney-
General and urged the court to deal immediately with the deliberate and
continuing affront to its dignity.

This is not a typical case and, if this is not a typical case, there is
no reason in my submission why principles which have been developed in relation to other circumstances should be applied to this
. . . The situation is simple. An order has been made by this court.
It has been disobeyed by companies guided by intelligent, mature,

well-advised men, who had all the time they required to think, and they have said "no."

Judge Clarkson's response, as we had come to expect, was rational and fair-minded; and he was not embarrassed about thinking aloud as he weighed the merits of the conflicting arguments. His obvious frustration over our refusal to obey his orders and his expressed fear that he might be accused of shuffling responsibility off to another court may have caused him to voice his displeasure. He made it clear that, if he were to exercise his right to punish the contemnors directly, he would indeed be very robust.

> *Judge Clarkson:* . . . If it is urgent and imperative that an order be complied with, it seems to me that the judge of first instance ought to see what he can do to get such compliance.
>
> *Caplan:* I would not wish to stop Your Honour giving any indication that Your Honour wishes to give, of course not.
>
> *Judge Clarkson:* The indication would be an unhappy one because I do not believe that I ought to impose a fine which is simply a financial penalty which the companies may decide it is preferable to pay rather than comply with the order of the court. It would have to be such a fine as would put their existence in peril.
>
> *Caplan:* I am grateful for such an indication.
>
> *Judge Clarkson:* Oh yes! It would be absurd simply to say, "a fine of £X,000," and they say, "We would rather pay that than do our duty." It would have to be obviously a fine that imperilled their existence.

Mr. Caplan replied that as it was, in the strict legal sense, neither urgent nor imperative that the judge deal with the contemnors directly, he ought to refer the case to the Attorney-General, who would then bring an action for contempt in the Divisional Court. At that point, said Mr. Caplan, the two companies would be free to challenge afresh the entire decision of the court by arguing that the judge ought never to have made or upheld the Production Orders. Although Judge Clarkson may not have welcomed this idea, he could see that if we succeeded in having the case referred to a higher court, via the Attorney-General, we would indeed seek to have his orders overturned. Such was Mr. Caplan's masterly exposition of the relevant legal precedents that he led Judge Clarkson to overcome his natural inclinations and to refer the case elsewhere.

Almost four months after the broadcast and nearly three months after the Production Orders had been issued, Judge Clarkson finally ruled that there would have to be yet another delay as the Attorney-General entered the affair and, in accordance with legal precedent, petitioned the High

Court to deal with the contempt. As the judge's ruling gives a fair summary of where we had arrived on January 22nd 1992 and was to be the basis of subsequent, highly-publicised proceedings in the High Court, I quote it at length.

Judge Clarkson: I have heard arguments in this hearing and I find the decision at which I have to arrive extraordinarily difficult, because it seems to me that over a period of time the authorities have established that the preferable practice, and of this I have no doubt on the authorities to which I have been referred, is that judges at first instance should not themselves deal with alleged matters of contempt where they are said to arise before them, but should follow a procedure which is initiated by the aggrieved party or, if not by them, by the Attorney-General himself under Rules of the Supreme Court . . .

Mr. Caplan, who appears yet again for Channel 4 and Box Productions, has made it abundantly plain that he does not dispute that this court has jurisdiction and power to exercise today where there is, as is beyond question, a plain considered disobedience to the order I have made, and defined at a further hearing, and an express assertion that neither of his clients has the slightest intention of complying with the order . . .

. . . It seems to be conceded that there is contempt in the sense that there is a declared unwillingness to obey the order that has been made. My inclination has certainly been to try to enforce my order by exercising some jurisdiction that would have that effect or would be intended to have that effect. I have indicated already that, in my judgement, to impose fines that were simply the price paid for the stand taken, and some would say (I have no doubt) honourably taken, by these two companies and their officers for reasons which are plain in correspondence and made plain at these hearings, would not serve any useful purpose if the court's order is rightly made and is to be enforced . . . I myself, if I deal with the matter summarily, would be inclined to impose penalties that, as I have said, imperil their continued existence, because that seems to me the only way that orders such as the present can be enforced.

I have given careful consideration, I hope everybody will accept this, to the arguments that Mr. Boyce addressed to me and my mind, I must confess, has hovered between acceptance of what Mr. Boyce has said and acceptance of the arguments that Mr. Caplan has placed before me. Without the authorities . . . I incline to the view that I ought to deal with this matter summarily today and form such view as I think is appropriate and impose such sanctions as I think appropriate. But I feel constrained on the authorities to say that this is not a matter that is of such immediate urgency and a matter that is so imperative, to use the epithet that appears in the cases, that I ought to do so.

This did not mean, however that the Attorney-General should allow even more time to pass before he took action, said Judge Clarkson. Given that much time had already gone by since the broadcast, he suggested, it was urgent that Source A be found so that the RUC could establish the truth of the programme's allegations. "Rather Irish" though an internal RUC investigation might be, Judge Clarkson was clearly not prepared seriously to contemplate the possibility that the investigation was designed to suppress the truth and protect the conspirators. So, while he would not deal directly with the contempt, he urged the Attorney-General to move with all possible speed.

> I was impressed by the argument that so much time has gone by, and is going by, that urgency is of the essence. It seems to me that the Attorney-General can see the urgency, if he chooses, of this matter and so can any court, such as the Divisional Court that is moved to consider the matter. It is not that by coming to the decision that I reluctantly have that I wish to add to the lapse of time, because I do not. And I sincerely hope that if the matter is referred to the Attorney-General, as there is no doubt that it will be now, he will be told that, in my judgement, it is imperative and urgent in so far as he is concerned; and if he does take the view that it should go before the Divisional Court, and I dare say he will, that that court too may be told and those who are responsible for listing it may be told that this is not a matter to be shelved. It is a matter to be got on with as urgently as possible because it is in the public interest that that view be adopted.

What would happen next? Given the judge's view of how urgent it was that the RUC find Source A, would we be appearing in the High Court within a week? And what would happen when the High Court discovered that Channel 4 and Box Productions intended to continue defying the Production Orders? These were just some of the questions I asked my solicitor, Brian Raymond, as we left Middlesex Crown Court, each of us taking comfort from the fact that the next hearing, whenever it came, would be heard in open court and be fully reported by the newspapers, radio and television. The prospect of one of Britain's four national television channels being shut down for contempt by a High Court judge and, moreover, because of a programme which had exposed RUC death squads, ensured that our next appearance in court would take place in the presence of media representatives sympathetic to, possibly even enthusiastic for, the stand that we were taking.

Brian was delighted by the fact that the case had been referred to this highly political figure in the British constitutional set-up, the Attorney-General. For Brian's long experience in representing champions of radical causes, people who had found themselves in conflict with the law, had led him to the view that judges were not, as they like the public to think, detached and independent arbitors like Prudence with her balancing scales of justice. "Don't forget this," Brian once told me after a legal conference at the Inns of Court in London in November 1992, "judges are just politicians with wigs on." And he later reminded me that Judge Clarkson's decision meant that our case had been referred to a party politician, a Cabinet Minister in the Conservative Government, Attorney-General Sir Patrick Mayhew—the very same man who had, during the Westland Affair a few years earlier, demonstrated how he was willing to bend the judicial process for party political advantage. It would be naive, Brian suggested, to think that Sir Patrick would not do so again.

Though Judge Clarkson had emphasised the urgency of dealing with the matter quickly he had, said Brian, overlooked the fact that a general election was looming and that the Conservative Government would not wish to risk the possibility of a highly public law case against Channel 4 being held as the voters prepared to go to the polls. Sir Patrick Mayhew would almost certainly wait, Brian suggested, until the election was safely over before allowing this potentially embarrassing matter to surface into public view.

This confident prediction proved to be entirely correct. As the weeks, and then the months of February and March, came and went without any visible move by Sir Patrick, I realised how shrewd Brian's instincts had been. And his cynicism about the supposedly apolitical character of Britain's judicial system was further consolidated when, on the day after the general election in April 1992 and with the Conservative Government safely returned to office, Sir Patrick—"another politician with a wig on"—petitioned the High Court to begin contempt proceedings against us. For reasons about which we can only speculate, those proceedings would not—despite Judge Clarkson's "urgency"—get under way until a further four months had passed and, even then, only after the newly elected Parliament had risen for the summer recess.

This convenient timetable ensured that when the Attorney-General eventually came to start his action against us in the High Court, there would be no prospect of any embarrassing questions in the House of Commons about collusion, RUC death squads or *The Committee*. Sir Patrick had ensured that the controversy, which would inevitably erupt after Channel 4 had been punished for its contempt, could be politically managed and safely contained—an outcome of direct personal interest to Sir Patrick because, immediately after the election, the Prime Minister agreed to give him the Cabinet post he most wanted, Secretary of State for Northern Ireland.

Notes

1   Although Sands later told us that the Committee had organised the murders of Patrick Shanaghan (August 1991) and Bernard O'Hagan (September 1991) this information came too late for inclusion in the Channel 4 dossier. [See Chapter 7]

2   The name, Jim Sands, was not one of the nineteen names listed in the Channel 4 dossier.

3   *In camera* proceedings mean that the press and public are excluded from the court room. Our lawyers warned us not to comment publicly on what was going on, fearing that we might commit contempt of court. As will become clear, the RUC did not feel similarly constrained and a steady stream of unofficial court reports, all favourable to the RUC, began to appear in the newspapers.

4   Brian Raymond, unpublished memorandum on the Prevention of Terrorism Act as an impediment to investigative journalism.

5   The seven people were Denis Carville, Patrick Finucane, Sam Marshall and the four Cappagh victims.

6   Sands did not indicate why he was so certain that the Nesbitt Inquiry was bogus. I would have to wait almost another four years before obtaining documentary evidence showing that Sands was quite right to be cynical about the ultimate verdict of the Chief Constable's "Inquiry." [See Appendix 3]

7   This was a reference to our researcher in Northern Ireland, Martin O'Hagan.

Chapter 7

THE PROFESSIONALS

From the moment the programme was transmitted on October 2nd 1991, there has never been any doubt in my mind about the far-reaching consequences the broadcast would have for the journalists who had made it, the television executives who had presided over it and, most especially, for the fifty to sixty individuals who had participated in the murder conspiracy. For Channel 4 had not broadcast the programme as a speculative theory about what might be happening within the province, but as a thoroughly researched documentary which put forward allegations of the utmost gravity. The Channel had stated as a *fact* that members of the business and professional classes—banking, accountancy, law, the church, the university as well as the owners of some of the biggest companies in the province— were meeting regularly to sanction and plan murder; professionals drawn from the Ulster Protestant community were, together with disaffected RUC officers, placing their skills and resources behind the Committee's assassination campaign.

These allegations were either true or they were false. If true, the fifty to sixty members of the Committee were, I believed, as guilty of murder as the men who actually pulled the trigger. If false, our careers in journalism, I also believed, would effectively be over; as with *The Sunday Times'* catastrophic blunder over the Hitler Diaries, our reputations would never recover. So, before the programme was screened, I well understood that the stakes on both sides could not be higher. This explains why those of us engaged on this project had stretched ourselves to the limit of our abilities and resources in establishing the facts before recommending to Channel 4 that it ought to broadcast the programme. And I think it also explains why those who have so much to lose if this story is believed, the murder conspirators and their protectors within the RUC and the British "security" forces, have gone to such lengths to discredit our journalism and why now, more than six years after the broadcast, all these people will do their utmost to prevent this scandal being fully exposed.

Armed with the Channel 4 dossier, which contained the names of nineteen conspirators and clues to the identities of several more, it should have been relatively easy for the RUC to track down the guilty men. Instead, as we have seen, the Chief Constable opted for a futile and unnecessary legal battle to force us to betray our principal source. As a result, the Committee remained intact and its members were given time to recover from the shock of the initial exposure. Before long, according to Sands, they were back in business and eventually in a position to resume their murder campaign; we shall see later that the British Government's reaction to the programme, which left the initiative with the RUC, resulted in the loss of further innocent Catholic lives between 1991 and 1994.

We had first encountered Source A [Sands] in 1991 and would continue to keep in communication with him until almost the end of 1992. At the time of the broadcast and during the subsequent legal actions which arose from it, Source A was our only source on the Committee; all our allegations about Abernethy, Ross and the others, ultimately originated from him. We knew that if he turned out to be a fraudster, we would be professionally ruined; and we also believed that, if he was telling the truth, which we were absolutely convinced he was, further investigation would, with luck, allow us to complete the picture he had painted of the conspiracy. I did not realise on the day of transmission, October 2nd 1991, or during the subsequent legal proceedings in 1991 and 1992, that I would still be investigating this murder conspiracy a full six years later; fortunately, since then I have not found a single reason to doubt that Source A was telling the truth as he understood it and, as we shall see, I have also established that the RUC's primary concern throughout has been to discredit the programme's allegations.

In 1991, we appreciated that Sands, as "Reverend" Hugh Ross's messenger and general assistant, was totally trusted but, at the same time, relatively junior among the conspirators; only much later would I realise that he was fairly exceptional in that most of the others were better educated and enjoyed the higher social status that their professional qualifications and money had brought them. We also appreciated that Sands did not have a complete grasp of all relevant details; we had, for example, noted his admission during filming in London that he did not know the identity of the RUC Assistant Chief Constable who was said to be a member of the Inner Circle. Still, Sands had given us a detailed picture of the overall conspiracy and, indeed, had provided much more information than we had been able to use in the programme.

We knew, for example, the identities of nineteen Committee members but we were unable, for legal reasons, openly to accuse any of these individuals by name of participation in the murder conspiracy; specifically, we were unable to state that Billy Wright was the notorious King Rat or to tell our viewers that—despite his denials—he had both murdered Denis Carville and carried out the Cappagh killings on behalf of the Committee. Similarly, we had also been legally obliged to take great care in handling the contribution of the only other Committee member to appear in the Channel 4 broadcast, Presbyterian Minister Hugh Ross.

As indicated earlier, we knew that Ross was a Jekyll and Hyde character, Christian minister in public, Loyalist terrorist in private. During our interview with him in the summer of 1991, we had judged it prudent to allow him to pose as a purely political and peaceful figure, though we would love to have asked him how he reconciled the murder of Denis Carville with the teachings of the Gospel—for example, "Thou shalt not kill." And, as with Billy Wright, we had also been careful not to give him the impression that we already knew about the existence of the Committee and about his role in the murder conspiracy. For we realised that we would not be able, under any circumstances, to ask Source A to come forward and point an accusing finger at either of these two men. Nor were we able, for exactly the same reason, to identify any of the other Committee members. We had found no-one who would be prepared, in the event of a libel action against us, to take the witness stand and declare: "Yes, I was present with these named individuals—X, Y and Z—when, together, we sanctioned and organised the murder of those named individuals A, B and C."

I imagine that Ross must have been greatly relieved to discover, while watching the broadcast, that neither he nor any of the other conspirators had been openly identified as Committee members. Nevertheless, he had made an appearance in a programme alleging that professional people, all drawn from the Protestant community, had thrown in their lot with the Loyalist terrorists. And, if this clergyman's subsequent testimony can be believed, his brief appearance in the film led some members of his congregation to conclude that he was not what he purported to be; they thought Channel 4 had accused him of being a terrorist. So, immediately after the broadcast, he sought to redeem his reputation by confronting the accusation head on. He accepted an invitation to appear on Channel 4's *Right to Reply*, a programme specifically designed to give aggrieved viewers a platform to answer their critics; Ross appeared on this programme just three days after the screening of *The Committee*.

He arrived at Channel 4's studios in London on Friday, October 4th, in the company of another politician from the province, none other than the man who had defeated him in the Upper Bann by-election the year before, the future leader of the Ulster Unionist Party, David Trimble MP.[1] Trimble had been invited to discuss the programme face-to-face with Channel 4's Karen Brown but Ross was allowed, first, to read a prepared statement which, given his key role in the assassination campaign, was of such shameless audacity and sheer chutzpah that it completely took my breath away. His brazen attempt to persuade the viewers that he was a peaceful man of the Gospel reminded me of Joseph Goebbel's infamous remark that the bigger the lie, the more likely it was to be believed. Sadly, unlike the programme makers, none of the viewers had been able to listen to Ross's assistant, Jim Sands, explaining to Ben Hamilton that his boss was one of the most ruthless fanatics in the Loyalist camp; so they would have had no reason to doubt the truth of the statement Ross was allowed to read out or to realise that his forthright denials were sanctimonious humbug. This is what Ross was allowed to state on the programme, unchallenged and under the cloak of respectability provided by his ministry in the Presbyterian Church:

> The interview I gave was set in the context of the Brooke talks. [*Secretary of State Sir Peter Brooke's attempt to start all party talks.*] I was given no indication whatsoever that alleged collusion between the security forces through a shadowy Inner Force linked to paramilitaries would form the basis and central theme of the programme. In my interview, I emphasised categorically that there was no connection between the Ulster Independence Committee and the Loyalist paramilitaries. Indeed, this important statement was deliberately excluded. The programme was presented in such a way as to imply that I had some unspecified association with paramilitaries, leading to the elimination of suspected members of the Irish Republican movement. The use of the Ulster national flag as a backdrop in the scenes dealing with the alleged Inner Force paramilitary meetings linked the Ulster Independence Committee with clandestine activities of which we have no knowledge. The Ulster Independence Committee was formed to promote the cause of a sovereign, united independent Ulster, carefully negotiated with England and based on an agreed constitution and Bill of Rights. This practical way forward would be gained only through political channels. It is disgraceful that this programme set up an innocent law-abiding person as a potential target for IRA gunmen. A totally false impression was given, and I stress again, I have no links with the alleged Inner Force or paramilitaries and neither has the Ulster Independence Committee.

As I watched Ross's performance, I recalled what Sands had told us in his filmed interview, namely that twenty-two representatives from the Ulster Independence Committee—President "innocent, law-abiding" Hugh Ross—sat on Abernethy's Committee alongside eighteen representatives of the RUC Inner Force. I also recalled that the only disagreement between Sands and Ross was on the single issue of whether the Committee ought to go public about its activities, whether the fifty to sixty Committee members should openly tell "the people of Ulster" (by which Sands and Ross meant, of course, the Protestants) what they were actively engaged in—seeking to wipe out the IRA and to defeat Irish Republicanism by counter-terror, to destroy the detested Anglo-Irish Agreement, prior to the creation of a new, sovereign and independent Ulster. The more cautious and pragmatic Ross obviously appreciated that such a public proclamation, while Her Majesty's writ still applied throughout Northern Ireland, was tantamount to booking overnight accommodation for life in one of Her Majesty's prisons, not just for himself but for all fifty to sixty Committee members. Hence, the necessity for an immediate and unambiguous denial of our allegations, delivered in the company and with the apparent endorsement of the apparently ever-so-respectable David Trimble MP.

Right to Reply's interviewer did not cross-examine Ross on any aspect of his statement. Instead, he put Ross's objections and criticisms to Channel 4's Karen Brown, who had elected to defend *The Committee* programme in the studio discussion. As an experienced journalist, alert to the pitfalls of libel, Karen knew that she could not confront Ross with the truth, namely that he was a prime mover in the murder conspiracy. For Karen fully understood that she would be unable to justify such a statement by calling Source A, Jim Sands, to testify against Ross in a court of law; Channel 4 lawyer Jan Tomalin had briefed Karen extensively on the libel dangers, with the result that she was forced to concede under questioning that the programme had not intended to suggest or imply that Ross was anything other than a peaceful politician—though she was able to point out that Ross, in his filmed interview, had declined to rule out the use of force to achieve his goals. Still, Karen's brief was such that she was unable to tell the viewers what we had discovered about him. So not for the first time, Britain's libel laws had helped a villain to prevent the public learning the truth but this was the only occasion, in my experience, where they could be said to have helped a criminal gang to get away, literally, with murder.

Karen was similarly constrained in the subsequent studio discussion with Trimble. As his constituency includes the notorious "murder triangle," we might reasonably have presumed that he would have been keenly interested in our revelations about how so many of his constituents had met their deaths. I have already noted Trimble's bizarre comment about the murder of one of his constituents, Denis Carville, a comment which fell far short of what we might expect from the constituency MP. As I watched his performance, I found it equally strange that his immediate public reaction was to denounce the programme for supposedly lacking credibility and to suggest that it was simply Republican propaganda. How would he have reacted, I wondered, if Karen Brown had been free to inform him that he was busily defending one of the principal murder conspirators. Little did I realise, at the time, that Trimble was well aware of precisely this fact and that he was using all his skills and status as a member of the House of Commons to do what he could to protect Ross and all the other conspirators, those responsible for many murders in his Upper Bann constituency and for numerous others elsewhere in the province.[2]

Only later would I realise that Trimble's televised scepticism about the existence of the Committee could not be accepted at face value; for, in June 1993, I learned via Jim Sands that Trimble regularly held secret meetings with the Committee's chairman, Billy Abernethy, and was aware of the fact that in doing so he was meeting the man who had sanctioned some of the worst atrocities of recent years, including the murder of Trimble's constituents—Denis Carville (19), Katrina Rennie (16), Eileen Duffy (17) and Brian Frizzell (29), to name but four. Unfortunately, we did not know this at the time Karen Brown faced Trimble in the studio but even if she had, thanks to our old friends the libel laws, she would have been unable to suggest that this newly elected Unionist MP had long been aware of the Committee's existence and had done nothing to stop its activities; as it had been with Ross, so it would have been with Trimble. So, both Ross and Trimble were able to exploit Britain's archaic libel laws and both were allowed to state categorically that "innocent" men had been irresponsibly accused of murder; and ironically—given what we knew about Ross and what we would later find out about Trimble—all Karen Brown could safely say, for legal reasons, was that we had never intended to name or to identify publicly any of the murder conspirators.[3] Fortunately, the libel laws did not require her to retract the whole story!

We quickly recognised that our inability to discredit Ross's robust denials on *Right to Reply* meant that he probably succeeded in persuading the casual viewer that he had been defamed. Certainly, his performance appears to have allowed him to rehabilitate himself with his congregation and it restored his confidence sufficiently to move him, in December 1991, to send Box Productions, through his solicitors, what the lawyers call a "letter before action." Given the detailed account Sands had provided about Ross's key role on the Committee, his close links to the other leading conspirators and the fact that he had much blood on his hands, his letter—quoted here in full—caused none of us the slightest concern.

> We write to you instructed by the Reverend Hugh Ross, 69 Farlough Road, Newmills, County Tyrone, in the following circumstances.

On June 18th 1991 our client gave an interview to Mr. Ben Hamilton and a Mr. Nick Reed [sic] of Box Productions. He was given to understand that this was an opportunity to advance the views of the Ulster Independence Committee (U.I.C.) of which he was and is President.

U.I.C. was formed to promote the case for negotiated independence for Northern Ireland by peaceful means and by consent of both sides of the sectarian divide. He gave the interview on that understanding. It was provided in his home between the hours of 9.30 pm and 1.00 am for a total filmed time of some two hours.

On June 19th the film crew returned to Black Skull to film Rev. Ross dedicating an Ulster National Flag symbol of the U.I.C. and a small band parade.

On Wednesday, October 2nd 1991 Channel 4 Television broadcast a programme "Despatches" [sic] in which they linked U.I.C., its flag and Rev. Ross with an alleged criminal Inner Force paramilitary organisation. A thirty-second extract from the Box Productions film, taken quite out of context, depicting our client against the backdrop of the Ulster National Flag was included in the material. The programme made no attempt to outline the real aims and objects of the U.I.C. Instead, the extract was [sic] in juxtaposition with the main subject matter and in a context which necessarily defamed our client's character and reputation and misrepresented U.I.C. The programme implied and indeed in the opinion of some who saw it directly suggested that Rev. Ross was involved in the Inner Force, that he gave political cover and credence to its aims and objects and that he was involved in acts of murder, deceit, subversion and conspiracy.

The programme further alleged that the members of the Inner Force were dedicated to the cause of the U.I.C. The producer deliberately excluded statements in the interview of June 18th which categorically denied and eschewed any links with paramilitary organisations.

The U.I.C. has been misrepresented as an extremist organisation. Persons have been described as amongst its membership who are not and would not be permitted to be.

Our client points out that he was not consulted at any time about the content of the Despatches [sic] programme before it went out.

Following the programme the "Right to Reply" producer invited our client to take part in the programme. That programme is broadcast at a time when it attracts few viewers. The producers of "Despatches" and "Box Productions" declined to appear. The occasion afforded no proper opportunity to reply. Neither Channel 4 nor Box Productions offered any excuse or apology.

Our client has since been interviewed by the R.U.C. Special Branch on at least two occasions and after-caution statements taken from him. He has had many telephone calls from persons who saw or heard the programme.

It is clear that our client's character has been defamed by an irresponsibly and recklessly produced programme. His personal safety has been placed in jeopardy.

We write to require an open retraction and apology and to claim damages for defamation. If we have not received a satisfactory response with [*sic*] seven days we shall commence proceedings.

Ross's letter had arrived in early December, while we were all preoccupied with the proceedings in Judge Clarkson's court, leading up to the contempt reference to Attorney-General Sir Patrick Mayhew. Four members of the production team, myself included, were still living in secure accommodation away from our homes and we knew, via Sands, that there was still a prospect that Abernethy and his friends might order a reprisal against one of us. Now, we were being threatened by a Committee member in a more orthodox manner, with one of the less worrisome hazards of our trade, the libel writ.

At first glance, it seemed that we now faced a serious threat. An apparently respectable Presbyterian Minister was alleging that we had accused him on national television of being involved, as the letter put it, "in acts of murder, deceit, subversion and conspiracy." In fact, we had little to worry about on the libel front because the script had been written in such a way that Ross's contribution had been embedded in the political section of the programme and deliberately kept at some distance from the section dealing with the Committee's assassination campaign—where, of course, he properly belonged and where he would have been featured but for the constraints imposed by the libel laws. Our Legal Counsel, Jonathan Caplan QC, had advised that the programme carried no significant risk of libel against Ross, Wright or anyone else. So, Ross was sent a curt reply by Channel 4's lawyer to the effect that, as Christmas was at hand, no effort would be made to meet his arbitrary deadline. And, as far as I am aware, Channel 4 did not bother to write to him again.

Ross's letter can now be seen, six years later, to have been exceedingly unwise. For he had stated that his character had been defamed and that he intended to begin a libel action against us if we did not retract, apologise and pay him damages. If he genuinely believed that false allegations of the utmost gravity had been levelled against him and, further, that they were especially damaging in view of his status as a minister of religion, there must have been an overwhelmingly significant reason why—once that letter-before-action had been written and had then been snubbed—he did not pursue the matter in the courts.

Since none of the allegations was retracted and the demanded apology was not forthcoming, we must assume that he did not feel sufficiently confident of success to make good his threat. Almost certainly, he was advised that any cross-examination in court in the course of a libel trial would have been a good deal more rigorous than the "after caution" interviews reportedly conducted by those indefatigable RUC inquisitors, Detective Chief Superintendent Nesbitt and Detective Inspector Chris Webster. If Ross had issued a writ, I would have entered a defence of justification and produced the evidence necessary to prove that everything Sands had said about his former boss is the absolute, copper-bottomed truth.[4] I would have argued in court that Hugh Ross is, as his solicitors so aptly put it, guilty of "acts of murder, deceit, subversion and conspiracy;" that he is as guilty of the murder of each one of the Committee's victims as if he had joined the death squads and participated in the attacks himself.

Ross is not the only professional person on the Committee to have perpetrated such crimes. Another is a highly successful lawyer with thriving practices in Belfast and Portadown, a member of the Law Society of Northern Ireland and someone who, until now, has seemed destined to reach the top of his profession, Charles Richard Pantridge Monteith. I first heard this solicitor's name when it was mentioned by Source A, Jim Sands, during his tape-recorded conversations with Ben Hamilton and I heard it again when Sands, during his filmed interview in London, named him as one of the Committee's most important and ruthless figures. Although we did not focus particularly on Monteith in 1991 or probe his past in any depth, I was later forced to do so because he chose to bring three separate libel actions in Northern Ireland over the programme, one against Channel 4 and two against me.

These legal actions demonstrated that Monteith was prepared to take considerable risks to protect himself and his fellow conspirators. For, as he would certainly have known, a plaintiff in any libel suit in the United Kingdom can have no certainty about what the outcome will be. Juries can be capricious; public cross-examination under oath is usually an ordeal and can be ruinous for a plaintiff especially if—as I would discover to be the case with Monteith—he has guilty secrets which he would understandably prefer to remain buried. But by launching his libel actions against Channel 4 and me in December 1992, Monteith made himself a focus of my attention for several years. Back in 1991, I had known only what Sands had told us about him—namely, that he had been a close friend of Abernethy's murdered brother and that, like several other Committee members and associates, he had supported the extreme Loyalist movement, the Ulster Clubs. Only later would I learn that this outwardly respectable lawyer had, for many years, been seriously implicated in Loyalist terrorism. Monteith had succeeded, like Hugh Ross, in leading a double life. In public, he championed peaceful, constitutional methods as the only legitimate approach to preserving the union with Britain; in private, he helped to direct the Loyalist terror campaign.

Yet, neither Ross nor Monteith were remotely as important—or as dangerous—as the man whose name was, according to Jim Sands, one of the best-kept secrets in Ulster Loyalism, that of the Committee's chairman, Billy Abernethy. Indeed, Sands had not dared to mention this name during his first tape-recorded dinner conversation with Ben Hamilton, preferring instead to scribble it on a piece of paper, which he then passed silently across the dinner table. Sands told Ben, as we have seen, that Abernethy was the Loyalist equivalent of Gerry Adams and that the Loyalists would not launch any significant terrorist action anywhere in the province without a prior nod of consent from him. Sands also told us that Abernethy was a leading figure in the Masonic Order, a member of a secret lodge known as "Sons of Ulster," together with senior RUC officers and businessmen, all of them dedicated to the Loyalist cause. Abernethy was clearly a man of some ability because he managed to combine his diverse extra-curricular activities with a full-time professional post of some seniority at the Belfast headquarters of the National Westminster Bank's main subsidiary in Ireland, the Ulster Bank.

It was, however, Billy Abernethy's status as a former part-time police officer and member of the RUC Reserve that had made him of particular interest to us. He had already shown Ben Hamilton his RUC credentials and given him a vivid demonstration of the freedom he enjoyed, courtesy of his Inner Force colleagues, to move around the province without the inconvenience or danger of road-blocks, car searches or troublesome security checks. Sands had told us that Abernethy's status as an ex-RUC officer meant that he had superb contacts within the police and ready access to high-level intelligence from Special Branch files. We took it for granted, therefore, that the identities of everyone involved with the Committee, including all those within the illegal RUC Inner Force, were known to the chairman, Billy Abernethy.

These three professional men—Abernethy, the banker; Ross, the Presbyterian Minister; Monteith, the solicitor—had used their talents and experience to give the Loyalist terror campaign a sense of purpose and direction, which it had lacked previously. They had mobilised and integrated the skills and resources of other professionals, such as a

Portadown accountant who specialised in money laundering and who had financed gun-running into the province to facilitate the Committee's campaign. This trio had ensured that there was no shortage of money because they were able to call on the skills and resources of some of the province's richest businessmen, such as car dealers David and Albert Prentice.

The professionals, as one might expect, were not the people who got their hands dirty in implementing the Committee's decisions. Other less affluent, less educated and less squeamish individuals were assigned the task of eliminating those whose deaths the professionals had authorised and organised. The Committee's two most important "hit men" were, as Sands revealed, Billy Wright [King Rat] and a man whose terrorist career, dating back to 1972, is so extensive and shocking that an entire chapter of this book is devoted to one of his killings.[5] Robin Jackson [The Jackal], as we've already seen, was responsible for some of the Committee's worst atrocities and there is good reason to believe that, thanks to the protection he has received from the RUC since the Channel 4 broadcast, he went on to murder several more Catholics between October 1991 and the declaration of the IRA and Loyalist ceasefires at the end of August 1994.

In the last chapter we saw RUC Detective Chief Inspector Samuel Ronald Mack's testimony, on oath, that the nineteen names of alleged Committee members listed in the Channel 4 dossier "do not all exist;" and we also saw his comment to Judge Clarkson that the alleged RUC conspirators on the Committee did not exist either. It is, I think, fair to say that Mr. Mack's overall testimony was designed to give the impression that the programme had been inaccurate and that the names of RUC Inner Force officers had been conjured out of thin air, invented to give spurious credibility to Source A's "revelations" and to malign the good name of "that highly reputable concern," the RUC. When Mr. Mack testified in Judge Clarkson's court in October 1991, he would certainly have known that one of those listed in the Channel 4 dossier as a full Committee member was an RUC officer well known for his support of the Loyalist cause, ex-Head of RUC Special Branch and former Assistant Chief Constable, Trevor Forbes OBE.

Sands had explained that Forbes had been "let go" by the former RUC's Chief Constable, Sir John Hermon, because he had been rather too enthusiastic in sharing the RUC's most sensitive intelligence files on Irish Republicans with Loyalists such as those who later formed the Committee. Despite Forbes's commitment to the Loyalist cause and his "shoot-to-kill" policy in the 1980s, he received all the protection he needed from Hermon during the abortive inquiry under the English detective John Stalker. Sands told us that Stalker had wished to arrest Forbes, which was the real reason why the Englishman had been removed from his inquiry and why he had then been comprehensively smeared by the officially inspired "dirty tricks" campaign against him. In short, by 1991, Forbes's reputation as an extreme Loyalist was well known to those at the top of the RUC and, following the Channel 4 broadcast, it would scarcely have been a great surprise for senior RUC officers to learn that Forbes's name was included in Channel 4's list of alleged murder conspirators.

So when Detective Chief Inspector Mack testified, in October 1991, about the alleged members of the RUC Inner Force, he would undoubtedly have known a great deal about Trevor Forbes, especially that this former RUC Assistant Chief Constable would most likely have been highly sympathetic to the goals and methods of Abernethy's Committee. Mr. Mack did, at least, admit in court that Forbes existed but his attempt to portray him as an entirely honourable and unremarkable police officer was disingenuous. For, as Sands had made clear to us, Forbes was one of the most important of the murder conspirators precisely because of his long experience within the RUC and his readiness to exploit his knowledge and contacts to ensure that the Loyalist squads operated with maximum efficiency.

It was this unprecedented coalition of Loyalist forces—businessmen and industrialists, professionals, gunmen and assassins, RUC and UDR Inner Force officers—which enabled the Committee to launch its assassination campaign in 1989, to boost its "kill rate" in 1990 and to strike terror within the Catholic community right across the province. By 1991, the Loyalists death squads were operating far beyond "murder triangle" and, as was noted at the time, they were able to do so with total impunity; for "mysteriously," not one Loyalist squad was ever intercepted by an RUC or UDR patrol and, equally "mysteriously," the subsequent police investigations routinely ran into the sand.

Jim Sands was unable to give us a comprehensive list of the Committee's killings but, in noting that the Loyalists murdered fourteen Catholics in 1989, sixteen in 1990 and twenty-three up to the end of September 1991—just before *The Committee* was broadcast—we should reflect on his claim that no Loyalist would pull a trigger anywhere in the province, without Abernethy's approval. The following list of eighteen murders, which Channel 4 gave to the RUC in October 1991, is sufficiently detailed to reveal the enormity of the scandal we had uncovered but which skilful media manipulation by the RUC, Northern Ireland Office and other British Government agencies has, until now, succeeded in discrediting in the public mind. Sands had something to say, during either his tape-recorded or filmed interviews, about the following murders.

Murder No. 1	1989 Pat Finucane
Murder No. 2	1990 Sam Marshall
Murder No. 3	1990 Denis Carville
Murder No. 4	1990 Tommy Casey
	1990 Brendan Curran (murder bid failed)

Tommy Casey was a Sinn Féin councillor who was shot dead by the Loyalists in Cookstown, County Tyrone on October 26th, 1990; Brendan Curran also worked for Sinn Féin but survived an assassination attack after the attacker's weapon jammed and the gunman was forced to flee to avoid being caught. No-one has ever been arrested or charged with either of these offences but Source A, Jim Sands, was able to reveal the details of both attacks to Ben Hamilton, when they held their tape-recorded conversation at the Silverwood Hotel in Lurgan on April 8th, 1991.

> BH: What about Casey, the Sinn Féiner?
> JS: That was in Magherafelt?
> BH: That's right.[6]
> JS: That was King Rat, it was King Rat and The Jackal. They worked together on that.
> BH: Were they helped by the Inner Force again on that?
> JS: Yes. The Inner Force brought them up and brought them back again, unless they were stopped along the way somewhere.
> BH: And . . .
> JS: And then Brendan Curran. He always went to his mother's house, his father's house, always went every Sunday night.
> BH: He told me he didn't. I went and talked to him.
> JS: According to the police, according to the Inner Force he did. They followed him. They set that one up. The Inner Force set it up.
> BH: And did they do it themselves?
> JS: No.
> BH: Did the Inner Force ever do killings themselves?
> JS: No.
> BH: They used Billy and. . .?
> JS: They use whatever squad is about.
> BH: So they rung up to see who was around?
> JS: They followed, for about five or six weeks, they followed him. And then they had men staking out the house as well.
> BH: What? The Inner Force did?
> JS: The Inner Force had men staking out the house. And then, they brought King Rat in and out.
> BH: Are you involved in either of those two groups? [The groups around King Rat and The Jackal]

JS: No.

BH: So how . . . Are you friends of theirs, or what?

JS: Yes. I went to school with Billy.

When Sands came to London in May 1991 we asked him, again, about the attack on Brendan Curran. His reply, more detailed than the one quoted above, is published here for the first time. Neither the murder of Tommy Casey nor the attack on Brendan Curran was featured in the programme, as we had gathered far too much material for the available air-time. We began this part of the London interview by asking Sands how it had come about that Brendan Curran had been suggested as a target and what had happened leading up to the attack?

JS: It was discussed at one of the Central Co-ordinating Committee meetings that there was a lot of young people from around the Craigavon area who were involved with Ulster Young Militants, who needed to progress, which meant getting the gun in their hands and going out. It was felt that since they came from the Craigavon area, that they should remove, to eliminate someone from the Craigavon area. So the Inner Force were asked, could they provide a name, so they came up with the name and with the file of Brendan Curran. So that was put to the Central Committee. The Central Committee agreed that it be carried out. They also agreed that King Rat go to lead the operation but that he also take some of the young people with him to let them get their first blood. So that was then left to the hands of the Inner Force, and between the Inner Force and King Rat, they would organise and carry out the operation. Brendan Curran was then followed and watched. They picked a date when they would carry out the operation. He was followed by a car containing members of the Inner Force who followed him. They thought, from his usual movements, that he was going back home to Craigavon but instead, that evening, he went to his mother's house. So when they were sure that he was staying in his mother's house they radioed then to another car, which was sitting parked up a lane between Craigavon and Lurgan, that the target was in place and for them to come in with King Rat and the other young fella who was with him. They were in another car, just parked behind the Inner Force car. They then led King Rat in, going in front, making sure that the road was clear. If they did happen to come upon any checkpoints, that they would be able to show their ID and that the second car would be able to come in as well. They led King Rat to Ballyduggan to Brendan Curran's mother's house. They met up with the other Inner Force car. King Rat was then shown the house. They went round to come round through the back door.

They went into the living room of the house and shot Brendan Curran. While King Rat was going to finish him off, the gun jammed. And while King Rat was trying to get the gun unjammed, to get it to work, Brendan Curran's father hit him with a chair. So they went from the house to get the gun working, in working order. By this time the young fella with him either panicked or for whatever reason of his own, he threw a stun grenade into the house. By this time the Inner Force felt that they were there too long and that they needed to get out of the area in case some of the neighbours, there's houses about, not just directly beside but there was houses in the same area, who may have heard the gunshot and they'd make it difficult to get out of the area. So the Inner Force told King Rat to come, so he got into his car and was escorted out of the area.

BH: Were either of those Inner Force cars on-duty patrols?

JS: They both were on duty. They were able to use their radios for contact to relay the information. One car followed Brendan Curran to see where his destination was. They were able to radio, then, to radio the second car, telling that the target was in place and to come on in.

BH: Could you tell us what happened at the report back, after Brendan Curran had been shot?

JS: As was the usual custom, it was reported back to the Central Co-ordinating Committee how the operation had went. They were disappointed that Brendan Curran had not been eliminated, but it was good that a young man had been taken out on his first job and overall they were disappointed but pleased that things went very well operational-wise. But, as was pointed out at the meeting, there will always be a next time.[7]

The Channel 4 dossier, given to the RUC, contained information on the following seven murders which, as we have seen, were carried out by the Committee's two top hit-men, King Rat and The Jackal.

Murders Nos. 5,6,7,8 1991 Cappagh—Dwayne O'Donnell; John Quinn; Malcolm Nugent; Thomas Armstrong
Murders Nos. 9,10,11 1991 Craigavon sweet shop—Eileen Duffy; Katrina Rennie; Brian Frizzell

Sands also gave us the inside story on a number of other murders organised by the Committee in the summer of 1991, during the months which followed his return from his interview in London in May. Security considerations and a desire to keep our distance from him in public prevented us from recording a second filmed interview about these additional murders. Sands told us that Abernethy's Committee was also responsible for:

Murder No. 12	1991 [10 August] James Carson, shopkeeper, Belfast
Murder No. 13	1991 [16 August] Thomas Donaghy, Sinn Féin worker, Kilrea
Murder No. 14	1991 [16 August] Martin O'Prey, Belfast
Murder No. 15	1991 [25 May] Eddie Fullerton, Buncrana, Co. Donegal; Sands told us that this murder had been organised for the Committee by Cecil McKnight, a Loyalist councillor in Derry who was subsequently murdered in retaliation by the Provisional IRA
Murder No. 16	1991 [April] John O'Hara, taxi driver, Belfast

Some time after Sands had returned home from London, he gave us information on three additional murders, one which had occurred in April 1991, the others in August and September. He told us that all three of them had been sanctioned and organised by the Committee.

Murder No. 17	1991 [August] Patrick Shanaghan, farmer, Castlederg, Co. Tyrone
Murder No. 18	1991 [16 September] Bernard O'Hagan, Sinn Féin Councillor. He was shot dead on arriving at the College where he lectured in Magherafelt, Co. Derry. Sands told us that the murder had been carried out for the Committee by a gunman, Alec Benson, who subsequently turned up to witness the funeral. Benson, who lived in Lisburn, Co. Antrim, also led the squad which murdered Belfast shop-keeper James Carson [Murder 12, above]

So, though the programme focused on just four Loyalist attacks (involving seven murders) organised by Abernethy's Committee, Source A had given us information about eighteen murders carried out between 1989 and 1991. Our information on at least ten of them was, as the reader is now in a position to judge, immensely detailed and authoritative because Source A had, on his own video-recorded admission, participated with named individuals in the discussions that had led to many such murders. We had tested and re-tested Sands's testimony against the accounts of numerous witnesses and had, after immensely careful and painstaking efforts, concluded that he had been telling the truth; he had given us an accurate, detailed account of the seven murders featured in *The Committee* and information about another ten murders which the Committee had organised. Seven years have passed since Jim Sands revealed information about all eighteen of these murders to Box Productions and Channel 4; yet, despite the fact that the RUC was given virtually all Sands's information immediately after the broadcast, not one of those who commissioned or organised the eighteen murders has been arrested, charged or convicted for any of them.

On the surface, the task assigned by the RUC Chief Constable to his two investigators, Nesbitt and Webster, had been an easy one. Since the Channel 4 dossier contained a wealth of information about the assassination campaign—including the names of nineteen key conspirators and clues to the identity of several more, the names of locations where the Committee had met and Sands's first-hand account of how the eighteen murders had been sanctioned—the investigators should have been able, on day one of their inquiry, to have detained the ring-leaders; then, the following day, they could have moved on to arrest the remaining Committee members, including their senior RUC colleagues, all eighteen representatives of the RUC Inner Force. Within a very short time, they would surely have succeeded in bringing the Loyalist assassination campaign to an abrupt end.[8]

Yet, we have only to envisage this scenario to realise that there was never even the remotest possibility of it happening. For it was always inconceivable, so it seemed to me, that the Chief Constable's two investigators would ever arrive at the conclusion that Sands had been telling the truth or publicly conclude that their boss's knee-jerk reaction—"an unwarranted slur on the good name" of the RUC—had been foolish and wrong. How could Nesbitt and Webster find in favour of Sands, if the result of that would be the almost certain abolition of the RUC itself? How could any police force in the United Kingdom survive, if it became accepted that its senior officers were running death squads? And how could the Chief Constable remain in office, if his own investigators were to admit that members of his force had been colluding with Loyalist assassins? Since the implications of any such findings would be horrendous for all concerned, it was blindingly obvious to me that a favourable verdict from the Nesbitt Inquiry had been guaranteed in advance. Given what was at stake, there was similarly never any possibility that Secretary of State Sir Patrick Mayhew would question the fact that the RUC was being allowed to "investigate" itself.

We will see later that Nesbitt's approach to his sensitive task was predictably partisan and that his investigation is vitiated by his own words in tape-recorded conversations which became available to me. In October 1991, however, the RUC appeared in public to be taking the Channel 4 allegations seriously and to be holding a genuine investigation. The Chief Constable gave the impression that the Official RUC Inquiry was energetically and genuinely seeking the truth. It must, in these circumstances, have appeared an ingenious ploy to the "investigators" to accuse the programme makers themselves of preventing the police from tracking down the alleged murder conspirators. How could the RUC be seriously expected to establish the truth of Source A's allegations, if both Channel 4 and Box Productions were deliberately refusing to provide the information the police so desperately needed? How could the alleged conspiracy be exposed, if those who claimed to know about it would not hand over the name of their key source?

Knowing that we were honour bound to resist such a demand, Nesbitt and Webster correctly assumed that, by deploying the Prevention of Terrorism Act against us, they would start a protracted court battle and thereby throw a legal blanket over the entire affair for months to come. The proceedings in front of Judge Clarkson would not come to a head for ten months from the date of the broadcast—not until the end of July 1992, when the Attorney General finally asked the High Court to deal with the contempt of court arising from our refusal to comply with the Production Orders. It is to these High Court proceedings that I now turn.

Notes

1 Trimble's involvement with the murder conspirators will be discussed in Chapter 15.
2 Trimble's performance in support of Ross and his effort to undermine the programme's credibility will be examined in detail in Chapter 15.
3 Britain's libel laws have enabled many criminals to muzzle the Press by preventing journalists from publishing the truth. During his lifetime Robert Maxwell, for example, was often informally referred to as "the bouncing Czech" but the British Press had to wait until he was dead and buried before safely informing the public that he was one of the greatest crooks of modern times.
4 See Chapter 11.
5 See Chapter 13.
6 In fact, this murder had occurred in Cookstown; Ben had made a mistake and Sands did not correct his error; but despite this inaccuracy there is no reason to doubt that Sands was speaking with inside knowledge of how the murder had been organised.
7 Brendan Curran is still alive in February 1998. However, the Loyalists murdered his girlfriend, Sheena Campbell on October 16th, 1992. She was shot dead by a masked gunman while having a drink in the York Hotel in Belfast. Sheena Campbell had been Sinn Féin's candidate in the Upper Bann by-election, contested by Committee member "Reverend" Hugh Ross and won

by William David Trimble MP, whose connections to the Committee are explored in Chapter 15.

8   In envisaging such an outcome, we would naturally have to assume that Nesbitt and Webster were genuinely seeking the truth. Such an assumption, as I was to discover, would never have been justified. [See Appendix 3]

Chapter 8

TELEVISION ON TRIAL

During the months that followed the broadcast, we had managed to keep open a reliable line of communication to Source A, Jim Sands. We had repeatedly reassured him that we would continue to protect his identity even when the Attorney General finally got round to bringing the contempt action against us in the High Court. And Sands, in reply, had indicated—during infrequent and necessarily discreet meetings with Martin O'Hagan—that he trusted us to keep our word and to resist all efforts to force us to hand over his name; we were assured by Martin that he remained supremely confident about his own ability to deflect any suspicion that might fall upon him, either from other Committee members or from the RUC. As we have seen, he had already fielded a visit from the Chief Constable's two "investigators" and been greatly amused by Chief Inspector Chris Webster's fervently expressed wish that one of Sands's Loyalist "friends"—which is to say, one of the Committee's assassins—should "rub out" the person most responsible for the entire controversy, "that wee Fenian over in London," namely myself. Naturally, I was somewhat shocked to learn of this police officer's proposal but I was reassured by a further message from Sands that Webster's suggestion was not, at that moment, being seriously considered. So, Source A himself remained the real focus of our concern and we continued to hope that his assessment of his own position was an accurate one; for if he had read his situation wrongly, we might wake up one morning to discover that the Committee had found "the traitor" and had dealt with him as it had with so many others before him.

Source A told us that, while the hunt for "the traitor" was going on, the conspirators' main concern, immediately after the broadcast, was to survive the initial exposure. All the Committee members, he explained, had been so stunned by the accuracy of our revelations that they had not dared to meet formally again. In consequence, the Committee's assassination campaign—which had been gathering momentum throughout the year—had been brought virtually to a halt, although freelance terrorist activity continued, with individual members reportedly acting without formal approval from the organisation as a whole. We were, naturally, gratified to learn that we had made such a powerful impact on the conspirators, that the broadcast had, if only for a time, induced near total paralysis among the Committee's leadership—especially Abernethy, Ross and Forbes. And it was immensely satisfying to know that our efforts had, almost certainly, saved the lives of those whom this unholy trio would have identified as targets for their death squads between late autumn 1991 and summer 1992.

Channel 4's decision to broadcast *The Committee* had, therefore, ensured that the Loyalist murder campaign was, for a time, significantly impeded; and, as later events would show, it was not to recover its full momentum until late 1993 and 1994, by which time the conspirators had recovered from the shock they had received in 1991, a recovery due in large measure to the activities of the Chief Constable's two "investigators," who had spent much of the intervening time assuring anyone who would listen that our revelations had been "a pack of lies."

As the date of the High Court hearing, July 27th 1992, approached and stories began to appear in the newspapers about the possibility of Channel 4 being taken off the air, Sands ventured the opinion that it would be a sensation in Northern Ireland if Billy Abernethy were to be named in open court as the Committee's chairman. And although Sands had once told us, long before the broadcast, that Abernethy was normally opposed to attacks on journalists, we were now informed, in mid-summer 1992, that there was a real possibility that he might decide to order a reprisal against us.[1] So, despite the passage of time, we remained alert to this continuing threat to our security, which resulted from the fact that the conspirators had been allowed to remain at liberty. As the High Court hearing loomed, we became somewhat less anxious because we thought the risk of violent action against us was reduced with each day that passed; we reasoned that if anything nasty were to happen to any of us at that time, the individuals listed in the Channel 4 dossier would, at once, become the prime suspects; and, in such circumstances, they would be likely to come under more intense scrutiny than they ever had before.

In the months leading up to the High Court hearing, I became more and more involved in our case and spent much time with my solicitor, Brian Raymond, who had by then mastered every aspect of the affair and emerged as our chief legal strategist, officially for Box Productions, unofficially and informally for Channel 4. Brian and I spent a good deal of time preparing my affidavit, which spelled out the significance of what we had discovered and gave the reasons why we felt unable to comply with the Production Orders. Once our distinguished barristers, Lord Williams of Mostyn QC and Jonathan Caplan QC, had approved all our affidavits, they were submitted to the High Court. Their contents, we thought, would have ensured that the judges had a good understanding of our position and would have led them to appreciate that we had meant what we said—that we were not, under any circumstances, going to give the RUC any document which would enable them to identify Source A.

In my affidavit, I had explained that my visit to Denis Carville's parents had left a deep impression upon me; it had made me determined to ensure that Abernethy's Committee, including its RUC Inner Force members, would be publicly exposed and that the conspirators be brought to account for their crimes. This is what Brian Raymond wrote on my behalf:

> Mr. and Mrs. Carville, who have no political connections whatsoever, were immensely distressed because they said that they knew that their son had been killed by Billy Wright. They said that the whole town knew who had killed Denis and indeed that the Police themselves knew but that they were doing nothing about it. I did not add to their distress by telling them what Ben Hamilton had been told by [Source] A, namely that Abernethy, together with other members of the Committee and RUC officers had been instrumental in arranging the murder of their son. Denis Carville Snr. was deeply distraught as he recounted to me his experiences in the weeks following his son's murder. He had been stopped by members of a UDR patrol who asked him whether or not he had another son who might be dealt with in a similar fashion. He had reported this outrageous behaviour by a member of the security forces to the RUC but nothing had been done about it.
>
> This meeting with the Carville family convinced me that it was my duty to ensure that the full circumstances of their son's death was brought to public attention. If it really was the case (as Source A was then telling us) that a significant proportion of the RUC were in collusion with Loyalist paramilitaries, then the tragedy that had befallen the Carville family would in all probability happen again to another wholly innocent family.

The public's right to know what we had found, that a significant proportion of the RUC was colluding with Loyalist death squads, was of paramount importance; there was an overwhelming public interest in exposing this scandal and in preventing the cover-up, which we rightly suspected would be the RUC's response to the broadcast. For these reasons, we were agreed that we could not, in good conscience, obey the Production Orders. My affidavit continued:

> I should like to make it clear that I very much regret the fact that my company, having made a serious documentary film on a difficult subject of paramount public importance, should find itself involved in these proceedings and threatened with the full force of

the Court's punitive powers for an alleged contempt. Neither in my journalistic career, nor in my private life, have I come into such potential conflict with the law.

The seeds of the proceedings in this Court were sown when I first endorsed and agreed to be bound by the undertakings given to Source A. Such undertakings, if they are to have any meaning or validity, cannot contain unspoken escape clauses or be given with mental reservations which will allow them to be abrogated at a later stage. To do otherwise, would be to engage in a deliberate and life-threatening deception of those to whom the undertakings are given. For this reason, such undertakings are not given lightly or without thought and deliberation, particularly when the consequences may be as grave as the proceedings in which I am currently involved.

No responsible journalist or broadcaster can be neutral about terrorism: if there is one issue upon which all parties to this matter can agree, it is the need to eradicate this scourge from the society in which we live. If there is evidence to show that the very institutions upon which we depend for our collective security contain a significant number of individuals who are actually engaged in perpetrating this evil, the public interest can only be served by bringing that evidence to public notice.

I hope that I have shown in the particular circumstances of this television investigation, the only means by which such evidence could be revealed in the public interest was by giving binding undertakings to protect the identity of our confidential sources. Had we not given these undertakings, our sources would not have agreed to be interviewed and the programme could not have been made.

Faced with the enormity of the allegations that Source A was making when we first encountered him and foreseeing the possible consequences which might ensue, we could have taken the easiest path and diverted our energies to a less controversial issue. I was given this option explicitly by Channel 4 last August when we became aware that a mercenary had been recruited and that our lives were in danger.[2] To have turned our backs on the corruption that we uncovered, however, would have been to renege on our duties as reporters of fact and as informers of the public. For if a police force is corrupted to very senior levels (as I believe our film shows the RUC to be), then it is incapable of performing its most fundamental functions and cannot be the agent of its own reform. The inevitable consequence, had we taken the soft and cynical option of abandoning this project, would have been firstly that the truth concerning the death of Denis Carville and others would never have been made known, and secondly that the murderous activities of the Committee would have been permitted to continue unhindered.

These are the reasons I respectfully believe that His Honour Judge Clarkson should not have made the Productions Orders against my company and Channel 4. The public interest, having regard to the circumstances in which we held the material we sought to protect, in my view demanded that nothing be done to impede the process of bringing these matters to public attention. Journalistic exposure of institutional corruption is always likely to commence with information given in confidence. If journalists can be compelled to disclose their sources in circumstances such as these, such corruption will survive unchecked. In a plural, democratic society, the public interest cannot be served by the creation of no-entry zones into which journalists may not stray: such areas will then become fertile grounds for unrestrained wrongdoing.

When the contempt proceedings finally opened in the High Court on Monday, July 27th 1992, all involved on our side—broadcaster, production company, television executives and programme-makers—were agreed and united behind the course we had taken. As all our affidavits had been submitted to the court in advance of the hearing, the judges would have known, from the outset, that those in charge of Channel 4 were prepared to have its assets seized and to see their network taken off the air, rather than betray Source A by giving his name to the RUC. Our Leading Counsel, Lord Williams QC, had come directly to the point on the first occasion we had met him; he asked Ben Hamilton and me to confirm that we would be prepared to go to prison rather than obey the Production Orders; when we had both indicated our readiness to face that prospect, he smiled and commented that our reply had made his task a good deal easier.

And so—seven months after Judge Clarkson had referred our case to the High Court as an "urgent" matter, "imperative" that it be dealt with quickly—contempt proceedings opened in front of Lord Justice Woolf and Mr. Justice Pill in a court-room packed with lawyers, police officers, television executives, reporters and members of the public. They had been drawn by the prospect, widely forecast in the newspapers, of a dramatic showdown over the media's most fundamental duty and responsibility—the duty to expose official wrongdoing of the gravest kind and the responsibility to protect a confidential source, even if that meant that the law would be broken. The court room benches and corridors were filled to capacity; most of those present were well aware of the issues and alert to the court's awesome powers to deal with the obstinate defendants. Accordingly, the mood was serious and sombre when the Crown's barrister, Mr. Andrew Collins QC, rose to open his case against Channel 4 and Box Productions.

Speaking in a quiet but confident manner, he proceeded to explain the significance of the various sections of the Prevention of Terrorism (Temporary Provisions) Act 1989—an act which, despite its name, had already been on the statute book for seventeen years and was now, for the first time, being used against journalists. Mr. Collins's argument was simple and clear: Judge Clarkson had made a valid order, which could not be appealed and which ought to have been obeyed; the two companies had deliberately placed themselves in contempt of the court and they ought to be punished; and it would be quite improper, now, for the High Court to open up, once again, all the issues the case had raised and to agree to decide afresh whether or not the Production Orders should ever have been made at all.

> Putting it shortly, in my submission, this court is not entitled to go behind the making of the order. Parliament has seen fit not to provide any right of appeal, and therefore the only right to remove the order, if I may put it that way, is by judicial review, on the basis that it was made *ultra vires*, or irrationally or whatever. No attempt was made and, indeed, it may well be that it is clear that no attempt could have succeeded, to suggest that this was an irrational order. At best it could be said that in the exercise of his discretion, the learned judge erred in the making of the order. My Lord, this is, in my submission, not a matter for this court, although I entirely accept that when, and if, the court has to come to consider mitigation, obviously all the relevant factors can be taken into account, but that is not quite the same point.

Mr. Collins then proceeded to review the history of the affair, the involvement of Box Productions and Channel 4, the encounter with Source A, his allegations about the Committee's murder conspiracy, the television broadcast, the removal of "sensitive material" from the court's jurisdiction and the refusal to bring it back, in defiance of the court order; he quoted, approvingly, from RUC Chief Constable Hugh Annesley's statement, published immediately after the broadcast the previous October—the one in which the Chief Constable had given his damning verdict on the programme's allegations, just before he announced the creation of the Nesbitt-Webster inquiry into whether or not they were true. Mr. Collins quoted a part of the Chief Constable's statement:

> On behalf of the Royal Ulster Constabulary, I utterly reject last night's television programme as an unjust and unsubstantiated slur on the good name of the Force. While I have no desire to give the programme a status it does not deserve, I owe it to the people of Northern Ireland to assure them that the integrity of their police force is sound and this television programme cannot be taken as the truth of the matter . . . The four crimes of murder mentioned in the programme remain under investigation. Two persons have already been charged and it is our firm resolve to relentlessly pursue our enquiries into these appalling crimes.

For Mr. Collins, the identification of Source A was "obviously the key" to the RUC's investigation, which could possibly show that Source A himself, as well as others on the Committee—if it existed—were "seriously involved in conspiracy to murder, if not actual murder." Mr. Collins explained that the dossier given to the RUC was insufficient to assist with this task and that, if Source A was to be found, the sensitive material taken out of the jurisdiction must be brought back and handed over.

> The reality is that in no circumstances is there an absolute right for a journalist to protect his sources as a matter of law . . . My Lord, as I say, so far as giving undertakings to sources such as this, the law in general is not that there is an absolute protection for journalist sources, it never has been, and therefore no journalist is able, properly, to give a complete undertaking to any source that he will, in no circumstances, disclose his identity. What he can say is, "I am prepared to break the law, if the law requires me to disclose your identity, and I am prepared to take whatever punishment and to undergo whatever penalty the law requires of me, if that should happen." If he does that, he does that at his peril. Those who give such undertakings must appreciate they give them at their peril . . .
>
> My Lord, all I am saying is that it is no doubt easy to raise special feeling on behalf of the media that this is a clash between their duty to their sources and other considerations. As a matter of fact, it is perfectly plain that Parliament has decided, and quite clearly decided, that it is not for the journalist to make that decision, it is for the court and, particularly in the context of a case like this, for the circuit judge, because one comes back to the public interest which must determine it and, however much they may like to think to the contrary, it is not the media who decide what is of public interest, it is the courts.

Mr. Collins was developing a powerful case. Parliament had tilted the balance decisively in favour of the police in terrorist cases and had brushed aside even the limited right to protect sources, a concession which journalists enjoyed in normal situations under the provisions of the Contempt of Court Act, 1981. The correct approach of the courts, said Mr. Collins, had been made clear by Lord Bridge in another case, earlier in 1991, when a journalist had been punished for disobeying a court order requiring him to identify a source.[3] Mr. Collins quoted Lord Bridge's ruling:

> The maintenance of the rule of law is in every way as important in a free society as the democratic franchise. In our society the rule of law rests upon twin foundations: the sovereignty of the Queen in Parliament in making the law and the sovereignty of the Queen's courts in interpreting and applying the law. While no

one doubts the importance of protecting journalists' sources, no one, I think, seriously advocates an absolute privilege against disclosure admitting of no exceptions. Since the enactment of Section 10 of the [Contempt of Court] Act of 1981, both the protection of journalists' sources and the limited grounds on which it may exceptionally be necessary to override that protection, have been laid down by Parliament. I have not heard of any campaign in the media suggesting that the law itself is unjust or that the exceptions to the protection are too widely drawn. But if there were such a campaign, it should be fought in a democratic society by persuasion, not by disobedience to the law. Given the law as laid down by Section 10, who, if not the courts, is to interpret it and to decide in the circumstances of any given case whether the protection is to prevail or whether the case is brought within one of the exceptions? The journalist cannot be left to be judge in his own cause and decide whether or not to make disclosure. This would be an abdication of the role of Parliament and the courts in the matter and, in practice, would be tantamount to conferring an absolute privilege. Of course the courts, like other human institutions, are fallible and a journalist ordered to disclose his source may, like other disappointed litigants, feel that the court's decision was wrong. But to contend that the individual litigant, be he a journalist or anyone else, has a right of "conscientious objection" which entitled him to set himself above the law if he does not agree with the court's decision, is a doctrine which directly undermines the rule of law and is wholly unacceptable in a democratic society. Any rule of professional conduct enjoining a journalist to protect his confidential sources must, impliedly if not expressly, be subject to whatever exception is necessary to enable the journalist to obey the orders of a court of competent jurisdiction. Freedom of speech is itself a right which is dependent on the rule of law for its protection and it is paradoxical that a serious challenge to the rule of law should be mounted by responsible journalists.

Lord Bridge's words applied to the situation in which Channel 4 now found itself, said Mr. Collins.

One is bound to say that, when Source A received the undertakings, he must have known that they were undertakings that were capable of being overridden by the courts and he chose, either for good or bad reasons, to make the allegations that he has made.

The net result of what has happened is that there has been presented to the British public as fact, "conclusive evidence" were the words used, very grave allegations against the integrity of the Royal Ulster Constabulary. These allegations may be complete rubbish *and probably are,* but none the less it is essential that they be investigated because if there is any truth in them a very serious situation is disclosed. [my emphasis]

It was not Mr. Collins' job, of course, to balance the Crown's case for disclosure against any competing interests or considerations, though he might have anticipated the arguments we would soon be presenting to the court. So Mr. Collins chose not to deal with any of the troublesome or complicating issues which appeared so obvious to us. For example, he did not raise the matter which had so troubled Judge Clarkson, namely the fact that the RUC was investigating itself and that it might not, therefore, be all that diligent in its effort to establish the truth about the Committee's existence and activities; nor did he question the RUC's claim that finding Source A was crucial to its investigation, a claim which downplayed the fact that the dossier had already given the police the names of nineteen other alleged Committee members; nor did he address the question whether Source A would have agreed to speak publicly, if he had been told that his name would be given to the RUC, should a PTA Production Order be issued against us; nor did he worry that the Committee's murder campaign would have continued unhindered with the loss of yet more innocent lives, if Source A had not had sufficient confidence in us to give us his video interview.

And while, as I say, none of the above matters may have been the Crown's concern, I wondered whether it was either necessary or wise for Mr. Collins to suggest that the programme's allegations were, probably, "complete rubbish." Was this not yet another example, as Brian Raymond had indicated, of the lawyer's wig slipping to reveal the politician underneath, an establishment figure instinctively opposed to investigative journalists and to what they produce?

Indeed, Mr. Collins was not content simply to rely on the technical arguments, outlined above, that the law was on his side. He seemed more than happy to advance the RUC's case that the programme's allegations had indeed been total rubbish, a hoax invented by a disillusioned Loyalist with a personal vendetta against the police. To this end, he proceeded to produce a sworn statement from an anonymous source of his own, a mysterious Witness X, who had reportedly told the RUC that he had been the inventor of the totally fictitious claims about Loyalist-RUC collusion, allegations which had then been unwittingly recycled by Channel 4 in its programme. Mr. Collins did not assert categorically that this anonymous, self-confessed hoaxer, Witness X, was our Source A but it was a possibility that he did not rule out. But, in a move clearly intended to undermine Source A's credibility, Mr. Collins went on to assert that Witness X had been the first person ever to allege the existence of an RUC Inner Circle:

Witness X says that he made up the story about the Inner Circle and he recognises, in the programme that was put out, some of the matters that he made up for his own ends.

Witness X's lengthy statement would have been of great benefit to the RUC, if Mr. Collins could have shown that its contents were true. For Witness X's claims went right to the heart of the allegations in the programme. Put simply, Witness X was saying that all our allegations were false, a malicious invention, a hoax based on X's own fictitious claims, which he had fabricated because of a personal grievance he had once held against the RUC. And, in his statement, he—X—suggested that well-known local journalist Martin O'Hagan—the same Martin O'Hagan who, as the reader knows, had introduced Ben Hamilton to Jim Sands—had exploited his [Witness X's] invention [an RUC Inner Circle], recycling this invention to perpetrate a hoax on a gullible Channel 4:

> I became completely disillusioned with the Special Branch in particular and the RUC in general. I considered I had been treated very shabbily and had had the dirt done on me . . . I invented a story about there being an Inner Circle in existence within the RUC and that members of this Inner Circle were prepared to take part in a coup in the event of a United Ireland . . . I knew of Martin O'Hagan, a journalist with the *Sunday World*. I knew he was an ex-internee on the Republican side and that he would use any means to attack the RUC. I phoned O'Hagan and told him I was a spokesman on behalf of the so called Inner Circle . . . I regenerated the story of the existence of the Inner Circle and I told him that members of the Inner Circle were prepared to act in collusion with Loyalist paramilitaries in targeting Republicans for assassination. These stories were untrue and made up by me . . . I watched the *Dispatches* programme which was broadcast last October. It was a lot of rubbish and quite a lot of the references contained in it were similar to the stories I had told O'Hagan.

So, here was testimony that the entire story about an RUC Inner Circle had been an invention by a disillusioned Loyalist, a fabrication eagerly promoted as a hard fact by a malicious Republican journalist. Mr. Collins was suggesting that Witness X's inventions had been recycled by Source A, possibly with the help of O'Hagan. The Crown did not advance any detailed account of how Witness X's inventions had made their way into the programme but X's statement to the RUC, said Mr. Collins, suggested that "there is another side to this" and that our refusal to identify Source A was hampering Detective Superintendent Nesbitt's earnest efforts to establish, beyond dispute, the absolute truth of the matter. "This is not a responsible attitude by the respondents."

Before completing his case for the Crown, Mr. Collins fired a warning shot across the bows of all those involved in the decision, taken by Channel 4 and Box Productions, to disobey the court orders. He suggested that if the directors of the two companies persisted with their present course, then the Director of Public Prosecutions might pursue the option of taking action directly against their personal assets. This produced wry smiles from the journalists but, for the highly paid television executives, it was a distinctly ominous development. While the implications of this threat reverberated round the court room, Lord Williams rose to his feet, waited patiently for silence to return and then, confident that he had the total attention of everyone present, began to outline the case for the defence.

My Lord, no one on behalf of Channel 4 or Box, or the companies themselves, doubts the deep seriousness of this occasion. It is necessary to remind oneself, I suppose, that this occasion depends on unique circumstances. The decisions to be made by your Lordships are, I submit, with great respect, and I shall develop this theme, infinitely more subtle than the blunt mechanical approach which is being presented. It is not simply a clash of principle. It is a question, and I shall put my submissions in these ways, of looking at matters in two distinct categories. First of all, and I need to develop this I am afraid at a little length by looking at the affidavits, it is a question of looking at the background and looking at what led up to the making of the order. It is then a question of deciding what the proper approach of this court should be. In that latter question, the subtle mechanisms arrive . . .

My Lord, I will be submitting that there are at least two currents here, one the law and one a different public interest which may eventually form one tide, I do not know. On the one side is the power of the law, which we recognise with deep respect, and on the other side is a public interest, the due requirement of journalistic enquiry and integrity. Each party bases its stance on a moral imperative: the Director on the authority of the law, which derives from the will of Parliament, and expresses itself through these courts; Channel 4 and Box, a journalistic duty to enquire fearlessly, to act with integrity and, I submit, a duty beyond that, a loyalty to those to whom you have given undertakings which may bring about their death. My Lord, at the end of the day Channel 4 and Box have to say, with reluctance and after due careful consideration, "We will bow the head but we cannot bend the knee." That is not in any way intended to be disrespectful, and I know it will not be taken as disrespectful, but it is idle for me to pretend that things would happen, when my instructions are that they will not. The stance adopted by both companies is that despite the power and authority of the law, and of this statute in particular, we cannot in conscience comply.

Lord Williams had struck the right note from the beginning. His tone and his manner, together with his status as one of the most distinguished lawyers in Britain, ensured that he was believed when, having explicitly recognised the supremacy of the law, he openly and frankly stated that we were not prepared, in the circumstances, to obey it. These unique circumstances, he said, provided the court with good and sufficient reasons for looking beyond the simple fact of disobedience, reasons which the court should weigh in coming to a judgement about the appropriate response. "We seek no martyr's crown," he said, also quoting Lord Bridge and implicitly recognising the authority of this judge's views, as read to the court earlier by Mr. Collins. Lord Williams then proceeded to flesh out the background to the events which had now culminated in this hearing in the High Court. His purpose was to paint a vivid picture of the unique circumstances of the case, thereby to win the sympathy and understanding of the court.

> There are, in Northern Ireland, creatures who will kill other human beings because of their name, or their accent, or their religious belief, or because of no reason at all.

There was, he continued, "conclusive evidence" that some of these creatures were Loyalist paramilitaries who had been supplied with police intelligence files. This was a matter of public record. It was not in dispute, he added, that the investigation of such matters was dangerous work for journalists and was undertaken for a wider purpose than mere self-interest. Slowly and carefully, he reviewed the history of the project to underline our seriousness of purpose and our resolve to stand by the commitment to Source A. He also noted Judge Clarkson's observation that, if we were to identify Source A as we had been ordered to do, the result could be death—and death not just for Source A.

> I would invite this court to proceed on the basis that this is an intact finding and ought to be the basis of your conclusion in this matter. I would submit that there is no material to disrupt that intact finding.

This difficult and dangerous investigative work had been carried out conscientiously, had been carefully scrutinised and conducted with the benefit of expert legal advice throughout. Precautions had been taken, at some expense, to minimise the dangers to Source A and to Box employees. Lord Williams was inviting the court to appreciate what had motivated the programme makers and what had led them to the view that they must continue to protect their sources, despite the valid legal orders that had been issued against the two companies.

> The Source A material was already out of the jurisdiction by September 26th, in other words pre first Production Order, which

was not made until October 31st. I do respectfully submit that on a whole and fair view of those affidavits, even if Box and Channel 4 were wrong, they were wrong for noble reasons.

There had been no hint of defiance, no suggestion that the media could be in any way above the law. So, our defence rested not on a clash of principle but on the particular circumstances that Lord Williams had reviewed and which had resulted in our appearance in the High Court. By stressing this seriousness of purpose and the care with which the programme had been made, he was seeking to give the judges a reason for looking beyond the mere fact of our disobedience of the law. Our conduct of the affair merited a more subtle and sympathetic response than the one Mr. Collins had argued for. As he put it:

> The mechanisms to be looked at are much more subtle than the question: Was there an order? Does it subsist? Have they complied? Answer: Yes, yes and no. Therefore, penalty must follow.

Lord Williams then moved on to the second aspect of his submission, namely to the suggestion that there is a strand in English law which indicates that there can be occasions when an individual may refuse to obey a court order to disclose information but without, *ipso facto*, being placed in contempt of court. He cited legal precedents, the case of a journalist, a Mr. Jack Lundin, who in 1982 had refused to answer a question when instructed to do so by a judge in a trial; when the Attorney General later prosecuted Lundin for contempt, the judge held that the question should not have been asked because it was already clear that the prosecution's case was going to fail. So, Lord Williams cited part of the ruling in the Lundin case by the judge, Lord Justice Watkins, a part which he considered most helpful to the defence that he was now presenting to the court:

> To defy deliberately, albeit politely as Lundin did, a proper order of a judge is a serious matter. When Lundin took this step he was fully aware of the possible consequences. So if his action was contemptuous he cannot complain if he is punished for it. However, refusal by a witness to answer a question in a criminal trial, even when ordered by a judge to do so, does not inevitably put that person in contempt of court.

These recondite legal points seemed to me, as I listened to the unfolding argument, to have made a favourable impression on the court because, just after this point, Lord Woolf intervened to comment as follows:

> What must be the situation is that the court, in deciding what is the appropriate course to take, must be entitled to have regard to all the circumstances. There is the conflict that there are the personal circumstances of the defendants who are concerned, which

attracts considerable understanding of the courts. There is also the factor that Mr. Collins referred to and that is that we have the intention of Parliament, as reflected in the legislation, and there is the problem with which the court is faced, that if that is the law, the law must be obeyed.

Lord Williams then moved on to cite other legal precedents and authorities in support of his argument that a person's refusal to disclose information, even when ordered to do so by a court, is not automatically a contempt of court and not an action which must necessarily be punished. After reviewing a number of relevant cases, he sought to demonstrate their relevance to our case.

> My Lord, may I draw my submissions together . . . The fundamental submission I make is that since there is no effective machinery of appeal provided by the statute and there is no prospect of judicial review in the overwhelming bulk of these cases, including this, then it must be for this court to exercise that protection which the citizen may require. I submit that what we look for is one of a proportionate response and if I may identify some of the strands that would be woven together to form the fabric of that proportionate response.

He mentioned, first, the extraordinary nature of the Prevention of Terrorism Act under which the Production Orders had been made—"No appeal. No remedy;" next, our motives had been "fine and noble," our conduct "responsible, diligent, careful;" if we had been prosecuted under Section 18 of the Act, we would have had ample reasonable excuses for not handing over the information—"the sanctity of undertakings," "human decency in not exposing other people to risk of death," the danger to the programme makers and to their families.

> I do submit that there is a legitimate public interest. I know that these are old friends wheeled out too often, and without sufficient cause on many occasions, for illegitimate motives. There is, I submit rightly and calmly, to be detected, a legitimate public interest in this case of the journalistic exposure of wrongdoing. If there was wrongdoing of this type, it corrodes the whole of society. I have constantly sought to say that I do not invite the court to conclusions because they are not capable of being brought but I do respectfully say that this type of corruption is infinitely worse than financial or ordinary political corruption, it corrodes everybody . . .
>
> It is with infinite regret that they [Channel 4 and Box Productions] cannot conform. They are not law breakers. My Lord, there is a more powerful Master, I am afraid, that controls them. You have heard nothing from me, on their behalf, of any bogus claims of immunity or press superiority. I simply put it on

that basis, that there is a greater Master that tries them and so I ask for your proportionate remedy.

We had been immensely fortunate in having Lord Williams to speak on our behalf. As I listened to him develop his argument and weave the fabric of our defence from the few thin strands of legal precedent available to him, I thought that he had succeeded in defusing the advertised confrontation between the Media and the Law, leaving the judges in no doubt that, as responsible journalists, we recognised and accepted the supremacy of the Law—except that in the unique circumstances of this case, we could not do so.[4]

As I studied the demeanour of the two judges on the bench, in an effort to gauge their reaction, I thought that Lord Williams had probably persuaded them that they ought to balance our considered disobedience of the order against the background circumstances he had so eloquently explained. He had mentioned the "intact finding" by the lower court, the judge's admission that disclosure would create a real risk of death for Source A; he argued that a binding undertaking could not honourably be broken; and finally, he reminded the court that our own lives had also been threatened. These, he said, were crucially important aspects of the affair, aspects which the court was obliged to take into account in coming to its verdict.

In reply, the Crown's Mr. Collins invited the judges to disregard most of what they had just heard in our defence, except in so far as it was relevant to mitigation of the sentence that ought now to be imposed for our wilful disobedience and contempt. The order ought to be obeyed and the background circumstances, as emphasised by Lord Williams, were largely irrelevant to that issue. The real public interest, said Mr. Collins, had been recognised by Judge Clarkson when he had made the order, so that the RUC could proceed with their investigation into the truth of the programme's allegations.

> It is in the public interest and it is difficult to see how that view could be contradicted, that these allegations should be properly investigated. Thus, if offences are being committed by anyone, and more particularly if there is this sort of corruption in the RUC, it should be rooted out.
>
> My Lord, the difficulty that we have is that the appeal is made to the legitimate public interest in the journalistic exposure of wrongdoing. I entirely accept there is that public interest but it is a public interest that is set at nil if the exposure can be made but nothing can be done to follow it up and to try to root it out because that is what has happened. The exposure is made but the failure to disclose the relevant information to enable the investigations properly to be carried out has—and this was the evidence

of Chief Superintendent Nesbitt before the learned judge—resulted in the situation that the wrongdoing cannot properly be discovered and rooted out if it exists. One has a paradox but that is the result. It, as it were, nullifies the whole purpose of the investigation if this attitude is adopted.

Mr. Collins wanted only a "proper," not an independent, investigation and he preferred to ignore Judge Clarkson's scepticism about the "rather Irish" situation in which the RUC was being allowed to investigate itself. Nor did he appear to see any inconsistency in arguing that the public interest required that the truth of our allegations be established, when a short time earlier he had himself declared that those very allegations were "probably rubbish." In sum:

> The court must . . . try to find a way of ensuring that the order is obeyed in the public interest not only as a matter of law, but because it is in the public interest that the information should be given.

This argument produced a series of exchanges with Lord Woolf in which Mr. Collins urged the judge to be ready to sequestrate Channel 4's assets and take the network off the air, if that proved to be the only way to ensure compliance with the order.

> Judge: Are you submitting to the court, therefore, that if we follow you down the possible step of sequestration, which you are suggesting, that might, in the situation which we are in, achieve the result which is the desirable result which you have identified?
> Collins: My Lord, yes. Initially perhaps the threat of it, or the indication that the court is going to do it because, obviously, it is perfectly proper to give Channel Four and Box the chance of reconsidering in the light of what the court may indicate would happen if they do not reconsider.
> Judge: Is that a realistic result, Mr. Collins? This is a decision which has been taken after careful deliberation. Rightly or wrongly this is the position the respondents feel compelled to take. Are they going to be affected by an order of that sort to change what they see as a principle of this nature?
> Collins: My Lord, it may well be. But if they appreciate that to stick to this decision, which is a wrong decision, will mean the end of Channel 4, then that surely will make them appreciate the seriousness of what they are doing.
> Judge: That will certainly bring home the serious consequence of what they have done, yes.
> Collins: My Lord, yes, but it will mean that it is, in effect, the only way in which the court can conceivably enforce the order that has been made . . . it must be to impose the sort of penalty which

ensures that unless there is compliance with the order, the alternative is really so drastic that those who were responsible should not, in the public interest and their own interests, contemplate [it]. . . .

Judge: . . . the first step is for the court to decide whether what the court would like to see achieved is achievable.

Collins: My Lord, that is right.

The barristers had argued the issues thoroughly over two days in a court-room crowded with an unusually large contingent of journalists and media executives. The arguments and the issues were reported in detail in the national and international press; television reporters also covered the proceedings for the nightly news bulletins. And when the two sides had completed their presentations, Lord Woolf had indicated that he and Mr. Justice Pill would do their utmost to deliver their judgement quickly—which, in fact, they proved able to do. Before considering that judgement, however, I would like first to deal with what Lord Williams had to say in the course of his presentation when he dealt with the statement by Witness X, the one from the anonymous, disillusioned Loyalist which the Crown had introduced on behalf of the RUC.[5]

Lord Williams managed to turn this development to our advantage because he drew attention to the fact that this statement, potentially as helpful to the RUC as it would be ruinous to our programme's credibility, had been signed by an individual whose name is already familiar to the reader and whose past activities will be discussed in some detail in a later chapter. Lord Williams told the court that the full significance of Witness X's statement could only be understood by reference to the contents of the Channel 4 dossier, which had listed the names of nineteen members of the Committee, as identified by Source A.

> Since life is redolent with irony, the statement is taken from someone who calls himself "X." "X" in fact is saying, I think I summarise it and paraphrase it fairly, "This is all a hoax got up by me." If your Lordship looks at the third page of "X's" statement, you will see that it was taken in the presence of a solicitor. I do not name him. Would your Lordship look at the . . . material provided by Channel 4. It says: "Category A consists of names of those who Source A confirmed unequivocally are members of the Committee." My Lord, this is part of the dossier which my learned friend Mr. Collins rightly indicated was handed over. It is nineteen members of the Committee. Category A is those confirmed unequivocally by Source A as members of this unlawful committee. Under the cross-head "Businessmen" in Category A, the third name down is the very person who was present as witness of the statement of Witness X, which was served on us a few

days ago. My Lord, that is simply an indication of the dangers that Channel 4 and Box have always feared and it is an indication that there is a very small world of inquiry in certain parts of Northern Ireland.

Lord Williams had drawn attention to the fact that the Channel 4 dossier, given to the RUC, had reported that Source A had unequivocally identified Portadown solicitor Richard Monteith as a member of the Committee. It was therefore a little strange, Lord Williams was suggesting, that of all the solicitors in Northern Ireland who might have witnessed the statement produced by the RUC's Witness X, the one chosen was allegedly a member of the actual murder conspiracy. As Lord Williams had said, this was evidence of the "very small world" we were dealing with; and the appearance of Monteith's name in both documents suggested that we had good reason to be suspicious. Were we not perfectly right to doubt the integrity of the RUC's internal investigation and to worry about the RUC's links to the likes of Monteith? If we were to give Jim Sands's name to the RUC, how long would it be before it made its way to Monteith, Abernethy, or one of the other conspirators? Whether Lord Justice Woolf and Mr. Justice Pill would seriously consider these questions was something we could only speculate about until the moment we heard their judgement. That moment would come just three days later, on Friday, July 31st 1992.

Brian Raymond, who had guided us unerringly through the legalities of the affair, assured us before the verdict that there was no prospect of the High Court acceding to the Crown's demand that Channel 4's assets be seized and the network shut down. Such a penalty would guarantee worldwide publicity for the programme's allegations and for the RUC's alleged role in facilitating the Loyalist death squads. Brian was sure that the astute Lord Woolf would find a more elegant and less draconian solution to the problem facing the court. I shared Brian's optimism because the judge had indicated, in his exchanges with Mr. Collins, that he had accepted the fact that we were not going to obey the orders, regardless of any penalty he might impose; he had (rightly) concluded that even if he were to shut Channel 4 down, we would still not give in. Lord Woolf had, perhaps reluctantly, accepted that the RUC was not going to be given any material which would identify Source A.

While we were waiting for the judgement to be handed down, we wondered how the judges would respond to our argument that we could not have made the programme without Source A's unique testimony; that we had only been able to persuade him to take part by giving the unqualified undertaking that we would protect his identity. Would the court accept the logic of our defence—no interview, no programme, no end to the Committee's assassination campaign? We also discussed whether the judges would share Judge Clarkson's doubts about an investigation in which the RUC was to be its own judge and jury; or whether they would side with the Crown's argument that we should indeed have handed over the name, with them taking it for granted that the RUC's investigation would be genuine. We also wondered how the judges would view the RUC's willingness to rely on the professional services of Richard Monteith, given his alleged role in the conspiracy. Would this development persuade the court that we were right to have been suspicious? Or, that we were right to fear that any information given to the RUC would soon leak to the Committee, leak from Nesbitt to Abernethy? I discussed these and other issues with Brian Raymond right up to the moment when, together with Channel 4's top executives Sir Richard (now, Lord) Attenborough, Michael Grade and Liz Forgan, we filed into the High Court to hear what the learned judges would say.

Everyone present in the courtroom rose and stood in silence as Lord Justice Woolf and Mr. Justice Pill, bewigged and enrobed, entered to take their places on the bench. Before delivering his judgement, Lord Woolf acknowledged the discomfort caused inside the court room by the heat wave we were experiencing that summer, telling the barristers that they were free to remove their wigs, if they wished to do so. He then spoke, without a break, for about half an hour and the following extracts give what I consider to be the most significant parts of his ruling. He began by outlining the background to the Attorney General's application and by reviewing the relevant provisions of the Prevention of Terrorism Act. Then, he continued:

> There is a substantial volume of evidence before the Court as to how the companies came to make the programme and to be in a position where the members of the board of both companies have unanimously come to the decision that they have to disobey an Order of the Court. Channel 4 can properly be regarded as being one of the more important public bodies in this country having regard to its role in the media. Box on the other hand is a company of modest financial resources but in its field it is highly regarded. The members of the boards of both companies are people of integrity and standing who should be well used to bearing heavy responsibility and making difficult decisions. I prefer to accept that in connection with their activities in relation to the programme they believe they were acting with propriety in a difficult situation. If they were not fully aware of the implications of what was happening, they certainly should have been.

Lord Woolf then proceeded to summarise the programme makers' account of what had happened and he quoted extensively from the affidavits submitted by Ben Hamilton, David Lloyd, Liz Forgan and me. He then moved quickly to dismiss the argument that the High Court had the power to consider whether Judge Clarkson ought ever to have made the Production Orders.

> Mr. Williams, Queen's Counsel, in his powerful and moving submissions on behalf of the companies argued, while fully recognising that this was not his best point, that although there is no right of appeal in respect of the Order made by the Judge on an application for committal for contempt, this court even where there is a clear breach of the Order, are entitled to decide that the lower Judge wrongly exercised his discretion under Schedule 7. In support of this argument he referred the Court to the Attorney General v Lundin, the law of contempt in Arlidge & Eady 1982, Paragraphs 487(b) to 487(d) and other authority. I cannot accept this contention. In my judgement, the law is clear . . . in my judgement the learned Judge exercised his discretion perfectly properly.

So, Lord Woolf had decided that the Order had been valid and ought, therefore, to have been obeyed. He continued:

> I fully accept that, throughout, both Channel 4 and Box were motivated by what they regard as being proper motives. I also accept that they now find themselves in a real dilemma. For genuinely held moral considerations, they feel compelled to disobey what they know well is their legal duty. However, in determining their responsibility it is necessary to identify how it is that they find themselves in this dilemma. In the passage of his Affidavit, which I have already cited, Mr. McPhilemy identifies the source of the problem when he says, "The seeds of the proceedings in this Court were sown when I first endorsed and agreed to be bound by the undertaking given to A." Whether they were aware of this at the time or not, both Box and Channel 4 should have appreciated that because of the provisions of the 1989 Act they should not have given an unqualified undertaking to A. They could properly give an undertaking that they would not disclose A's identity unless they were ordered to do so by the Court and that they would do everything in their power to protect his identity but they were not in a position to give the undertaking which they did. It was and should have been obvious to them, particularly having regard to the legal advice which they were receiving, that if they were going to act or might act on the information which A provided, there was at least a substantial risk of an Order being made in the terms of the Order which was actually made. This is particularly true in the case of Channel 4 who only became subject to the undertaking on deciding to go ahead with the preparations of the programme with a view to its being broadcast.

So, in Lord Woolf's judgement, we ought not to have given Source A an unqualified undertaking. We should have told him that, if he agreed to give us an interview, we would not identify him unless a court asked us to do so. This view seemed to me, as soon as I heard Lord Woolf announce it, to have been totally unrealistic about what Source A's likely response would have been—had he been presented with such a proposition. A qualified undertaking of the kind proposed would have strengthened Source A's fears that his name would eventually be disclosed to the RUC and, then, leaked (by the RUC Inner Circle/Inner Force) to the Committee; fears such as these would, I thought and I continue to think, have led Sands to withdraw completely from the project. Lord Woolf's proposal, therefore, would—if implemented—have meant no interview, no programme and, almost certainly, many more murders by the Committee. In short, the eminent judge's solution to our problem would not have worked; and had we followed the course he proposed, the Committee would have murdered even more people throughout 1991 than it, in fact, managed to do.

Lord Woolf went on to castigate the two companies for a second reason; the stand we had taken had, he argued, frustrated the RUC's investigation into the programme's allegations.

> Both companies must have appreciated what would be the consequences of the programme, that almost inevitably there would be an inquiry as a result of the programme and A's role would be crucial. Why did they otherwise send a dossier to the RUC immediately the programme was over? That the immediate effect of the programme would be to undermine the confidence of the public, particularly in the Province of Northern Ireland, in the RUC and an inquiry would be essential if the damage to that confidence was to be kept within limits. They should also have appreciated that, however careful the companies had been, there would remain a risk. A risk confirmed by the evidence filed on the behalf of the directors that A's allegations may have been untrue and were possibly designed to achieve the undermining of the confidence in the RUC. It was, and should have been, obvious that if the investigations into the RUC took place, which after all is now claimed to be one of the hopeful benefits of the programme, the security forces would inevitably want to identify A and follow up his involvement. That would be necessary if A was speaking the truth to eradicate a canker within the RUC and it would be necessary if he was not speaking the truth to show the RUC had been gravely slandered to the disadvantage of the Province.

This second part of the judgement seemed to me to be even less satisfactory than the first. We shall see, later, that the RUC "investigation," which was actually carried out between October 1991 and February 1993, turned out to be an entirely bogus exercise designed to protect the force by discrediting the programme and its sources; I will later present evidence to show that Detective Chief Superintendent Nesbitt's inquiry fully merits this harsh denunciation. But even in July 1992, there was sufficient reason for Lord Woolf to ask himself whether the official response to the broadcast, an *internal* RUC inquiry, was an adequate or proper way to deal with allegations of such gravity from a respected national television network. If ever an independent investigation into the activities of a police force was merited, surely this was such an occasion; yet unlike Judge Clarkson, Lord Woolf did not express any unease about the RUC's investigating itself, nor did he consider whether there was even a remote possibility that Mr. Nesbitt would vindicate our programme. It was always, in my opinion, unthinkable that this RUC inquiry would ever admit that senior officers in an RUC Inner Force, an Inner Circle and a secret Committee were running death squads under the direction of former RUC Reserve officer, Billy Abernethy.

It is important to stress that, once we had given our unqualified undertaking to Source A, we could not hand over his name to *any* inquiry, independent or otherwise. However, as I have already stated, our undertaking to Sands did not extend to protecting him from the consequences he deserved to face for his role in the murder conspiracy; it simply meant that we could not honourably identify him to the police. I readily admit that I would have had no qualms of conscience if a police investigator, working from the clues contained in our dossier—including the list of names of the nineteen alleged conspirators—had managed to identify Sands in this way. Indeed, I believe that a conscientious investigator, genuinely determined to find out the truth, would have interrogated all nineteen individuals on the list and would, on the basis of Sands's testimony, have succeeded in identifying all fifty to sixty members of the Committee.

We would later discover that Mr. Nesbitt's inquiry team did not even bother to arrest or hold any of the nineteen alleged conspirators for interrogation, as the emergency terrorist legislation, the PTA, entitled them to do; the RUC preferred, instead, to direct its fire power against us in the courts. None of this greatly surprised us. For, to answer Lord Woolf's question, when we handed over our dossier to the RUC we had done so on legal advice and with no optimism that it would be used to establish the truth. Subsequent events, as we shall see, showed that we were fully justified in holding such a view and it seems to me that Lord Woolf was unrealistic in suggesting otherwise.

Perhaps the most bizarre aspect of Lord Woolf's thinking was his conclusion that the Witness X statement, the one the Crown presented in support of the RUC, "confirmed" the risk that Source A's evidence was untrue. I suggest that the proper inference to be drawn from the introduction of Witness X's statement to the court was the one put forward by Lord Williams, namely that X's testimony was highly suspect, given that it bore the signature of one of the alleged murder conspirators, Richard Monteith. And it seemed to me, though not to Lord Woolf, that the RUC's readiness to use Monteith's professional services raised an obvious worry about the integrity of the RUC's internal inquiry. We know today, with absolute certainty, that Witness X never had anything to do with the programme; we also know that his claims were totally irrelevant to what we had learned about the Committee from Sands. All of this is also known to the RUC, today, for it was to discover in November 1992 that Source A was not—as the police claimed to the court—Witness X but was, in fact, one of Hugh Ross's Loyalist foot soldiers, James Alfred Sands.

So, what should we have done when, in the spring of 1991, Sands demanded from us the unqualified undertaking that we would protect his identity, no matter what the consequences? Lord Woolf had no doubt about the course we should have taken:

> Even if they decided improperly to adopt this approach [to give the undertaking] they should have at least tried to secure A's cooperation by qualified undertaking or sought legal advice at the highest level of government, which should have been available in view of Channel 4's standing as to the propriety of the action they were proposing. If, however, they felt that either or both of these possibilities would not realistically produce any result then they should have borne in mind the nature of the issue at stake. They should have borne in mind that what they were proposing to do would inevitably undermine not only the reputation of the RUC but also, and possibly more importantly, the rule of law and must help to achieve the very result that the terrorists on both sides in Northern Ireland are seeking to bring about.

If Channel 4 had, as Lord Woolf recommended, informed the Government about what our researches into collusion had unearthed, I believe the outcome would have been exactly the same as what would have happened if we had taken up the judge's other suggestion, namely to have offered merely a qualified undertaking to Sands—in both cases, there would have been no documentary, no broadcast and no exposure of the scandal. For the British Government has never had any enthusiasm for investigative journalism in Northern Ireland and, least of all, for that which has exposed the misconduct of the security forces, whether in Derry on Bloody Sunday in 1972, in the Stalker "shoot-to-kill" affair in 1982 or in countless other killings in the province. And if the transmission of our documentary investigation can be said to have tarnished the reputation of the RUC, as it undoubtedly has in some people's eyes, that is not the fault of journalists but of a Chief Constable who failed to thwart the illegal activities of his senior colleagues within the RUC Inner Force. It is they who facilitated the murder of Republicans and innocent Catholics in the province and who, as a result, have undermined confidence not just in the RUC but in the rule of law which the entire force is supposed to uphold. *Pace* Lord Woolf, the Catholic community in Northern Ireland is unlikely ever to have confidence in a police force which has been so corrupted to such a high level that senior RUC Inner Force representatives chose to sit on Abernethy's Committee and, according to the testimony of their colleague, Jim Sands, to approve assassinations such as that of the innocent youth, Denis Carville.

In Lord Woolf's judgement, Channel 4 and Box Productions had to be punished because they had broken the law; the law ought to have been obeyed.

> Whatever you may personally think of the 1989 Act, it is an Act which is the law of the land and like any other law it has to be observed while it is in force. An institution with the status and responsibility of Channel 4 must surely be required not to act in a way which will or even may result in flouting the law. If Channel 4, and I emphasise their part because everything that Box did was under their supervision and with their approval, are seen to be able to flout the law with impunity, what is the example that this sets to those who do not have their standing and reputation?

The judge then quoted at length the words of Lord Bridge which had already been read to the court by Mr. Collins, the passage which pointed out that freedom of speech is dependent on the rule of law and that it is paradoxical that a challenge to the rule of law should be mounted by responsible journalists. Lord Bridge's ruling, endorsed by Lord Woolf, articulated the court's fundamental criticisms of our conduct: first, that obedience to the law takes precedence over all other considerations; second, if we feel that this law is unjust and we wish to change it, we should seek to do so by persuasion, not by disobedience.

Both findings seem to me to be inappropriate to the circumstances that arose in 1991, when we encountered Source A and came to believe in the truth of what he was saying. I would respectfully argue that saving lives, the lives Abernethy's Committee would have destroyed had the broadcast not stopped the killing, took precedence over all other considerations— including the possibility that we might find ourselves in conflict with the law, if an Order were ever to be issued against us. I find it hard to believe that such a civilised and humane judge as Lord Woolf could seriously argue that, in the circumstances we faced, we should have refused to give Source A the undertaking he demanded—when the consequence would have been yet more assassinations by Abernethy's Committee. I also believe that the second court finding—a campaign to change the PTA by persuasion—was not a realistic proposition for us in 1991. For we had uncovered a truly astonishing situation which nobody in Parliament had ever envisaged; our unique source, who we were convinced was telling the truth, had revealed that a sizeable part of a British police force was *promoting*, rather than preventing, terrorism in the province. Quite rightly, our top priority in 1991, once we had learned that eighteen RUC Inner Force officers were members of Abernethy's Committee, was to place our discoveries in the public domain—not to launch a political campaign against the Prevention of Terrorism Act. That can be our priority today and, indeed, Brian Raymond quickly produced a pamphlet for that very purpose and which argued that the PTA ought to be removed from the statute book.[6] And, a few days after the High Court ruling, I gave my own views on this second proposal from the judges:

> Parliament must be persuaded by a campaign of reasoned argument to remove a blind spot in the law relating to terrorism, the PTA, which refuses to envisage the possibility that officers of a police force could be systematically promoting terrorism rather than preventing it—which is what the Channel 4 programme claimed to have found.
>
> Until the day arrives when that law is reformed . . . each of us will have to decide our own course of action. I confess that I will be reluctant to make another programme on Northern Ireland, but if I were to meet Source A for the first time tomorrow and he were then to tell me the full story of Denis Carville's murder, I would like to think I would do exactly the same again.[7]

Lord Woolf imposed a fine of £75,000 jointly on Channel 4 and Box Productions and stated that it was a substantially smaller sum than it would otherwise have been as we "may not have appreciated . . . the dangers which were implicit in giving an unqualified undertaking" to Source A. And then he delivered an ominous warning to anyone who might give such an undertaking in similar circumstances in the future: "This will not apply to the future but is a compelling factor in the present situation."

Mr. Justice Pill agreed, in a separate judgement, with what Lord Woolf had said and suggested that our conduct had frustrated the RUC's investigation, which he implicitly accepted as a genuine search for the truth.

> The result of the Respondents' contempt of Court is that the authorities and the Courts have been deprived of the opportunity to investigate the extremely serious and inflammatory allegations

which have been made. If the allegations are true, urgent and thorough investigation is required. Prosecutions would be likely. If the allegations are untrue, they should be exposed for the dangerous and pernicious falsehoods they are. The public has the worst of it. They endure the distrust, fear and distress which are bred by the allegations, without the opportunity to have the truth of the allegations properly investigated. The danger to society if falsehoods of this kind go uncorrected needs no underlining, neither does the degree of concern to be felt if Source A is telling the truth.

Mr. Justice Pill chose to ignore the fact that we had given the names of nineteen alleged Committee members to the RUC; he preferred to accept the claim that Source A's identity was crucial to the success of the investigation. We shall see, in a later chapter, that the RUC did eventually succeed in finding Source A and we shall consider how the force coped with the discovery that his allegations were *true*, that he was—as he claimed—a close political associate of Abernethy, Ross, Monteith and the others. Instead of opting for the prosecutions which Mr. Justice Pill had thought "likely" in such an outcome, the RUC chose instead to pretend that they were *untrue*, that they were—in the judge's words—"dangerous and pernicious falsehoods." As a result, no prosecutions have taken place and nobody has been charged with any of the murders examined in the programme, murders which the Chief Constable publicly declared his resolve "to relentlessly pursue" [*sic*].

After the two judgements had been delivered and the judges had retired to their chambers, we all—solicitors, barristers, Channel 4 executives, programme makers—filed out of the court room and huddled together in the corridors in an effort to agree what we would say to the press and television cameras gathered in the street outside. The case had made front-page news in most of the national newspapers and had been reported worldwide as one of the most important clashes between the Media and the Law in recent times—despite Lord Williams attempt to defuse the confrontation. Fortunately, I was able to call, yet again, on the services of my quick-witted and resourceful solicitor, Brian Raymond, who had scribbled a short soundbyte for me on a piece of paper. He told me to memorise his few words and then, within minutes, I found myself standing on the steps of the High Court facing what seemed like an ocean of reporters, photographers, camera crews and on-lookers of all kinds. After Sir Richard Attenborough had explained why Channel 4 had taken such a principled stand, I then uttered Brian's words to the sea of faces in front of me.

> If we had not given an unqualified undertaking to our sources, no one would ever have known that members of the RUC have been running death squads.

I was then invited by Channel 4 to join Chief Executive Michael Grade and Director of Programmes Liz Forgan at a press conference where we all called on the Government to set up an independent inquiry into the programme's allegations. Although the newspapers gave some space to what each of us said, there is no doubt about the words which caused most offence when they were heard at the RUC's Headquarters in Belfast. Brian Raymond's soundbyte, which I had published outside the High Court, provoked the Chief Constable to retaliate with a press statement, which he later published as a half-page advertisement in the leading newspapers on both sides of the Irish border. In view of subsequent developments, which I will deal with in later chapters, it is worth quoting the press advertisement in full; for the text will help the reader to appreciate the extent to which the RUC's version of events differs from the truth about how the Committee, relying heavily on its eighteen RUC Inner Force members, "eliminated" many Republicans and Catholics between mid-1989 and 1991.

ALLEGATIONS AGAINST THE ROYAL ULSTER CONSTABULARY
A statement by the Chief Constable, Sir Hugh Annesley

On Friday 31 July, on national television, Mr. Sean McPhilemy, Chief Executive of Box Productions, commented:
"If we had not given an unqualified undertaking to our sources, no one would ever have known that members of the RUC have been running death squads."
Box Productions is the television production company which made the Channel 4 "Dispatches" programme alleging that the RUC was colluding with Loyalist paramilitary organisations. The allegation was denied when the programme was broadcast in October 1991. It was an outrageous allegation then. It remains an outrageous allegation.
Now that the court proceedings involving Channel 4, Box Productions and the RUC have concluded, the RUC wishes to set out the facts and these are as follows.
Extensive investigation has now established that the allegation of an Inner Circle/Inner Force within the RUC was an invention. The author of the invention [Witness X] has made a statement describing in detail how he set out to discredit the RUC. The alleged existence of an Inner Circle/Inner Force was central to the Channel 4 "Dispatches" programme which claimed collusion between the RUC and Loyalist paramilitaries in a murder campaign.
Furthermore, the RUC investigation team is satisfied that there is no overall organising "Committee" comprising members of the

security forces, paramilitaries and prominent members of the community, as alleged by an anonymous source in the Channel 4 programme.

INNER CIRCLE/INNER FORCE

In a written statement [by Witness X] to the Police, made in the presence of his solicitor [Richard Monteith], a witness has said, *inter alia*:

"in early 1985 the riots took place in Portadown when the RUC banned the Orange processions and this was followed by serious disorder and confrontations between the RUC and the Loyalist community. I considered that the RUC was being used to implement the Anglo/Irish Agreement and to suppress any Loyalist opposition to it. I believed that this was carried out on the directions of the Dublin Government and that this was being done to give the RUC credibility among the minority community.

I decided that I would attack any credibility that the RUC had been given by the minority community as a result of this exercise. I invented a story about there being an Inner Circle in existence within the RUC and that members of this Inner Circle were prepared to take part in a coup in the event of a United Ireland. I also thought that if the powers in the RUC thought they could not control their own members it would slow up the implementation of the Anglo/Irish Agreement."

The witness then describes how he telephoned a journalist [Martin O'Hagan] whom he believes to be hostile to the RUC. Using a code word but remaining anonymous he gave the journalist a statement purporting to come from the Inner Circle. The story was published. On other occasions the witness telephoned the same journalist, using a code word and repeated the story of the Inner Circle and stating that the members of the circle were prepared to act in collusion with Loyalist paramilitaries in targeting Republicans for assassination.

The witness states: "these stories were untrue and were made up by me. The whole story of the Inner Circle and the activities I described to (the journalist) were a complete fabrication on my part. I watched the "Dispatches" programme which was broadcast last October. It was a lot of rubbish and quite a lot of the references contained in it were similar to the stories I had told (the journalist)."

The journalist involved has been interviewed by the Police and has agreed that he originated publication of the Inner Circle story. He confirmed that he did so on the basis of telephone calls from an unidentified man; he never met the man face to face, and had no other information to support the allegation of an Inner Circle. This journalist co-operated with the "Dispatches" TV programme.

Another journalist interviewed in the same programme [John Coulter] about an alleged interview with a member of the Inner Circle has told the police that he did not know whom he interviewed. This journalist claimed he was misrepresented by the programme makers.

THE COMMITTEE

The Channel 4 programme, using an unidentified source, alleged the existence of a "Committee" comprising members of the security forces, Loyalist paramilitaries and prominent members of the community. Channel 4 supplied a dossier to the RUC but after prolonged enquiry, my investigation team is satisfied that no Committee exists as alleged by the Channel 4 source.

CHANNEL 4

Despite repeated requests, and notwithstanding a court order, Channel 4 has refused to reveal to the RUC the identity of a source who professed to be a member of the "Committee" which sanctioned acts of terrorism. If this source exists, and if he was indeed involved in crime, the RUC considers it essential for the protection of the community that he should be made amenable to the law.

Channel 4's refusal to co-operate with the RUC in this crucial respect was not confined to us. They similarly refused to co-operate with the Metropolitan Police.

THE RUC

The RUC believes strongly in the freedom of the news media within the law. We have no desire whatever to muzzle the news media or hinder responsible journalistic investigation. However, the primary and inescapable duty of the RUC is to save life and protect the community; to investigate crimes and to bring those responsible to justice, whoever they may be. It is that duty which has impelled the RUC in this case involving Channel 4. The RUC also has the right to defend itself robustly against allegations which it believes to be false and which would unjustly undermine public confidence in its integrity and impartiality.

The RUC has not hesitated, at considerable sacrifice to its officers, to confront Loyalist extremism, whether in dealing with violent disorder on the streets or in bringing Loyalists to justice for terrorist crimes.

CONCLUSION

I have stated before, and I state again, that the RUC should not be above criticism or scrutiny. Inherent in this proposition is a reasonable expectation of balance and goodwill by those who televise or write about us. In short, power should be accompanied by responsibility.

The High Court in London called upon Channel 4 and Box Productions to reconsider their position in refusing to disclose the source who claimed to be a party to a series of murders. The

RUC, in the interests of justice, now again asks Channel 4 and
Box Productions to provide their information.

In taking the unusual step of issuing a statement in such detail,
the RUC wishes to assure the people of Northern Ireland and
beyond that the allegations, as portrayed in the Channel 4 television programme, are without foundation.

This RUC press statement, which was issued the day after the High
Court judgement (August 1st 1992), is extremely important because it
shows that the Chief Constable, Sir Hugh Annesley, was entirely satisfied,
on that date, that the programme's allegations were false. There had never
been an RUC Inner Circle nor an RUC Inner Force, he said, as these
were—supposedly—the mere inventions of the disgruntled Witness X,
whose entirely credible statement had been signed by his respectable solicitor, Richard Monteith. Nor had there ever been a Committee of the kind
alleged; although the RUC had persuaded Lord Woolf and Mr. Justice Pill,
only the day before, that the allegations could not be properly investigated without access to Source A, Sir Hugh's inquiry team had miraculously
managed, just 24 hours later, to convince their boss that they now knew,
quite definitely, that all our allegations were false. In short, the RUC had
put its authority behind the "hoax" theory, the claim that Channel 4 had
been duped by Witness X and others and that the RUC had been grievously maligned.

Unfortunately for Sir Hugh, Witness X had played no role in the story
we had learned from Source A, Jim Sands. Witness X's statement contains
nothing to refute any part of the extensive, convincing and first-hand testimony we obtained from Sands about the eighteen specific murders
attributed by him to the Committee. The RUC had, therefore, already
committed itself to this "hoax" theory long before it discovered Source A's
true identity or had an opportunity to examine his detailed account of the
murder conspiracy. The reader should bear this in mind because, when
the RUC finally did manage to discover Jim Sands and study his evidence,
it quietly abandoned its reliance on Witness X but, ironically, maintained
its allegiance to Witness X's "hoax" theory, transferring the blame from
the disillusioned Loyalist featured so prominently in the RUC's press
release to the one whose identity we had gone to such lengths to protect.

Notes

1   We felt that this was a real prospect because one of Martin O'Hagan's colleagues on *Sunday World,* Jim Campbell, had been nearly killed during an earlier period of the troubles. In 1984, he had been running a series of critical articles on the top Loyalist assassin, Robin Jackson [The Jackal]. The reward for his courageous journalism had been a bullet in the stomach.

2   We were informed by Sands that Abernethy and three other Loyalists came to England at the beginning of August 1991, as he (Sands) had predicted. They did not, in fact, visit our homes (as we had been led to believe they would) but, instead, had recruited a mercenary, who had agreed to take action against us, as and when required to do so. All this information, which emanated from Sands, was discussed at the time with Channel 4.

3   Lord Bridge of Harwich; judgement in "X Ltd. v Morgan-Grampian Ltd., 1991."

4   Perhaps wisely, Lord Williams chose not to allude to the "blind spot" in the law, which makes no allowance for the possibility—the actuality, we had discovered—that a significant part of a police force might be promoting, rather than preventing, terrorism.

5   I never learned the identity of Witness X, nor did I try to do so. I always viewed him as a distraction.

6   Brian Raymond; "A Shield Full of Holes," Chapter 88, London, 1992.

7   *Broadcast Magazine,* London. August, 1992.

Chapter 9

DIRTY TRICKS

The Chief Constable's unprecedented use of the PTA against us had back-fired badly on his force. For, once the court case had ended, his officers had found themselves returning home to Belfast without the name of Source A but with the damaging allegations about RUC death squads ringing loudly in their ears. The entire legal exercise had been a spectacular public relations disaster because far more people had heard about the death squads as a result of the High Court hearing than had done so from watching the programme, ten months earlier, on Channel 4. So, it was to be expected that those in Government charged with the task of shaping public opinion on these delicate matters would try to restore the RUC's battered reputation by launching a propaganda exercise of their own.

We would later discover that, while the court case was running in London, a small number of officials inside the Northern Ireland Office at Stormont Castle in Belfast and RUC Headquarters, also in Belfast, had been working overtime to ensure that an effective counter-attack got under way immediately after the court had delivered its verdict. This little group was highly experienced in the practice of media manipulation, an art form which encompassed an encyclopaedic range of "dirty tricks," including misinformation, misrepresentation, fabrication and deception. The group would, in the months that lay ahead, display a cynical contempt for the wider British public by feeding them false and confusing information about the programme, all of it designed to prevent the truths contained in the broadcast from being recognised and believed. This media manipulation was so successful that before long it had created near unanimity among supposedly well-informed commentators on Irish affairs that we had got the story badly wrong.

The Committee had been an extremely rare, if not a unique occurrence, in British current affairs television in that it had exposed high-level, ongoing police corruption, which had led to the murder of many innocent people. For this reason, it presented an even bigger problem for the media manipulators, the dirty tricks brigade, than the one they had faced back in

1988, when they had tried to discredit *Death on the Rock*. Such was the ferocity of their attacks on that documentary that Thames Television, in a futile attempt to placate the Thatcher Government, had been forced to set up an independent inquiry into the conduct of the programme makers—a conspicuous victory for the dirty tricks brigade who had managed to shift the focus of the controversy from what the programme had claimed to how the programme makers had behaved; the ensuing row centred less on the conduct of the SAS soldiers and much more on the conduct of the producers and on the credibility of their witnesses. We would soon find ourselves subjected to similar techniques, with our critics ignoring Source A's testimony about the murder conspiracy, preferring instead to muddy the waters by injecting polluted information about our sources and ourselves.

The Committee presented a particularly serious threat to the reputation of the British security forces—especially the RUC—because it had claimed that corrupt Police and Army officers had been prepared to murder not just IRA terrorists but totally innocent Catholics as well; the lesson we had drawn from Denis Carville's murder was that these RUC officers, the eighteen members of the RUC Inner Force on Abernethy's Committee, posed a threat to the life of any and every Catholic in Northern Ireland. It was clear to me that, if our programme's allegations came to be believed and if what Sands had told us were to be accepted as the truth, the RUC's very future would be in jeopardy. But, fortunately for the RUC and the dirty tricks brigade at Stormont Castle, the *Dispatches* programme had contained two weaknesses, both of which they now proceeded to exploit to the full. First, our key source had been anonymous, so his testimony and even his existence could plausibly be denied; second, as his identity had still to be kept secret, we could not conclusively disprove that any bogus claimant—such as the RUC's Witness X—was an impostor, someone who had no connection to Source A.

Both of these weaknesses were quickly identified by the dirty tricks brigade who, we soon learned, were briefing their favoured press reporters, those who could be trusted to follow official guidance on how best to undermine our story's credibility. The outlets regarded as most reliable by the Stormont Castle and RUC spin-doctors were the two right-wing, mass-circulation Sunday newspapers which had, back in 1988, led the attack on *Death on the Rock*. These two newspapers—Rupert Murdoch's *The Sunday Times* and Lord Stevens's *Sunday Express*—would, over the ten months from August 1992 to May 1993, deploy their tried and tested techniques in a relentless campaign against the programme and the programme makers. The sustained abuse heaped on Channel 4 and Box Productions during this period, together with a series of false and malicious reports emanating from the RUC and Stormont Castle, were eventually to succeed in persuading many commentators that the programme had been deeply flawed. For example, on the anniversary of the broadcast—October 1992—*The Independent's* Belfast-based "Ireland Correspondent," David McKittrick, felt able to agree with the Chief Constable's verdict that our allegations had been unfounded and lacking in credible evidence—a flawed programme which, in his "expert" view, reflected our naiveté, ignorance and gullibility.

> If even a small proportion of the allegations levelled against the programme are ever substantiated, it could go down in history as one of the worst television programmes ever shown in Britain.
>
> Box Productions, which made the programme, stands accused not just of getting the story wrong but of complete naiveté, misrepresenting interviewees and even of fiddling expenses . . .
>
> Insofar as there can be said to be a consensus about anything in Northern Ireland, the feeling is widespread among public figures and journalists that *Dispatches* got it wrong. The common view is that, although collusion between members of the security forces and extreme Loyalists has been shown to exist, credible evidence has not been found for the highly structured and formalised procedures which *Dispatches* depicted.
>
> Some of its sources are widely known and have reputations for unreliability. At the same time, the widespread assumption has been that the programme was made in good faith and represents an honest error of judgement caused by lack of local knowledge.

When these words were written, we were still in constant touch with Source A and so felt able to shrug off such comments, secure in the knowledge that we retained access to sufficient material—still held outside the court's jurisdiction—to enable us, one day, to prove the truth of what the programme had alleged. But it is a tribute to the skill of the hard-working dirty tricks brigade that they had managed, by October 1992, to contain the scandal, to foment scepticism about the programme among the British Press's specialist Ireland Correspondents and, most important of all, to convince the public that the RUC, that "highly reputable concern" (Judge Clarkson), had been grievously maligned.

How could anybody seriously believe that fifty to sixty people, supposedly some of the most affluent and well-connected citizens in the province, would regularly and freely congregate to sanction and plan murder? Was such a proposition not too ridiculous for words, so far fetched that it could only be advanced by someone who had no knowledge of Ulster or of the Ulster Protestant mind? This rare "consensus," this "common view" about our "complete naiveté" and "honest error of judgement," owed much to the efforts of the two Sunday newspapers which had worked closely, for many months, with their friends in the RUC and Stormont Castle. Sadly, many people were all too ready to believe the black propaganda against us, presented in the form of "revelations," "scoops," "exclusive findings" and "special investigations" in the two newspapers. Coverage in *The Sunday Times* was provided by Belfast-based correspondent Liam Clarke, whose copy was rewritten in London by the newspaper's editor, Andrew Neil; while the *Sunday Express* relied on the skills of a "reporter" who, when previously employed by *The Sunday Times*, had shown himself decidedly reluctant to let the facts stand in the way of a "good story," Barrie Penrose.

One might reasonably have expected that this trio's "reporting" on *The Committee* would have met with a degree of scepticism elsewhere in the media because it was *The Sunday Times*, edited by Andrew Neil, that—aided and abetted by the very same dirty tricks brigade—had been so reckless and so indifferent to the truth in its "reporting" on *Death on the Rock* that it had incurred huge libel damages and costs. The ignominious end to that previous journalistic crusade—the newspaper's total capitulation on the steps of the High Court in London—confirmed what many observers had long known, namely that the "reporting" on the SAS in Gibraltar by Andrew Neil's reporters was as reliable and truthful as *The Sunday Times*'s earlier and equally unforgettable triumph, the exclusive serialisation of the "Authentic Diaries of the Fuhrer of the Third Reich, Adolf Hitler."[1]

"HOW TV TEAM WERE DUPED IN ULSTER" was the bold headline over Barrie Penrose's double-page article in the *Sunday Express* on August 2nd 1992, published just two days after Lord Woolf had given his ruling. Though the RUC's team of sixteen investigators had failed to find Source A in the ten months since the broadcast, the intrepid Penrose appeared to have encountered no difficulty at all in tracking him down. Remarkably, within just forty-eight hours of the end of the High Court proceedings, Penrose was in a position to inform his readers that he had managed to identify the elusive Source A; he had no hesitation in declaring that Source A, whom we had gone to such lengths to protect, was none other than the RUC's mysterious Witness X. Penrose's "discovery"—which, of course, was not a discovery at all and totally wrong—also seemed to me to be an implausible, if not incredible, story because the RUC itself had been careful not to make this explicit claim, either in the court room or in the Chief Constable's lengthy press release. Indeed, careful reading of the RUC's detailed statement suggests that the police knew that Witness X had *not* been our source and that they believed that someone else had probably appeared in our film, where he had then parroted Witness X's supposed inventions. Perhaps Penrose thought that the RUC's version of events would be too complicated for *Sunday Express* readers to understand and this was the reason why he had chosen to opt for the simpler, balder assertion that Source A and Witness X were one and the same person—an equation which made it much easier to assert that we had all been duped.

Penrose's first big revelation was superficially embarrassing for us in that he had managed to find and to highlight a link between the IRA and the programme:

> A convicted IRA terrorist was behind Channel 4's Inner Circle story and was paid a four-figure sum to help research the programme . . . Former IRA man [Martin] O'Hagan, who had been jailed for seven years for arms possession, claims that over . . . seven months he was paid a four-figure sum for helping Channel 4.

Penrose's revelation was partially correct but it was also totally misleading in that he was inviting his readers to infer that O'Hagan's limited involvement with the programme makers meant that the documentary was, for that reason alone, deeply flawed and that its allegations could be safely ignored. It is perfectly true that Belfast-based journalist Martin O'Hagan had been, in the early 1970s, a member of the Official IRA—sworn enemies, we should note, of the Provisional IRA—and that he had also been convicted in 1972 for possession of two weapons, an offence for which he had served four years in prison. What Penrose did not tell his readers, however, was that O'Hagan had, since his release in 1976, put his past behind him and built a successful career in journalism over fifteen years; by 1991, he had become a well-known reporter on the Belfast tabloid *Sunday World* and regularly published front-page stories on extraordinary "human interest" topics, as well as on political and paramilitary developments on both sides of the sectarian divide.

When Ben Hamilton first met O'Hagan in early 1991 and had, with my approval, hired his services we were fully aware of his past conviction and we also knew how he had reformed and established himself in his new career. We had checked him out and had, for example, discovered at an early stage that he was sufficiently trusted by the RUC to be allowed to carry a personal weapon for his own protection, a concession which would never have been granted to him if there had remained any suspicion that he was involved with the Provisional IRA.[2] So Martin's conviction dating back nearly twenty years was, we had judged, irrelevant to the limited roles we asked him to play—introducing Ben to his paramilitary contacts, coming to London for Sands's interview and providing background information on personalities and incidents in which we were interested.

Having smeared our Belfast-based researcher as a closet IRA terrorist and having also smeared us for the "four-figure sum" we had paid him—a detail probably leaked to Penrose by the RUC from our programme accounting records—Penrose then offered a detailed account of the catastrophic blunder Channel 4 was supposed to have made in broadcasting *The Committee*.[3] For it turned out, according to Penrose, that O'Hagan and Witness X—equated with Source A and then named—had each independently played a role in perpetrating a "hoax" on Channel 4. These two paragraphs followed immediately from Penrose's revelation about O'Hagan's terrorist past:

> What the film makers did not know was that O'Hagan's source was a hoaxer who called himself Mr. X. He was a disgruntled Loyalist angry at the RUC after the Portadown, County Armagh riots in 1985.
>
> O'Hagan, who helped set up the meetings for Channel 4 with a string of leading Ulster Loyalists, some convicted terrorists, said: "I had written an article about the Inner Circle five years previously, but it was a flier—there was no hard evidence for it. I handed the newspaper cuts [press cuttings] and telephone numbers to Hamilton.

I have no idea what *Sunday Express* readers may have made of all this but the elaborate "hoax," though not clearly explained by Penrose in his article, seems to have worked like this. The seeds of the eventual Channel 4 blunder were sown five years before we ever encountered O'Hagan, when the convicted IRA-man-turned-journalist hoaxed his own newspaper readers by inventing and publishing a report on a mythical RUC Inner Circle. This fictitious report was then read, quite by chance, by a disgruntled Loyalist, a Mr. X, who subsequently telephoned O'Hagan and hoaxed the journalist into believing that his caller was, in fact, a member of the non-existent RUC body which O'Hagan himself had invented. So— *if* Penrose can be believed—the hoaxer O'Hagan was himself hoaxed by the disgruntled Loyalist. At this point in Penrose's story in the *Sunday Express* Witness X, having become aware of the controversy over the *Dispatches* broadcast, stepped forward and admitted to the RUC that he was partly responsible for the lies and smears that had somehow been recycled on Channel 4. Penrose then quotes approvingly from the RUC Chief Constable's version of events, which conveniently supports his own.

> "Using a code word, but remaining anonymous he [Witness X] gave the journalist [O'Hagan] a statement purporting to come from the Inner Circle," added [RUC Chief Constable] Sir Hugh [Annesley].

Finally—*if* Penrose can be believed—O'Hagan completed the "hoax" on Channel 4 by dumping this intricate web of fictitious and malicious nonsense into the lap of the young, inexperienced researcher, Ben Hamilton; then, Hamilton's credulous employer, Box Productions, invited Witness X to come to London and repeat his lies in a filmed interview;

and eventually, this jumbled mess was, somehow, approved for transmission by Channel 4.

As if this was not sufficient for one article, the redoubtable Penrose then produced his biggest revelation of all, the actual name of Channel 4's top-secret Source A.

> When the programme was transmitted last October, Channel 4 handed over nineteen names to the police but refused to identify a man dubbed "Source A."
>
> The programme blacked out the Loyalist's face as he claimed there was widespread and systematic collusion between the security forces in Northern Ireland and Loyalist death squads. To name him, Channel 4 later told police and High Court judges would put his life at risk. Last night John Whitten, 50, a prominent Loyalist activist from Portadown, County Armagh, admitted he was Channel 4's source and provided the key Loyalist witnesses for the programme.
>
> Whitten, a builder and convicted terrorist, told the *Sunday Express*: "The programme was completely wrong from start to finish. The Inner Circle was never mentioned to me."
>
> Whitten said he had at least three meetings with Hamilton. O'Hagan had been the intermediary, he [Whitten] had been told.

Barrie Penrose, the grandly titled "Investigations Editor" of the not-so-grand *Sunday Express*, had triumphed again. He had defeated all comers by tracking down the elusive Source A and managing to do it within hours of the end of the High Court proceedings in London. It was a magnificent journalistic coup and one which, as we shall see, was generously recognised and saluted on the same day by his arch-rival on the story, the Ireland Correspondent of *The Sunday Times*, Belfast-based Liam Clarke. Though Penrose told his readers relatively little about his Source A/aka Witness X/aka John Whitten, Clarke was much more forthcoming:

> Last night, the man was identified as a fifty-year-old prominent Loyalist activist from Armagh. His name was published in the *Sunday Express*, which alleged that a convicted IRA man had been involved in setting up the Channel 4 film.

Clarke, having recognised that Penrose had published a wonderful "scoop," then proceeded to take issue with Channel 4's Liz Forgan, who had earlier justified our refusal to identify Source A by saying that he had "helped us to prevent terrorism." Clarke wrote:

> Far from being an opponent of terrorism, he [Source A/aka Whitten] is a former leader of the banned Ulster Volunteer Force and of Ulster Resistance, a shadowy Loyalist paramilitary group. He has been cited in arms smuggling conspiracies, the IRA have

made an attempt on his life and he has been at the centre of Loyalist terror for twenty years. He is a godfather of violence.

So—*if* Penrose and Clarke could be believed—the *Sunday Express* had managed to track down Source A and to expose him as a criminal and a hoaxer. This well-known and utterly disreputable character, according to Penrose, had turned out to have been assisted in his deception of the gullible Channel 4 by an equally disreputable convicted IRA terrorist; together, these two unscrupulous and malicious individuals had slandered a respectable police force by inventing a series of allegations which were— Penrose concluded—totally lacking in any foundation in fact. Penrose's in-depth "investigation" had laid out the facts and his readers could, therefore, be absolutely satisfied that there had never been any truth whatsoever in any of the allegations in *The Committee*. Indeed, it was now established beyond dispute—*if* Penrose could be believed—that there had never been a Committee of murder conspirators, nor had there ever been an Inner Circle, nor an Inner Force. Every allegation contained in the programme—*if* Penrose could be believed—could be safely disregarded, including all Source A's testimony about the murders of Denis Carville and Sam Marshall, the killings at Cappagh, the mobile sweet shop murders and the murder of Belfast solicitor, Pat Finucane.

If Penrose could be believed, it was clear that there would be no future for Box Productions and that the career prospects of the Channel 4 personnel most involved with the programme would be blighted, if not also ended. But could Penrose be believed? Had he really found Source A? John (Jackie) Whitten had turned out to be the RUC's Witness X (according to Penrose) but was he also our Source A? Penrose ought to have been able to answer these questions very easily. To make certain that his journalistic achievement was copper bottomed and that he would win a British Press Award for his "Scoop of the Year," all Penrose had to do was follow normal journalistic practice and put two simple questions to Jackie Whitten. First, were you interviewed on film or video by Box Productions for Channel 4? And second, if you were, did the programme makers bring you over to London secretly to film the interview? If it had occurred to Penrose to ask Whitten either of these two questions, the *Sunday Express*'s Investigations Editor would surely have realised that his published account was total nonsense. Penrose would have had to press the delete button on his word processor and begin his investigation all over again. [4]

Though Penrose had not found Source A, he had encountered two other members of the Committee, Billy "King Rat" Wright and Hugh "innocent, law abiding" Ross. Penrose quoted King Rat's opinion that "the programme was a shame and a disgrace," while Ross was allowed to say that he had been "seriously misrepresented." Penrose did not, of course, inform his readers that Billy Wright was a notorious Loyalist terrorist and that he was widely believed to have murdered Denis Carville; as for Ross, *Sunday Express* readers were kept in the dark about him as well. Unfortunately, *Sunday Express* readers would have had no reason to doubt the truth of what they had been told and most of them, presumably, would have concluded that one should be careful not to believe everything shown on television. These readers would not have known how utterly implausible and ridiculous Penrose's account really was because he had been careful not to report the stringent supervisory and vetting process that this sensitive programme had gone through before reaching the screen. Penrose must have known from his attendance at the High Court that Box Productions was, in Lord Woolf's words, "highly regarded in its field"—investigative documentaries—and that some of the most experienced executives in British television had scrutinised every aspect of the production; yet *Sunday Express* readers were assured that, without any trace or shadow of doubt, the entire programme had been a monumental hoax. And readers of *The Sunday Times* would similarly have had no way of realising that they, too, were being deliberately misinformed. We would later discover from an unhappy freelance journalist, who had worked alongside that newspaper's correspondent in Belfast, Liam Clarke, that "he [Clarke] was never off the phone to [Detective Chief Superintendent] Nesbitt, the head of the Chief Constable's "investigation."[5]

Clarke, having acknowledged Penrose's success in finding Source A, treated his readers to a detailed analysis of what the supposed Source A— incorrectly said to be the exact same person as the *Sunday Express's* Witness X, aka John Whitten—was, wrongly, assumed to have told us. It did not appear to have occurred to Clarke, any more than it had to Penrose, to find out whether we had ever interviewed Whitten on camera or whether we had brought him to London. If Clarke had taken the trouble to ask Whitten either of these questions he, too, would have learned, at once, that neither *The Sunday Times* nor the *Sunday Express* had succeeded—despite their claims—in finding the real Source A.

The rest of Clarke's published comments were sloppy and inaccurate, as the reader will readily perceive. For example, this is Clarke's contribution on the murder of Denis Carville:

> Much of what he [Source A] says is inherently unlikely. He claims that the murder of Denis Carville, an entirely innocent Catholic shot *at random* in revenge for the killing of an Ulster Defence Regiment soldier in similar circumstances, had been carried out with police connivance. Yet what need is there for intelligence involvement in the death of a person chosen *at random*? [my emphasis]

As the reader knows, Source A had explained in great detail how a small group of Committee members had met in the Dolphin Bar in Lurgan at the end of September 1991. It was at that meeting that they planned their retaliation for the IRA's murder of the young UDR soldier, Colin McCullough. The conspirators had all agreed that their intended victim would be a Catholic, preferably a known Republican; he would be of much the same age as Colin McCullough; and he and his girlfriend would have parked their car at the beauty spot on Lough Neagh where the UDR youth had been murdered. And as the reader also knows, Sands reported that both the intelligence and the logistical support for the murder had been provided to the Committee's assassin, Billy Wright, by members of the RUC Inner Force. Denis Carville's murder was not described by Source A as a random killing—contrary to what *The Sunday Times* claimed—but was said to be the result of careful planning and collusion between Abernethy's Committee and the RUC Inner Force.

Although the disinformation published by these two newspapers can easily be refuted, it was repeated uncritically by other media outlets, with the result that casual readers and television viewers came to form the impression that Channel 4 had, for some undefined reason, blundered into broadcasting a dud programme. Our calls for an independent investigation into what we had uncovered were, predictably, ignored; and our efforts to cope with this officially inspired dirty tricks propaganda against us failed to stop the whispering campaign in the media that the programme had been fundamentally flawed. Still, we did our best within the constraints imposed upon us—the libel laws which prevented us from naming the conspirators, the continuing need to protect Source A—to deal with the criticisms we faced. And it was for this reason, the defence of our journalism, that Channel 4's Director of Programmes, Liz Forgan, decided that I should accept, on the Channel's behalf, an invitation from BBC Northern Ireland to appear in a live interview on the local news magazine programme, *Inside Ulster*.

So, on the Monday after the *Sunday Express* and *The Sunday Times* had tried to discredit the programme, I made my way to Channel 4 where I was briefed on what I could safely say, reminded of the pitfalls of libel, and advised that I should be careful not to mention any of the names of those whom we knew to be the murder conspirators. Liz Forgan suggested that the Government's refusal to concede an independent inquiry was one of our strongest points. For it suggested to many that the RUC had something serious to hide.

I had little doubt, as I prepared for the interview with the BBC in Belfast, that the questioning by *Inside Ulster* would be both aggressive and dismissive. For, over the years, I had frequently visited my native province and regularly listened to local news coverage of the political and paramilitary conflict; and I had long held the view that, though there had been the occasional, high-quality local BBC current affairs television programme, the BBC Newsroom in Belfast could be safely regarded as little more than an extension of the RUC Press Office.[6] And I surmised that there would also be a natural, understandable resentment of our claim to have uncovered one of the biggest stories of the troubles—the existence of the Committee—within a few weeks of our young researcher's arrival in the province. Even more galling, perhaps, would have been the fact that the Committee's chairman, Billy Abernethy—the man responsible for most of the horrific murders committed by the Loyalist squads, incidents which local BBC News reported at length virtually every single day—was working in the Ulster Bank, a few hundred yards away from BBC Broadcasting House in central Belfast. My expectations were soon shown to have been fully justified because it was immediately evident that the BBC's interviewer in Belfast had taken his cue from the RUC Press Office. The transcript of the short interview shows that, exactly ten months after the broadcast, we were a very long way from convincing our fellow journalists in BBC Belfast of the truth of what we had said.

Q: Mr. McPhilemy, you are the executive producer of Box Productions which made this programme for Channel 4. It's looking increasingly like you have been sold a pup by disillusioned Loyalists.

A: I think the first thing I should say is that, if we had made a serious mistake, I would readily admit it because no good purpose would be served by saying something is true if it were false.

Q: The RUC's witness says your programme is a lot of nonsense, sir.

A: None of the allegations, none of the central allegations, in our programme rests on anything said by this Mr. X produced by the RUC. I would just make two points about Mr. X. It shows that the RUC themselves recognise the need to protect sources. But much more significantly, the name of the solicitor who witnessed the statement is the same name on the nineteen, on the list of nineteen people that we gave to the RUC in our dossier on the 7th October last year.

Q: But given that the dossier seems to be completely unfounded, according to the RUC, there is no reason why they should not use that solicitor.

A: Well, that brings us to the heart of where we go from here. The Chief Constable destroyed his own inquiry by giving its verdict before setting it up—something reminiscent of the old Soviet Union. What is now needed is a thoroughly independent inquiry. These are extremely grave allegations. The programme was made under the rules of the Independent Television Commission. My company has, as the judge said last week, a high reputation and I am very, very jealous to defend it. The researcher who we sent to Northern Ireland met the Chairman of this Committee and, perhaps, it is important that your viewers hear some of the things that they do not know.

Q: Why should we believe this researcher? I mean, none, many respected journalists have made many years' study of Northern Ireland and say that there seems to be no substance to your allegations. No one outside the parameters of your programme has any knowledge of these allegations.

A: Well, the head of the RUC internal investigation [Nesbitt] confirmed to me that the Chairman of the Committee, as alleged by us, is indeed a member of the RUC Reserve. And he took my researcher in a convoy with paramilitaries. He showed him his police medal; he brandished a revolver at him. He told him "it makes you think who runs this place" and he then introduced him to what we were told was the Commander of the Armagh Brigade of Ulster Resistance.

Q: Mr. McPhilemy, without names, these allegations are a waste of time. Are you going to name names?

A: Well, you say without names they are a waste of time. You should realise that we made this programme under extremely difficult circumstances. Under the Prevention of Terrorism Act, it is a criminal offence to obtain information and not hand it over to the police. We gave the police 99.9 per cent of our information. Now, instead of going to Channel 4 in the four weeks after we handed it over and saying, discreetly, calmly, "Could you help us further? Would you like to indicate to us how you found this piece of information or that?" they didn't do any of this. There was no contact whatsoever.

Q: Mr. McPhilemy, I am sorry . . .

A: . . . Just to finish my point. They [the RUC] went for the aggressive use of the PTA which backfired on them last Friday and they had to go home without the name of Source A.

Q: We shall await further revelations from you or the RUC but, Mr. McPhilemy, in the meantime thank you very much indeed.

The emergence of Witness X and his bogus claim that he had invented the supposedly non-existent RUC Inner Circle had, unquestionably, helped the RUC to undermine the credibility of our programme. And our continuing inability to name Source A—Jim Sands—or to identify publicly any of the other nineteen known Committee members, the individuals listed in the Channel 4 dossier, also meant that we could not conclusively disprove the RUC's emphatic assertion that we had been the victims of a "hoax." The severe limitations upon us—the continuing need to protect

Source A and the libel laws (which prohibited naming those listed in the dossier, without our being able to rely on Source A)—so restricted what I could safely say in the BBC *Inside Ulster* interview that I had to admit, as I left the studio in London's West End and discussed the exchange with Ben Hamilton, that we were losing the public relations battle. For we were, now, simply asking the viewer to take it on trust that Witness X had not been Source A, and to trust us in our claim that this anonymous individual really existed and that he had been telling us the truth. I realised that, unless and until we could persuade Sands to come into the open, or until we could induce another member of the Committee to confess to the murders, or otherwise obtain convincing proof of the conspiracy—all highly unlikely scenarios—we would never succeed in converting the sceptical about what *The Committee* had claimed.

The official counter-attack had got off to a good start and it continued on the following Sunday, August 9th 1992, with another double-page spread in the *Sunday Express* by the ever resourceful Penrose. I knew that we could expect a second instalment from him because, in the week leading up to his article, he had made a nuisance of himself by managing to find and call the ex-directory numbers of four members of the production team, each of whom had moved into "safe" houses in response to the security alert that had arisen during the summer. Penrose, displaying the cavalier attitude to the truth that we had come to expect, had chosen a quite different theme for his second article. "Yard to quiz TV team in RUC 'death plot' inquiry" was the headline over his second "investigation," which enabled him to unveil "two serious deceptions" that the programme makers had perpetrated on the ever gullible Channel 4.

Where his first article, analysing the elaborate "hoax" on the broadcaster, had exposed us as fools unable to distinguish fact from fiction, his second suggested that we were knaves who had defrauded Channel 4 on a large scale. Since £83,000 of the £273,000 programme budget was said to be "unaccounted for," Penrose's "discovery" that Ben Hamilton had supposedly fiddled his expenses was evidence that he was not to be trusted. As the RUC was the only body, apart from Box Productions and Channel 4, in possession of the programme's accounts, it was pretty clear to us where the *Sunday Express* had obtained its tainted and misleading information. And a further clue, as the reader may recall, was that the Chief Constable's chief inquisitor, Detective Chief Superintendent Jimmy Nesbitt, had also told Judge Clarkson that a smaller amount, £80,000, was allegedly unaccounted for in the programme's accounts.

The other "serious deception" uncovered by the assiduous Penrose was that the "claimed assassination plot to kill Box Productions employees" had been a "fiction." Apparently, we had known all along that this claim had been untrue, for we had simply invented the threat scenario ourselves in order to induce Channel 4 to spend £50,000 in providing us with unnecessary, if temporary, second homes. So our "two serious deceptions" had defrauded Channel 4 of around £130,000—criminality on a sufficient scale to suggest that little credibility should be attached to our efforts in the journalistic field and, especially, in our programme on the RUC.

> In May last year Hamilton told Channel Four they [Box Productions] had received death threats from Ulster Loyalists who wanted to stop the programme.
> Police believe these threats were baseless although they have not yet established who may have fabricated them.
> Hamilton claimed "Source A"—whom he said was an Ulster terrorist—had identified the Loyalist gang who would assassinate his Box colleagues.
> He said the gang had spied on the Oxfordshire farmhouse of Box Productions chief Sean McPhilemy, executive producer of the disputed programme.
> Detectives say this is laughable.
> But on August 6 last year Hamilton said the murder gang would return to the British mainland the following weekend.
> McPhilemy alerted Special Branch and Channel 4 Chief Executive Michael Grade. But detectives found no evidence that the men had visited London and dismissed the claim as groundless.

Although Penrose had obviously been extensively briefed by the RUC, which was the only possible source he could have had for these sensitive, security-related aspects of the production, the account he actually gave his readers was inaccurate and misleading. For example, I was on holiday abroad when Ben Hamilton had learned from Source A about the new threat to our security and, as the reader is aware, I had returned home to find Channel 4 executives deeply concerned about our welfare. It was, in fact, Michael Grade who alerted me to the threat, not the other way round.

Penrose had shown that he had little regard for the truth, which is possibly the reason why the RUC felt able to feed him sensitive information about us; they knew Penrose could be relied on to help them with their dirty tricks against us.

> Researcher Hamilton said Source A named assistant bank manager Billy Abernethy from Portadown and BT engineer Graham Long from Tandragee as two of the gang members. But police say they are respectable people with no criminal connections. They can prove to detectives where they were in May and August.

These two names—Billy Abernethy and Graham Long—had been submitted to the RUC by Channel 4 in the confidential dossier handed over in October 1991. Both men had been identified unequivocally by Sands as members of the Committee and, for the avoidance of doubt, as full members of the murder conspiracy. Both of their names had also been given to Scotland Yard's Special Branch by Michael Grade in August 1991, as soon as he had learned about the imminent arrival of the "murder gang" from Belfast. So the fact that Penrose had been given these names and allowed to publish them proved to us, beyond any doubt, that he was now working openly with the RUC to discredit the programme. He had abandoned any pretence of being an independent journalist, a reporter interested in the truth either about what the programme had claimed or about how it had been made.

Having claimed, incorrectly, that I had alerted Special Branch and Michael Grade in August 1991 to what Ben Hamilton had been told, Penrose then adopted an even more reckless position when he told his readers what my state of mind had been at the time. He felt able to assure them that I had never taken the threats to my life at all seriously. I had deceived Channel 4 and, indeed, the High Court itself when, in my sworn affidavit, I had suggested otherwise.

> But McPhilemy says he took the threats against his life very seriously.
>
> In a sworn affidavit he says his family and his colleagues decided to move to "safe" houses and press ahead with the programme.
>
> He says: "Since May 1991 my family and I have therefore been living in rented accommodation . . . at some considerable distance from our family home. I believe there is a continuing danger to our lives."
>
> It is true that McPhilemy, his wife Kathleen and four children rented a £900-a-month flat in Oxford a year ago—twenty minutes from the dilapidated 17th-century property he bought five years ago.
>
> But since then he and his family have regularly been seen at New Barn Farm in Ditchley.
>
> John D. Wood, who have been trying to sell the property for £350,000 said last night: "They certainly have been living there. Absolutely. They were in semi-residence." His colleague Jacqueline Falkeld [sic] added: "The family have been living there. They were there on and off, weekends and things."
>
> Asked why he had been at his farmhouse when he had sworn he and his family would be in mortal danger to be there, McPhilemy said: "It is a lie. I deny I have ever lived at the farmhouse."
>
> But when pressed he admitted: "I have attended my farmhouse. I have not lived there since I left last year."

Asked if this applied to his wife and children, he said: "Yes." But on Friday a *Sunday Express* reporter saw Mrs. McPhilemy and two of her children at the farmhouse.

Channel 4's Liz Forgan had warned the *Sunday Express*'s lawyer, on the eve of publication, that if the newspaper's editor dared to print the defamatory material he had been preparing, the newspaper would be "showered with libel writs." But undeterred, the editor had gone ahead and published what Penrose had written. Perhaps the editor thought that Liz Forgan was bluffing and that Penrose's allegations, which accused me of both fraud and perjury, would go unanswered. The *Sunday Express* was gambling that it was worth taking the risk of a libel action in the effort to persuade its readers that the programme makers were totally lacking in integrity and that their allegations were, therefore, worthless.

Penrose's "two serious deceptions" were nothing of the kind. The alleged theft of programme money led Channel 4 to commission an independent audit of the entire programme budget. All money was satisfactorily accounted for and, significantly, the RUC subsequently dropped this allegation and, by implication, accepted that its original claims had been unfounded.[7] As for the second "serious deception," the truth can be simply stated. Everyone involved in the programme was convinced that Abernethy and his co-conspirators, having sanctioned multiple murder in the province, would take whatever steps they considered necessary to further their aims. That is why I agreed with Channel 4, which proposed to relocate the four key members of the production team, that we should do everything possible to minimise the risks we faced while, nevertheless, pushing ahead with the programme. Penrose's published account, suggesting that my wife and I did not take the threat seriously, was untrue. After I moved, with my family, from our farmhouse in September 1991 we did not spend a single night there until it was judged safe for us to return in November 1992.

Penrose launched his third assault on the programme the following Sunday, August 16th 1992, when he reported on the activities of a notorious "hoaxer," calling himself "Patrick," who had telephoned Channel 4 to say he had sensitive information for sale. Although we were intensely suspicious about this man's phone call, we agreed to send him £250 simply to hear what he had to say. When our suspicions proved well founded, the hoaxer broke off further contact and handed his story to the *Sunday Express*. The episode would not be worth mentioning except that it illustrates Penrose's motivation.

> If they're prepared to deal with a man called Patrick on the phone and send him money immediately, without checking anything, how could anybody trust the allegations made in their documentary?

Penrose's conduct was something of a puzzle. I can well understand why Stormont Castle and the RUC were prepared to go to almost any lengths to discredit *The Committee*. But why did it matter so much to Penrose? Why did he persuade himself so easily that the programme had been a hoax? Why was he so keen to discredit the story and to exonerate the RUC? Even more puzzling was the fact that, as I discovered later, he decided to attack the programme even before he had found an opportunity to view it![8]

Whatever the answer, he was back in action two months later, on October 4th 1992, when both the *Sunday Express* and *The Sunday Times* carried prominent reports that the RUC had made a breakthrough in their investigation into the making of the programme. The RUC rewarded the two newspapers for their enterprising coverage by handing them another "exclusive" story, the news that the police had finally managed to identify one of the anonymous contributors to the programme. This individual was *not* the crucially important Source A but a much less significant figure, the Scotsman to whom Ben Hamilton had given a lift in his car during the summer of 1991. Edward Quinn had surprised Ben, as the reader will recall, by confessing that he had been involved in the murder of a Republican and that members of the RUC had colluded with the Loyalists who had carried out the killing.[9] Subsequent to Ben's initial encounter with Quinn, we decided to film an interview with the Scotsman and we eventually included a small part of his testimony in the final programme. But now, in October 1992, Quinn was singing a different tune—*if* Penrose and Clarke could be believed. First, Penrose:

> A key contributor to the Channel 4 programme that alleged Britain's security forces conspired with Loyalist terrorists in Ulster has admitted lying.
>
> Edward Quinn, a middle-aged Catholic, claims he was paid by Channel 4 film-makers to appear on the programme posing as a Loyalist terrorist who had turned informer . . .
>
> Quinn has told friends he was instructed what to say on the documentary and paid for it . . .
>
> Last week a TV researcher appeared at Horseferry Magistrate's court in London, charged with perjury.

If what Penrose reported about Quinn were to turn out to be true, we would have been in deep trouble. For the report was alleging that the programme makers had invented everything Quinn had said in the film and had paid him to recite these blatant lies in front of the camera. Penrose's account of Quinn's alleged recantation also offered a possible explanation for an incident which had occurred a few days earlier, at the end of September 1992. Ben Hamilton had been arrested at dawn by a team of

Scotland Yard detectives who, acting on behalf of the RUC, had suddenly arrived and detained the young researcher at his London home on a charge of perjury, an offence he had allegedly committed when he had sworn an affidavit for the High Court contempt proceedings. Before taking Ben away for questioning, the detectives searched his home and found a number of documents relating to the programme. We would later receive confirmation that the perjury charge—which received huge publicity, thanks to the efforts of the dirty tricks brigade—had resulted from what Quinn had reportedly claimed about his role in the programme.

Although Penrose's story had been highlighted with bold headlines in the *Sunday Express*—"I LIED ON TV ABOUT ULSTER TERROR KILLINGS CONSPIRACY;" "CATHOLIC PAID TO POSE AS LOYALIST HITMAN"—the version presented in *The Sunday Times* was altogether more sophisticated, a masterpiece of propaganda in that it seemed to undermine completely whatever vestige of credibility might still be attached to our documentary. If what Clarke now reported were to turn out to be true, it surely would deserve the description given a week later in *The Independent* as "one of the worst television programmes ever shown in Britain."[10] Liam Clarke and his colleague, Ian Birrell, wrote:

> Police sources say they believe a witness described as "a former Loyalist informer" when he appeared in a controversial Channel 4 documentary on Northern Ireland was actually a Catholic paid to repeat a script.
>
> Edward Quinn, who appeared anonymously in the programme, is understood to have given detailed statements to the Royal Ulster Constabulary casting doubts about his role in a *Dispatches* documentary that alleged collusion between the RUC and Loyalist terrorists.
>
> In the programme, entitled *The Committee*, the "informer" is seen with his face in dark shadow to prevent identification. He confirms the existence of a group of police officers known as the Inner Circle, who supposedly plotted with Loyalist death squads to murder suspected IRA members.
>
> Quinn, who is now understood to be dismayed by the way he was used in the programme, contacted the police after the documentary, broadcast a year ago, became the subject of fierce debate . . .
>
> In the *Dispatches* programme, the witness was filmed saying he was a "kind of liaisons officer" between the Ulster Volunteer Force (UVF), an outlawed Loyalist terror group, and the so-called Inner Circle. Quinn is understood to have told police that he repeated a prepared text, which he was paid to deliver and which alleged he had brought two UVF members to meetings with the Inner Circle in Belfast at which an envelope full of money and a name was handed over.

This article in *The Sunday Times*, published in an early edition, was illustrated with a photograph, taken from the documentary, of a man's blacked-out head and shoulders, a silhouette filmed with a bright window and a venetian blind in the background. Readers of *The Sunday Times* might have thought that this was a photograph of the "former Loyalist informer," Edward Quinn. But it was not; although the image was taken from our film it was, in fact, a blacked-out photograph of Source A, Jim Sands. And the overall effect of the report and picture, taken together, was to suggest that the programme had been total nonsense or, as the RUC had told one newspaper, "a pack of lies."

The article went on to state that Ben Hamilton had been arrested and charged with perjury over the affidavit he had sworn for the contempt proceedings in the High Court. It reported that:

> SO1, Scotland Yard's serious crime branch, intends to continue its investigations into the programme. It is interviewing the actors, cameramen, and sound technicians who took part to see if they support the claims that the film contained suspect interviews.

Scotland Yard's serious crime branch investigating the programme makers; actors participating in a supposedly factual documentary; a witness paid to repeat a prepared script; the researcher facing a perjury charge. *The Sunday Times* was leaving its readers in no doubt that the Channel 4 documentary on the RUC had been deeply flawed, an embarrassment for the broadcaster and possibly ruinous for the programme makers, who might well find themselves in the dock before the affair had finally ended. And little wonder that a consensus was hardening in the media, especially among those reporting on Northern Ireland, that an embarrassed Channel 4 had made a catastrophic blunder in broadcasting *The Committee*.

On the day after publication of these two reports in the *Sunday Express* and *The Sunday Times*, I was surprised to find that our solicitor, the cheerful and diligent Brian Raymond, was even more optimistic and confident than normal about our prospects for coping with these assaults on our professional reputations. For Brian had made a startling discovery after he had obtained all that had been written about us in the various different editions of *The Sunday Times*. He had noticed that later editions of that newspaper had carried a significantly different account from the one, quoted above, which had appeared in the earlier, Irish edition.

While the first two paragraphs of the story in the later editions remained more or less the same as those printed above, the rest of the report was significantly different. Instead of the categoric assertion that we had invented allegations against the RUC and paid Quinn to recite them as if they were his own, the amended article contained an admission by Quinn that what he had said in our programme had been *true*—that he and other Loyalists *had* colluded with RUC officers in the murder of a Republican.

Inquiries by *The Sunday Times*, however, have established that, though Quinn, 58, was born a Catholic, he claims he is a former British Army soldier who made Loyalist contacts while serving in the army and afterwards became involved in Loyalist activities. He denies he has ever been a Loyalist "supergrass."

In the programme, Quinn, described on screen as a "former UVF informer," is seen with his face in dark shadow to prevent identification. *He confirms the existence of a group of police officers known as the Inner Circle, which supposedly plotted with Loyalist death squads to murder suspected IRA members.*

Quinn says that when he spoke to the makers of *Dispatches* about his Loyalist activities, they asked him if he would repeat what he had told them for the documentary. He agreed, and went to Belfast to make the recording in a hotel room. But he says that before the recording he was taken into a side room and given guidance on what to say. Quinn now maintains that words were put in his mouth.

Nevertheless, he does also maintain that collusion between RUC and Loyalist paramilitaries is well established. He says senior RUC officers had provided him with intelligence on what would be a clear time to make a "hit" against IRA suspects, and when to leave the area.

But he did not know about the existence of a large committee, part of the central thesis of the documentary—he was told about that by the programme makers. He did think that there might be a small, unnamed group of people involved. He says that most of the *Dispatches* programme was *true*, but that exaggerations had been added. [my emphasis]

What caused *The Sunday Times* to change its story so dramatically? In the early editions, we had been accused of fabricating the entire story and bribing Quinn to lie in front of the camera. We were said to have engaged in utterly disreputable conduct which, had it been true, would have left us unfit to be employed in journalism, in any capacity, ever again. But then, astoundingly and within a matter of a few hours, the later editions of the same newspaper were flatly contradicting the original account and quoting the self-confessed murder conspirator Quinn as saying that the Dispatches programme had been "true;" he was admitting that RUC officers had, after all, colluded with him in the murder of an unidentified Republican. This was, surely, one of the most bizarre and most rapid about-turns in the history of what passes for journalism at *The Sunday Times*; and this sudden change between editions left us puzzled over why it had occurred.

We noted that both versions of the article had, apparently, been written by the same two reporters, Liam Clarke and Ian Birrell. We knew, of course, that Clarke had been immensely hostile to us and that he still enjoyed the closest possible relations with the dirty tricks brigade in the Northern Ireland Office and RUC Press Office in Knock Headquarters in Belfast. We knew nothing about Ian Birrell's contribution to the two articles, the only clue to the changes coming from an italicised by-line at the end of the second report, which stated: "Additional reporting by Ian Birrell and Tricia McDaid." Perhaps these two reporters had discovered something new, something which would explain the sudden decision to discard the original, defamatory report in favour of an incoherent replacement which, nevertheless, acknowledged that *The Committee's* allegations about collusion had been true. It would be many months before we discovered the reason for this sudden somersault in the newspaper's reporting, an explanation which would show that Brian Raymond's optimism over the significance of his discovery had been completely justified.

"INFORMER WHO DUPED TV TEAM IS HELD BY POLICE—FORMER IRA MAN MADE UP STORY FOR DOCUMENTARY," were the headlines in the *Sunday Express*, on January 17th 1993, for yet another "scoop" by Investigations Editor, Barrie Penrose. More than fifteen months after the broadcast and nearly six months after the High Court hearing, Penrose was able to report that the RUC had finally succeeded in tracking down "the key informant in the Channel 4 documentary"—Source A—the anonymous individual who had revealed details about the Committee's assassination campaign. The reader will appreciate that the RUC's success must have been somewhat embarrassing for Penrose because he had, some months earlier, published another "scoop" which had enthusiastically asserted that Source A was the RUC's Witness X, the "disgruntled Loyalist" and former UVF terrorist, John (Jackie) Whitten. Had not Penrose explained to his readers, at great length, how Witness X/aka Whitten and the IRA-man-turned-journalist Martin O'Hagan had conspired together to hoodwink the credulous Hamilton, Box Productions and Channel 4? What had Penrose to tell his readers about all this, now that the real Source A had turned out to be somebody else? The answer is, simply, nothing at all; understandably, the *Sunday Express*'s "Investigations Editor" remained totally silent about Witness X and he seems to have decided that John Whitten's name ought also to be quietly forgotten. However, Penrose was able to put some of his previous work to good use:

> Police have arrested the key informant in a Channel 4 documentary which claimed Britain's security forces conspired with Loyalist terrorists to murder Republicans and Catholics.
>
> The man, in his forties, from Portadown, County Armagh, admitted he was paid to appear in the programme to make false claims about the police involvement.

Martin O'Hagan, a convicted IRA terrorist-turned-journalist who coached the unemployed Protestant on what to say has also been arrested. Both were released on police bail.

O'Hagan hoodwinked Channel 4 by introducing the man as a hardened terrorist closely involved in multiple murder. The man has no paramilitary links.

Presumably, few *Sunday Express* readers paid sufficiently close attention to Penrose's journalistic triumphs over the months to realise that O'Hagan was supposed, in an earlier "scoop," to have teamed up with another, quite different Loyalist trickster to hoodwink the young television researcher. And even fewer readers, I imagine, would have recalled that Penrose had been able to rely on the RUC Chief Constable himself when he had, in his earlier version, pinned all the blame on O'Hagan. For, as we have seen, Penrose had quoted approvingly from Sir Hugh Annesley's press release, which had claimed that Witness X and O'Hagan were, together, responsible for perpetrating the "hoax" on Channel 4. Now six months later, with the discovery by both the RUC and Penrose that Witness X and Source A had always been two different people, they must both—Penrose and Annesley—have realised that their earlier "explanations" had been entirely wrong. Yet, undeterred by his previous blunders, Penrose felt able to give his readers a detailed account of how O'Hagan and Source A had, allegedly, "hoaxed" Channel 4.

Dubbed Source A by programme makers Box Productions, he says he now regrets giving the bogus interviews.

Senior Scotland Yard officers are providing Channel 4 chairman Sir Michael Bishop with evidence that Source A's interviews were fabricated . . .

Source A told detectives earlier this month that O'Hagan instructed him to use the name Robert McGrath and paid him £500 for the fake interviews.

O'Hagan invented a terrorist body called the Ulster Central Co-ordinating Committee, which he falsely claimed was made up of members of the RUC and Army, Protestant paramilitaries and senior members of the province's business and professional classes.

He convinced Channel 4 that McGrath belonged to the non-existent UCCC and was prepared to talk about its murderous activities. McGrath was rehearsed in what to say at the journalist's terraced house in Lurgan before going to London.

He says he was unhappy about performing for the camera but says he was frightened by O'Hagan's former terrorist links.

The *Sunday Express* is concealing McGrath's identity to protect him from genuine Loyalist terrorists who have threatened to kill Source A.

The source regrets the bogus interviews; Scotland Yard providing Channel 4 with evidence; interviews were fabricated; O'Hagan paid Source A £500; O'Hagan invented the Committee and falsely claimed that RUC and Army officers were involved; McGrath (Source A) was rehearsed in what to say; he was frightened by O'Hagan's former terrorist links. Like *The Sunday Times*'s first report on the discovery of Edward Quinn, the *Sunday Express*'s latest "scoop" was going all out to undermine whatever lingering credibility the programme might still retain and to convince anyone who had not yet been converted by Penrose's "reporting."

Surprisingly, few specialist commentators or Ireland Correspondents asked themselves why these two newspapers, both well-known for their indifference to the truth, were so strident in their efforts to discredit a programme which had, after all, been shown only once on Channel 4 and had been largely ignored by the rest of the media when first screened. And nobody bothered to draw attention to the obvious inconsistencies, contradictions and implausible allegations contained in both newspapers. Penrose must have won plaudits from his high-level contacts at Stormont Castle and the RUC when he suggested that the problem with *The Committee* lay in the fact that it had been made by one of the small independent companies which had sprung up to supply Channel 4, companies which were so poorly resourced that they had to hire young, inexperienced researchers like Ben Hamilton.

> The problems facing investigative film-makers have escalated since many started tiny independent companies. Most have smaller budgets than when they worked as members of ITV and BBC, leading to cut-backs in fact-checking research.
> Michael Townson, editor of the [ITV] Cook Report, said: "We never use young inexperienced researchers. You have to be right—there is no margin for error. The majority of our budget goes on research."

Sunday Express readers may have inferred from all this that Box Productions was run by amateurs with no money to do proper research and what money they did have must have gone on something else, possibly fiddled away with their expenses. What would they have felt if Penrose had told them the truth, namely that the budget for *The Committee* had been £273,000 (the most expensive factual programme Channel 4 had ever made), that it had been commissioned and supervised by one of the most senior figures in British current affairs television (David Lloyd), that it had been scrutinised by eminent lawyers from its earliest moments and that we could prove that Source A was, as he had claimed, a close political associate of the murder conspirators he had identified—Abernethy, Ross and Monteith? As Penrose reported only those facts which the dirty tricks brigade wished the public to hear, we must assume that his poor, unfortunate readers accepted on trust that it had been a colossal blunder for Channel 4 to commission and screen *The Committee*.

By January 1993 the RUC seemed to have the affair under control. Two national Sunday newspapers had published a series of "revelations" which had demonstrated that the programme had been produced unprofessionally, if not criminally, by a team of journalists combining incompetence and malice in more or less equal proportions. The programme had been effectively discredited in the eyes of the publics which mattered most to the dirty tricks brigade, the two communities in Northern Ireland and the opinion formers within the British media specialising in Irish affairs. And once the RUC had found Sands and published his "hoax" version of events through the medium of their favoured reporters—Penrose and Clarke—it seemed as if the danger which the programme had posed to the RUC's reputation had been completely removed. *The Committee* could now be seen to have been a ghastly mistake; for there had never been a Committee; nor had there been an Inner Circle, nor an Inner Force; nor had there ever been systematic and widespread collusion of the kind alleged; and whoever was responsible for the murder of so many Catholics and Republicans between 1989 and 1993, it had certainly not been a Committee of RUC Inner Force officers, professional and business people from the Protestant community, working hand in glove with an assortment of Loyalist terrorists such as King Rat and The Jackal.

The definitive newspaper rebuttal of the documentary came in *The Sunday Times* on May 9th 1993 with the publication of the results of an "investigation lasting ten months," headlined "FILM ON ULSTER DEATH SQUADS A HOAX, SAYS MISSING WITNESS." Before considering what "Ireland Correspondent" Liam Clarke wrote, we should remember that Source A, Jim Sands, had talked freely to Ben Hamilton for nearly three hours in audio-recorded conversations, that his long interview in London had been recorded on video and that all his testimony about the murder conspiracy has been carefully preserved and is available to contradict misinformation. In view of what the RUC would later claim about his interview in London, the reader should know that the entire film crew—camera operator, sound recordist, film director, producer, researcher and production manager—all later confirmed, independently, that Sands had not been coached, pressurised or otherwise influenced about what he should say.

The reader will recall that Liam Clarke had doffed his cap to Barrie Penrose, just after the High Court case, when the *Sunday Express* reporter had stated, unequivocally, that he had unmasked Channel 4's anonymous Source A, the "disgruntled Loyalist" and "hoaxer," John (Jackie) Whitten. But by May 1993 this journalistic triumph, so generously acknowledged by *The Sunday Times* nine months earlier, was being quietly buried and forgotten as Clarke, once again, agreed with his rival's entirely new discovery about Source A. Both Clarke and Penrose were again united in singing, without any sign of humility or hint of embarrassment, a new tune but a tune with a familiar theme. Their "joint exclusive" explained that the RUC had, finally, got to the root of the affair. They had tracked down the elusive Source A. [We knew that this, at least, was true because we had learned from Martin O'Hagan that Sands had been arrested.] Source A had—Clarke and Penrose revealed—turned out to be a born-again Christian with no paramilitary connections of any kind. Yet despite this alleged spiritual rebirth, he was nevertheless a "hoaxer," a liar who— Clarke and Penrose were claiming—had pretended to be involved in a murder conspiracy and had slandered the RUC for a mixture of reasons, including greed and fear. *The Sunday Times* stated:

> It seemed the television scoop of the year, revealing the existence of an official conspiracy to murder Republicans in Northern Ireland. This weekend, however, the makers stand accused of producing little more than a collage of unsubstantiated rumours and fabrications, condemned by the very man whose identity they went to court to protect.
>
> "Source A," the anonymous central witness in the sensational Channel 4 documentary, *The Committee*, has now described the programme as a hoax and claimed he was tricked into appearing. The man, who appeared on the film with his face masked to say he knew about nineteen such killings, claimed he was promised £5000 to recite a prepared script about events on which he had heard rumours but about which he had no personal knowledge. He said he was assured his interview would not be screened.
>
> This weekend he said: "At the time I didn't know if what I was saying was true or not. But the programme makers told me that they had checked it out so I thought it must be right. They took me to London and I felt trapped."
>
> His testimony undermines, perhaps fatally, suggestions raised by the *Dispatches* programme, screened in October 1991, that there were sinister death squads in Northern Ireland controlled by a committee of police officers, Protestant businessmen and Loyalist terrorists.

Liam Clarke had abandoned, from the outset, any pretence that he was offering his readers a neutral report on how Source A had, following his arrest, recanted his testimony. "It seemed the scoop of the year" was language chosen to convey the message that the programme had, in fact, been no such thing; it would soon become clear that, if *The Sunday Times* could be believed, it had been the "hoax" of the year. Nor was Clarke remotely interested in what we would have said about his "discoveries" because he had made no effort to contact us during his "investigation lasting ten months," until he finally called our office (which was closed) on the Saturday before publication, leaving a message on our telephone answering machine—enabling him to write that "we were unavailable for comment." We were, of course, unavailable only on that Saturday afternoon but would have happily talked to him at any other time during the ten months he said he had devoted to his "investigation."

Clarke was asking his readers to believe in the truth of a series of preposterous propositions. We had bribed Source A by offering him £5000 to deceive the Channel 4 audience into swallowing "a collage of unsubstantiated rumours and fabrications" as solemn facts. We had invited our source to London and filmed an all-day interview at considerable expense, yet we had also promised this man that the interview would not be screened. Source A had been persuaded to recite a prepared script containing detailed allegations about specific attacks, allegations which he did not know to be true or false but which he repeated in front of the cameras, simply because the programme makers had assured him he was speaking the truth.

If the article's first four paragraphs invited ridicule for its implausibility, the rest of Clarke's report suggested that the dirty tricks brigade, the spin-doctors in the Northern Ireland Office and RUC Press Office, were losing their touch. For the story fed to Clarke about what Source A was supposedly claiming to the RUC, after he had been identified and apprehended, was virtually identical to the earlier reports on how Channel 4 had been "hoaxed" by Witness X/aka Whitten, when he had been identified, wrongly, as Source A.

> "He [the "new" Source A] told *The Sunday Times* that he first learned about the Inner Force from newspaper reports, mostly written by Martin O'Hagan of the *Sunday World*, a Dublin-based tabloid. Other details came from other rumours heard while working for a youth organisation in a Loyalist heartland.
>
> Source A said he had been a long-standing contact of O'Hagan, who used him to pick up rumours. "Martin would ring me up and I told him the local gossip. Sometimes he said he had heard that the Inner Force were involved and I didn't know if he was right or not."
>
> It is known that a disenchanted Loyalist was spreading such rumours and had been phoning O'Hagan claiming to be a member of the Inner Force. The rumours were starting to be believed by Republicans.
>
> Source A said that in 1991 O'Hagan asked him to meet a television researcher called Ben Hamilton: "Martin asked me to tell Ben the rumours."

If this appears familiar to the reader, it should not be a surprise. For Clarke was here repeating the same convoluted argument that Penrose had advanced the previous August, when he had explained to his *Sunday Express* readers how the "disgruntled Loyalist"—Witness X/aka Source A—had passed on the idea of an RUC Inner Circle to O'Hagan, who had then given it to Ben Hamilton. Now, in May 1993, in Clarke's latest version, the "new" Source A also turns out to have read the very same article by O'Hagan, in the very same tabloid *Sunday World*, where he also learned for the first time about the existence of an RUC Inner Circle. The only twist missing in Clarke's version of the "hoax" was the claim, pioneered by Penrose, that the concept of an RUC Inner Circle had been invented by the "IRA-man-turned-journalist" O'Hagan as a means of smearing this valiant police force. Perhaps Clarke dropped this additional component from his "hoax" story because he felt that even readers of *The Sunday Times*, those who had forgiven or forgotten the episode of the Hitler Diaries, must have still possessed some credibility threshold, a point beyond which a story such as Clarke's would begin to engender a sense of *déjà vu* or *déjà lu*.[11] However, the rest of the article must have led quite a few readers to approach this threshold because Source A's story, as reported by Clarke, became ever more fantastic and implausible.

> Before the meeting [between Source A and Hamilton] O'Hagan went through various terrorist incidents with Source A and explained his theories. "He told me Channel 4 would look after anyone who helped them. He mentioned £5000 and that seemed a lot of money," Source A said.
>
> He said that when he met Hamilton he repeated the rumours, pointing out that they were only rumours. He claimed Hamilton later told him they had been confirmed by police, Loyalist and Republican sources.
>
> In the summer of 1991 O'Hagan asked Source A to travel to London to be interviewed again. "Filming was never mentioned. Martin told me the film had already been made and the interview was only for the lawyer's records," Source A claimed.
>
> The day before the interview, O'Hagan showed him a checklist of points to repeat. The next morning Source A was taken to a flat, where he was surprised to find cameras were set up; he claimed he was assured the film would never appear on screen.
>
> He was then given a detailed script of what to say during the eight-hour interview. "When filming started, they got me to make each separate point with the camera switched off and when it was okay they filmed it. If there were any mistakes, they filmed it again."
>
> He said that when filming was concluded Sean McPhilemy, the managing director of Box Productions which had been commissioned by Channel 4, told him he would be paid a bonus.

Clarke's account of the "hoax" seemed to waver between pinning responsibility entirely on O'Hagan and suggesting that Box Productions had also participated in the deception of Channel 4. O'Hagan was said to have schooled the pliable Source A in what to say, taking him—on the day before the London interview—through a "checklist" of points to repeat in front of the cameras. We found it particularly difficult to believe this particular claim for two reasons. First, nearly everything revealed by Sands in his long interview, video recorded in London in May 1991, had already been discussed with Ben Hamilton in the tape-recorded conversations the two men had held over dinner in the Silverwood Hotel in Lurgan, two months earlier, in March 1991.[12] So how could O'Hagan have devised a "checklist" of incidents to be covered in the interview, when Sands had already described these incidents—Cappagh, Denis Carville, the mobile sweet shop and so on—at great length in his tape-recorded dinner conversations? The second reason for doubting the truth of Clarke's "checklist" allegation is that Sands simply did not have the intelligence to absorb such a vast amount of information in such a way, to master a brief which would have challenged the intellect of the most accomplished barrister in Britain. As we have seen, Sands had been able to answer our questions at great length, without any obvious difficulty or sign that he was regurgitating rumours which he did not believe. The freelance film crew—none of whom had any reason to participate in such a deception and whose career prospects required them to behave professionally—would later be unanimous in denying that Sands was given a checklist at the interview, rehearsed in his answers or supplied with a script, detailed or otherwise.

Clarke's report, presumably based on a briefing from the RUC, seemed to concede that O'Hagan could not have pulled off the "hoax" on his own, that the deception could not have worked without, at the very least, the participation of Ben Hamilton and myself. Hence, according to Clarke, Ben knew that Sands's testimony was no more than "unsubstantiated rumour and fabrication"—even though the Loyalist had claimed, during his filmed interview, that he was providing a first-hand account of what had gone on at meetings of the Committee. As managing director of Box Productions, I supervised the "hoax" and—according to *The Sunday Times*—was so impressed by the bogus interviews (scripted and rehearsed answers) that I promised Source A a "bonus" on top of the £5,000 already offered. I have already noted that Clarke on his own admission did not see any urgent necessity in obtaining my reaction to these exceptionally grave allegations until he called my office on the day before publication.

We will see, in the next chapter, that the results of Clarke's "investigation" in *The Sunday Times* dovetail neatly with the conclusions reached by the Nesbitt Inquiry's official report on the programme. Fortunately for us—

and unfortunately for Clarke and the RUC—the three audio tape-record-ings of Ben Hamilton's conversations with Jim Sands, held in March 1991, were never handed over to the RUC. These conversations are, possibly, of even greater importance to us than the seven half-hour video recordings, quoted at length earlier in this book. Although much of what Sands told Ben during those dinner conversations in Lurgan, County Armagh was subsequently repeated in his formal London interview, some of his taped remarks are—as we shall see—especially helpful in enabling us to refute the allegations that he was fed a prepared script and bribed to fabricate stories about collusion between RUC officers and the Loyalist squads.

What *The Sunday Times* failed to explain is why Ben Hamilton or I would ever have wished to participate in such a "hoax" on Channel 4. By 1991, Box Productions had become an established independent produc-tion company, with a proven track record in investigative journalism, with warm and close relations with Channel 4 and with good prospects for expansion as the BBC, ITV and other outlets were opened up to inde-pendent production. Why, therefore, would any rational person suddenly decide to risk everything by deceiving his main customer? Why would Ben Hamilton or I decide to abandon our standards of personal and profes-sional conduct, suddenly betray our friends and colleagues by trying to hoodwink experienced television executives and lawyers or, most impor-tantly, why would we wish to dupe a million viewers of Channel 4's flag-ship current affairs programme? Would it not have been insane to attempt such a deception?

These questions had, I thought, only to be stated for the conclusions of Clarke's "ten month investigation" to be seen as absurd nonsense. How, I wondered, could anyone who knows anything about the way television documentaries are made believe a single word of what Clarke had written in *The Sunday Times*? Sadly, I was to discover, as the months and years went by, that many people were indeed taken in by Clarke's "reporting." Even though every one of his allegations against us can, quite easily, be refuted, the cumulative effects of the orchestrated campaigns in both *The Sunday Times* and *Sunday Express* were immensely damaging. Liam Clarke's final article had accused us of utterly disreputable conduct and it is not surprising, I suppose, that after the screening of *The Committee* we would find it increasingly difficult to win programme commissions as we had in the past. For example, after describing how we had foisted the "hoax" on Channel 4, Clarke reminded his readers that Ben Hamilton had faced perjury charges over the programme, though they had later been dropped. He added:

> Senior security forces have confirmed that the Director of Public
> Prosecutions in Northern Ireland is considering a file recom-

mending prosecution of Source A and Martin O'Hagan for their part in the programme. *London detectives are also preparing a file on Hamilton and others associated with the programme.* [my emphasis]

Connoisseurs of the art of propaganda might savour those words, an apparently straightforward statement of fact, simultaneously suggesting that criminal acts had been committed on both sides of the Irish Sea—by the two hoaxers, Source A and O'Hagan, in County Armagh and by Hamilton and, presumably, his boss at Box Productions in London. "Senior security forces have confirmed" can, I suggest, be safely interpreted as, "RUC Detective Chief Superintendent Jimmy Nesbitt has told me." *The Sunday Times* was ending its full-page "investigation" by suggesting that three, four or more people had committed criminal offences by duping Channel 4 into broadcasting a series of entirely false allegations against the RUC. Nesbitt's investigation was making great headway, Clarke implied, in exposing the real RUC scandal—a media conspiracy, not a murder conspiracy—in which a small group of journalist-hoaxers had fooled a national network into broadcasting these baseless allegations. Belatedly, a reluctant Channel 4 was also gradually recognising that it had been deceived, according to Clarke; it was slowly coming to terms with the distressing fact that Nesbitt's Inquiry was coming to the same conclusions as had Penrose and Clarke:

> Channel 4 is now understood to be co-operating fully with the police in both investigations. It is believed to have released documents about the programme which it had previously withheld.

What Clarke "now understood" was, in fact, quite correct because—as he had no doubt learned directly from Nesbitt—Channel 4 had eventually decided to give the RUC a copy of our filmed interview with Sands. For, once we were sure that Source A (Sands) had been identified and arrested, there was no longer any point in withholding material which we had kept back, at an earlier stage, solely to protect Source A's identity. Clarke's report ended by saying that Channel 4 was still standing by the programme makers; but, by this time, the reader would probably have concluded that, whatever Channel 4 might feel obliged to say in public, it would be more wary of Box Productions in future and would be highly unlikely to commission a programme from Box Productions about Northern Ireland ever again.

It is fitting, perhaps, that the last word in this analysis of the dirty tricks brigade's propaganda against the programme goes to the Machiavelli of the British Media, Barrie Penrose. On the same day that *The Sunday Times* published a full-page article on its "investigation," Penrose opted for brevity with a report under the headline "£1M TV TERROR HOAXER EXPOSED"

Denis Carville, shot dead October 1990. "He was just picked out because he was a Roman Catholic."

Sam Marshall, shot dead March 1990. "The Inner Force like to see the operations are done professionally. They bring their RUC training to good use."

Pat Finucane, shot dead February 1989. "The actual job was carried out by Ulster Resistance with help from the Inner Force."

Eileen Duffy.

Katrina Rennie.   Brian Frizzell.

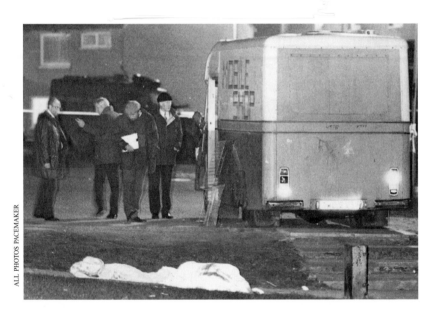

March 1991: A body lies at the rear of the mobile sweetshop in the Drumbeg South area of Craigavon, Co. Armagh; three victims were shot dead. "The Committee felt the Jackal's gang and the Inner Force had co-operated very well."

Dwayne O'Donnell.

Malcolm Nugent.

John Quinn.

Thomas Armstrong.

Four shot dead, Cappagh, March 1991: "An Inner Force car from Portadown took King Rat and his squad to Dungannon. Then an Inner Force car from Dungannon took the squad up to Cappagh."

Tommy Casey, shot dead October 1990. "It was King Rat and the Jackal. They worked together on that."

Eddie Fullerton, shot dead May 1991. His death was "organised for the Committee by a Loyalist councillor in Derry."

Patrick Shanaghan, shot dead August 1991. The RUC kept the doctor and the priest away until he was dead.

Thomas Donaghy, shot dead August 1991. Sinn Féin worker, murdered by the Committee.

Bernard O'Hagan, shot dead September 1991. Source A said that Committee member Alec Benson committed the murder.

Martin O'Prey, shot dead August 1991.

The Cairns family a short time before Rory *(back row, left)* and Gerard *(back row, right)* were shot dead by Loyalists.

Kathleen O'Hagan, shot dead August 1994. "This savage, barbaric and cold-blooded murder will be vigorously investigated." —RUC press statement. But, three years later, the murder is still officially "unsolved."

Six people died in the Loughinsland pub massacre in June 1994. Would it have happened if the Committee had been arrested?

Adrian Rogan.

Barney Green.

Patrick O'Hare.   Malcolm Jenkinson.

Dan McGreanor.   Eamonn Byrne.

Committee members *(left to right)* Lewis Singleton, "Reverend" Hugh Ross, Nelson McCausland.

The Committee's chairman, Billy Abernethy.

Committee member Richard Monteith.

Former RUC Assistant Chief Constable Trevor Forbes, OBE. Source A named him as head of the Inner Force.

Billy Wright, "King Rat," one of the Committee's two key assassins. He was murdered in prison in December 1997.

Channel 4's Source A—Jim Sands.

Committee member Philip Black.

Frazer Agnew. Source A said that Agnew was given RUC files by Inner Force chief Trevor Forbes.

"An accomplished liar"—Committee member Ken Kerr.

William David Trimble, MP. Held secret talks with the Committee's chairman, Billy Abernethy.

Drew Nelson, solicitor. Swore affidavit in support of Committee member Richard Monteith.

R. J. "Bob" Kerr. Not charged "for operational reasons."

Sir John Hermon, ex-RUC Chief Constable. "Rosemary, you read too many fairy stories."

Sir Hugh Annesley, ex-RUC Chief Constable.

RUC Sergeant Joseph Campbell, shot dead February 1977.

RUC Detective Chief Superintendent Jimmy Nesbitt.

and with the first published photograph of the man who had caused the entire controversy, Jim Sands. As it would be difficult to find a better illustration of the propagandist masquerading as a reporter of fact, I have chosen to quote it in full as it appeared in the *Sunday Express*.

> A HOAXER who cost the police and Channel 4 £1 million after a controversial TV programme can be revealed today.
>
> He is Jim Sands, who the documentary claimed was a terrorist with inside knowledge of sectarian murders in Northern Ireland.
>
> But he has no convictions or paramilitary links.
>
> "It's all very unfortunate and I'm very sorry," he said. "I wouldn't hurt a fly."
>
> Sands, a former youth leader who until recently ran a women's football team in Portadown, was paid £500.
>
> After the broadcast, Channel 4 and programme makers Box Productions were fined £75,000 plus costs for refusing to disclose Sands's identity.
>
> It is estimated Channel 4 has spent a six-figure sum on lawyers' fees and in rehousing the TV team who were said to be in fear of their lives from Sands and his killer associates.

It would be churlish to deny that Barrie Penrose and Liam Clarke demonstrated enormous commitment and energy to their common goal of defending the RUC by undermining the credibility of *The Committee*. Their enthusiasm for their work, however, caused them to be reckless in their disregard for the facts about how the programme had come to be made. Naturally, I paid close attention to every aspect of their "reporting" and I consulted my solicitor, Brian Raymond, about the serious allegations they had printed against us. Brian assured me that the *Sunday Express* would find it very difficult to defend any libel action I might bring against it over its coverage of my conduct in response to the security threat that had arisen against my family and me; for, in brief, Penrose had accused me of deceiving Channel 4 and of extracting money from the network by false pretences. Brian also told me that both Martin O'Hagan, Ben Hamilton and I had good grounds for a separate libel action against *The Sunday Times* because the newspaper had accused us of the most reprehensible conduct imaginable for any journalist; in brief, we were said to have bribed witnesses, fabricated evidence and duped both the broadcaster and the viewing public.

Fortunately, Britain's libel laws do not require a plaintiff to begin proceedings in haste. Anyone who wishes to sue for libel can issue a writ at any time during the three years subsequent to publication. This meant that I could afford to wait until August 1995 before deciding whether or not to take any action against the *Sunday Express;* and I had even longer to make up my mind about what to do over the much more serious libels committed by *The Sunday Times*. So, I decided that I would take full advantage of the period for reflection which the law allowed. For I knew that nobody should embark lightly on a libel action, no matter how spurious the allegations or how aggrieved one's feelings.

I was aware that libel has been rightly called "a rich man's sport" and that it was, therefore, not a sport that I could afford to play. Still, I recalled that Channel 4's Liz Forgan had warned the *Sunday Express* in August 1992 that it would be "showered with writs," if it proceeded with its attacks upon us. And I realised that any decision to launch libel proceedings would, ideally, be taken in conjunction with Channel 4 because, quite apart from the fact that we—Martin O'Hagan, Ben Hamilton and I—had been made the scapegoats for the channel's journalism, only the broadcaster could afford to incur the enormous bills that such legal actions would inevitably involve. Any sane individual would, I felt, need to be in fairly desperate circumstances to risk embarking on one—never mind *two*—expensive libel actions against two national newspapers, both of which had vast resources to spend in their defence.[13] So, after discussing all relevant matters with my solicitor Brian Raymond, I decided that the wisest course was to keep a careful note of everything that was being written or said about us and to wait until the appropriate moment arrived for me to reach a decision.

Notes

1 *The Sunday Times* had attacked the reputation of Carmen Proetta, the Gibraltar resident who had witnessed the SAS in action and whose testimony flatly contradicted the official, spin-doctored (i.e. false) version of events. Andrew Neil was forced to withdraw unreservedly his allegations against her and admit that the "facts" he had printed about her were untrue. The newspaper did not abandon its crusade against her until, literally, the moment of truth had arrived—a date for Andrew Neil and his reporters to defend their lies and their reputations in the libel court.

2 By 1991, the Official IRA had long since withered away and, if it could be said to remain in existence at all, had become little more than a criminal gang.

3 Martin was paid the normal rate for television research. I later discovered that Penrose had omitted to tell his *Sunday Express* readers that he, too, had hired Martin for his journalist expertise—a fact which, if his readers had known it, would have undermined Penrose's attempt to portray Martin as an IRA terrorist sympathiser.

4 I later discovered that Penrose, when he had made his big "discovery" about Source A's identity, was being heavily briefed by the RUC. So he knew that we had brought Source A to London to be interviewed on film.

5   See Chapter 11.

6   The local BBC *Spotlight* programme has produced a few worthwhile documentary investigations into collusion between the Loyalists and the security forces.

7   See Chapter 6, p. 102.

8   See Appendix 3, p. 393. Penrose: *"I'd not seen it at the time."*

9   See Chapter 5, pp. 73–74.

10   See Chapter 9, p. 165.

11   See Chapter 9, p. 168.

12   Fortunately, copies of these tapes are still available and, in the unlikely event of a genuinely independent inquiry into this affair, they would be available for the investigators.

13   Desperate circumstances would, for example, include the ruination of one's reputation or the destruction of any business predicated on that reputation—such as an independent television production company.

Chapter 10

THE ARISTOCRATS OF ULSTER

It is not difficult to imagine how shocked and frightened Jim Sands must have been when, in November 1992, RUC detectives arrived at his Portadown home to detain him for questioning about the role he had played in *The Committee*. For, despite desperate efforts by fellow Committee members, Loyalist paramilitaries and the RUC to identify our elusive source, Sands had managed—for well over a year—to outwit all concerned and to give the impression that he was as anxious as everyone else on the Committee to unmask the traitor in their midst. He had been greatly amused, we were told, by the RUC's continuing failure to find "the traitor" or "the animal"—as his co-conspirators had dubbed Source A— and he had remained supremely confident that the controversy would eventually fade away, without anyone ever suspecting that he had been the anonymous interviewee on Channel 4.

For our part, we had been careful not to contact Sands directly, fearing that we might inadvertently expose him to the risk of identification. We relied mainly on Martin O'Hagan, who remained in touch with him and who sent us the occasional, necessarily discreet message about what was going on. We were assured that all was well and that Source A felt that there was no danger of his being exposed as a result of any blunders he might make; he was said to remain totally confident of his ability to keep his colleagues off the scent for as long as necessary. This satisfactory situation might well have lasted for years but for a failure on our part which, unfortunately, was to lead the RUC to his door and to enable the force to turn the tables on us all.

The police breakthrough in the hunt for Source A occurred in September 1992 when Scotland Yard detectives, acting on behalf of the RUC, had launched their "dawn swoop" on Ben Hamilton's London home. The real purpose behind this sudden raid had been the one we suspected, a "fishing expedition" designed to catch a shoal of documents which would, the police hoped, lead the RUC directly to their man. Although Ben had removed nearly all sensitive materials from his home, he had held on to a number of programme documents which, regrettably, fell into the hands of his police visitors. Among them were copies of letters from Martin O'Hagan to Brian Raymond, one of which contained an indirect reference to Sands but which was, nevertheless, sufficiently specific to enable the RUC to identify him. So, soon after the Metropolitan Police's raid on Ben's home, RUC detectives arrived at Sands's modest council house in Portadown. The year long hunt for Source A was finally over.

As relations between the RUC and Channel 4/Box Productions were, by the end of 1992, a good deal colder than glacial, we received no official information, at that time, about the fate that had befallen Sands. Our only reliable source about RUC activity relating to the programme was, as always, Martin O'Hagan; and this source would soon dry up because Martin also received an unwelcome visit from the RUC, when detectives came to his door in early January 1993. Like Sands, Martin was detained for questioning and, while in custody, he had to cope as best he could, without any help from anyone at Channel 4 or Box Productions. We would, of course, later learn in detail about what had happened to Martin but it would be some years before we were to discover precisely how the RUC had dealt with Sands, the man who had accused the force on national television of helping Loyalist death squads to eliminate the individuals chosen for them by the Committee to which he belonged.

Although we had been, for a long time, genuinely concerned about what might happen to Sands if his identity became known, we were not especially worried, in December 1992, about his personal security following his arrest by the RUC; for we thought it inconceivable—rightly, as it turned out—that any harm would befall him, in view of the immense publicity that had been generated by the High Court proceedings. Our anxieties were, therefore, directed elsewhere and were focused on the methods the RUC would, in all likelihood, use to persuade Sands that the information he had given us in 1991 should be withdrawn, recanted and denounced as completely unreliable, if not utterly fictitious. So we began to speculate on the strategy the Chief Constable's "investigators," Nesbitt and Webster, would devise to allow them to come up with a definitive refutation of the programme's allegations. They needed a new strategy because, with the arrest of Jim Sands, they would have discovered—if they hadn't known already—that the "disgruntled Loyalist," Witness X and Source A had always been two different people; so they would have realised that the Chief Constable had been mistaken when, in August 1992, he had publicly declared the programme a "hoax" on the basis of what Witness X had claimed.

We suspected that those RUC officers who had arrested Sands would, together with Nesbitt and Webster, devise a new version of the "hoax," allowing them to confirm the substance, if not the detail, of the Chief Constable's stance. For we remained absolutely confident that, for the RUC, the only acceptable outcome of the Nesbitt Inquiry would be one which, however it came about, would endorse the Chief Constable's verdict and dismiss all allegations about collusion as entirely false.[1] Yet devising a coherent version of the "hoax," we realised, would not be easy because the RUC had been denied access to some of the most sensitive programme materials. Nesbitt had, for example, been given only an edited version of the transcript of Sands's London interview; as a result, he could not be certain about the significance of the small amount of missing material. Nor had he been given any of the three tape-recorded dinner conversations between Ben and Sands. So, those questioning Sands with a view to producing a knock-out blow against *The Committee* had to consider the risk that sensitive materials in our possession, once produced, might enable us to blow apart whatever version of the "hoax" thesis they might settle on as their official verdict on the programme.

Our first clue about how the Nesbitt Inquiry was dealing with Sands came from a by-now-familiar quarter. On January 11th 1993 Tony Coldwell, the cameraman who had filmed the London interview with Sands, received an unexpected phone call from someone who claimed to have worked with him in the past—none other than the "Investigations Editor" of the *Sunday Express,* "dirty tricks" specialist Barrie Penrose. Although I had never worked with or even met Tony Coldwell before we hired him on this project, he was to support us magnificently throughout the entire affair; and on the day in question, Tony had the good sense to switch on his tape-recorder before allowing Penrose to ask any questions. I do not know whether Tony had seen Penrose's attacks upon us but he was, thankfully, properly suspicious about the purpose behind the call. Only two days earlier, Penrose had broken the story that the RUC had found Sands; now, he wanted Tony to confirm that it was he who had filmed the interview in London.

> BP: But, I mean, you did do some filming in London, did you?
> TC: I did some filming on the Box Productions film but I wouldn't really like to say what I did on it exactly or where I was.
> BP: Obviously I'm a professional in the same way that you are, but it was just in terms of Source A and there's been a lot of publicity in the press and the High Court and a lot of leading articles . . . I just wondered, as a matter of record, whether you might be the person that shot that interview.
> TC: I think the person to ask, really, about everything to do with that programme is Sean McPhilemy. He's the producer and Ben, he's the researcher . . . and rather than me say anything to do with the programme, I'd rather you speak to Box Productions.

BP: Why is there such a mystery surrounding this, such secrecy about it?

TC: Well, absolutely. But then again we've all read the papers,
we've all seen the news, and I've got to keep my future clients
happy and you ought to refer your questions to them about any
filming.

Fortunately, Tony Coldwell was more than a match for Penrose, who
carried on with his questions until he realised that he was not going to
learn anything at all that he could use against us. Penrose took the hint,
said that he might call Box Productions directly, as suggested, and then
rang off. The most significant aspect of his conduct, by far, was the fact
that he had called Tony Coldwell at all. For we had deliberately not put
Tony's name on the programme credits, screened at the end of the film, so
that it would be impossible for Penrose and his ilk to contact the cameraman and quiz him about our source. So where, then, had Penrose obtained
Tony Coldwell's name? Well, the only people in possession of the name—
apart from those involved at Channel 4, Box Productions and the legal
firms providing advice—were the RUC officers working on the Nesbitt
Inquiry. We had handed over Tony Coldwell's name, together with a vast
amount of other information, as we were legally obliged to do in obedience
to the Production Orders issued by Judge Clarkson. So there can be no
doubt at all that Tony Coldwell's name had been given to Penrose either
by RUC Detective Chief Superintendent Jimmy Nesbitt himself or a member of his Inquiry team.

A few days later, on January 16th 1993, Penrose called again and, after
the preliminary introductions (giving Tony Coldwell sufficient time to
switch on his tape-recorder), the *Sunday Express's* Investigations Editor got
down to work.

BP: I thought that out of courtesy I'd give you a call to tell you
that, since I last spoke to you, events have rather overtaken what
I was asking you so that there's no need to mention you at all. If
I can just tell you, in confidence, what's happened. Martin
O'Hagan has been arrested in Belfast.

TC: Who's Martin O'Hagan?

BP: He's the Belfast-based journalist who was the researcher at
Box Productions; and also the Protestant who was flown over
from Portadown to be filmed in the flat where I think you were—
he's also been arrested in Portadown and he's made a full confession. And by the way, this is not a criticism of Box as such, it's a
criticism of Martin O'Hagan. The Source A has said that he was
rehearsed in what to say by O'Hagan at his home in Lurgan, in the
hut in the garden that he uses as an office. Obviously, no-one else
knew that. And he was brought over, he said he was somewhat

frightened of O'Hagan because O'Hagan, you may not know this, has a conviction as an IRA man going back some years . . . He served time for that. And Source A said he was frightened and that if he didn't go ahead and go on camera, he thought that he was just going to be tape-recorded in Northern Ireland, which he was, and then they asked him to appear and they gave him, O'Hagan provided a combat pullover and bomber jacket and that his hair was ruffled for the interview and he did what he was told. It's just that when I spoke to you, I mean, I wasn't aware of all this, so events have rather overtaken what I was talking to you about before. So there have been two arrests and they've now been released on police bail. So there we are, but you probably haven't given it a thought. But I shan't be mentioning that you did some filming along with some other people, I mean it's now rather been marginalised, so er . . .

TC: Well, I have to admit that my ideas have been on something else at the moment. My wife's just had a baby so I've been . . .

BP: No, No, you know sometimes people think, oh golly, I wonder if anything is coming this Sunday, so I just wanted you to know that there was no real reason to press you on that.

Thanks to Tony Coldwell's shrewd handling of the conversation, the devious Penrose again learnt absolutely nothing from his call but he had given us a good indication of the RUC's emerging strategy for containing the scandal. His account confirmed and expanded upon the two Sunday newspaper reports about Sands's recantation, which had just been published. We now knew that the RUC would be trying to prove that Channel 4 had been hoaxed, that it had screened a series of totally false allegations about the force. Apparently and conveniently, the entire blame for the fiasco could be rested on the shoulders of one journalist, the mischievous, if not malicious, Martin O'Hagan; since his past membership of the Official IRA and his conviction, in the early 1980s, for a terrorist offence were undeniable facts, they could and would be easily exploited to undermine the programme's credibility. So, it seemed that the RUC's case would be that the wicked O'Hagan had intimidated the born-again Christian and "women's football team" manager, Jim Sands, into participating in a hoax. O'Hagan had secured the Loyalist's participation, partly by blackmail, partly by bribery, before taking the stooge to a hut in his garden and schooling him into reciting a series of utterly false accusations about the RUC. According to Penrose, the RUC's new version of the "hoax" would claim that Sands, manipulated by puppet-master O'Hagan, had performed brilliantly in front of the cameras in London; the unlikely duo, Sands and O'Hagan, had duped the film makers—"not a criticism of Box as such"— and thereby Channel 4.

It was obvious that Penrose enjoyed close relations with Nesbitt and that he had been given a preview of the emerging "official" RUC verdict on how the programme had come to be made and shown on Channel 4. It always seemed to me to be an implausible scenario but, in passing judgement on Nesbitt's investigative skills, we should bear in mind that the task he had been assigned always required him to stand the truth on its head. From the outset, it had always been unacceptable for him to conclude that Jim Sands had been telling the truth; for such a conclusion would, most probably, have entailed the abolition of the force to which he belonged. Still, we were hearing a version of events which, I felt, failed adequately to appreciate the significance of the material which we had sent abroad before the broadcast and which Nesbitt had never seen. Nesbitt was, if the Penrose synopsis accurately reflected the emerging official RUC verdict, opting for a version of the "hoax" which would be easily refuted once we brought the materials back from France. For, as we shall see, they leave no room for doubt that Sands had been speaking on the basis of personal experience about what he had witnessed at meetings of the Committee; our tape-recordings show that he could not have been schooled by O'Hagan in the days leading up to his London interview because he had given exactly the same information in his various conversations with Ben Hamilton almost a month earlier.

When Penrose called Tony Coldwell for a third time, on January 20th 1993, we were able to see even more clearly how the RUC was going to justify the verdict it would eventually deliver on *The Committee*. For Penrose was now indicating that O'Hagan and Sands had been assisted in their deception by members of the Box Productions' team who, in an attempt to disguise their true role in the production, had committed perjury in the High Court. But he began this third conversation by explaining that a "mutual acquaintance" had suggested to him that he telephone the cameraman because his professional reputation as a programme maker was at stake.

> BP: . . . eventually there will be a very important court case following these arrests in Northern Ireland. But in a nutshell, what the article describes was Source A being flown over, he flew over on his own to London back in Spring, April '91 and with Martin O'Hagan who was also in London. Do you remember O'Hagan, the Belfast journalist?[2]
>
> TC: I can't say anything about it, Barrie.
>
> BP: Right, you feel under some kind of restriction?
>
> TC: Well, as I said before, until Box Productions contact me about anything to do with that programme, I'm not willing to say anything about it.
>
> BP: No, the problem is, as you know, in the High Court case

that you may have not followed that closely is people from Box, of course, said that they didn't meet Source A and, of course, they were present in the flat which Source A describes. I mean he now tells of it in great detail that a) he wasn't connected in any way with the paramilitaries and in fact was rehearsed in what to say by O'Hagan. I think I mentioned that to you before. We carried that story on Sunday. Obviously, it has received a lot of media attention and for that reason we are anxious to get as much background information for further pieces. But, I mean, you feel restricted from saying anything about it?

TC: Well, the whole project was obviously cloaked in security problems and secrecy and when I worked on the project, I realised that the last thing I should be doing about it is talking to anyone about it at all.

BP: But I mean if the police approached you, for example, as indeed they must do in due course . . .

TC: If the police approach me then, obviously, I'll have to speak to them in the presence of a solicitor.

BP: . . . There's no criticism of you at all and I'm sure you know that but the fact is that in the affidavit in the High Court, Box Productions people swore, quite openly, it was read out in court, that they didn't meet Source A. The fact is that Source A has identified those people as being in that room when he was given a sort of pullover, had his hair ruffled by the girl who was there from Box and was given a leather bomber jacket to wear and was then filmed and interviewed on camera, as we saw on the screen, talking about things of which he now has made absolutely plain and can demonstrate he has no connection with whatsoever; a) he had no connection with paramilitaries, b) he had no convictions or special knowledge, and he can demonstrate from notes given to him by O'Hagan—who is, I've met him a couple of times in Belfast over the years, he's a sort of fairly small Belfast journalist working for the *Sunday World*—who had actually found, well not found, he knew this chap from Portadown in his forties and said to him would you like to earn a few shillings and offered him £5000 and eventually gave him £500 in cash and then rehearsed him in a shed at the bottom of his garden in Lurgan.

Now Source A, so-called, was given the name Robert McGrath, you may have known him as that. That was the name given to him by O'Hagan to use in front of people like yourself, but you can see that we are getting into very serious waters here. So this is not just a mistake by journalists, heavens above we can all make mistakes, but this is something, as we said on Sunday, was sheer fabrication. And, by the way, I don't say it was the reason, but you may well have wondered why your name didn't appear on the screen afterwards in the programme.

So, Penrose was clearly convinced that I—the only person at Box Productions, other than Ben, to have sworn an affidavit for the High Court—had committed perjury when I had, supposedly, stated that I had never met Source A. He was also suggesting that Ben and I had been fully aware that Sands's story was "sheer fabrication" and we must, therefore, have known that O'Hagan was, ultimately, the man behind the hoax. Penrose was evidently quite happy to accept and promote this line of argument, which he could only have obtained from the Nesbitt Inquiry. His remarks to Tony Coldwell in this, his last conversation with the cameraman, suggested that this would be the official police verdict on how *The Committee* had come to be made.

> BP: But you did the key interview and you may well have been used as a sucker, if one wants to be cynical, because your name and that of your sound recordist didn't go on the credits and that was so the authorities—the police—could not trace you and therefore you would not be questioned about Source A. What happened now, Tony, and I know you didn't see the programme go out, so I'll go through it very quickly now, nineteen names were given over to the police by the Box people. On the screen, they said the police have now been given the names of nineteen people that belong to this so-called Inner Circle, this Committee who have been responsible with the army and police in murdering Catholics and Republicans, but there was one name they wouldn't hand over and that was Source A. Well, we all know why now, because Source A was simply a fabrication by O'Hagan who hoodwinked Channel 4.
>
> I mean we've always said in articles we've written and so has *The Sunday Times* that Channel 4 have acted honourably in protecting a journalistic source, that is something that we all do, and something that must be done. But, when of course a source is fabricated, we're in a different ball game altogether, so that is why obviously your knowledge of filming Source A in the circumstances I've described, and I won't bother to describe them again, I think you get the drift of what it was, I mean Source A has now confessed to the police. So you can see that you will be a crucial person for them to be, obviously they are aware of your name. They have Channel 4 records. They had them by warrant last year. Are you with me?
>
> TC: Well, as I've said Barrie, I'm listening exactly to what you're saying but . . .
>
> BP: I'm trying to help. I'm putting my cards on the table in a good American manner, if you know what I mean, I mean we're all journalists at the end of the day and the fact is that you were the cameraman who recorded Source A, and obviously you must find it particularly disturbing that the person you were filming was

not just flakey but was an out and out fake. And I wondered, and the reason for me calling you is, whether you had any suspicion that there was something a bit strange about him.

TC: I can't say to you, Barrie, that I did that interview or not.

BP: Sorry, you said to me at the beginning, sorry, when we first spoke, you mentioned that you did the London interview. Well, that was the only London interview.

TC: No, I never said anything of the kind to you. And I'll tell you why I never said anything of the kind, Barrie, because I've got a recording of every conversation we've had so far.

BP: Well, fine, I'm pleased with that because . . . well, it may be my memory. But I thought you mentioned you were in London to do the er, Box . . . well, it doesn't matter, I mean if you didn't mention it, then it's my mistake. I'm sorry to get it wrong but you know, as I say, the important thing is this what Source A says happened and he was rehearsed by O'Hagan in what to say.

Penrose obviously preferred to back off, recognising that Tony Coldwell was not going to give him any significant information about the production. The grudging apology was, presumably, judged to be the best way of disengaging and certainly preferable to revealing that he had got Tony's name directly from the RUC. The conversation had not been entirely fruitless, from his point of view, because Penrose had established Tony's readiness to give the RUC a statement in the presence of his solicitor, if such was requested. We can assume that Penrose immediately reported this back to the Nesbitt Inquiry because, less than twenty-four hours later, Tony received a telephone call from RUC Detective Sergeant Elliott asking for a formal interview.

Channel 4 had acted honourably, while Box Productions had conspired with O'Hagan to fabricate the evidence against the RUC. Since that was the latest version of Penrose's thesis, no doubt reflecting further extensive briefings by the RUC, it seemed sensible to him to write to the person most directly affected by these "discoveries," the individual who had taken the decision to broadcast the documentary, Channel 4's Director of Programmes, Liz Forgan. His letter strongly suggests that he did not appreciate that, if his thesis could be shown to be true, he would be about to bring Liz Forgan's career as a high-flying television executive to an abrupt end.

3rd February, 1993

Dear Liz,

I won't disguise the fact that I find this a difficult letter to write . . . Of course, there has never been any doubt in my mind that you and Michael (Grade) have behaved throughout in the best possible tradition of protecting journalistic sources . . . If you think a private meeting might be helpful please call me. As I say, there are matters you should know about now rather than later.

The ingratiating, oleaginous style, his presumption in addressing Liz Forgan on a matey first-name basis, the use of his personal notepaper, the offer of private word-in-your-ear advice all invited a snub on the grand scale. Instead, Liz Forgan's reply was a model of restraint but she must have derived some amusement from giving Penrose advice, tongue-in-cheek, about where he should send any damaging information he might acquire about the programme.

5th February, 1993

Dear Barrie Penrose,
. . . I am however getting a little tired of running after rumours which one by one turn out to be untrue and whose origins I can only assume to be malicious.
Since we are all apparently the object of such rumours and since the matter is a very sensitive one in which people's safety is at risk, I would ask you to put any evidence that you may have of deceit or invention by any source or anyone working on the production of *The Committee* in writing to me. My strong feeling would be that a copy of anything sent to me should also be sent to the RUC whose officers, we are assured, continue actively to investigate the events surrounding the programme if not the allegations made in it.

Penrose, ever the optimist, wrote back to Liz Forgan in an effort to persuade her, in the Channel's own interest, to agree to meet him. He explained that he had carried out a lengthy tape-recorded interview with Sands and he said that he would be happy to play it for her benefit. Then, he repeated the libellous remarks about me, which he had made a few days earlier during his telephone call to Tony Coldwell.

When Mr. S was brought to London to be interviewed he says he was rehearsed into what to say by two researchers working for Channel 4. He also says he met—and was entertained in between filming—by Sean McPhilemy and other Box employees. You will recall that Mr. McPhilemy says in his affidavit he never met Source A. What is clear is that Mr. S had no knowledge or involvement with what appeared on the screen. He admits it was a fabricated interview. Part of what he says is confirmed by one of your cameramen who was not credited on the film. He also says Mr. McPhilemy was present with Source A.

As the reader now knows, Penrose's claim about what the cameraman, Tony Coldwell, was alleged to have said to him was totally untrue. Nor was there any truth in Penrose's further allegation that I had sworn an affidavit containing an untrue statement about whether I had met Source A. My affidavit, written largely by my solicitor Brian Raymond, had deliberately left it unclear about whether I had been present at the interview or not; Brian had not wished to make it any easier for the RUC to find Source A, by indicating precisely who had met him and knew his name. Penrose's second letter provoked a sharp response from Channel 4's solicitors, who warned him of the dangers he was running with his campaign of denigration and abuse.

> I am concerned that you may be contemplating writing an article based on information which is not accurate. By way of example, you are under a serious misapprehension concerning the contents of Sean McPhilemy's Affidavit, which clearly you cannot have seen.
>
> Let me make my clients' position quite clear. They have received no information which has caused them to doubt the truth of the programme or of the information it contained. If any such information exists, it should be made available to the proper authorities forthwith . . .
>
> . . . Should further damaging and unwarranted allegations be made against my clients you may be sure that they will not hesitate to take such action as might be necessary to protect their reputation. I have no doubt that the production company, who are separately represented, would take the same view.

This correspondence between Penrose and Channel 4 took place around three months after Sands had been arrested and detained by the RUC. Apart from the limited information we had obtained from Martin O'Hagan, after his release on bail, our only source of information about what Sands was saying had been Penrose. He was obviously in close touch with the Nesbitt Inquiry and had, so he claimed, been allowed to carry out a lengthy tape-recorded interview with Sands. On the basis of his letters to Channel 4, his telephone calls to Tony Coldwell and his published articles in the *Sunday Express*, we inferred that the Nesbitt Inquiry had, after a period of some uncertainty, finally settled on the view that Box Productions had also been a party to the deception of Channel 4. Though Martin O'Hagan was unquestionably the principal villain—*if* Penrose's account could be believed—he had been helped in the deception by both Ben and me. Our role, it seemed, had been to fabricate the evidence, to invent a plausible story, to school the puppet and, generally, to coax and cajole our willing accomplice into doing what he was told.

I found it hard to believe that Nesbitt and his team, knowing how closely Channel 4 had supervised the production, would plump for such a scenario. However, given that the programme had to be discredited at all costs, I admit it was not easy to see what plausible alternative theory was available to them. In any case, all speculation was rendered pointless when, eventually, an RUC delegation, led by Nesbitt and including the Scotland Yard officer who had charged Ben with perjury, Detective Chief Inspector John Butler, arrived at Channel 4 on Wednesday, February 10th 1993. Sixteen months after the broadcast and six months after Sands had been arrested, the RUC was finally in a position to deliver its verdict. The delegation was received, if not welcomed, by the Channel's Director of Programmes John Willis—who had replaced Liz Forgan after her move to a top job at the BBC—lawyer Jan Tomalin and the editorial executive who had commissioned the programme, David Lloyd. These three executives listened intently for almost two and a half hours as the RUC's most senior detective guided them through the "conclusions" he and his team had reached. Jan Tomalin's memorandum on what was said forms the basis of the account which follows.[3]

Nesbitt began his report by saying that he had approached his task with an "open mind" and had not started out by investigating the programme makers. He had, he said, begun his task by focusing on what the programme had alleged. The various venues where the Committee was said to have met, all listed in the Channel 4 dossier, had been checked out and the police were satisfied that the management of all the venues were people of impeccable reputation. No meetings of the Committee had ever taken place at any of these venues.

The nineteen names in the dossier fell into two distinct categories, according to Nesbitt. Two of those named, Robin Jackson and Billy Wright, were "well-known terrorists" who had, he said, been arrested on numerous occasions. So, these two individuals occupied one category—known Loyalist terrorists. The remainder of those named in the dossier, he said, were "respectable members of the community;" all of them had been interviewed shortly after the broadcast and all had categorically denied having any knowledge of the alleged organisations—the Committee, the Inner Force or the Inner Circle. "A few of these people were members of the Ulster Independence Committee, which is an entirely different thing." Some of those listed in the dossier, the owners of large businesses, had been interviewed in their board rooms and had been "appalled and horrified" by the allegations. "They were not the sort of people to fraternise with terrorists. All these people come from impeccable backgrounds and are leading community members." He then mentioned two leading businessmen named in the dossier—a Mr. **** of ******, David Prentice of Prentice Garages—and described them as "the aristocracy of the country."[4]

Nesbitt then discussed the names of the RUC men listed in the dossier. The following passage is a verbatim account of Jan Tomalin's note of what he said:

Turning to the police officers named in the dossier, all these, apart from one, do not exist. The records have been checked extensively and these people have never been members of the RUC. As far as Trevor Forbes is concerned, he is an ex-Assistant Chief Constable from Special Branch who was in the RUC for thirty-eight years. He has an OBE and was decorated for his work against terrorists.

Nesbitt proceeded to report on what various people interviewed for the programme, including Hugh Ross and Billy Wright, had said about the way their contributions had been distorted. Again, what follows is taken from Jan Tomalin's note.

The Reverend Hugh Ross will say that he was totally misled and misrepresented. He was asked to give an interview in order to give the programme balance. He gave a four-hour interview and only a few minutes were used, out of context, and juxtaposed with a UVF marching band.

Billy Wright was interviewed on the programme. He has been arrested many times. He has no liking for the RUC and said when he was interviewed on the programme, he was asked by Ben Hamilton about the Inner Circle and the Inner Force. He said it was absolute rubbish and he confirmed that the RUC took firm action against Loyalist paramilitaries. When his interview was transmitted, however, that bit was edited out.

Nesbitt next mentioned four other interviewees, only one of them listed in the dossier as a Committee member, who had told the police that they were unhappy with the way they had been treated. Jan Tomalin's memorandum adds:

Mr. Nesbitt told us that he had proved beyond reasonable doubt that there was no Ulster Central Co-ordinating Committee and all the people named as members were totally exonerated.

Later in the meeting, Nesbitt is recorded as being even more blunt in his assessment of the programme. Again, the Channel 4 memorandum states:

Nesbitt said that to be frank, the murders and how they were committed, as described in the programme and the dossier, was "a complete and utter lot of balls." The way in which the murders were alleged to have been carried out could be proved to be "bunkum."

So Channel 4 had now been told, officially, by the RUC that all the central allegations in *The Committee* had been totally false. Most of the nineteen people identified by Jim Sands as his fellow conspirators were—

if they existed at all—innocent, respectable people from impeccable backgrounds. Some of them were of such high social standing, he said, that they could be described, without exaggeration, as the aristocracy of Ulster. The three Channel 4 executives, who did not challenge anything that was said to them, needed no explanation of the significance of what they had heard. For, *if* what they had just been told was true, a million viewers had been totally misled and the programme had grossly slandered the RUC.

So how had such a flawed programme managed to make its way on to the television screen? Nesbitt proceeded to describe a series of events which will be more than familiar to the reader because his account was very similar to what Penrose had led us to expect and to what had already been printed by the *Sunday Express* and *The Sunday Times*, as reviewed in the last chapter. The following account, the official RUC version of how Channel 4 had been "hoaxed," is taken from Jan Tomalin's written account of what Nesbitt had told the channel's executives.

> Mr. Nesbitt went on to say that in 1985, a journalist named Martin O'Hagan published a story in a local newspaper called the *Sunday World*. This is not a very reputable paper. The story was about the Inner Circle and the Inner Force and a man, who was not named, had told the journalist [O'Hagan] about it. The police then traced a man called Witness X who admitted that he was the man who had fabricated this information anonymously over the phone to Martin O'Hagan. He told the police that he had laughed when he had read it in the newspaper. He said it was all made up. Witness X is anti-RUC because they banned Orange marches in Portadown. His motives were malice and a wish to make a fool out of O'Hagan. At no stage did he say that he was a representative of the RUC or a spokesman for them. He simply wound O'Hagan up and, for example, would ring O'Hagan at home and tell him his phone was bugged, thus persuading Martin O'Hagan to telephone him from a callbox.

The reader may have noticed that this account differs somewhat from what Penrose laid before his readers immediately after the High Court case in August 1992. Where Penrose had blamed O'Hagan for inventing the notion of an RUC Inner Circle, Nesbitt accused Witness X who, having fabricated the existence of an Inner Circle and an Inner Force, was said to have implanted these malicious ideas in O'Hagan's mind. It is worth noting that Nesbitt chose to skate over the issue of the Chief Constable's embarrassing press release, the one where he had wrongly asserted that he had found our key source, the "disgruntled Loyalist," Witness X. And we should also note that the RUC now admitted, implicitly, that Witness X had always been the wrong man; for Nesbitt confirmed that Source A was, indeed, Jim Sands. Again, this is the note of what he said.

Then, said Nesbitt, the RUC discovered the identity of Source A—the one that all the controversy had been about. Eventually they got his name. Source A was interviewed and he said that he was approached by Martin O'Hagan and told there were people in Northern Ireland making a programme who had lots of money. "A" said that O'Hagan told him that if they played their cards right, there would be lots of money in it for them. "A" said he was given a dossier of information and various press cuttings and was schooled by Martin O'Hagan in what he had to say. "A" had a connection with O'Hagan in the past because he had given him some gossip stories.

"A" was then introduced to Ben Hamilton. He met Ben Hamilton on a number of occasions and these interviews were taped. He told Ben Hamilton stories about the Inner Force and the Inner Circle, along the lines indicated by Martin O'Hagan.

"A" was then asked to come to London to be recorded. He assumed that this was another [audio] tape-recording. He was brought to a flat in London and he discovered that he was expected to go on camera. The night before the interview was filmed, at a hotel, he had a conversation with Ben Hamilton and discovered the interview was on camera and he refused to do it. He thought that this had gone too far. However, Ben Hamilton offered him £5000 to go on with the programme.

The next day "A" was taken to a flat in London. He was told that his identity would be concealed by his face being darkened and his clothes changed. He had his hair fluffed and his jewellery was removed. The interview was then recorded.

The night before the interview—said "A"—O'Hagan and Ben Hamilton went over the script with him and he was rehearsed through the whole thing and told what to say and what not to say. This script was available to him at the interview.

After the interview, "A" had a conversation with Ben Hamilton and Sean McPhilemy. Sean McPhilemy had said that he had done so well he would be given an additional bonus as well as the £5000 originally promised.

He [Source A] alleged that he was used to get money from Channel 4 and coached by Ben Hamilton and Sean McPhilemy. That was his side and he will be charged . . . Nesbitt said that what Channel 4 had to say could have a bearing on what people would be charged with.

This, then, was how the "hoax" programme had reached the television screen, according to the man who had led the Chief Constable's investigation over a period of sixteen months. Channel 4 had been hoodwinked, not just by O'Hagan and Sands but by two key members of the production team, Ben Hamilton and myself. Knowing that Sands was an impostor and that there had never been a Committee, an Inner Circle or an Inner Force, we had nevertheless happily, indeed enthusiastically, gone along with the deception. Ben Hamilton was said to have promised Sands £5000 and, so thrilled had I been by the impostor's performance, that I had even offered to pay him a bonus. So, the RUC's considered verdict, delivered in person by the Chief Constable's hand-picked investigator and documented by the Channel 4 lawyer, was that Box Productions had duped Channel 4 into broadcasting a series of malicious falsehoods against the RUC. *The Committee* had been a hoax.

Nesbitt's account had one great merit. It was clear. He had reached and delivered a stark and simple verdict. He made it clear that O'Hagan and Sands were in deep trouble and that Sands, at least, would be charged with a criminal offence.[5] And he added that if Channel 4, having spent £273,000 on what would undoubtedly be the biggest hoax in the history of British television, wished the police to take action against the other rogues implicated in the deception—Ben and me—they would be happy to bring charges against us as well. Martin O'Hagan and Jim Sands had already found themselves on the wrong side of the law, he said; O'Hagan had "convictions for possession of firearms and IRA connections," while Sands has "a serious criminal record." He was suggesting that, in view of the grim facts he had solemnly laid before the three executives, it would not be all that long before Ben and I had acquired criminal records as well.

Surprisingly, Nesbitt had little new to say about Jim Sands. Our source was said to have "had a connection with O'Hagan in the past because he had given him [O'Hagan] some gossip stories;" "Sands was prominent in the Orange Order" and had once had a "meeting with [ex-RUC Special Branch boss] Trevor Forbes to discuss the re-routing of marches." The three executives were told nothing else about Sands's background, about his political activities or, most importantly, about any possible connections he might have had to the "aristocracy," such men as Abernethy, Ross, Monteith and Prentice. Instead, Nesbitt focused on the fact that Channel 4's own trouble-shooter, the former Army Intelligence man—known as "Neil"—had discovered Sands to be telling lies; this should have convinced Channel 4 that the entire programme was based on a hoaxer's testimony. Jan Tomalin summarised this part of Nesbitt's account as follows:

> "A" will say, emphatically, that "Neil" gave him quite a grilling and caught him out telling numerous lies. It became very obvious to "Neil," Nick Read and Ben Hamilton that "A" was talking non-sense and telling lies. After the grilling, "A" went into the car park with Ben Hamilton who was no longer friendly towards him and appeared no longer to want to know him . . . He felt it fair to add

that they [the RUC] had a document which was a note from Nick Read to David Lloyd giving a watered down version of the interview in which Neil expresses doubts about the credibility of "A" and Ben Hamilton says, "We still have a story because, perhaps, he was just treated aggressively."

Nesbitt did not even try to begin to explain why Ben and Nick, the film's researcher and director respectively, would be writing notes to David Lloyd about possible weaknesses in Source A's testimony, if the entire production company was, at the same time, busily engaged with Sands in hoaxing Lloyd and Channel 4. Nor did Nesbitt tell the Channel 4 executives that he had arrived at his "hoax" verdict in spite of the fact that Tony Coldwell, who had filmed the interview with Sands in London, had emphatically denied to the RUC every single one of its allegations against the programme makers.[6] Nor did Nesbitt choose to dwell on the troublesome question of motive. Why, he might have asked himself, would the programme makers have conspired together to deceive the television network in the manner described? Would such conduct not have been totally irrational?

Ben Hamilton was, in 1991, a young television researcher with a natural ambition to advance in his career; would he not have realised that such an escapade was bound to end in exposure, disgrace and the ruin of his career? Nick Read was a freelance television director, who had never worked for Box Productions before; having joined the project after Sands had been interviewed in London, what possible reason would he have had for taking such a risk? Why would the freelance director who supervised the London interview with Sands have agreed to help us dupe the network which commissioned most of her work? And finally, what was my motive supposed to have been? Hatred for the RUC? Sympathy for the IRA? Boredom with the everyday demands of routine television production? A professional death-wish? Perhaps wisely, Nesbitt chose not to raise any of these questions and he moved on swiftly to other matters, seeking to hammer the nails, one by one, into the coffin containing the corpse of our reputation as a producer of factual television documentaries.

He reported his conclusion on the role played by Edward Quinn, the Scotsman who had confessed to involvement in the murder of a Republican, carried out in collusion with members of the RUC. The reader will recall that *The Sunday Times* appeared to experience great difficulty in establishing the facts about Quinn and had dramatically altered its reporting between two different editions of the newspaper. This is Jan Tomalin's account of what Mr. Nesbitt said.

Edward Quinn is a Scottish Roman Catholic living in Londonderry, away from much of the other information in Ulster.

He told the police an "amazing story." He said that he was walking along the road and a man stopped and gave him a lift, saying
that he was making a television programme. The man took Quinn
to a pub and bought him a drink. He was asked whether he would
like to appear in the programme which was about Northern
Ireland, giving both sides of the story, and was told that he would
be given something to say. Nesbitt observed that Quinn was
unemployed and not particularly intelligent. He was given £20 as
a gesture of good faith and picked up the following morning. He
was taken to a hotel in Belfast and given half a bottle of whisky to
drink. He was then taken to another room where he was told a
story about the UVF and a committee meeting with police officers
involved, he was told to say that the police officers would ensure
the road was clear for the killing. It was clearly implied that the
man was Ben Hamilton.

The Channel 4 executives listened in silence as Nesbitt told them how
the RUC had investigated Quinn's story and had interviewed him jointly
with officers from the Serious Organised Crime department from New
Scotland Yard in London. The Metropolitan Police had been called in
because Ben had sworn an allegedly false affidavit about the Quinn interview. "They [the RUC and the Metropolitan Police] were satisfied that he
[Quinn] was telling the truth."

It was embarrassing enough for Channel 4 to learn that Jim Sands had
been bribed, rehearsed before his filmed interview and provided with a
script to ensure that his "evidence" was precisely what the producers/hoax-
ers had wanted to hear. Now, it appeared that Ben had shown breathtak-
ing cynicism and duplicity in his readiness to lubricate his stooges with
generous portions of whisky, shortly after their breakfast and immediately before their interviews in front of the cameras. It was surely obvious to
all, Nesbitt was suggesting, that since Ben's conduct had been so disreputable and contemptible, no respectable television executive could, any
longer, credibly assert the truth of any of the information contained in *The
Committee*.

A few days after the meeting, Nesbitt wrote on behalf of the RUC to
Channel 4's solicitors to set the record straight. His letter, quoted here in
full, gave the RUC's formal and unambiguous verdict on the programme.
It invited the Channel to co-operate so that criminal charges could be
brought against all those responsible for the deception which had caused
so much damage to the reputations of both the RUC and Channel 4.

The information given to Mr. Willis, Mr. Lloyd and Jan Tomalin
at our meeting in the Channel offices is accurate.

I can confirm that exhaustive enquiries carried out have established beyond doubt that the allegations made in the programme

and the information provided by your clients to the RUC are without foundation.

The investigations have revealed that no meetings took place at any of the alleged venues, that the so-called Ulster Central Co-ordinating Committee does not exist and that none of the names provided by Channel 4 are involved in any terrorist conspiracy or collusion. In fact the police officers who were named as being involved in the conspiracy do not exist.

The investigation into the terrorist aspect of the enquiry has therefore been concluded. However, other matters of a criminal nature have been uncovered.

The person who appeared on the programme and who was referred to as "Source A" has been interviewed. He has admitted that the entire contents of his interviews with the programme producers were a fabrication and that he was acting in concert with a journalist for the purpose of obtaining money from Box Productions/Channel 4.[8]

In view of these circumstances the Channel may now wish to provide information to support a complaint, for example, that money was obtained from them by deception or that they were the victims of a conspiracy to defraud.

In addition, documents in our possession indicate the existence of original tapes which would corroborate or refute the allegations made by "Source A" of the involvement of other persons in the deception.

Such information would be included in a file to be submitted to the Director of Public Prosecutions to determine the nature of the criminal charges to be considered.

"Source A" and the journalist were arrested under PACE [Police and Criminal Evidence Act] legislation and tape-recorded interviews were carried out.

I confirm that there is no suggestion of possible terrorist related charges against any of the persons under investigation.

Most of the contents of Nesbitt's letter are in harmony with what he said earlier at the meeting at Channel 4—no Committee; no Inner Circle; no Inner Force; the listed police officers do not exist; the others listed, including the "aristocracy," are not involved in terrorism or collusion. However, his letter differed significantly in one respect; he was no longer placing Ben and me in the category of villains who could be said, unequivocally, to have joined in the deception of Channel 4. One interpretation of the letter, which I held to for a time, suggested that he was hedging his bets over his earlier claim, giving himself the option of treating Box Productions as he had Channel 4, as a victim of the Sands/O'Hagan "hoax;" he was keeping an open mind until he heard the tape-recordings referred to in his letter, tapes which he believed—rightly—would settle this aspect of the affair once and for all. Still, whatever the precise nature of the alleged hoax, his basic finding remained the same. The programme's allegations had been false. In his own words, they had been "a complete and utter lot of balls."

So, by February 1993, the RUC had turned the tables on Channel 4. Its media allies, *The Sunday Times* and the *Sunday Express,* had created a public consensus that we had blundered badly and got the story wrong. Privately, the head of the RUC's inquiry had confirmed the newspaper reports that the programme had been a hoax. His distressing verdict meant that the Channel's executives now had to consider seriously the horrible possibility that he was right. Perhaps, despite all the precautions taken, something awful had occurred. The RUC's message had now raised the stakes so high that the Channel could no longer take anything on trust. Its reputation as a credible broadcaster had been challenged and the accusation was so serious that it could not be sidelined or left unanswered.

A few days after the meeting with the RUC, Channel 4's Chief Executive, Michael Grade, summoned Ben and me to his office. He told us that, while we continued to enjoy his full confidence, the Board of Directors had decided to commission an independent investigation into the programme. A national network, he said, could not ignore the formal verdict of a police inquiry that one of its programmes, especially one as controversial as *The Committee,* had been fabricated by the production company. This was why he was calling in one of Britain's leading barristers, the Hon. Michael Beloff QC, to conduct the investigation. Mr. Beloff would be given a free hand to look into any and every aspect of the programme, so that he could give the Board an informed and independent opinion on the affair. He would be given all the time and resources he needed to enable him to determine whether there was any truth in the RUC's allegations against us. So, the Nesbitt Inquiry was to be followed by the Beloff Inquiry, which was asked to decide whether the RUC or Box Productions was telling the truth about *The Committee.* Had Channel 4 been hoaxed or not?

Long before the RUC's visit to Channel 4, I had become ever more confident that Sands would be persuaded to recant. Once I had learned that he had been arrested, I thought that an officially induced recantation would be by far the best way to exploit the weakness in our position. As the programme's allegations had come from an anonymous source, I felt that the public—with the assistance of the dirty tricks brigade—could be manipulated into believing that our source had not been genuine. No-one would have sufficient information to question such a judgement; and if the public was told often enough and forcefully enough that he had recanted, this would chime perfectly with the scepticism about the programme that was already widespread in the media. Then, it would be quite plausible for the RUC to "reveal" that the source, once found, had turned out to be a hoaxer; and who better to blame for the hoax than the hoaxer's unlikely but acknowledged Republican friend, the convicted IRA-man-turned-journalist Martin O'Hagan? Finally, for this ingenious ploy to succeed and the RUC's reputation to be restored, it would be necessary to keep the troublesome Sands out of reach until the controversy had subsided. Channel 4's "scoop," once discredited, would soon be forgotten.

Our suspicions that such a strategy was being followed were strengthened some time after Sands's arrest, when I received what might be called a Christmas present from the Committee—a libel writ which had been issued against me in Belfast. The plaintiff was none other than Richard Monteith, who was arguing that I had libelled him in my interview on the BBC's *Inside Ulster* programme in August 1992. Although I had not mentioned him by name, I was alleged to have given sufficient information to identify him as a member of the Committee and, thus, as a murder conspirator. Although Monteith's argument was specious, the fact that he had issued a libel writ indicated that he felt he was on strong ground. It suggested that the only person whose testimony I could expect to rely on in such an action—Sands—had indeed turned against us; it appeared that once he had found himself in the clutches of the RUC, he had begun to sing an altogether different tune. As the weeks went by in early 1993, we prepared ourselves for the worst. Our suspicions soon proved well founded and we later learned that, following his arrest, Sands had dismissed the solicitor chosen for him by his wife and had appointed someone with a keen personal interest in his welfare—the Committee's very own solicitor, Richard Monteith.

Nesbitt's visit to Channel 4 and his subsequent letter had confirmed that the expected recantation had occurred. We have seen that he referred, in his letter, to the original tape-recordings of Ben's initial conversations with Sands and that he recognised that they would "corroborate or refute the allegations made by 'Source A' of the involvement of other persons in the deception." While this judgement was absolutely correct, I knew that these tape-recordings would prove of far greater importance than that; for, unlike Nesbitt, I had listened to every word that Sands had spoken to Ben and, therefore, knew just how explosive his revelations had been. The tape-recordings in our possession contained first-hand testimony about meetings of the Committee Sands had attended, murders he had helped to plan, the identities of the assassins and, crucially, the role named RUC officers had played in the entire collusive process. I knew that this material was more than sufficient to blow apart *any* recantation, no matter how determined or creative the RUC might be in devising a structured argument for the luckless Sands to proffer as his own.

We have seen that Nesbitt found it difficult to make up his mind whether or not to include Ben and me in the hoax that Sands and O'Hagan were said to have engineered. This ambivalence was deeply puzzling and I was not able to explain it for a very long time. For Nesbitt and his team proved exceedingly reluctant to give us transcripts or copies of their tape-recorded interviews with Sands, the ones which he had referred to in his letter. Without a detailed account of what Sands had claimed, following his arrest, it was obviously impossible for us to challenge the reported recantation. Our frustration persisted even though Channel 4, following Nesbitt's visit, authorised its lawyers to give the RUC copies of the filmed interview with Sands, recorded in April 1991; as we were all satisfied that Sands had been identified, arrested and been turned against us, we saw no reason to go on refusing to hand them over.

Yet the RUC clearly felt no obligation to reciprocate and a further two years were to pass before I would finally manage to obtain the transcripts I had sought, a verbatim account of the RUC "interrogation" during which Sands had "recanted" his testimony about the Committee. As soon as I was able to read these transcripts, I was to understand the RUC's reluctance to let us have them because they show that Mr. Nesbitt's top priority had been the creation of a plausible recantation by Sands. He had devised a story which was intended to free Sands from his predicament and, far more importantly, to conceal the fact that RUC Inner Force officers had routinely attended meetings of the Committee where, as Sands had told us in London, they "would come with a file [from RUC Headquarters] and would advise that maybe the time is right now to eliminate known terrorists."

By a quirk of fate, these RUC transcripts made their way to me from a court room in California, where they were produced by the British Government in its effort to have an IRA escapee extradited back to Northern Ireland to complete his prison sentence. The Californian proceedings had centred on the defendant's claim that his life would be threatened if he were to be returned to prison, with his lawyers arguing that *The Committee* had shown evidence of the type of collusion their client feared. Although this case was heard in November 1993, I did not obtain the transcripts produced for the trial until the summer of 1995.[9]

These documents, which run to 213 pages, purport to be a verbatim record of the original interviews conducted with Sands by the RUC following his arrest. As we shall soon see, they are not at all what they purport to be and are, in fact, a transcript of a well-rehearsed Sands being spoon-fed with questions, designed to elicit answers to a script written in advance by his interrogators. If that sounds familiar, it is because the RUC appears to have done precisely what it accused us of having done in

London in May 1991—to have schooled Sands with a fictitious script and then had him parrot it for the benefit of the tape-recorder. Having spent many hours studying these documents and pondering their significance, I began to feel sorry for Nesbitt and his team because they had to struggle heroically to mould a coherent story from their dim-witted, inarticulate and, no doubt, terrified interviewee. Sands had to be led by the nose through the recantation, nudged constantly to give the "right" answers, provided with lengthy, structured questions which frequently provoked unconvincing, monosyllabic grunts in reply. I believe it is scarcely an exaggeration to say that, in the 213 pages of transcript, Sands does not manage to articulate a single coherent, grammatical sentence, however short. And when the tongue-tied Sands did eventually find some words to express his thoughts, he managed—fortunately for us—to expose the entire exercise for what it was, a crude and amateurish attempt by his "interrogators" to produce a credible "recantation" of the unique and devastating revelations he had made in his interview for *The Committee.*

Sands's orchestrated performance is so unimpressive that it is possible to expose the fraudulent nature of the "interrogation," even without drawing on the so-far-unpublished information contained in our audio tape-recordings. That information, as we will see in the next chapter, proves beyond doubt that Sands was what he claimed to be, a full member of Abernethy's Committee and, as such, one of the few people in the province in a position to provide authentic, first-hand testimony on the systematic and widespread collusion between RUC officers and the Loyalist death squads, in 1989, 1990 and 1991. Sands's tape-recorded "recantation," together with other documentary evidence I have uncovered during the past three years, will demonstrate that what Nesbitt reported at the Channel 4 meeting and later repeated in his letter was totally untrue. It will be obvious that the "aristocracy of the country" had indeed sat on Abernethy's Committee and that the biggest mistake they made was to overestimate the intelligence and underestimate the fanaticism of their fellow conspirator, James Alfred Sands.

Ironically, by another quirk of fate, we obtained further recantation documents from another unlikely source, someone who believed that he might eventually succeed in detaching the reputable broadcaster from the disreputable production company responsible for the "hoax." In an effort to secure an interview with Channel 4 in May 1993, Barrie Penrose sent the Channel's solicitors an affidavit which Sands had sworn just two weeks after the RUC had visited the Channel in February; he also provided the transcript of an "interview," which Sands had given to Liam Clarke's wife, Kathryn Johnston. When these two documents—the Sands affidavit and the Johnston interview—are studied alongside the transcript of the RUC's interviews with Sands, a plausible explanation emerges for Nesbitt's ambivalence about whether to blame Ben and me, as well as Sands and O'Hagan, for the supposed hoax we had all engineered together.

For it is strikingly evident that Sands was also unable to answer, whether through fear, confusion or just plain stupidity, a most basic question: What precisely did he think he was doing throughout the seven months he had been dealing with Ben, Box Productions and Channel 4? Had he been merely passing on unsubstantiated rumours, which he had picked up on the streets of Portadown and which he had admitted to Ben were nothing more than that? Or, had he been deliberately misleading Ben and everyone else into believing that he was a member of the secret body running the Loyalist murder campaign? Surely Sands would have realised that it was not possible for him simultaneously to answer "Yes" to both of these questions, wouldn't he? Evidently not!

This is what Sands said in paragraph four of his affidavit.

> Early in the New Year, 1991, I met a reporter from Box Productions, London, Ben Hamilton, with Martin O'Hagan in the Silverwood Hotel, Lurgan. After speaking to him briefly, he questioned me about Loyalist killings. I made it clear to him that I had no personal knowledge of any of the events he questioned me about and that anything I told him about was based solely on local rumours.

His affidavit, at least, is coherent and his meaning is clear. And what did he say in the associated interview?

> . . . Just before he [Ben] came, Martin O'Hagan told me that when I met him, as well as the Independence thing, just sort of tell him the sort of rumours that were going about, about Loyalist killings, and all that, just general talk on the ground . . .
> . . . So I met him, it was in the Silverwood Hotel in Lurgan . . . Martin O'Hagan said, "Tell Ben about the rumours," you know, the rumours about Loyalist killings, the rumours of who had been involved . . .

Again, though Sands is less than eloquent, there is no doubt about his meaning; he is saying that he was dealing solely in rumours, not hard facts.

And what reason did he give his interviewer for the visit to London? Was he invited just to talk about rumours? Evidently so!

> Shortly after that, Martin O'Hagan came to me and asked me about going over to London . . . At this time I actually thought they wanted me to talk about the rumours that were going about, they wanted me to talk about them on more professional [audio] tapes.

In short, Sands's affidavit and his associated interview make it clear that, in all his dealings with us, he was claiming that he had no personal knowledge about terrorism or collusion, that all his comments were nothing more than local rumours and that he had told us this was the case.

So what was his story when he was "interrogated" by the RUC on December 11th and 12th 1992? What did he say about his meeting with Ben at the Silverwood Hotel in Lurgan in 1991? Had he admitted that he knew nothing but unsubstantiated local rumours? This is a verbatim extract from the tape-recorded police interview:

Q: '91, right. Ah, go on ahead, then what happened next then?

A: Well I arrived down and there was no one, no one about.

Q: Uh huh.

A: And I sat in the foyer and then Martin O'Hagan and Ben Hamilton, I didn't know his name then. He came, they came in and Martin O'Hagan went into the lounge bar and Martin O'Hagan introduced me to Ben Hamilton, introduced him as coming from Channel 4.

Q: Right.

A: And we sat talking in the lounge bar. Martin O'Hagan wanted me to sort of tell him about the rumours. But he wanted, he told me on the telephone before meeting him, he sort of wanted the rumours to sound as if they were actual facts.

Q: Right, I want to get this absolutely straight now. Are you saying to me that prior to you meeting Ben Hamilton, that Martin O'Hagan either met you or phoned you up, right?

A: Yes.

Q: And what exactly did he ask you to do. Let's clear this up, what exactly did he ask you to do?

A: He asked me if I would relate rumours that I had given him in the past.

Q: Right.

A: If I would relate them to the researcher who came over.

Q: Right.

A: But not to, sort of say that they were rumours. Now he said because he had checked on a lot of the things and that he had found them to be correct.

Q: So you had to. Yes, go ahead.

A: So I had sort of to put them across as actual facts.

Q: And I mean, actual facts in what way. Actual facts of things that were, which were supposed to be in your knowledge.

A: Yes.

Q: So go on ahead then, right. Give me an example, just one example of the sort of thing that, that you told Ben Hamilton at this stage.

A: There was just, relating things that happened in the Portadown area.

Q: For example?

A: Well it was relating to Loyalist gangs, killer gangs going out and not getting caught, yet everyone knew who they were.

Q: Right.

A: Ordinary people in the street knew who they were as well as the police and yet nobody was ever arrested.

Q: Uh huh.

A: People weren't even pulled in to be questioned, there was rumours of members of Loyalists going about freely, walking about, driving about Portadown yet they were allowed to go.

Q: Uh huh.

A: There was ah.

Q: When you say they were allowed to go now.

A: Allowed to go about their business, allowed to go about.

Q: By who?

A: By the Security Forces, cause they were never stopped, you know, they were always. But these were always rumours but.

Q: But when you were talking to Hamilton, you were, you portrayed as being facts that you were aware of.

A: Yes.

Q: Is that what you're trying to tell us?

A: Yes. That they were actual facts.

Q: So. It must've been a case that if you are portraying these facts to be true right?

A: Yes.

Q: You understand what we're getting at here?

A: Yes, yes.

Q: That you must've been able to convince Ben Hamilton that you were involved in these things in some shape or form?

A: Yes.

So Sands, with what appears to be a little help from his police interviewer, is putting forward an interpretation of his conduct which flatly contradicts the other two versions. This extract shows that, contrary to what Sands stated in his affidavit and in the associated interview, he told the RUC that he had been seeking to mislead Ben, to dupe him into believing that he was hearing the inside story about collusion, reliable factual information from a well-placed source who was in a position to speak from personal experience about what he had witnessed first-hand.

Two further short extracts from the transcripts reveal what Sands had to say to the RUC about his visit to London. What impression was he seeking to convey once he had arrived? Was he offering unsubstantiated rumour or pretending to possess sensitive factual information about the Loyalist murder campaign?

Q: And you're still convincing them that you know what's going on, that you are in actual fact, how did you describe yourself to him exactly?

A: As a member of the UIC [Ulster Independence Committee].

Q: Yes, and what as?

A: Well he, he got the impression that I was a sort of UIC representative to the Ulster Central Co-ordinating Committee.

Q: But, ah yes, you've explained that to me, but again.

A: And he, and I didn't, I didn't do anything, I didn't do anything till [to] take away that impression.

Q: Uh huh, did you by any way at all give Ben Hamilton the impression that you were a terrorist, you know what I mean.

A: No, no.

Q: A Loyalist terrorist?

A: No.

Q: Did you, at any stage, ever give Ben Hamilton the impression that you were present when people were killed?

A: No, no.

Q: Did you at any time give Ben Hamilton the impression that you were present at meetings where possible targets were discussed?

A: Yes.

Q: You did?

A: Yes.

Q: Can you remember what targets you told him was discussed at meetings that you were present at?

A: I honestly couldn't, couldn't say.

Q: Can you remember any at all?

A: No, no.

Q: Eh?

A: No, for like 100% honest to you I couldn't, no so.

Q: That's what I'm wanting, 100% honesty.

A: I couldn't, honestly no I couldn't say.

Q: Right, OK then that's fair enough then . . . I want to just jump back here, a wee thing, to clear absolutely up, you said towards the end of the conversation that you had mentioned to Ben Hamilton about the reliability of this information.

A: Yes.

Q: Now it doesn't mean to say that you were portraying to him that your information was unreliable, were you still portraying yourself as a guy who knew what was going on?

A: Yes, yes, yes.

Q: And what you were asking him was, if I've got this right, or if we have it wrong, tell me, what you were asking Ben Hamilton was, do you have any other stories apart from me?

A: Yeh.

Q: That backs up all these stories?

A: Yes.
Q: Is this true?
A: Yes.
Q: Is that the way it was?
A: Yes, yes that's the way it was.
Q: The way it was supposed to be?
A: Yes, yes.
Q: OK right go on.
A: See ah, in my own mind I still wasn't happy about it.
Q: Yes. But you weren't portraying that to Ben Hamilton?
A: I wasn't.

These extracts make it clear that Sands, in this version of events, had been presenting himself as a member of the Committee, someone who claimed to have been present when targets were selected, that he was an insider who knew what was going on. The glaring inconsistencies between his answers in these two extracts and the claims in his affidavit and press interview would, in normal circumstances, be sufficient to convince any experienced interrogator that Sands was not being entirely candid or truthful about his role. But the circumstances in which Sands found himself, following his arrest in November 1992, were anything but normal. For if he had insisted on telling the truth and had refused to participate in the bogus recantation, he would have been telling his interrogators something which they would, most certainly, not have wished to hear. So, far from confronting him with the obvious contradictions in the various statements he was making, his RUC interrogators glossed over his inconsistent and incompatible statements; they helped him to devise what, they must have hoped, would be a plausible account of his role, one which would release him from the mess he had created and, simultaneously, enable the RUC to declare that there had been no truth in any of the allegations broadcast on Channel 4.

So, what version of Sands's story was finally awarded the RUC's imprimatur? Was it that he had deliberately misled and hoaxed us all by pretending that his rumours were facts? Or, was it that the programme makers knew full well that he was just a rumour monger, a rogue willing to join them in a hoax of their own making, someone who would say anything required just to get £5000 in his pocket? We have seen that Nesbitt, like Sands himself, found it exceedingly difficult to make up his mind. The version he had presented at the meeting with Channel 4 was, unequivocally, the latter with, as the reader will recall, Nesbitt inviting the Channel's co-operation so that he could bring charges against Ben and me, as well as Sands and, presumably, O'Hagan. But within days of delivering this verdict, the RUC's top detective was—as we've also seen—hedging his bets, apparently unable to decide but seeming to prefer Sands's first version of events, with Ben and me now among the deceived, rather than among the deceivers. The reason for this ambivalence in the "official" RUC version of the "hoax" would not become clear until much later.[10] However, Nesbitt's indecision was never a problem for the dirty tricks brigade and its media allies; they disregarded his equivocation and plumped unreservedly, as we've seen, for the more comprehensive version of the "hoax," one in which the programme makers were said to have joined the other villains, O'Hagan and Sands, schooling the ever willing and pliable Source A until he was word perfect in reciting the slanderous script we had given him; the version in which he was supposedly persuaded to regurgitate rehearsed and bogus "answers" to our questions about collusion, the RUC Inner Force and the Committee's assassination campaign.

Nesbitt's equivocation about Ben's role and mine contrasted with his certainty about the identity of the real culprit in the affair, Martin O'Hagan. The IRA-man-turned-journalist emerged, in the "official" RUC version, as the programme's supreme hoaxer, a Machiavelli, a Rasputin and a Svengali, all rolled into one and wrapped in the Republican tricolour. O'Hagan, the crafty and mischievous tabloid hack was conveniently found—in this "official" RUC version—to have manipulated the venal Sands and, simultaneously, to have hoodwinked or recruited the novice researcher to join them in the "hoax;" one way or the other, Box Productions had managed to deliver Channel 4 what the naive broadcaster considered "the scoop of the year," as *The Sunday Times* would later disparagingly describe the programme. The RUC transcript shows that Sands was guided by his "interrogators" into adopting this official version of events, one in which Martin was made the prime mover both in devising and executing the "hoax." All three documented statements by Sands pin the blame on Martin who, if Sands's affidavit could be believed, had being planning the "hoax" even before the moment Ben had arrived in the province. These are the second and third paragraphs of Sands's affidavit.

> Shortly before Christmas, 1990, Martin O'Hagan of the *Sunday World* newspaper, Belfast, asked me to meet some journalists from Channel 4 and assist them in making a documentary about the Ulster Independence Movement.
>
> Between Christmas, 1990 and January, 1991, I met with Martin O'Hagan in the shed at the back of his house in . . . Lurgan, where he showed me newspaper cuttings from the *Sunday World* which stated that there existed a Loyalist conspiracy within the RUC, the Inner Force. This Inner Force was supposedly composed of policemen who colluded with leading members of the community and Loyalist paramilitaries to organise the murder of Catholics.

And Sands repeated much the same story in the Johnston interview.

Before Christmas 1990 Martin O'Hagan came to me and told me that people from Channel 4 were doing a programme on politics in Northern Ireland and when they came over, could I meet them. At that time I was involved with the Ulster Independence Committee and Hugh Ross. He said to me that it would be good publicity for Independence. He said that by helping them out, there would be some money in it. They would pay whatever, that was alright [*sic*], I didn't mind. So then they came over, Ben Hamilton came over, probably early in the New Year 1991. Just before he came, Martin O'Hagan told me that when I met him, as well as the Independence thing, just sort of tell him the sort of rumours that were going about, about Loyalist killings and all that, just general talk on the ground.

And when we study the transcripts of Sands's "interrogation" by the RUC, we again discover that Martin O'Hagan is the central figure in the story. However, we find that it is not Sands who singles him out for blame but the RUC officers in charge of the proceedings, Detective Chief Inspector William Hetherington and a member of the Nesbitt Inquiry who subsequently joined the delegation to the Channel 4 meeting, Detective Sergeant Chris Webster. Sands is deftly guided through the scenario that Nesbitt described when, during his meeting with Channel 4, he explained how the "hoax" had been perpetrated on the broadcaster and its viewers.

Q: Right now hold on a second. The point that I'm trying to make is this, that from the outset of this whole incident, right, before Ben Hamilton ever came across to Northern Ireland, and again correct me if I'm wrong, listen to what I have to say and listen to it very carefully. If Martin O'Hagan and you got together, Martin O'Hagan told you, if I'm right, that these boys were coming across they have got a lot of money to spend and if youse got together you could take a lot of money off them. Is that right?
A: Yes.
Q: Am I right in saying that?
A: Yes, yes.
Q: Again, if what you are saying is correct, you are telling me that you prepared the deception for Ben Hamilton, insofar as Martin O'Hagan and you met up before you met Ben Hamilton, you researched your stories through old newspapers of the *Sunday World*, through notebooks of Martin O'Hagan's, again stop me if I'm wrong . . . youse [*sic*] discussed with Ben Hamilton, I believe and a sum of some 5000 odd pounds was talked about.
A: Yes, yes.
Q: Right, bear this in mind.
A: Mm.

Q: You've done all that preparation, you went to great lengths
. . .

A: Yes, yes.

Q: To deceive Ben Hamilton, alright [*sic*] to take Ben Hamilton
on . . .

A: Yes, yes.

Q: And in actual fact it would appear that you have done that
alright. It is true?

A: Yes.

Q: Would that be a true assessment of the thing?

A: Yes, yes.

So we can see that the same story emerges from the affidavit, the
Johnston interview and the transcripts of Sands's question and answer session with the RUC. All three documents contain statements by Sands that
Martin O'Hagan, whom he admitted having known for five years, had
bribed and threatened him from the outset of the affair. Although all three
accounts are, more or less, in harmony with each other that does not, of
course, guarantee that they are true. In fact, if we consider the two paragraphs quoted from Sands's affidavit, we can easily establish that they are
both false.

Sands states that Martin O'Hagan approached him "shortly *before*
Christmas 1990" and, having asked him to meet some journalists from
Channel 4, had begun to brief him *between* Christmas 1990 and January
1991. If these statements are true, Martin O'Hagan must possess unrecog-
nised telepathic powers because, as the reader may recall, Ben's interest in
the Loyalist assassination campaign was aroused only towards the end of
February 1991—around two months after Martin is supposed to have
recruited Sands to participate in the alleged hoax. We can, therefore, dismiss the first of Sands's two quoted paragraphs as false because it is a fact
that, before February 1991, Ben would not even have known of Martin's
existence, let alone have spoken to him on the telephone or met him in
Belfast.

And we can be equally confident in dismissing as false the other quoted paragraph of Sands's affidavit because Martin—never having heard of
Ben, Box Productions or me—would not have had any reason to have
behaved in the manner alleged. Sands's account can be disregarded
because Ben did not set foot in Northern Ireland until nearly three months
later than Sands would have us believe the "hoax" began. A genuine
inquiry, one committed to establishing the truth, would have quickly
realised that Sands's account was false and that Martin O'Hagan had been
unjustly accused. However, if the inquiry was bogus and was actually an
exercise designed to exonerate the conspirators identified by Sands, its primary goal would have been to discredit the entire story by locating its

Achilles heel—the fact that the programme's principal source had been introduced to us by someone whose reputation could, it was felt, be savaged with impunity—even though this person, Martin O'Hagan, had put his Official IRA past firmly behind him fifteen years previously and, to his considerable credit, built a successful new career in journalism.

A close reading of the transcripts suggests that the decision to pin the blame on Martin, together with the invention of the scenario in which he was said to have bribed and threatened Sands to do his bidding, was taken by Nesbitt and his team. It shows that Sands was guided step-by-step through the scenario, which was carefully rehearsed before the tape-recorder was switched on. We saw, in the passage quoted, how the "official" version was articulated by the police interviewer; we have also seen that Sands's modest contribution to the exercise was, at each stage, simply to grunt in agreement with what he had just been told. Though the overall exercise was conducted to simulate a genuine interrogation, there remained signs that Sands was not answering the RUC's questions for the first time. We can see this when he is being asked about what happened after his arrival in London.

> Q: And what happened around nine then, or what?
> A: Well, then we got a taxi, well no it was only a mini, cab.
> Q: A mini-cab?
> A: A mini-cab, and we went just round London . . .
> Q: . . . So really the only thing you saw when you were out was where Box Productions or what was pointed out to you as a Box Productions office?
> A: Yes, yes.
> Q: And it was just as you happened to be walking past it and that's basically it?
> Right, OK, what happened then?
> A: Well ah,
> Q: I mean did youse go back to the hotel or whatever.
> A: We went to a Greek restaurant.
> Q: Right, uh huh.
> A: It was a wee small, wee, *now I told the boys this morning*, it was a wee small, wee place, maybe about six tables. [my emphasis]

"Now I told the boys this morning." When I first read those words in the RUC transcript, I immediately thought that someone had made a serious mistake. For this tape-recorded interview with Sands—which, strangely, was begun at 9:33 pm at night (according to the transcript)—purports to be a record of his official interview by the RUC after his arrest. Yet, we discover on page 211 of the transcript that he had been discussing, earlier in the day, the character of the Greek restaurant where we had taken him during his trip to London. Who were these "boys" who had been ques-

tioning him that morning? Why was Sands talking to them about the Greek restaurant? What else did he talk to them about that morning or, indeed, in the afternoon? The more I thought about this tell-tale phrase, the more I realised that the transcript could not be taken at face value and was, most probably, the record of a conversation that had been rehearsed with Sands before the tape-recorder was switched on.

We find another clue, a little earlier in the interview, to suggest that this was the case. According to the transcripts, the interviews with Sands were carried out, as already noted, on December 11th and 12th 1992, presumably a short time after his arrest. Yet an exchange between Sands and his interviewer, Detective Chief Inspector Hetherington, reveals—unintentionally, I believe—that this was not the case at all.

> Q: Right, minutes of meetings, did you give him [Ben] any minutes of meetings?
> A: He had seen minutes of the UIC meetings.
> Q: Which particular ones?
> A: The ones that's in.
> Q: That's the ones that you gave me.
> A: Yes.
> Q: *On, I think it was the first of December, when I called at your house.*
> A: Yes. [my emphasis]

So we discover that, though the interviews took place on December 11th and 12th 1992, Detective Chief Inspector Hetherington had called at Sands's home in Portadown on what the officer thinks was "*the first of December.*" This indicates that Sands was, almost certainly, unmasked by the RUC as our Source A on that date. Though it is possible that he was visited and identified even earlier, some time in November, we now know from the transcripts that he was known by the RUC to have been our source for *at least ten days before these tape-recorded interviews were carried out.* So the question that arises is what were Sands and the RUC doing during this long period? There are other signs in the transcript that, by December 11th, the RUC interviewers were satisfied that they were dealing with a "hoaxer" rather than a seasoned terrorist or conspirator to multiple murder. His interrogators call him by his first name and the questioning is gentle and friendly, giving the impression that most, if not all, of the wrinkles in his story have been ironed out in advance of the preparation of the "official" record. None of Sands's replies appear to cause the RUC any surprise or puzzlement about how they should interpret the significance of what he is saying.

The transcripts strongly suggest, therefore, that the tape-recorded interviews with Sands came at the end of a long process, lasting ten days or more, during which he was persuaded to "recant" the allegations he had made in the *Dispatches* programme. Since he had, in truth, become a regular source for Martin O'Hagan during the five years they had known each other, he must have felt he had no other choice but to go along with the entirely false scenario outlined above. Even when at liberty, Sands had inhabited a small world limited by his inarticulacy and lack of education. Once under arrest and under pressure, he would, I believe, have quickly succumbed and agreed to do exactly what he was told. After the Nesbitt Inquiry team had debriefed him on his involvement with us and quizzed him about his role in Abernethy's Committee, he would have been in no position to resist when instructed by his RUC handlers on the reconstruction of his story to which he would henceforward rigidly adhere. This reconstruction, centred on Martin's alleged bribery and culminating in the "hoax" supposedly broadcast by Channel 4, was painfully and unconvincingly extracted from Sands, who evidently found great difficulty in regurgitating what he had been fed, as if spontaneously, for the benefit of the tape-recorder. Fortunately, Sands was not up to the task required of him and his tortuous performance is easily recognised for the fabrication it is—as we shall see in the next chapter.[11]

Notes

1 Our conviction that the Nesbitt Inquiry was a bogus exercise would be proved correct when, in September 1996, we managed to obtain transcripts of Nesbitt's conversations with Barrie Penrose, held just after the High Court case in August 1992. Part of the transcript of these conversations, showing the true character of Nesbitt's "investigation," are printed in Appendix 3; they demonstrate that Penrose and Nesbitt worked closely together to discredit the programme.

2 The article Penrose is referring to is the one which the *Sunday Express* published on January 17th 1993—the day after Penrose's conversation with Tony Coldwell. [See Chapter 9, p. 183]

3 All Nesbitt's quotations, cited below, are taken from Jan Tomalin's memorandum, which she wrote on the basis of notes she had taken at the meeting.

4 As Source A was not absolutely certain about some of those he named as Committee members, I have decided not to name the businessman to whom Mr. Nesbitt was referring. In contrast, Source A was unequivocal in his assertion that David Prentice was a member of the Committee. [See Appendix 1]

5 In fact, this was never to happen. Instead, Jim Sands and his entire family

were moved from Portadown shortly after he had been unmasked by the RUC. As far as I am aware, he has been living under RUC protection in Northern Ireland ever since.

6 Tony Coldwell told the Nesbitt Inquiry's Sergeant Elliott, in a tape-recorded conversation, that we had behaved professionally during the interview with Sands. "The whole interview appeared like a normal interview. It was a standard current affairs interview. The subject matter just happened to be quite important." Q: "You did not see the interviewee examining or using any script material?" A: "No." Q: "Would you say that he answered the questions of his own accord?" A: "I would say he answered the questions of his own accord, in a precise and confident manner."

7 See Chapter 9, pp. 179–183.

8 This is, presumably, a reference to Martin O'Hagan.

9 The IRA escaper, John Joseph Smith, eventually lost his legal battle and was returned to Northern Ireland in 1995 to complete his life sentence.

10 We shall see that, towards the end of 1996, we finally obtained documents which threw fresh light on Nesbitt's inability to choose between the two contradictory versions of the "hoax." [See Chapter 14 and Appendix 3]

11 The RUC has never released these tape-recordings of Sands's supposed recantation. I have had to rely on the transcripts of those conversations which, as explained, first surfaced in court proceedings in California. Any investigator, wishing to probe the way in which Nesbitt and his team— Webster, Hetherington, Elliott et al—covered up the scandal after the October 1991 broadcast, will need to obtain these tape-recordings from the RUC.

Chapter 11

THE "HOAX"

By May 1993 *The Committee* had become the most controversial and expensive documentary programme in Channel 4's history. Ever since the broadcast, the Channel's Board of Directors had publicly supported the programme makers because they believed that we had satisfied all the requirements laid down by the network's editorial executives. But, following Nesbitt's visit to the Channel and his disturbing claim that the network's executives had been duped by Box Productions, the Board decided that it could no longer afford to take anything on trust. If, in the light of the RUC's verdict, Channel 4 was to continue to insist that the programme's allegations were true, it obviously had to be absolutely certain that the programme makers had behaved properly. Understandably, the Board wished to have the reassurance that could only come from a rigorous and independent inquiry—which was why it decided, within days of Nesbitt's visit, to set up the top secret Beloff Inquiry.

If the Beloff Inquiry were to conclude that anyone working for Box Productions—especially Martin O'Hagan, Ben Hamilton or I—had bribed, bullied, cajoled or otherwise pressured any of the programme's participants into presenting false statements about the RUC as if they were factual truths, then the Channel would be facing a calamity of unprecedented proportions; if Beloff did not acquit Box Productions completely by dismissing all the RUC's charges against the programme makers, then the entire rationale for the broadcast and for its subsequent defence could lie in ruins. Liz Forgan had spelled out that rationale in an article for *The Observer*, published in July 1992, shortly before Channel 4 and Box Productions faced the contempt proceedings in the High Court:

> Television programmes about Northern Ireland are the wrong place to look for media self-interest. The mystery is why anyone makes such programmes at all. Viewers turn off at the very mention of the subject. The story has been hopelessly going round in circles for decades. There is no sex, no laughs, no charm, no hope. The place is such a hall of mirrors that getting anywhere near the

truth is difficult, dangerous and often prohibitively expensive.
So why do it? There is only one reason for making programmes .
about Northern Ireland, and that is because it is the biggest, nastiest, most important domestic political issue of our times.

Ten months after Liz Forgan's article, Channel 4 found itself under even greater pressure over the programme. For, by then, the RUC had formally delivered a written verdict, stating that the programme had been a "fabrication," a hoax.[1] And, on May 9th 1993, *The Sunday Times* had printed a full page "report," which claimed to provide an explanation of how the alleged hoaxers—Martin, Ben and I—had successfully duped the network.[2] Even worse, one of the murder conspirators identified by Sands, Portadown solicitor Richard Monteith, had recently issued a libel writ against me in the High Court in Northern Ireland; and it seemed probable that he would also launch separate proceedings against Channel 4 (which he subsequently did.) David Trimble MP was continuing his attacks on the programme in the House of Commons. And, in the absence of any effective response from Channel 4, it had by mid-1993 become the conventional wisdom in the media that *The Committee* had been little short of a calamity for all concerned.[3]

So, throughout most of 1993, Channel 4 found itself in the unhappy position of fielding attacks from the RUC and its allies while, simultaneously, waiting and hoping that the Beloff Inquiry would provide much needed reassurance that the programme had been properly made. Michael Beloff, realising the importance of his assignment, worked at full speed in an effort to establish what the Channel 4 Board most wanted to know—whether *The Committee* had been a hoax or not. As for the programme makers, we had no alternative but to co-operate fully with the Inquiry, even though we all knew that the RUC's "hoax" allegation against us was totally without foundation. In any case, we welcomed the Inquiry because we appreciated the situation facing the Channel 4 Board and we hoped that a favourable verdict, which we all confidently expected, would result in the Board continuing to support us as vigorously as it had since the broadcast in October 1991.

So we ensured that all programme materials—scripts, interview transcripts, audio and video tapes, correspondence, contracts—were readily made available to the Inquiry team; everyone involved in the production, including the freelance camera crew members and technical staff, agreed to be interviewed; every request for information was acted on immediately so that the Inquiry could report as soon as possible. Each person was interviewed individually, with a tape-recorder running so that verbatim transcripts could be prepared and sent to us for correction and signature. By the end of the summer it was my turn to be interviewed and, during two lengthy conversations with Michael Beloff, I was forced to defend various decisions I had taken while making the programme in 1991 and to justify my belief that the programme had got the story right. After meeting Mr. Beloff, I had no doubts that the Channel 4 Board had appointed the right person to conduct the investigation; for I saw at once that he was a skilful and experienced inquisitor and that, if any of us really had committed the misdeeds alleged by the RUC, he would have detected any such wrongdoing and would not have hesitated to say so. But, as the RUC's allegations against us were utterly spurious, I was confident that the Inquiry would eventually deliver a verdict that would give the Channel 4 Board all the reassurance it needed.

As the Inquiry proceeded during 1993, I was forced to spend a good deal of my time on the libel case which the Committee's solicitor, Richard Monteith, had brought against me in Belfast. By opting to bring proceedings for criminal libel, nowadays an extremely rare form of litigation but one which remains available to a plaintiff who feels especially aggrieved, Monteith was indicating his confidence that I would never be able to prove that he had been a member of Abernethy's Committee. His Statement of Claim, which accompanied the writ, left my legal advisers in no doubt that Monteith would, if successful, be pressing for my imprisonment; criminal libel carries a maximum sentence of two years in jail. When I had read what Monteith was claiming in his affidavit, it had reminded me of the effrontery of his fellow Committee member, "Reverend" Hugh Ross, who had also vehemently protested his innocence and threatened to launch libel proceedings, unless we gave in to various demands.[4] Unlike Ross, Monteith had actually issued the libel writ and showed in his sworn Statement of Claim that he had no inhibitions about perjuring himself even before he was called into the witness box.

> When I first read the article in *The Sunday Times* on August 2nd 1992 and heard, and read a transcript of the statement made by Mr. McPhilemy, the reference to myself was clear and unmistakable. My reaction was one of horror and fear and one of anger. I immediately realised that the lives of my wife and two infant children and my own life were thereby exposed to grave danger. In effect, I was being identified and accused of being a sectarian and mass murderer. The enormity of these allegations has had a devastating effect on my wife and myself. It is well known in Northern Ireland that even the suggestion of suspicion of involvement in sectarian and paramilitary activity is enough to invite retaliatory action and murder. On many occasions the wives and families of innocent suspects have not been spared by terrorists. Because of these defamatory statements I have to take and continue to take extra precautions for the security of my home and family and

myself. I have no doubt that these statements have made me a particular target for terrorists. The dangers and consequences must have been especially obvious to Mr. McPhilemy before he made the allegations against me as the *Dispatches* programme dealt with the murder of Mr. Patrick Finucane, which was allegedly planned and executed by the Committee.

Although, contrary to what Monteith was claiming, I had been extremely careful not to identify him in my interview on the BBC *Inside Ulster* programme, he had been able to find two people willing to testify on oath that they, at least, had been convinced that he was the solicitor about whom I had been speaking during the television interview. One of these was another Loyalist solicitor, Drew Nelson, who stated that he had "no doubt" that Monteith had been the person I had been referring to. Was it really possible, I asked myself when I first saw Nelson's affidavit, that this man had been able to reach such a view about Monteith, merely on the basis of what I had said on the BBC and not for some other, possibly more interesting, reason? A possible answer to this question would surface later, as we shall see.[5] The other witness, who also swore that he had "absolutely no doubt" that I had identified Monteith as a Committee member, was his representative in the House of Commons, William David Trimble MP. I must confess that, when I learned that Trimble had felt it necessary to come to Monteith's aid, I was more convinced than ever of the Portadown solicitor's guilt and of his consequent vulnerability; I also thought that Trimble's readiness to swear an affidavit for Monteith's benefit was extremely foolish because, as a result, the MP might one day be obliged to testify in court about his dealings with this solicitor and about meetings he had secretly held with Committee chairman Billy Abernethy and Ulster Resistance leader John McCullagh during the period they were organising the assassinations.

Nevertheless, the appearance of these two apparently respectable citizens as supporting witnesses—together with Monteith's "I-was-horrified" affidavit—convinced me that, if I was to be certain of winning any libel case against him, I would have to find sufficient admissible evidence to mount a defence of justification; in other words, I would have to be able to prove that Monteith, despite the claims of his two witnesses, was one of the murder conspirators—or, as he put it himself, "a sectarian and mass murderer." Otherwise, there was a serious risk that my reputation as an investigative journalist would be destroyed and my television career brought to an ignominious end. And since criminal libel is an imprisonable offence, I also realised that a defeat in the High Court in Belfast could result in my losing my liberty as well.

So for these reasons, as well as a keen desire to see Abernethy, Ross, Monteith and company brought to justice, I decided that I would have to concentrate my efforts on finding the evidence I needed to prove that Monteith was one of Sands's co-conspirators. As I remained absolutely convinced that Sands had been telling the truth as he understood it and, further, that we had barely scratched the surface of Monteith's criminal past, I began in earnest to explore the Portadown solicitor's past involvement in Loyalist paramilitary activity. I soon discovered that this supposedly respectable lawyer was involved with Loyalist terrorism for a long time before he joined Abernethy's Committee and before he participated in the Loyalist assassination campaign in 1989, 1990 and 1991.

Lord Williams QC, who had advised me to plead justification in my defence to the criminal libel action, scored a decisive victory over Monteith in the High Court in Belfast when, in March 1993, he persuaded the judge, Mr. Justice Carswell, to refuse permission for this criminal prosecution against me to go ahead. While this undoubtedly proved a setback for Monteith, I anticipated that he would soon return to the attack and issue a civil libel writ, again alleging that I had identified him, in the BBC interview, as a member of the Committee. Although he did, in fact, subsequently issue this second writ in May 1993, I would not hear about it until much later, after he had served it, together with his Statement of Claim, in September 1994. Then, once again, I pleaded justification—pointing out that his name was listed in the Channel 4 dossier as one of the nineteen Committee members—and I set about finding the evidence to prove in court that, contrary to what Trimble and Nelson had claimed, Monteith had been a member of the Committee.[6] Ironically, I would probably never have made Richard Monteith the focus of such a prolonged and intensive investigation but for the two libel actions he chose to bring against me; Monteith's conduct had left me no other choice.

Although I would later obtain more than sufficient evidence to prove the truth of what *The Committee* had revealed and to refute the RUC's "hoax" verdict on the programme, I was not in that happy position in May 1993. Then, it looked as if we would never succeed in countering the endless stream of propaganda against us. Ever since the transmission, we had been mired in a series of lengthy, expensive and exhausting legal actions, including contempt, perjury and criminal libel; and we had been subjected to a barrage of propaganda, emanating from the RUC and amplified by the *Sunday Express*, *The Sunday Times* and other media. Though the RUC's divide-and-rule strategy had, fortunately, failed to detach Box Productions from Channel 4, the "hoax" verdict had nevertheless forced Channel 4 to set up the Beloff Inquiry; and this very fact, the existence of this secret Inquiry, added to the strains upon us. For I feared that news about the inquiry might leak out, with the result that our company's reputation would be damaged still further. Who in the television industry

would commission Box Productions to make sensitive factual programmes, if it became common knowledge that we were being investigated for having hoaxed Channel 4?

It was during this tense and troublesome period that suddenly, without
warning, an unexpected development occurred which gave me hope that,
provided we kept our nerve, the truth would eventually emerge and we
would manage to convince the sceptics that, despite what they had so far
been told, the journalism in *The Committee* had been accurate. The development in question began with a phone call to Channel 4 from a freelance
reporter, Tricia McDaid, whose by-line had appeared in *The Sunday
Times*, during the previous October, when the newspaper had changed
dramatically, between editions, its account of what UVF informer, Edward
Quinn, was saying about the RUC, collusion and his dealings with Ben
Hamilton. This sudden change, we had speculated at the time, might have
been due to the contribution mentioned at the bottom of the article, an
acknowledgement which read, "*Additional reporting by Tricia McDaid and
Ian Birrell.*"[7] McDaid had phoned Channel 4 to offer us evidence which
would prove that *The Sunday Times* had been using dirty tricks against us.

Channel 4 had referred Tricia McDaid to me and, after hearing what
this freelance reporter had to say about her former employer, I decided to
pass her on to my solicitor, Brian Raymond, who invited her to come to
his office next day, Thursday, May 20th 1993. Brian, who had been
informed that she was offering to sell us a tape-recording of an interview
she had conducted with Quinn, had obviously decided that his conversation with her should be recorded for posterity. Brian had switched on his
tape-recorder before the conversation began. As her remarks throw considerable light on that newspaper's motivation and methodology, I quote
her at length:

> BR: Right, I want to hear what you have got to say—I mean—let
> me tell you straightaway what the context is. Obviously the whole
> issue, rather all the issues surrounding this programme, are on-
> going matters.
> TMc: Yeh.
> BR: It's not dead, it's not finished and in particular . . .
> TMc: Why do you say "it's not finished?"
> BR: Well, for example, as *The Sunday Times* itself reported and
> as the . . .
> TMc: The RUC may press charges on Sands.
> BR: On Sands—that's right and on O'Hagan also whom they
> arrested, so that may happen and there are civil proceedings hang-
> ing around against a number of newspapers in relation to com-
> ments made after the programme, including against *The Sunday
> Times*. We've just been to Belfast and successfully beat off an

attempt to do both *The Sunday Times* and McPhilemy for criminal libel—that was a strange case where everybody found themselves on the same side. [*Monteith had also sued* The Sunday Times *because it had printed comments, attributed (wrongly) to me, about the solicitor.*]

TMc: Monteith.

BR: Monteith. Also there is the—I won't hide from you the fact that the question of taking civil proceedings for defamation against *The Sunday Times* possibly, at least, other newspapers as well, have been under consideration for many months.

TMc: *The Sunday Times.*

BR: Well, that would be the prime candidate if we decided to go. That has been under consideration for some time. No decision has been made yet but it's a strong possibility, I think, particularly in view of *The Sunday Times* . . .

TMc: My piece.

BR: You're in the 4th October. [*Brian was referring to the newspaper's different versions of what Quinn was supposedly saying in October 1992.*]

TMc: November—October.

BR: October, yes, yes—the date is engraved on my mind! So, and the point about it is that these—there have been some appalling injustices taking place in relation to this case. When the full facts are known and brought out, those associated with it really—how far this extends, I don't know—the people that are directly concerned [will] have had their journalistic credentials very severely dented. There's no question about that. Now, therefore, I would obviously be very interested in what you have to say about your direct involvement with it and, as it appears from the conversations you have had with Sean . . . that you did not approve of the methods that were being used at the time. Well, then, it is only fair to you that it should be known and that you should not be tarred with the same brush that is going to blacken them— almost inevitably. So that is the reason why I am interested to hear what you have got to say and to discuss the question of this tape with you.

TMc: Well it is not really clear that I did not really approve of the methods that were being used.

BR: Do you mind if I make notes while you talk or would you rather I didn't?

TMc: I'd rather you didn't.

BR: OK—all right. [*Tape noises indicate pencil and notebook being put in Brian's desk!*]

TMc: It's just a case of, I went there on the job and, from hindsight, it seems the editor who actually wrote our story and . . . .

BR: This is Andrew Neil.

TMc: Yes. It seems we were all under the impression, which was the line we were being fed—that it was a load of old bollocks and that, you know, we were going there to get the witnesses. We understood he was homosexual and this is what had happened.

BR: Quinn was homosexual?

TMc: Yeh, between Ben and him and that's why he had been picked up.

BR: Oh really.

TMc: I mean, that actually put us off finding him for a while because we spent time looking in gay bars and things—and obviously . . .

BR: Where did that information come from that?

TMc: Well, it's one of those things automatically comes out when you are under suspicion—it is one of the first things that is put out about you, isn't it, that you are homosexual.

BR: Well sure, I was just wondering—oh yes, it is an obvious sort of smear—was it Clarke or was it from London where that smear came from?

TMc: London.

BR: London.

TMc: It was going round London and, you know, by the time it filters through to the Press—it is most likely that it started with the RUC.

BR: Yeh.

TMc: Them putting out this as their Press Office line.

BR: Sure sure.

TMc: Anyway, I went there as a journalist, completely independently, did my own thing and, you know, we filed and essentially I was freelance and I had, after listening to the thing—the tape—it is obvious that Quinn supports and vindicates Ben Hamilton—now I am not quite sure whether it is just luck because, frankly, you know—knowing how the other end operates—if it had been me saying to them, "Oh look, I've got this," you would just have been snapped off your feet and, obviously, this operates differently and so, I mean he was a bad witness anyway and I know, I know he is just a small player in this but . . .

BR: Yeh.

TMc: But the fact is he does say things like he was beaten and given a hard time by the RUC and they were asking him to say this and this and this.

BR: Did he say how the RUC found him in the first place?

TMc: Yes.

BR: How was that, through his son?

TMc: No, he says it in the tape. So um . . .

BR: I thought he had a son in the RUC—this is what we were told.

[The conversation continues with McDaid saying that she has a tape-recording containing about two and a half hours of Quinn's testimony.]

TMc: It is just him going on about how he says he wasn't paid and he vindicates [Ben]. Essentially, you know, obviously from your point of view it means that if you have this, then it says this is what they did to Quinn, they . . .

BR: Yeh.

TMc: So, no doubt, Sands is the same and . . . [8]

BR: Well, Sands may be in a different category. I am amazed to hear you say that Andrew Neil wrote the story.

TMc: Yes.

BR: His name does not appear on it.

TMc: Of course not. He is the editor and doesn't have a role in the by-line.

BR: Why is a lofty individual like him taking an interest in an issue like this? I don't understand that.

TMc: Well it—the editor likes to think that he knows about Ireland.

BR: [Acknowledgement]

TMc: And the trouble is nobody, you know, Ireland is as Ben Hamilton found out, is a pain in the neck to get involved in because the politics are knitted—it's not just—you can't take a line in Ireland 'cause it's so tied up—I mean, for example, you know, now Ben Hamilton—the IRA would knock him off or the RUC would knock him off, the UVF would knock him off and he has upset the whole damn lot.

BR: Right, well we'd better stay out of it then.

TMc: Well, you know, that's what I mean, that the editor is involved but I don't know how obviously he—I mean—it's top PR isn't it, getting *The Sunday Times* to take your line.

BR: But the attack of *The Sunday Times* has been directed also against Channel 4, I mean it's been very much an anti-Channel 4 thing.

TMc: That's the editor and Michael Grade.

BR: How do you mean?

TMc: Well, there is just a bit of competition between them, symbolism and . . .

BR: Do you know that first-hand or is that just rumour?

TMc: No, it's obvious anyway and if you read *Private Eye*, *UKPG* [Press Gazette] or any of the in-house magazines and I know Andrew Neil anyway, I know the sort of things . . .

BR: How was it received when you filed your, you say you did your interview and filed your stuff and how was it received back at Wapping?

TMc: Well, I was very embryonic in *The Sunday Times* at that time and I had a senior journalist, a so-called senior journalist with me, who actually had nothing to do with, I had to buy him sweets and chips and pizza to keep him actually on the story.

BR: Who was that?

TMc: Because he was not interested. Well, it's a guy from *The Sunday Times*, I don't think it's fair unless, you know he is on the tape so I mean it is not fair to mention other people because he is not coming to you. It is only me who is freelancing, he is still employed by the paper. But, anyway, it was all oh wonderful, well done and great stuff and Andrew Neil directly on the phone, not by-passing . . .

BR: This is after you found that Quinn was going back on his whole story. That was all wonderful and well done was it?

TMc: Well the—no—what happened was the guy—Andrew Neil had written the story anyway—then we found the guy—we found Quinn and so then my colleague went on the phone to Andrew Neil and Andrew Neil said this is how it is, blah blah and got my colleague to say and didn't give him a chance, and if you are dealing with Andrew—the guy had never dealt with Andrew Neil on a story before and Andrew Neil is like God in *The Sunday Times*, so the guy wasn't able to—because he was speaking to the editor and he had never done that before on a story out on the road, he got carried away with the emotion and Andrew Neil saying down the phone: "Well done, well done, you stood it up and we'll do this and this and this."

BR: So this is when you had found him but had not actually heard what he had to say?

TMc: No, that is one when we had heard what he had had to say. So that is what I am saying—the guy got carried away with the emotion of Andrew Neil saying this is . . .

BR: Oh you mean you didn't communicate properly what Quinn had said.

TMc: No because he was overawed by the fact that the editor was saying well done, you have found him, and well done, you have stood up my story.

BR: But of course you hadn't stood up his story—you had demolished it.

TMc: Yes.

BR: Right, well was it that Andrew Neil hadn't understood that from what was said?

TMc: Well, it was that the guy was so terrified of Andrew Neil he wasn't, he didn't dare say . . .

BR: But eventually they did print it. It did knock a hole in their story and it shows in the later edition, does it not?

TMc: Yeh, yeh but that is after we filed. I mean the guy didn't completely—you know—he let them go half way but he did say well, you know, we didn't completely stand up the story.

McDaid then proceeded to give Brian her opinion why it was she and not Liam Clarke, *The Sunday Times'* correspondent in Belfast, who had found the elusive Edward Quinn.

> TMc: Because, you see, my involvement was very brief because the actual MI5, the Home Office line was not to find Quinn and I was new on the paper and hadn't been there that long. Liam Clarke hadn't heard of me and then the editor dispatched me from London and inevitably I know Northern Ireland.
>
> BR: Sure.
>
> TMc: So I found Quinn, which was a big balls, a big whole because I wasn't supposed to. Nobody else would have but, unfortunately, there was not only me being very keen and new on the paper but there was me knowing Northern Ireland.

So, according to one of the reporters covering the story for *The Sunday Times,* the RUC had beaten Quinn and forced him to lie about his various encounters with Ben. Although we were unable, for legal reasons, to buy the tape-recording McDaid was trying to sell, we knew from the later editions of her newspaper that Quinn had confirmed his involvement in the murder of a Republican, a crime in which RUC officers were said to have colluded with the Loyalist killers. Significantly, it was only *after* the publication of this story, as a consequence of McDaid's success in finding Quinn, that the police dropped the perjury charge they had brought against Ben. Clearly, it had been the RUC's intention to deliver Quinn to the Metropolitan Police so that he could help secure Ben's conviction for perjury; Quinn was to be used by the RUC to tell lies about Ben, under oath in the court room in London.

McDaid's sudden appearance had given us an insight into how the RUC and *The Sunday Times* had combined forces to discredit the programme. Her revelations suggested to us that the RUC—meaning, Jimmy Nesbitt—wanted to get Ben convicted for perjury; no doubt he felt that, if he could achieve that, there would not be a single person in Britain, Ireland or anywhere elsewhere, who would any longer believe in the truth of the allegations contained in *The Committee.* As McDaid had perceptively commented to Brian, it was also likely that the RUC would have subjected Sands to similar treatment so that, as with Quinn, he would also "recant" his testimony about collusion—and, indeed, about the RUC Inner Force, the Committee and its chairman, Billy Abernethy.

Within minutes of the reporter's departure from his office, Brian phoned me with a full report of what she had said. We then realised, better than we had ever done before, that we were engaged in a bare-knuckle fight with the RUC, which would not end until one side was victorious, the other defeated.[9] It was, I felt, a great pity that we had not been able to persuade McDaid to part with her tape-recording but we had, at least, managed to make our own recording of what she had said. After discussing the benefit we might yet be able to draw from this unexpected development, Brian and I agreed that we would meet and review the position over lunch, during the following week. His conversation with his visitor had filled him with optimism and he was even more confident than usual that we would, somehow, triumph over all the adversities the programme had generated. At last, fate had dealt us a card to play and we looked forward to discussing how we could use it to our best advantage.

Tragically, however, that telephone conversation was to be our last. For, two days later on Saturday, May 22nd 1993, Brian suffered a heart attack and died at his home. I will never forget the shock I received when Channel 4's lawyer, Jan Tomalin, phoned next evening to tell me what had happened. Brian's sudden death, at the age of just forty-four years, was a catastrophe for his family and an irreplaceable loss for his friends and colleagues at Bindman and Partners, the solicitors practice which he had played a big part in making one of the most respected legal firms in Britain. Although many of those who attended his funeral had known him longer and better than I did, I grieved for the loss of someone whom I had trusted, admired and come to value as a friend. Brian's death had removed the one individual who had mastered every detail of this affair and who had emerged as the strategist to whom we all looked, both at Channel 4 and Box Productions, for advice and guidance on how we should defend the programme and seek to restore our reputations. After Brian's death his partner, Geoffrey Bindman, took over my case and I soon discovered that I had all the support I needed to continue my struggle. As the months and years have gone by since that terrible weekend in May 1993, I have also come to trust, admire and rely on Geoffrey Bindman in the way I had depended on Brian Raymond.

Although we still do not know precisely what happened to Sands after he had been identified and arrested by the RUC in November 1992 it is, I think, reasonable to assume that he would have suffered a similar fate to Quinn and would have agreed to do whatever he was told. We may never know what pressures, physical or psychological, induced him to retract his allegations and to recant his story. But ever since the RUC informed Channel 4 that he had recanted, we have known that his new version of events—the version which provided the main evidence for the official "hoax" verdict—would not be credible unless it harmonised exactly with the account he had given Ben during their tape-recorded dinner conversations in April 1991. Fortunately for us, Sands's RUC handlers within the Nesbitt Inquiry team were denied access to these tape-recorded conversations and they had, therefore, to devise their recantation story in the knowledge that we retained material which might, in time, enable us to undermine their efforts. This explains, I believe, the RUC's reluctance to give us either copies of Sands's tape-recorded recantation or the transcripts which I later obtained from California. For, as we shall now see, the official version of events as laid out in the 213-page transcript of Sands's interview with the RUC in December 1992 is utterly discredited by the series of revelations he made to Ben in April 1991.

At an early stage in his RUC interview, Sands admits that he had been, in 1991, the secretary of the Portadown branch of the Ulster Independence Committee, [UIC]. This admission immediately struck me as odd because Nesbitt had omitted any mention of this rather significant fact during his meeting at Channel 4; one of Nesbitt's few revelations about Sands, on that occasion, was that he had "a serious criminal record." Sands began by portraying himself as a local political activist for the UIC and proceeded to claim that it was his occupancy of this post which had put him in a position, supposedly, to hoodwink Ben; he claimed he had merely passed on the names of prominent UIC members— Abernethy, Ross et al—but led Ben to believe these were the murder conspirators belonging to the Loyalist Committee. This superficially plausible story, developed in the early part of the interview, begins with Sands describing what he had told Ben during their first meeting, which took place at the Silverwood Hotel in Lurgan, Co. Armagh.

Q: What position did you tell Hamilton that you held that you could in actual fact have the knowledge of these things that you were telling him?

A: Well, at this stage, I had told him that I was a member of the Ulster Independence Committee, the Portadown Branch, I was the Secretary of Portadown Branch.

Q: Right.

A: And over a meal in the hotel we just talked, and that's, know, it was just about general, general things.

Q: Uh huh, right.

A: Relating to Ulster Independence to, there wasn't really much, you know, actually talked at that first meeting.

Q: Right, fair enough. At this stage, now, on the first meeting, did you suggest to Ben Hamilton that the Ulster Independence Committee was giving political cover to Loyalist terrorists?

A: No.

Q: Not at this time?

A: No.

Q: Right, go on ahead. So, what we're saying now is that we have just general chit-chat over the first meal with Ben Hamilton in the Silverwood Hotel?

A: Yes.

Q: And.

A: And Martin O'Hagan he was, he was there as well.

Q: Uh huh. Did Martin? Yea, go ahead.

A: It was. Ben Hamilton asked questions about Ulster Independence and also about ah, the Loyalist gangs and.

Q: Well, yes. Did you supply any names at this stage? I mean you were talking about Loyalist gangs and what have you. Did you supply Ben Hamilton or tell Ben Hamilton about any names of these gangs?

A: Well, Ben Hamilton had names. He already, Ben Hamilton already had names.

Q: Right, what sort of names did he have? Can you remember any of those names?

A: Billy Wright.

Q: Uh huh.

A: And Robin Jackson were the only two names, the other names he had were people who belonged to the Ulster Independence Committee.

Q: Did he get any names of the Ulster Independence Committee from you, Jim?

A: Well he had, he had the list of members.

Q: Now what list of members are we referring to?

A: Of the Portadown, Portadown Branch.

Q: Right, and where did he get those?

A: He got some of those names from me.

Q: Right.

A: Other ones he already had.

Q: Uh huh. Right . . .

At a later stage in this interview, the RUC officer asks Sands to reveal what he had told us about each of the individuals listed in the Channel 4 dossier, those said to have been running the assassination campaign; the interviewer takes Sands through the list, one-by-one, asking him what he had said about each of the alleged conspirators.

Q: So we'll start off with Category A. *[Category A in the dossier consisted of those individuals whom Source A had confirmed unequivocally to be members of the Committee, according to Channel 4/Box Productions.]*

A: Yes.

Q: Now this category, again, I'll remind you, consists of the names of those who you, as Source A, have confirmed to be members of the Committee. And it starts off, "Senior Members—No. 1—Billy Abernethy—he is described as the Chairman and as Assistant Branch Manager of the Ulster Bank." Is this true? Did you mention him as, in this light?

A: He was. He was one of the names that was on the list.

[Sands was referring, here, to a supposed list of names presented to him by Ben after his arrival in London in April 1991. Sands had referred to this list earlier in his RUC interview.]

Q: Yes, but I mean, did you confirm to them that he was?

A: They asked me to, for, to read off. They'd given me a list of names.

Q: Uh huh.

A: It was on this, these pages at this time.

Q: Right. But had you, before now. What I'm saying to you is this, before they had given you this list.

A: Yes.

Q: Right. Had you given them the names for them to put on to the list?

A: Well, I'd given them names of people who belonged to the UIC.

Q: So, I assume from you saying that, members who belonged to the UIC. I'll run them over here. Is Billy Abernethy, alright.

A: Yes.

Q: He's a UIC member . . . Isobel McCulloch?

A: Yes.

Q: Right. Ah, Reverend Hugh Ross?

A: Yes.

Q: Nelson McCausland.

A: Right.

Q: A fella called John McCullagh. Do you remember John McCullagh?

A: I know him, yes. I don't know whether I.

Q: Did he sit at any of your meetings whenever you were Secretary of the UIC?

A: I think he did. I think he did. Yes.

Q: So the chances are.

A: Yes.

Q: Right. And a Graham Long. Do you know Graham Long?

A: No.

Q: Do you know of Graham Long?

A: No. Not at this time.

Q: What do you mean not at this time?

A: I know of him later. Not in the context of the programme.

Q: Not in the context of the programme. Well, was Graham Long's name mentioned at this, at any time during the filming of the programme?

A: Yes, yes.

Q: Was he described as Ulster Resistance?

A: Yes. He was described to me as the Ulster Resistance Leader in County Armagh.

Q: Right.

Q: Who described him to you as that?

A: On this, it was on this. Now this was the first time I had actually.

Q: Uh huh.

A: You know.

Q: Right.

A: Knew anything about him. [*Sands seems, at this point, to be finding it rather difficult to remember the lines he was supposed to have learned in his early morning rehearsal!*]

Q: So. Then they go on to say now. Yes.

A: Now from what I was told he was one of the men that Billy Abernethy had brought Ben Hamilton down to meet. When he came to Portadown.

Q: Graham Long was.

A: Yes. Now I don't know. That was what I was told.

Q: Right. That's okay. No. We'll come onto that at a later stage, alright because I can appreciate what you're doing there. [*This puzzling exchange suggests that Sands and his interviewer were, at this point, conducting some form of non-verbal conversation, an exchange they did not wish the tape-recorder to pick up.*][10]

A: Right.

Q: Now this, according to Channel 4, are the Committee members. Now I want to go on them from that there to the businessmen, because they say these lads belong to it as well. Is Davy Prentice of Prentice's Garage?

A: Yes. I know, well I know him by name. You know.

Q: Right. Charlie Moffett an Accountant.

A: Well, he's a member of the UIC.

Q: Right. Richard Monteith, Solicitor.

A: I know Richard Monteith.

Q: Was his name mentioned in connection with this at all?

A: Yes.

Q: Right. And Cecil Kirkpatrick. Do you know Cecil Kirkpatrick?[11]

A: I know him by name.

Q: You don't know him personally.

A: I don't know him personally.

Q: So in actual fact.

A: I think he's a member of the UIC as well.[12]

Q: You think he's a member of the UIC as well. Alright. Now. I want to take you a wee bit further. That you then, according to them, went on to mention the Inner Force members, alright. And there's two names here, and I want you to think about them and tell me what happened. A lad called Will Davidson, and he was described as the Inner Force National Representative. Do you know a Will Davidson?

A: No.

Q: Have you ever heard of a Will Davidson?

A: No. The first time I heard of him was through this programme.

Q: And who told you about him or what?

A: Ben Hamilton asked me about him.

Q: Right.

A: Ah. That he'd been told that he was ah, sort of, the senior spokesman for the Inner Force.

Q: Right. Did he tell you what he done. Did he suggest that he was a policeman or anything like along that line?

A: Yes.

Q: So this. I want to get this straight. This man Will Davidson, who's supposed to be a spokesman for the Inner Force is supposed to be a policeman.

A: Yes.

Q: And where does he come from?

A: I don't know.

Q: You have absolutely no knowledge of this man?

A: Now I was asked was he from the Portadown area.

Q: Yes. And, what did you say?

A: I didn't say anything.

Q: Right. So as far as you're concerned.

A: No, I didn't.

Q: Now. I want to go on to another name then. Ian Whittle, who is described as the Inner Force Portadown representative.

A: Yes.

Q: Do you know an Ian Whittle?

A: I think I know him by, I think I know him by the name.

Q: Now how do you think you know him? Who is he or what do you know about him, or think you know about him?

A: If it's the same person I can picture. He's from Portadown Police Station.

Q: Right. Uniformed policeman or?

A: Yes. Yes. I think he works in the office.

Q: He works in an office?

A: In the office. Now if that's the same person I'm thinking of. But at this time they, I had given them no names of any policemen.

Q: Right. So the names of these policemen in actual fact did not come from you.

A: No. they were actually on the list.

Q: Right, okay.

A: Now the first time I heard of Davidson, your man Davidson, was when Ben Hamilton had told me at one of the meetings in the hotel, in the Silverwood Hotel in Lurgan.

Q: Yes.

A: When he asked me, know.

Q: Did you know Davidson?

A: Was he the sort of spokesman for the Inner Force.

Q: Well, this is the point. Did you confirm that he was? I mean, you know, now remember that what you had said was that you were portraying yourself to know all this. [*The interviewer clearly felt that Sands needed to be reminded, yet again, of the line he had been told to adhere to.*]

A: Yes. Yes, yes.

Q: Did you confirm to Ben Hamilton that his information was right, or probably right or whatever?

A: Yes. Yes.

Q: And the same thing applies as far as Ian Whittle was concerned?

A: Well up to this time I didn't, Ian Whittle hadn't been mentioned until now.

Q: Until now. Right. But again, you're playing your part as a man who knew everything that's going on.

A: Yes.

Q: Did you confirm to him that?

A: Yes.

Q: That's fair enough. That's alright.

A: So you confirmed to him that you knew both Davidson and Whittle.

A: Yes.

Q: Alright. And that they, so far as you were concerned at that stage, they were members of the Inner Force.

A: Yes, yes.

Q: Alright. Now. We'll go one wee step further and ah, they then categorise this, as far as paramilitaries are concerned, right. And the paramilitaries that are mentioned here are Billy Wright, described as Portadown UVF. Was Billy Wright's name mentioned?

A: Yes.

Q: And described as a UVF man?

A: Yes.

Q: Right. You know Billy Wright of course.

A: I know him by reputation and to see.

Q: Right. Okay. The second man is Robin Jackson, described as the Donacloney UVF.

A: Yes.

Q: Do you know Robin Jackson?

A: No. Just by name and reputation.

Q: Right. Okay. Now. The third name is a chap called Alec Benson. Now he is described as the Lisburn LRDG. Alright. Do you know an Alec Benson? [*LRDG, an abbreviation of Loyalist*

Retaliation and Defence Group, is one of the smaller Loyalist terror organisations.]
    A: No. No.
    Q: Where did this name crop up from?
    A: That was. It was mentioned at the second meeting I had with Ben Hamilton at the Silverwood Hotel.
    Q: Uh huh.
    A: In Lurgan.
    Q: And again, if the name was mentioned.
    A: It was confirmed.
    Q: You confirmed it.
    A: Yes, yes.
    Q: Even though you didn't know him.
    A: I didn't know him. Didn't know who the name was.
    Q: But you confirmed to Ben Hamilton that this boy did exist. Have you ever heard tell of the LRDG. What does the LRDG stand for?
    A: I don't know.
    Q: You have never heard tell of it?
    A: I never even heard tell of it, that's.
    Q: Did anybody ever discuss the LRDG with you?
    A: No, no.
    Q: And you don't know what the LRDG is?
    A: No, I don't. Even that Saturday there was nothing that was mentioned. It was. Alec Benson was described as a Loyalist para-military from Lisburn, that's all, you know.
    Q: Right, that's alright. Right. I want to move on now. That will cover Category A.

These two extracts, together with those discussed in the last chapter, provide a vivid illustration of the process by which the RUC reconstructed our involvement with Sands to produce a superficially plausible account of how the "hoax" had occurred. Sands—in this official version—had been a well-placed, low-level political activist for the Ulster Independence Committee; this explained how he knew the names of some of the more prominent Loyalist politicians and paramilitaries in and around Portadown, individuals such as Abernethy, Ross, Wright, Jackson and Monteith. His constant need for money and his instinct for self-preservation explained the readiness with which he consented to the proposal from IRA-man-turned-journalist, Martin O'Hagan, to join him in stringing along the young television researcher, who had come over from London and located himself inside "murder triangle." So Sands—the official version continues—was persuaded by O'Hagan to pick up whatever local rumours he could find about murders, collusion, gunmen and related topics; he would discuss them with O'Hagan, enrich them with other colourful material and, then, recycle them as "facts" which he could allegedly vouch for on the basis of his own experience. But—again, according to the official version—by far the boldest idea in the "hoax" dreamt up by this unlikely pair, Sands and O'Hagan, was their decision to pretend to Ben that the "innocent, law-abiding" Hugh Ross and his supposedly harmless Ulster Independence Committee was, in reality, the supreme terrorist body controlling the Loyalist murder campaign; Sands joined in the "hoax" with enthusiasm, partly out of greed for the promised £5000, partly out of fear of O'Hagan's alleged [Provisional] IRA connections. This official version of events, carefully extracted from Sands and documented in the 213-page transcript of his RUC interviews, formed the basis of the Nesbitt Inquiry's final verdict that the programme had been a "hoax" and, what's more, one which O'Hagan and Sands had planned more than nine months before transmission!

How easily can this story—the recantation based on the RUC's reconstruction of our involvement with Sands—be reconciled with the confidential information Sands divulged to Ben during their tape-recorded conversations at the start of the project in 1991? Can we detect any contradiction between what Sands was saying then and what he subsequently stated in reply to the numerous questions he faced from his RUC handlers? What did he say in 1991 about those whom he had identified unequivocally, during audio and video-taped interviews, as members of the Ulster Loyalist Central Co-ordinating Committee? And did he have anything special to say, back then, about the Category A Committee members—Abernethy, Ross, Monteith, David Prentice, Isobel McCulloch, John McCullagh, Cecil Kilpatrick, Nelson McCausland, Charlie Moffett, Graham Long, Will Davidson, Ian Whittle, Billy Wright, Robin Jackson and Alec Benson—fifteen individuals whom he identified and whose names are listed in the Channel 4 dossier? Did he reveal anything about them which would lead us to challenge the subsequent judgement of RUC Detective Chief Superintendent Jimmy Nesbitt that some of these splendid citizens are nothing less than the aristocrats of Ulster?

Fortunately, Sands provided us with more than sufficient information on both the conspiracy and the conspirators to undermine the entire "recantation" and the associated cover-up. His detailed revelations, recorded in Lurgan in March and April 1991, blow apart the RUC-orchestrated cover-up of the Committee's murder conspiracy. Having presented the reader with copious extracts from the transcripts of Sands's "recantation," I will now quote extensively from the 1991 conversations to show the dramatic contrast between the two versions of events. It will then be clear that Nesbitt and his team protected the murder conspirators and, as we shall see later, enabled the Committee to remain in existence and to plan the resumption of its assassination campaign. This is what Sands told us in 1991 about some of the leading members of the Committee:

Robin Jackson (The Jackal)

Somebody pulled up at The Jackal this morning and asked him could he come down to the Seagoe Hotel in Portadown. And he went down this morning, it must have been round about ten-thirty or eleven o'clock this morning. And he was handed a file with copied papers on John McCann. He was told that that was the man that planted the bomb yesterday morning.[13] And he was told that certain people would look very favourably if he was removed; that's the way it was put, that certain people would look very favourably if he was removed.

The Jackal is meeting his squad tonight to discuss it. He's meeting his squad of people tonight to make arrangements. The contact from the Inner Force tomorrow . . . so that they can work together with the Inner Force on safe roads in and safe roads out.

[BH: Do you know The Jackal quite well then?]

Yes. We go a long time back, go a long time.

Graham Long

There's another fella that was involved with the killing of Adrian Caroll in Armagh, a fella called Graham Long. He's ex-SAS; he's a Loyalist. He has worked with the Loyalists through British Intelligence. He was involved with the killing of Adrian Caroll. Now there's four UDR men in prison at the moment for that.

[BH: But it was actually done by The Jackal and Graham Long?]

No. The Jackal didn't do that, now; it was a squad came from Armagh. Davy Paine, he's in jail now, he was actually bringing guns from Graham Long's house. Those UDR men were picked up for it for political reasons but British Intelligence wanted somebody quick before the finger would point too long at Graham Long, because British Intelligence through Graham Long was getting certain Republicans removed. So they wanted Graham Long protected.

[BH: Is Graham Long from England?]

He's originally from Belfast but he lives outside Tandragee now, just outside Portadown, on the Armagh side of Portadown. He was involved, through British Intelligence, in the organisation of the assassination of Adrian Carroll. He was involved in that, in bringing the people in from Belfast to do it and bringing them out again. That was his job. And British Intelligence had to protect him, that was why they had to get somebody quick. The police were going to bring him into Gough Barracks but somewhere along the line they were stopped; policemen were going to bring him into Gough Barracks to question him on it but somewhere along the line word came down that, no, so probably British Intelligence were pulling strings somewhere to stop it.

[*Next, Sands discusses how an RUC Special Branch man, called "Bertie" colluded with Loyalists, including The Jackal, to target the owner of the mobile sweet shop, John Jenkinson. Three innocent Catholics were murdered in this attack. See Chapter 4, pp. 51–53.*]

[BH: Just tell me again what you were telling me earlier about Robin meeting this guy [*"Bertie"*] this morning.]

They met him this morning to discuss John McCann. He was supposed to have blown up David Jameson yesterday.[14] They had a file of photocopied papers and Robin was to meet his squad tonight.

[BH: And this file was the file of details about the man, McCann?]

It's police files. There's photocopies of his description, his address, some safe houses that he would be in, his movements.

William (Billy) Abernethy

There's another man coming today as well. Now, he's not supposed to be known. He's actually the third highest man in the Ulster Bank in Northern Ireland. (*At this point in the conversation, Sands chose not to use Abernethy's name; he only did so later, when he came to describe the history of Ulster Resistance.*)

[BH: And what does he do?]

He would be something like the Loyalist equivalent of Gerry Adams. Nothing happens except it goes through him, militarily or politically.

[BH: In the whole Resistance?]

In the whole of Northern Ireland. In the whole of Ulster.

[BH: What? Even down to the guy who was killed in the bakery the other day?]

Yeah, everything goes through him.

[BH: And how's he becoming involved at the moment?]

He's coming down tonight to meet Robin. That'll be sure to give it the official go-ahead.

[BH: Right. And then what are they doing tomorrow?]

[John McCann] He'll probably go and be buried inside two weeks. Robin will check it out. It'll be done very professionally. Then the Inner Force, then, will meet to sort of give the go-ahead when they can go, so that they can have roads cleared, road blocks removed and things like that, so he'd have a clear road in and a clear road out.

John McCullagh (Ulster Resistance) and Billy Abernethy

There's a fella called John McCullagh. He's from Ballynahinch, outside Lisburn. He would be the main man [in Ulster Resistance]. He
took over from Charlie Watson. You see this whole idea came about
through Charlie Watson; Charlie Watson is a folk hero in Ulster. He
was ex-UDR and ex-RUC Reserve and he was very prominent in
the Orange [Order], the Black [Preceptory], Apprentice Boys, the
Masonic. He was very prominent within the political parties and he
supported Ulster Independence. He was murdered by the IRA four,
five, maybe six years ago. He lived in Clogh outside Newcastle, Co.
Down. He actually had a group around him, from that sort of north
Down, middle north Down area, parts of south Down where there'd
be disgruntled RUC men. And he had sort of grouped together, sort
of, it was his idea of bringing all the Loyalist groups together. He
actually started the Ulster Resistance, bringing all these groups,
bringing the groups within Co. Down together. When he died, then,
Colin Abernethy—he was murdered on the train going to work from
Lisburn, that's about '86, '87—he was treasurer of the Ulster Clubs,
he took over from Charlie Watson and his idea was the same, to
bring all Loyalist groups together under one banner, politically and
military. When he was killed on the train, so his brother took over,
Billy Abernethy. Now you never heard that name![15]

[BH: OK.]

That's the man I was telling you about from the Ulster Bank.
He works in the Ulster Bank headquarters in Belfast. He's the
third highest man in the Ulster Bank in Northern Ireland. He lives
in Lisburn and he carried on the work of bringing everyone
together. He had connections with UVF, UDA, so with a lot of
the UDA leadership inside, Tommy Little, people like that all
inside, Jackie McDonald they're all inside, so it was very easy to
bring the UDA into it.

[BH: Into?]

The Ulster Resistance, it's an umbrella, you see the UDA will
have four representatives on the Ulster Resistance Council.

[BH: So the Ulster Resistance has its own council?]

Yes, yes. There would be, then, the UVF will have so many representatives, the Protestant Action Force, the Ulster Freedom
Fighters.

[BH: I thought the Protestant Action Force were the UVF?]

Not really. They're separate organisations. Robin Jackson
would be UVF but Billy Wright would be Protestant Action
Force. That's why there are two groups in the area working
because they are, you know, both different organisations.

[BH: The UVF claims the things Billy Wright does, don't
they?]

No. Protestant Action Force claims them.

[BH: The UVF claimed Cappagh, didn't they?]

Yes. But it was Billy Wright. [Laughs] That happens regular, you know, happens regular. It throws the police off the scent. That's why it's done, deliberate. In other cases, it's done deliberate. They claimed it for the UVF, well the UVF, they don't mind, it's good publicity for them. So then the police would be looking for the UVF squad, but they would then have an alibi.

Everything is controlled by a central council, with so many representatives from the Ulster Independence Party would be on the political welfare side, with so many representatives from Ulster Resistance, making sure that the UDA has a voice, UVF, Protestant Action Force, UFF all have voices. But there are so many representatives from Ulster Resistance, Ulster Independence Party and so many representatives from the Inner Force. They would be, sort of, overall control.

[BH: And what's the name of that council?]

It's the Loyalist Central Co-ordinating Committee. Billy Abernethy is Chairman.

[BH: And they meet once a month?]

They meet roughly about once every six weeks, just to discuss how things are going.

[BH: When's the next meeting?]

The next meeting will be end of April, no date set yet, probably the last Saturday in April in Dungannon.

[BH: Where do they meet?]

Inn on the Park, Dungannon. [BH: Inn on the Park?] Hotel, Dungannon. It's a Loyalist hotel, it's owned by the Orange Order.

So far, we have seen that Sands had told Ben an awful lot more about Robin Jackson, Graham Long, John McCullagh and Billy Abernethy than he had admitted during his interviews with the RUC. Contrary to what the RUC would subsequently claim, after recording his rehearsed "recantation," Sands had made it crystal clear to Ben that the Ulster Independence Committee was a totally separate and distinct body from the Ulster Loyalist Central Co-ordinating Committee, the umbrella organisation running the assassination campaign and chaired by Billy Abernethy. Sands had explained at some length how Abernethy had emerged as the top man in Loyalist terrorism and how he had personally to sanction every Loyalist killing, such as the one he had come to Portadown to discuss with Robin Jackson on that night, in April 1991, when Sands was talking to Ben. Naturally, Sands told a very different story to the RUC when he was guided through his "recantation" in December 1992—as this excerpt shows:

Q: Did you tell them, that is the TV production team, that Billy Abernethy was the chairman of the Committee, now as distinct from the UIC, the Committee, did you tell them that Billy Abernethy was the Chairman of that?

A: No.
Q: You didn't?
A: No. We never went into, in connection with the Central Co-ordinating Committee, we never actually went into office bearers or anything like that, it didn't come out till the actual Saturday of this programme.
Q: You never told them that Billy Abernethy was the chairman of the Committee?
A: No.
Q: Did you tell them at any stage, if you can remember this, that he was maybe the Chairman of the UIC?
A: I told them that he was the Chairman of the UIC in Portadown.
Q: But not the Committee?
A: Not the Committee.

Leaving aside the question whether, in April 1991, Sands had been merely recycling rumours or telling Ben the truth as he understood it, the extracts already quoted are sufficient to prove that the RUC's tape-recorded "recantation"—the basis of the RUC's "hoax" verdict—is worthless. For Sands's account of Billy Abernethy's rise to prominence within Ulster Resistance, the Ulster Independence Committee and the quite separate terrorist umbrella organisation—the Committee—contradicts his assurance to the RUC that he had not identified Abernethy as the Chairman of the Committee. Our tape-recording also falsifies Sands's claim that he had hoaxed Ben into believing that the Committee's membership was solely and exclusively drawn from the Portadown Branch of the UIC, where he was branch secretary. The assassin Robin Jackson, for example, was a member of the Committee but did not belong to the UIC.

So what do the April 1991 tape-recordings reveal about the other Category A Committee members listed in the Channel 4 dossier? Did Sands provide the same information about them to Ben over dinner at the Silverwood Hotel that he subsequently gave his RUC handlers in December 1992? Did he, for example, also tell Ben that he knew Billy Wright, the notorious King Rat, simply "by reputation and to see?"

Billy Wright
The following extract, taken from Ben's first conversation with Sands on April 8th 1991, deals with the failed assassination attempt on local Sinn Féin councillor Brendan Curran. Mr. Curran, though shot and seriously injured by King Rat is—as we saw in Chapter Seven—one of the very few targets to have survived an operation sanctioned by Abernethy's Committee, an attack carried out with the operational assistance of the RUC Inner Force. Let us recall what Sands told Ben about King Rat's role in this attack.

And then Brendan Curran, he always went to his mother's house every Sunday night.

[BH: He told me he didn't. I went and talked to him.]

According to the police, according to the Inner Force, he did. They followed him. They set that one up. The Inner Force set it up.

[BH: And did they do it themselves?]

No.

[BH: Do the Inner Force ever do killings themselves?]

No.

[BH: They use Billy and . . .?]

They use whatever squad is about.

[BH: So they ring up and see who is around?]

They followed, for about five or six weeks, they followed him. Then they had men staking out the house as well.

[BH: What, the Inner Force did?]

The Inner Force had men staking out the house. Then they brought King Rat in and out.

[BH: Are you involved in either of those two groups? (*The groups around King Rat and The Jackal*)]

No.

[BH: But you're friends of theirs or. . .?]

I went to school with Billy.

So much for the claim that he knew Billy Wright simply "by reputation and to see."[16] Earlier in their conversation, Sands had given Ben a detailed account of the Committee-approved attack at Cappagh a few weeks earlier.[17] Once again, we can see that there is a dramatic difference between that account and what he subsequently stated in his "recantation" to the RUC.

[BH: How did the RUC men who were on duty, what would their superiors have thought they were doing?]

Just patrolling. Probably their superiors were involved as well, with the Inner Force. So they would have been allowed.

[BH: And who were the people they brought in?]

That was the killer, King Rat.

[BH: He's some man, isn't he? He drove one car, did he?]

No.

[BH: Did he actually go there himself?]

He was there himself, yes.

[BH: So how was the team organised? How did they do that?]

They went in. They would go to the pub but the people in the pub seen them coming and they barricaded the door. Then there was a car drove up with men coming to the meeting of the East Tyrone brigade. And they just shot those ones in the car.

[BH: So why did they need three cars to take the team in?]

They didn't know who they were going to meet. They were

expecting a shoot-out. They were expecting the IRA to have men around the pub.

[BH: Gosh, it could have been quite a big battle. So how many men did they bring in?]

They had ten altogether, ten men. That was the whole Rat Pack.

[BH: Was it?]

The whole Rat Pack.

[BH: That lot has got nothing to do with Jackson's squad?]

No. [BH: Separate?] Separate.

[BH: They're much younger men, are they?]

King Rat would be thirty. The rest of the pack would be between nineteen and twenty-four.

[BH: Who was involved in the shooting?]

The whole squad.

[BH: Did men not see four cars go in, obviously not?]

It was a country area.

[BH: I'm just wondering how one could try to establish the truth of what you're saying.]

[Laughter] Well, there's no, nothing actually put down. And the Inner Force as well, they like to keep themselves, probably, more than likely, the squad of men who went in, the Rat Pack, probably didn't even know who the two policemen [the two uni-formed RUC Inner Force officers] were. They probably had no contact, just they were picked up at the motorway roundabout, Dungannon, and were brought down to the pub and led back again, probably would never even have spoke.

[BH: So who looks after the King Rat? Is he protected then?]

He has protection, he has a certain amount of protection, from the Inner Force and from various other people.

[BH: Is there a man who's his handler or . . .?]

Yes. He gets, the usual police patrols, they would drive past his house. They keep an eye on him, the usual patrols. So people don't really realise how big the Inner Force actually is, how well. You see, it's only in the last two years that the Loyalists have been organised. You see, before, you would have had wee groups all over, doing their own wee thing. Now the Loyalists have been put into a central command, everything is now controlled.

On the basis of what Sands had told Ben at their first meeting, we can be totally confident in stating that the RUC "failed" completely to estab-lish the truth about our source's relationship with his friend and former school companion, Billy Wright. It ought to have been a simple matter for the sixteen police officers employed in the Nesbitt Inquiry to have discov-ered that Sands and Portadown's most notorious resident had spent years together in the same classroom at their primary school; the RUC would then have quickly learned that Sands knew Billy Wright not simply "by reputation or to see" but as a close friend who shared his chilling view on how best to deal with their perceived enemies. The scale of the RUC's "failure" in this respect becomes even clearer when we discover what Sands told Ben about Billy Wright a week later, during their second meeting at the Silverwood Hotel. After describing how Billy Wright had murdered Denis Carville with the help of members of the RUC Inner Force, Sands went on to provide a personal assessment of his friend's operating methods.

> Billy is very professional. When he goes out, it's always shirt and tie and suit. He actually goes to some of the funerals.
> [BH: Which ones?]
> The ones he does.
> [BH: Really? Did he go to any of the ones in Tyrone? *(The funerals for the four Cappagh victims)*]
> No, I don't think he went to any of those. He was going to go but I think he was advised not to. He's been in the chapel a few times, getting used to their forms of worship. [Laughter]
> [BH: He doesn't have a lot of time for that type of worship?]
> No. He puts, a lot of it is mental fear, putting a lot of mental fear. That's why he does a lot of driving about different estates, putting a lot of mental fear in people.
> [BH: He has been inside, hasn't he, when he was young?]
> Yes.
> [BH: About three times, hasn't he?]
> Could have. I know at least twice, anyway.
> [BH: At what age? What were they for?]
> I think they were mostly robberies or handling stolen goods. Wee small things.
> [BH: Nothing big?]
> No. He's only been in a few months and out again.
> [BH: I think he was in four years when he was sixteen.]
> He was in, I think he got a four-year sentence but I don't think he stayed the full [term], with remission and all, that was in the young offenders' centre, I think he got a year or so, fifteen or fourteen months, something like that.
> It was shortly after he came out after that, that he actually did his first killing. He was only about seventeen or maybe coming eighteen at the time he done the first one.

All of these extracts demonstrate that, if there had been any genuine desire on the part of the Nesbitt Inquiry to find out the truth, the investigating officers would have been able quickly to establish that Sands and King Rat knew each other very well; and they could not have seriously doubted that what Sands had said about his friend on the Committee had

been based on the two men's active participation in the murder conspiracy. So, having failed to extract any significant part of what Sands really
knew about Billy Abernethy, Graham Long, John McCullagh, Robin
Jackson and Billy Wright, how did the RUC fare with their questions
about the other Category A members of Abernethy's Committee? Did
Sands reveal to the RUC his true feelings about the President of the Ulster
Independence Party, Reverend Hugh Ross? It would appear not, on the
basis of what he told Ben in April 1991.

Reverend Hugh Ross, President, Ulster Independence Party
The Ulster National Party, Independence, they are the Ulster
hard-liners. Paisley would put himself to be a hard-liner but, in
reality, he just bluffs his way along. Well, his bluff is going to be
called by the Loyalist people. They're involved in talks now and
the only reason for the talks is a negotiation for a united Ireland
but Unionists have nothing to negotiate. And the Unionists are
looking for a way out of the talks. Well, the Unionists are going to
be blew away from the table. I wouldn't be surprised if Unionist
Party Headquarters are blew up some night, it wouldn't surprise
me if the DUP headquarters are blew up some night, it wouldn't
surprise me if Unionist politicians happened to be found with a
hood over their heads, with a bullet in the back of their head,
inside the next couple of months. And they'll be seen, the Ulster
National Party will be seen to be the hard-line Loyalist party, so
coming up to a June election or an autumn election, general election, they'll be standing in the elections against the likes of
Molyneaux and Paisley, if they are still living at the time. They are
the party, the hard-liners. No-one knows what Molyneaux and
Paisley are up to, everyone knows that they are betraying Ulster.
Protestants have a thing that, they see the British as their friends,
we're British. What these talks are going to show is that the British
are not our friends. The British want a united Ireland; the British
want to wash their hands of the whole affair. They want to negotiate a way into a united Ireland. Ulster Protestants will not accept
a country that is ruled by Rome. So the Ulster National Party can
play on that fear of being ruled by Rome and as well as showing
that Molyneaux and Paisley have been betraying Ulster, therefore
you will get a lot of votes. As well as that, people within the
Unionist Party are going to be afraid to stand against people from
the Ulster National Party in elections. Because like, are you going
to stand against Hugh Ross, knowing that it means certain death?
. . . Paisley will bluff for what he'll do but he never actually does
it. Whereas people like Hugh Ross, the Ulster National Party, will
not bluff and inside the next few months there'll be things happening in Ulster that will show that.

Anyone who tangled with Hugh Ross, according to what Sands had told Ben, risked "certain death." Source A was not exaggerating because, as Ross's factotum, he knew exactly what was going on within Ulster Loyalism and he appreciated his boss's fanatical devotion to their common cause.

[The Ulster Independence Party] will replace the Unionist Party within a few years' time.

[BH: And that's who the Resistance is working for, is it?]

Yes. The Resistance would be the military wing. It [UIC] would be Protestant Sinn Féin, just as you have Sinn Féin and the Provisional IRA, so you'll have the Ulster Independence Party, they'll change their name to the Ulster National Party. And Ulster Resistance will be the military wing.

[BH: And that includes the Inner Force people and this Ulster Bank guy?]

Yes.

[BH: Does Robin Jackson want an Independent Ulster?]

Yes.

[BH: And Billy Wright as well?]

Yes. It will be to their advantage.

[BH: If someone asked them, is that what they'd say?]

Probably would.

[BH: And the Inner Force people, they don't want to stay part of Britain?]

No. The way they look at it is that, at the moment, their hands are tied. The police's hands are tied, they know who the people are but they can't touch them. There's a lot of disillusioned policemen . . . The Ulster Independence Party puts on a nice respectable face, that it is against all forms of terrorism from both sides and a lot of people from the Inner Force that are that gullible, that gullible that they have been sucked in. But there are other people who know what they are doing. You see, the Inner Force is split into two; there's the Inner Force, which is just disgruntled members of the RUC; and then there's the Inner Circle which is the more militant Loyalist element in the Inner Force. The members of the Inner Circle would actually be the ones involved in the setting up the terrorists, the Loyalist squads.

[BH: So the Inner Force is just people who are unhappy about the way things are? Which group has the stronger links to the Independence Movement?]

The both really. A lot of people within the Inner Force would see an Independent Ulster as, at last, they would be free to be policemen. Their hands would be untied and they wouldn't be, they would be able to police in an impartial manner without having to look over their shoulders to the politicians . . . they should be able to police the same way no matter who is in power, no matter what political party is in power, that at the moment that doesn't happen.

So what Sands—the UIC's Portadown branch secretary—really believed about his boss, the Reverend Hugh Ross, was that the Presbyterian Minister liked to put on "a nice respectable face" and to keep his distance in public from the sordid side of his organisation's activities. But, in fact, the "innocent, peace-loving" clergyman was secretly engaged in eliminating "Ulster's enemies" and was, ironically, simultaneously adopting their political model by creating a Protestant Sinn Féin—Ulster Independence—together with an associated military wing similar to the IRA, Ulster Resistance; he was both a theoretician and a practitioner of Loyalist terror. Sands did not divulge a single word about any of this to his RUC handlers and, as a result, the 213-page official recantation transcript says scarcely a word about the Presbyterian Church's "Reverend" Jekyll or the Committee's Mr. Hyde.[18]

Sands was equally reticent in his RUC interview about all the other Category A members of Abernethy's Committee. His police handler took him through the names, one by one, prompting him to say whatever he judged appropriate. Throughout the recantation, Sands stuck to the position that as he had known nothing but rumours (presented as "facts"), that his role had been largely confined to "confirming" the truth of information provided to him by Ben. Sands emerges from the transcripts as a very different individual from the Loyalist fanatic who, back in 1991, provided us with an insight into life and death within "murder triangle" in County Armagh. His stunted vocabulary, his abrupt answers and his rigid adherence to a few simple themes, alongside questioning which gently nudges and pushes him along, give an overwhelming impression that he is carefully making his way through material with which he is familiar and which he has been rehearsed to answer in a particular manner. Consequently, he reveals little in his recantation, adopting the position that he had played a passive role in his dealings with Ben who—contrary to what we have seen in the extracts from 1991 already quoted—was supposed to have been the driving force in their conversations. The following passage illustrates the posture he adopted in his interview with the RUC.

> Q: What else did youse [sic] talk about then after these names and what have you, and he's [Ben] throwing names about and you were saying yea or nay or whatever. What else sort of?
> A: Well he talked about then, ah sort of a, structured organisation.
> Q: Yes.
> A: Or no, a structured group.
> Q: Okay.
> A: Where ah, terrorists, Loyalist terrorists and the police sat down together.
> Q: Yes.

A: To plan and discuss.
Q: Good. Right, go ahead.
A: Well, then again. Again, I gave him the impression that this was true.
Q: Uh huh. Was there any names given for this ah, grouping or whatever?
A: There was names of, he said they were policemen. There was names that ah, well said they were businessmen, some I knew.
Q: Uh huh. Can you remember any?
A: Well there was one, David Prentice.
Q: Yea.
A: From Portadown.
Q: Uh huh.
A: I knew him, know, being a businessman in Portadown.
Q: Yep.

David Prentice

Anyone who listens to our 1991 tape-recordings will realise, at once, that what Sands told the RUC in 1992 about the other Category A Committee members was totally untrue. For example, the above passage suggests that one of the names Ben was "throwing about" was that of the Portadown millionaire businessman, David Prentice. However, our tape of the April 1991 conversation reveals that it was Sands who divulged David Prentice's membership of the Committee; it would have been astounding if Ben had been able to do so, as he had been working on the project for just a few weeks and had arrived in the province for the first time not long before this recording was made. Sands, speaking in hushed tones, identified the two brothers who own Prentice Garages in Portadown.

Prentice, the motor people. David and Albert Prentice.

Sands made no further comment about these brothers during those early meetings with Ben but he subsequently confirmed their membership of the Committee, when we interviewed him in London. He also told us that David Prentice was extremely well-connected within the legal and political worlds though, unlike Nesbitt, Sands did not suggest that either brother belonged to the aristocracy of Ulster.

We have seen that Sands, when contrasting the supposedly dovish Ian Paisley with the hawkish Hugh Ross, compared the Ulster Independence Party to Sinn Féin. Our tape-recordings have preserved what he had to say about that.[19] But by December 1992, however, he was attributing this comparison to Ben and, as the transcript shows, his RUC handler guides him to a point where it is Ben who is credited with authorship of the idea of an [Ulster Loyalist] Central Co-ordinating Committee.

Q: You were talking about a structured organisation that Ben Hamilton mentioned . . . Tell me more about that or are you talking about the same thing?

A: No he, this was so far ah, what he talked, what he described as a Protestant Sinn Féin type organisation.

Q: Right, yes.

A: That ah, the UIC is sort of that type of organisation and that they were sort of some way involved.

Q: Using the UIC as what?

A: As sort of a political cover.

Q: For?

A: For killings.

Q: Right . . . So what you're saying is that you portrayed to him, and again correct me if I am wrong here, that the UIC was like a sort of a Sinn Féin organisation, giving political cover to Loyalist terrorists?

A: Yes.

Q: Right?

A: Yes. And ah, in amongst those Loyalist terrorists we had policemen and businessmen and . . .

Q: Yes. Alright. Is that fair to say that?

A: Yes. Yes.

Q: Right.

A: But a lot of that, he brought that up, but I didn't correct him on it.

Q: Yea. Uh huh. Was there any talk that at these meetings of the UIC that, there, specific plans were made to carry out killings, for example like, as you said, the Cappagh killings, or indeed the Sam Marshall killing?

A: No. Not within the UIC.

Q: Not within the UIC?

A: Not within the UIC. Nothing.

Q: So at no UIC meetings did this ever take place.

A: No. No.

Q: Was there ever any discussion about these plans being made at any sort of meetings?

A: Well at this sort of, grouping, that he, he called it the Central Co-ordinating Committee.

Q: Right. Yes. Tell me about the Central Co-ordinating Committee.

A: Now this was a, this was, he had this group. Now this was what he described it as, know, the Central Co-ordinating Committee.[20]

Q: And how does he describe it or what way was it?

A: Well he talked about and I gave him the impression that it, that it existed.

Q: Uh huh. Right. And what was this, what did this Central
Co-ordinating Committee do?
A: It was supposed to be where, a place where members of the
UIC, where Security Forces, businessmen, terrorists all met.
Q: Uh huh.
A: And so. Discussed things.
Q: For example?
A: Policies and killings, and policy.
Q: And killings?
A: And killings.

So Sands told the RUC that Ben had invented the concept of an Ulster
[Loyalist] Central Co-ordinating Committee, the organisation said to be
running the Loyalist death squads. And the RUC handler, guiding Sands
through the questioning, does not seek absolute precision from his captive
interviewee on the relative status of the UIC—Ross's political party—and
the ULCCC, Abernethy's Committee. This lack of precision is, however,
of no consequence because what Sands told the RUC was, as we know
from what he said to Ben in 1991, a total fabrication. Contrary to what he
said in his "recantation" and contrary to what the RUC chose to believe,
Sands had explained to Ben how he attended the regular sessions of
Abernethy's Committee, where he and fifty to sixty other Loyalists had
sanctioned and planned multiple murder in 1989, 1990 and 1991.

Brian/Trevor Forbes OBE, RUC Inner Force/Inner Circle
Sands did not divulge the names of the two Inner Force representatives,
both allegedly "Category A members" of Abernethy's Committee, until he
arrived for his interview in London in 1991. Once in front of the camera,
he proceeded to name Will Davidson as the Inner Force National
Representative—the nation being "Ulster"—and Ian Whittle as the Inner
Force Representative for Portadown, where he worked in the local RUC
Station. The only member of the Inner Force whom he had earlier identified to Ben, during their conversations in April 1991, was Trevor Forbes
OBE. Nesbitt subsequently confirmed to Channel 4 that Forbes had been
an RUC officer for thirty-eight years, had been Head of Special Branch
and an Assistant Chief Constable, as well as having been decorated for his
efforts in combatting—as opposed to promoting—terrorism. Obviously,
implied Nesbitt, such a distinguished police officer would not have participated in any of the activities which the "hoaxers" had included in their
fabricated programme. Nesbitt also told Channel 4, as we've seen, that
none of the other alleged RUC Inner Force personnel had ever existed.[21]
What did Sands tell the RUC about the Inner Force and Trevor Forbes?
The following extract, taken from the RUC transcript of Sands's interview
after his arrest, makes reference to the fact that Ben had sworn an affidavit

for the High Court in London; Ben had stated in this affidavit that Sands had told him that a Deputy Chief Constable in the RUC was the highest ranking officer in the Inner Force.

Q: It is alleged in the affidavits that you supplied names of Police Officers who were allegedly members of the secret Committee to the TV production team, did you in fact do so?

A: No.

Q: i.e. I'm talking about police officers who were allegedly members of the secret Committee.

A: No.

Q: Did you tell them or did they tell you that the Committee was composed of around sixty people?

A: They asked me roughly the strength of the Committee, roughly a figure and I said fifty to sixty.

Q: OK, so that information would in fact have been supplied by yourself?

A: Yes.

Q: . . . Did you inform any person connected with the programme, Ben Hamilton in particular, that a Deputy Chief Constable in the RUC was the highest ranking police officer in the Inner Force?

A: No.

Q: Did they suggest to you that a Deputy Chief Constable was the highest ranking officer in the Inner Force?

A: No, no. They only referred to this one man who they referred to as a high ranking Police Officer.

Q: The term Deputy Chief Constable, was it ever used in your presence?

A: No, it was never used.

Q: It was never used?

A: No.

Q: Did they refer to a person of a high rank by name?

A: They referred to Forbes.

Q: Did that come from you or did it come from them?

A: It come from them.

Q: So if Ben Hamilton, if Ben Hamilton was to make an affidavit stating that ah, that you had told him that there was a Deputy Chief Constable involved in the, in this Committee, the Central Committee, that would be untrue?

A: Yes.

Q: And if he were to make an affidavit to that effect, that it would be totally false?

A: Yes.

Q: You are certain?

A: Yes.

Q: Are you certain that you never told that to him?

A: Yes.
Q: You are certain about that?
A: Yes.
Q: Did he ever suggest it to you and you would have agreed to it?
A: No.
Q: OK.
A: No. There was no ranks.
Q: There was just reference to a senior police officer and the name Forbes was mentioned.
A: Yes, yes.
Q: OK.

When I read this exchange, I though that it had been very unwise of the RUC to seek such explicit answers, even though they had no intention of giving us a transcript of what Sands had said. For, as I shall now show, the above answers fell somewhat short of total accuracy. The following extract is taken from Sands's conversation with Ben on April 8th 1991.

[BH: In Lurgan and Portadown, the Inner Force are about ninety per cent [of the force]. Do they include the top officers in those places?]
Yes.
[BH: What, the very top?]
Yes. They need to, they need to, to be able to run the thing smoothly. I can give you a name at the very, very top but he is retired now.
[BH: Could you?]
Yes. Head of Special Branch in Northern Ireland.
[BH: You're joking!]
Yes, Brian Forbes.
[BH: You're joking!]
Now, he took early retirement or he was forced to take early retirement.
[BH: That was because of Stalker, wasn't it?]
No, not because of Stalker. It was round about the same time but he took early retirement because they found out he was actually very prominent within the Inner Force.
[BH: Do you think he would be prepared to talk about it?]
Very unlikely, he may do, you never know, he may do, he may do.
[BH: How do you know he was Head of Special Branch?]
I've met him. (*Nesbitt confirmed this at the Channel 4 meeting, when he confirmed that Sands had met Forbes in the past to discuss the rerouting of marches in Portadown.*)
[BH: You've met him?]
Yes.
[BH: And he told you?]

Yes. He was the Head of Special Branch in Knock Headquarters. He gave a lot of his information to Frazer Agnew. He's Mayor of Newtownabbey Council now, he's an Official Unionist.

[BH: He's an Official Unionist?]

He's the Mayor of Newtownabbey Council.

[BH: And how is he involved then? Is he involved in the Resistance, then, no?]

Well, he had connections with various groups.

[BH: What, paramilitary?]

Yes. But he wouldn't tell you that. You know the way the Unionist people are, nice people. *(Sands's tone of voice makes it clear that he is being sarcastic about how the "respectable" Ulster Unionists manage to keep their distance from their Loyalist terrorist friends.)*

[BH: But how do you know . . .?]

Brian Forbes gave a lot of his information to him because he trusted him.

[BH: And he used to give the information to the paramilitaries? Do you know what "hits" he was involved in giving information for?]

Every single file that was in Special Branch cabinets was photocopied and given out . . .

[BH: . . . to Frazer Agnew?]

Yes. Every single file. Anything that went into the filing cabinet was photocopied before it went in and Brian Forbes brought it out.

[BH: Really?]

So that's how big the Inner Force is. It goes to the very top of Special Branch. He was forced to take early retirement.

[BH: Who by?]

Political! People from the Northern Ireland Office because they had discovered that he was Inner Force. Different things came out from Stalker, found that he was involved with the Inner Force. But then to maintain what they'd always said, that there was no such thing as an Inner Force, they had to make a sacrifice. He got a wee handshake.

[BH: Did he?]

He got something like £50,000 in a handshake. It might have been more. Some people have said it was £150,000. He got a good handshake for taking early retirement. Plus all the benefits, he still gets all the benefits, you still have all the benefits.

[BH: Is he still involved?]

Yes.

[BH: With the Inner Force and the Resistance?]

Yes. You see, the Inner Force is made up of ex-RUC and RUC, it's made up of both and he still is involved. He has good connections within the force as well.

It would be difficult to construct two more diametrically opposed accounts than those between what Sands told Ben in April 1991 and what Sands told the RUC in December 1992. His detailed revelations about the Inner Force and the fact that this illegal body's tentacles reached to the very top of Special Branch undermine completely the subsequent "recantation" which, despite the efforts of his RUC handlers, gives a strong impression that a cowed and obedient Sands is repudiating that which he knows to be true and parroting that which he knows to be false, all in an effort to please those in charge of his fate. His second tape-recorded conversation with Ben is, arguably, even more damaging to this "official version" than the first; it is certainly enlightening about Forbes, the unnamed Assistant Chief Constable and about the RUC Inner Force, the RUC Inner Circle and their links to Ulster Independence, Ulster Resistance and Abernethy's Committee.

[BH: Is Forbes a member of the Inner Circle?]
Yes.
[BH: So it goes that high up, the Inner Circle?]
Well, he's actually retired now. Somebody who is an Assistant Chief Constable, don't know who he is, don't know the name, but he's involved, he's the highest ranking, that's why they couldn't put a Northern Ireland man in as Chief Constable. Impossible to do that because they didn't want a member of the Inner Force as Chief Constable.[22]
[BH: Inner Force or Inner Circle?]
Inner Force. You see, the British Government didn't want a member of the Inner Force as the Chief Constable. So they had to get someone from outside. (*Sands is referring to the fact that Sir Hugh Annesley was brought over from the Metropolitan Police in London to replace the Ulsterman, Sir John Hermon.*)
[BH: So how different are the Inner Force and the Inner Circle?]
Well, the Inner Circle is the more militant members of the RUC, of the Inner Force. They would be the ones that would be involved in terrorist activity.
[BH: Are they the ones who guide the hits?]
Yes. The Inner Force would be more or less disgruntled RUC members, who want everything done fairly, without political interference. And they are involved with the Inner Force. It started off as a sort of a pressure group within the RUC, it started off in about '85, '86 and sort of gradually built up. And then certain people seen that it could be used to their advantage. Then certain people moved in and took control of it.
[BH: How did they take control of it?]
Putting certain people into different positions. And it was more organised; before there were a lot of disgruntled policemen who

were disgruntled about being used for political reasons. They were not allowed to get on with their job as an impartial police force, that they were constrained by political decisions. And they were disgruntled, just groups of people in various police stations. When people seen that this could be used to their advantage and they brought in people who were more militant to come and take control. And to organise it more on police stations, bring the disgruntled policemen together.

[BH: So how is it organised in Lurgan? How are the disgruntled policemen organised together?]

Well, there would be a group of the Inner Force. Now they would be policemen based in Lurgan police station. Well, then there's overall control by a divisional committee. Lurgan would be part of J Division, so there would be a J Division committee to look after the affairs of J Division. So many representatives then from each police station, which makes up a committee.

[BH: This would be an unofficial Inner Force committee?]

Yes. And then they would sit on a J Division committee, and then there would be so many representatives from J Division would sit on the Ulster Council. That would be a representative of each Division. They would be in overall control of the Inner Force.

[BH: And who else would sit on the Ulster Council [of the Inner Force]?]

There would be observers from the Ulster Independence Party, there would be observers from Ulster Resistance, there would be roughly about four observers from Ulster Independence Party, four observers from Ulster Resistance and about twenty people from the Inner Force.

[BH: Are you one of those observers?]

Yes.

[BH: How often does the council meet?]

Once a month. Now there's, the way it's organised, the representatives from each police station would be more militant, sort of from the Inner Circle and, therefore, each Divisional committee would be militant and controlled by the Inner Circle and, therefore, the ruling body, the committee would be militant members of the Inner Circle.[23]

[BH: And who would the representatives of the Ulster Resistance be?]

There's a fella called John McCullagh. (See above p. 253)

These two extracts show that, within two weeks of their first meeting, Sands had explained to Ben in some detail how those in control of Loyalist terrorism, those responsible for the eighteen murders discussed in Chapter Seven, as well as many other murders committed in the period leading up to the ceasefires in August 1994, had subverted the Royal Ulster Constabulary, the British Government's most important security organisation in Northern Ireland. He had described how this unofficial, illegal Inner Force had emerged in the years since the signing of the Anglo-Irish Agreement in 1985, becoming a police force within a police force. With its own militant elite—the Inner Circle—this Inner Force owed its allegiance to Ulster Loyalism, which was represented on the controlling Inner Force Council by representatives of the Ulster Independence Party (Sands), Ulster Resistance (McCullagh) and also, presumably, the Chairman of the Ulster Loyalist Central Co-ordinating Committee and the most important figure in Loyalist terrorism, Billy Abernethy. This illegal police force within the RUC had its own distinct loyalties, agenda and priorities—which it furthered through systematic and widespread collusion with the Loyalist death squads.[24]

So, despite what Sands told the Nesbitt Inquiry, he had already admitted to Ben that he sat as an observer on the controlling body of this terrorist police force within the RUC. He was, therefore, speaking from a position of authority and experience when he had told us, in April and May 1991, that the Inner Force was able to draw on the services not merely of the ex-Head of Special Branch (Forbes) but of another, serving—though unnamed—Assistant Chief Constable as well. On this testimony, we must assume that the RUC's Chief Constable Sir Hugh Annesley would, unknowingly, have interacted on a regular basis with this unnamed individual and, further, we can reasonably conclude that the high-level intelligence available to the RUC Inner Circle would have flowed freely to the membership of Abernethy's Committee. Sands had, therefore, confirmed that a significant part of the RUC was, in effect, a terrorist organisation working for the Committee; a fact which, regrettably, entirely eluded the Stevens Inquiry team when it had investigated RUC/Loyalist collusion in 1989.

Sands had been able to give us such a comprehensive and accurate account of the murder conspiracy because he had access to some of the most secret and sensitive intelligence information in RUC files. His membership of the Ulster Independence Party in Portadown brought him into close contact with those planning a future for Northern Ireland outside the United Kingdom; his observer status on the RUC Inner Force Council brought him into regular contact with RUC officers working for the Committee; and his membership of the Committee itself enabled him to give us a first-hand account of the murders he had helped to plan. His firm grasp of the most intimate details of the conspiracy was, I believe, the reason why he had been able to discuss the personalities involved and to describe what had happened in the various attacks, without ever contradicting himself or appearing discomfited by any of our requests for explanation or elaboration. And it was the fact that he was so knowledgeable and so trusted by Abernethy, Ross, Monteith and the others that made his decision to talk on Channel 4 such a potentially catastrophic development for all concerned.

Sands and his family have been living under RUC protection ever since he and his family were moved out of Portadown, shortly after he was unmasked by the RUC in November 1992. He has been living at a secret location in Northern Ireland, kept under constant police surveillance so that the RUC does not have to worry about him deciding, for a second time, to talk to the likes of Ben Hamilton about the matters contained in his interview for *The Committee*. So, Sands is alive and well. And if there should ever be an independent inquiry into what he revealed to us in 1991 about the Committee, the RUC Inner Force and the RUC Inner Circle, I suggest that a good starting point for any investigation would be a fresh set of interviews with the man who helped us to break the story in 1991, Channel 4's Source A, "Reverend" Hugh Ross's political assistant and King Rat's old school friend, James Alfred Sands.

Since the Nesbitt Inquiry's "hoax" verdict rested largely on Sands's recantation, as laid out in the detailed 213-page transcript, we are able to dismiss that verdict as a deliberate attempt to discredit the programme, regardless of truth or justice. Since the RUC-inspired recantation has now been shown to be bogus, it follows that Sands's original allegations remain unanswered and that the murder conspirators have been protected by the RUC ever since the broadcast in 1991. The scandal we exposed on Channel 4 was unprecedented in that it revealed that a significant part of a British police force was running death squads. Now, we can see that the official response to the programme's revelations constitutes a new scandal; the British Conservative Government's failure to set up an independent inquiry and its cynical acceptance of the RUC's "hoax" verdict meant that those responsible for upholding the law and administering justice in Northern Ireland failed in their duty to apprehend and to prosecute the murder conspirators.

This official cover-up has now lasted for over six years. On August 1st 1992, RUC Chief Constable Sir Hugh Annesley denounced my statement that his force had been running death squads as "an outrageous allegation . . . without foundation;" and he repeated his pledge, given initially in October 1991, that the RUC would do everything possible to track down those responsible for the seven killings featured in the programme—the murders of Pat Finucane, Sam Marshall, Denis Carville and the four Cappagh victims, Dwayne O'Donnell, John Quinn, Malcolm Nugent and Thomas Armstrong. Yet, despite the Chief Constable's pledges, not one of these seven murders has been solved and there is no sign whatever that the

RUC, if left in charge of the investigation of these crimes, will ever place any of the culprits on trial. This remarkable failure to bring the conspirators to justice is not, of course, the result of any inability by the RUC to identify those responsible; the Chief Constable's "investigators" have, since October 1991, known the identities of at least nineteen Committee members—indeed they have long known the names of *all* the conspirators—as well as the identities of *all* the victims, including the names of the eighteen Catholics murdered by the Committee in 1989, 1990 and 1991, as described in Chapter Seven.

I have long accepted the fact that, left to itself, the RUC will suppress the truth about the Committee forever; that not one of those eighteen murders will ever be properly investigated or solved by the RUC itself. And I have also accepted that Jim Sands is not going to volunteer to come forward and admit that his elaborate "recantation" was bogus; we can be sure that the RUC will keep Sands under control and rely on the fact that, as time passes, media interest in long forgotten murders in Northern Ireland will wither until it has vanished entirely.

As the months and years since *The Committee* was broadcast passed, I nurtured hopes that I would somehow be able to persuade Channel 4 to complete the project on which we embarked together in early 1991; but, reluctantly and belatedly, I abandoned such hopes and came to accept that the network would not commission Box Productions to make another documentary based on the material I had uncovered about collusion; and I also realised that no other British broadcaster or newspaper, aware of Channel 4's traumatic experiences over *The Committee*, would dare to dip a toe into the quicksands of "murder triangle" a second time. So, the choice I faced, in late 1993, was either to forget about the Committee and the "unsolved" murders it had organised, to drop the story as Channel 4 had chosen to do, or to persevere. I decided to carry on.

Notes

1   Nesbitt letter to D.J. Freeman, solicitors to Channel 4, February 1993.
2   See Chapter 9, pp. 186–192.
3   Channel 4 had insisted from an early stage that we should not say anything in public about the controversial issues arising from the broadcast. This had also been the message from our lawyers, who warned of the dangers of committing contempt of court through commenting about matters which were the subject of legal action.

4 Although we gave in to none of his demands, Ross wisely decided not to make good his threats—most probably because he knew he would find himself in the witness box, where he would have to testify on oath about what Sands had said about his role in the murder conspiracy.

5 See Chapter 15, p. 356 and Appendix 1.

6 See Chapter 12, pp. 291–4.

7 Ian Birrell had co-authored with Liam Clarke some of the earlier, hostile articles in *The Sunday Times*. Patricia McDaid's name appeared on just one article. [See Chapter 9, pp. 180–3]

8 We can only speculate how Sands was treated, at least initially, after his arrest in November/December 1992. The transcript of his subsequent "recantation" suggests that he was coaxed and cajoled during his later "interrogations"—as we shall see later in this chapter.

9 McDaid's revelations made me realise that Nesbitt was prepared to take considerable risks to protect the murder conspirators; I later learned that Quinn was not the only programme contributor "roughed up" by Nesbitt— journalist John Coulter was given similar treatment at the RUC Castlereagh Detention Centre. [See Chapter 14]

10 This answer suggests that the Armagh commander of Ulster Resistance, the man whom Abernethy had introduced to Ben Hamilton in 1991, was Graham Long; Ben was not given a name during the meeting.

11 Although, as I later learned, the Nesbitt Inquiry had interviewed a Cecil Kilpatrick after the broadcast, this RUC transcript does not correct the misspelling which, I believe, resulted from the fact that Sands suffers from a slight speech impediment.

12 In fact, Cecil Kilpatrick was a member of the Portadown branch of the Ulster Independence Party which Sands, as Portadown branch secretary for eight years, would presumably have known.

13 I have no reason to believe the truth of this allegation about John McCann who, according to Sands, was a member of the Provisional IRA in County Armagh.

14 I have no evidence to support Sands's claim about this IRA murder of UDR officer, David Jameson.

15 Charlie Watson, a former UDR soldier and prison officer, was murdered (in front of his wife and ten-year-old child) by the IRA at his home in Clogh, County Down in May 1987. His successor in creating the Loyalist umbrella organisation (which evolved into the Committee), Colin Abernethy (aged 29), was also murdered by the IRA just over a year later, in September 1988. At that point, according to Sands, Billy Abernethy took over his brother's role. The Watson family did not, however, fade from the scene; Charlie Watson's 32-year-old brother, Delbert Ivor, was involved in the murder of a Catholic businessman, Jack Kielty, in January 1988—a crime for which he was convicted and given a life sentence; his sister-in-law Doreen, Charlie Watson's widow, was convicted of manslaughter for her role in the Kielty killing. Q: The solicitor who represented Delbert Watson at his trial? A: The Committee's solicitor, Richard Monteith.

16 See this Chapter, p. 248.
17 Sands gave us an identical account of the Cappagh killings, when we filmed an interview with him in London in 1991. [See Chapter 4, pp. 53–56]
18 In July 1995, Ross was secretly photographed at a meeting of the Committee, attended by Abernethy and other leading conspirators. Ross was photographed talking to various Loyalist paramilitaries, including a close associate of Billy Wright, Alex Kerr.
19 See this Chapter, p. 260.
20 Compare this with what Sands told Ben in 1991—see this Chapter, p. 254.
21 Ian Whittle, the person whom Sands identified as the RUC Inner Force representative in Portadown certainly does exist. One of my informants sent me a death notice from the *Belfast Telegraph*, dated June 7th 1995. The death notice reads: "WHITTLE, EDITH—July 6, 1995 (peacefully) . . . Funeral from the residence of her son, Ian . . . [the notice then prints Ian Whittle's address in Portadown.]
22 This is Sands's explanation as to why Hugh Annesley was appointed as RUC Chief Constable in succession to Trevor Forbes's former boss, Sir John Hermon.
23 Some months after we had learned from Sands of the existence of the RUC Inner Circle, we managed to secure an interview with one of these Loyalist police officers. We commissioned journalist John Coulter to conduct the interview on our behalf. [See Chapter 5, p. 74 and Appendix 4]
24 Sands admitted to us in 1991 that he did not know the identity of the Inner Circle's most senior serving member within the RUC, the Assistant Chief Constable. Several years later, another Committee member, Ken Kerr, sought to mislead me about the identity of this man. [See Chapter 14]

Chapter 12

Flaws and Slip-Ups

From late 1993 until I finished this book in early 1998, I have pursued two quite different strategies in my attempt to bring my investigation of collusion to a successful conclusion. Although it seemed inconceivable that, given what had befallen Sands, I would ever succeed in persuading a second member of the Committee to talk to me, I nonetheless believed that I had—as my first strategy—to try to achieve just that; consequently, I spent a good part of the past five years edging my way closer and closer to the centre of the murder conspiracy, never doubting for a moment that what Sands had initially told us was true, but occasionally asking myself whether it was worth the effort to persist with such a costly and unpromising enterprise, week after week, month after month, year after year.

Eventually and against all rational expectations I managed to arrange a meeting, in April 1996, with a middle-aged, softly-spoken man who—once I had explained who I was and what I wanted—frankly admitted to me that he had been, like Jim Sands, a full member of the murder conspiracy. Naturally, given my desire to learn everything I possibly could about the Committee, I had readily agreed to this man's demand for absolute confidentiality; I assured him that, *if his offer of assistance was genuine*, I would never disclose his identity to the authorities, not even if I was again dragged in front of Lord Woolf and Mr. Justice Pill. It *seemed* that my first strategy had, against the odds, paid off in that I had found a second source on the Ulster Loyalist Central Co-ordinating Committee; our initial, brief meeting, which took place at a hotel bar in Derry, ended with the source confirming that Sands had told the truth in 1991 and promising to provide supplementary details on the murder conspiracy. Source B, as I chose to call him, would have remained anonymous but since it became evident, beyond dispute, that his only loyalty was to his co-conspirators on the Committee and that he had been deliberately giving me false information, I have no qualms about identifying him as Ken Kerr. His elaborate attempt at deception will be described later.[1]

My second strategy, which I pursued simultaneously with the first, was

to try to demonstrate the truth of Source A's original revelations by exposing the flaws in the RUC cover-up and the confusions in the associated
dirty tricks campaign against us. It often happens in conspiracy cases—
Watergate being the classic example in modern times—that those who spin
the tangled web of deceit become ensnared in their own inconsistencies,
contradictions and falsehoods; and when the cover-up begins to unravel,
the official denials—Nixon: "I'm not a crook;" Annesley: "An outrageous
allegation"—only serve to confirm the truth of the original allegations. In
the Watergate affair, the White House managed to suppress the embarrassing details until President Nixon had been safely re-elected; but, after
his election, when the cover-up began to come apart, unexpected evidence
(in the form of tape-recordings) emerged to show that Nixon had known
about the Watergate burglary from the start. In *The Committee* affair, the
RUC also managed to suppress the truth; but, ironically, this cover-up
would also be undermined by the existence of tape-recordings. For, as we
have seen, the taped conversations between Jim Sands and Ben Hamilton,
which have still not been given to the RUC, totally undermine the "official" recantation and demolish the "hoax" verdict that formed the basis of
the cover-up. As a result, Source A's revelations remain unanswered and,
as we shall see, they do so for a very good reason: because they are, each
and every one of them, absolutely true.

So—even if, for the moment, we leave to one side what can legitimately be inferred from Ken Kerr's efforts to mislead me about the
Committee—we can safely dismiss Sands's "recantation" as an elaborate,
RUC-inspired fabrication; and, consequently, we can regard the original
allegations contained in *The Committee* as having been reinstated and, in
early 1998, as remaining unanswered. This raises further questions:

a) is there any evidence—independent of Sands—to corroborate
part or all of what he told us back in 1991?

b) aside from the transcript of Sands's "recantation," are there
any other RUC documents that suggest the truth of the original
allegations or which tend to undermine Nesbitt's "hoax" verdict?

c) have any of those identified by Sands as members of
Abernethy's Committee acted in a manner which, since 1991, has
thrown light on their past conduct and alleged participation in the
Committee's murder conspiracy?

d) Is there any independent evidence to show that Sands, contrary to what the RUC told Channel 4, was in 1991 a trusted con-
fidant of the "respectable" citizens whom he identified as his
co-conspirators in the Committee's assassination campaign?

(a) Corroboration from California
One of the murders featured in *The Committee* was that of Sam

Marshall, who was shot dead shortly after he and two friends had left Lurgan RUC station in March 1990. In summary: the programme reported that the town's Catholic community had accused the RUC of collusion but that no evidence had been produced to justify their claim. That remained the position until Source A agreed to give us the inside story of how the Committee had organised the murder. As we've seen, it contained an extract in which Sands described how two off-duty RUC Inner Force officers from Lurgan police station had teamed up with the Loyalist squad, including Robin Jackson [The Jackal], to carry out the attack; one RUC officer had been in the red Maestro, the other in the red Rover, along with Jackson; while the three Republicans were inside the RUC station, two of the Maestro's occupants had hidden in the sentry box outside the building. Sands also described what happened some days after the killing, when the Committee met to discuss why the squad had failed to kill all three men, rather than Sam Marshall alone.

Sands's account, as the reader is also aware, was subsequently dismissed by the RUC as a total fabrication; Nesbitt concluded that Sands's televised version of the killing, revealing the nature of the collusion that had led to the murder, had supposedly been part of a prepared script given to Sands by Ben and me before the interview in London. The RUC transcript of Sands's "recantation" about the Marshall killing makes this clear:

> Q: And anything that was written down, you answered it, to obviously Ben Hamilton's eventual satisfaction . . . Right, so they spent some considerable time getting the Sam Marshall one right?
> A: Yes, yes.
> Q: OK, was there anything of any significance he wanted you to emphasise on that there, or bring out or . . .
> A: To bring out that the police car, cars came out of the police station and that done the killing and went back in again after the killing.
> Q: Right.
> A: And that when the men were walking out that the actual killers were in the sentry box, you know, at the police station.
> Q: So, in other words, what they wanted to do was to try and emphasise the fact that there was evidence which would suggest that police were actually involved in the Sam Marshall killing?
> A: Yes.
> Q: . . . as far as the Sam Marshall killing was concerned was to try and emphasise the fact that there was police involvement?
> A: Yes.

Fortunately, we are again able to dismiss this part of the "recantation" because it is directly contradicted by what Sands told Ben in one of their earliest conversations, recorded on April 8th 1991. Contrary to what

Sands was prompted to say by his police "interrogator," the account of how RUC officers had colluded in the Marshall murder had been initially provided, not by Ben but by Sands himself. Our tape-recordings reveal that Sands knew the inside story of how the attack had been planned; they show that he was able to tell Ben that the Loyalists had been tipped off about the bail signing times by the RUC officer in charge of Lurgan police station, RUC Inner Force member, Inspector Alan Clegg.

[The Jackal] was tipped off that Sam Marshall would be going to the police station inside a certain time. So he just sat; there was an off-duty policeman sat in the back seat of the car pointing the man out, when he was coming out of the police station.

[BH: I mean it didn't seem like The Jackal. The shots went all over the street, didn't they? It wasn't as accurate as the other ones.]

Well, you never know with The Jackal. [laughter] He was trying to hit as many as he could hit.

[BH: But he only got one, didn't he?]

Only got one. He was in a bad mood because he didn't get the other two. Well, the gun actually jammed, the gun jammed . . .

[BH: Who was in the Maestro?]

That was part of The Jackal's gang. There was an off-duty policeman with them. They hadn't decided whether to hit him going to the police station or coming out from the police station. You see, there was too much traffic. They were actually going to hit him but there was too much traffic to get away, so they decided then they'd hit him coming out.

[BH: So the off-duty policeman was in the Maestro, not the Rover?]

There was two off-duty policemen, one in each car.

[BH: What, Lurgan off-duty policemen, from the Inner Force, obviously?]

Yes.

[BH: Who could have told them what time the bail, I understood bail times were kept very secret?]

He had to be there at certain hours, he had to be there from four to six, you know . . .

[BH: But I understood it was negotiated by the solicitor and then an Inspector. Well, that Inspector must have told them mustn't he?]

Yes.

[BH: Is he in the Inner Force?]

Yes. Lurgan is ninety per cent Inner Force.

We should recall that Sands also told Ben that he sat as an observer on the RUC Inner Force Council, a position he enjoyed due to his status within Ross's Ulster Independence Party. So when, in reply to Ben's question, he confirmed that Inspector Alan Clegg was a member of the Inner Force and had tipped off Robin Jackson about the time of the bail signing, he was doing so as a member of the highest level of command within this terrorist branch of the RUC. Whether he was fully aware of what he was saying or not, Sands was accusing RUC Inspector Alan Clegg of participating in the murder of Sam Marshall.

So it is clear that, despite the "recantation" and the reassuring verdict of the Nesbitt Inquiry, Sands had been consistent in his accounts of the Marshall murder, which he gave during his filmed interview in London and during his dinner conversation with Ben some weeks earlier in Lurgan. His inside story of the killing provided details which had never before appeared anywhere else. Specifically, he claimed that the two cars—the red Maestro and the red Rover—had each contained an Inner Force officer and that, as witnesses to the shooting had claimed, the three Republicans had been under surveillance from the moment they left their homes to walk to the police station; and he also revealed the fact that the two men in the external security post had earlier been in the Maestro, where they had been hoping to find an opportunity to attack and kill all three Republicans, even before they arrived to sign on for bail at the RUC station.

Sands's two accounts of the Marshall killing are, therefore, entirely consistent with each other. But that does not necessarily mean that they are true; before we can accept them as an accurate version of events, we need to find independent corroboration of one or more of the exclusive components of his story. And this is exactly what we managed to obtain when we studied transcripts of a court case in California which, to our great surprise, centred on precisely these allegations of collusion by the RUC in the Marshall murder. They had been made in court by lawyers acting for an IRA member, who had escaped from prison in Northern Ireland and fled to the United States; in November 1993, his lawyers were fighting an attempt by the British Government to have him extradited back to the province to complete his jail sentence.[2] They argued that the revelations in *The Committee* about Sam Marshall's murder had demonstrated that their client's life would be in jeopardy, if the court were to decide to send him back to Northern Ireland. The British Government fielded a high-level team to fight the case, including the most senior civil servant in the Northern Ireland Office, Sir John Chilcot, as well as nine or ten RUC officers, including RUC Inner Force Inspector Alan Clegg.

Inspector Clegg was cross-examined under oath by the IRA man's lawyers and was asked about the status of the red Maestro car—license plate KJI 1486—which had been seen before and after the shooting by local residents and other witnesses to the murder. By November 1993, the

RUC's Chief Constable had already gone on record about this red Maestro, stating that it had been eliminated from police enquiries into the murder; the Chief Constable had confirmed this in reply to a letter from British Labour MP, Mr. Terry Fields, who had written to him on behalf of the Marshall family. By that time, of course, the RUC had officially dismissed all Sands's revelations as sheer invention and had, therefore, not felt it necessary to issue a specific refutation of Sands's claim that the red Maestro had contained an off-duty Inner Force officer and had been part of an official surveillance operation on the three Republicans. So, we might have expected that Inspector Clegg, when cross-examined in California, would have sided with his Chief Constable rather than with the supposedly discredited "hoaxer" (Sands). Surprisingly, Inspector Clegg—whom, as we've seen, Sands had accused of collusion in the Marshall murder—conceded that this key aspect of Sands's testimony had been correct. He confirmed that the red Maestro had indeed been a security force car and that it had been on surveillance duty at the time of the murder. The cross-examination continued:

> Q: Now, the two men who were with Mr. Marshall at the time of his death, were interviewed by the police shortly after; were they not?
>
> A: They certainly, they named two cars, Your Honour, but the direct association with the murder, I don't think was as clear as that.
>
> Q: Well, one car was a red Rover, and that's the one that was carrying the gunman; isn't that true?
>
> A: That is correct.
>
> Q: And the other that they told you about was a red Maestro with a license plate of KGI 1486, and they told you that that car had been following them before the murder; isn't that true?
>
> A: They'd seen it in the area of fire, Your Honour.
>
> Q: And, in fact, they told you that it was an undercover police car?
>
> A: That was their . . . they made that allegation.
>
> Q: And they told you that they believed that they had been followed for the preceding few days, as well, and that they'd seen that car following them; isn't that true?
>
> A: That's correct, Your Honour.
>
> Q: Now, the police traced the Rover, despite the fact that witnesses . . . had gotten a couple of the letters or numbers in the license plate wrong; isn't that true? They gave you a number, and it turned out to be slightly off?
>
> A: That's correct . . . [*The Rover had been stolen a few days before the killing and was found burnt-out after the killing, forty-five miles down the motorway from Lurgan.*]

Q: Now, reading through your report, I note that after the history of the Rover is traced . . . there's no discussion of what happened, whether there were any efforts made to trace the Maestro? Did you make efforts to trace the Maestro, Sir?

A: Of course that was part of the investigation, every allegation made, every unidentified vehicle that came into investigation were traced, or as far as possible traced, and that the Maestro did become part of the, obviously the investigation.

Q: Well, can you tell us why there's nothing about the tracing of the Maestro in your report?

A: I can't answer the question.

Q: And could you state for the record why you can't answer it, please?

A: It's part of the *national security*. [my emphasis]

Q: That car belonged to the police, didn't it, Inspector Clegg?

A: The car did not belong to the police, Your Honour.

Q: It was associated with the police; wasn't it, sir?

A: The vehicle, Your Honour, there was a number of surveillance operations going on in the Lurgan area because of an upsurge in terrorism in the area, and a course, or as a reaction to that, there would be surveillance going on in relation to a number of suspects or suspect terrorists, both from the Protestant paramilitary side and on the Provisional IRA side.

Q: Sam Marshall was under surveillance by the police at the time of the murder; wasn't he?

A: There was a general surveillance operation going on in the Lurgan area which included a number of people.

Q: And he was being surveilled by people in that red Maestro that eyewitnesses saw within seconds of his murder?

A: The *vehicle certainly was involved in a surveillance operation*, Your Honour, but he was not the target on that particular evening. I don't know who the target was, but there was general surveillance on, and the vehicle was not in the vicinity of the shooting when it took place. [my emphasis]

Inspector Alan Clegg's testimony in California is highly significant. For, more than two years after *The Committee* had been broadcast, a crucially important component of Sands's unique testimony—that the red Maestro car had contained an off-duty RUC officer on surveillance duty—had been partially confirmed by the person in charge of Lurgan RUC station on the night of the murder. The RUC Chief Constable had managed, previously, to evade giving an explicit answer to this question, stating simply that the red Maestro had been ruled out of the murder investigation. Inspector Clegg's reply, which was made under oath, was also circumspect and, no doubt unintentionally, his revelation raises more questions than it answers. He had admitted that the Maestro had been involved in a surveillance operation though, strangely, he claimed that it had not belonged to the RUC. So the question arises: If the car did not belong to the RUC but was involved in a surveillance operation, who was carrying out the surveillance? And what "national security" reason prevented Inspector Clegg from referring to the Maestro in his official report on the murder?

Inspector Clegg's reply—guarded and incomplete as it is—nevertheless confirms Sands's claim that the red Maestro had been involved in a surveillance operation at the time of Sam Marshall's murder. Obviously, Inspector Clegg did not feel able to tell the whole story but, if Sands's version can be believed, it is scarcely surprising that this RUC officer would wish to be circumspect about any statement he might make, under oath, about the murder of Sam Marshall. For if Sands's revelations are as accurate about Inspector Clegg as they were about the status of the red Maestro, it means that the man in charge of the bail signing was one of those who enabled Robin Jackson (The Jackal) to shoot Sam Marshall dead.

(b) The Annotated List
The most sensitive document created during the production of *The Committee* was the list of alleged Committee members which Channel 4 submitted to the RUC a few days after the broadcast in October 1991. This list contained the names of nineteen individuals, fifteen of whom were classified as Category A members because Sands had confirmed unequivocally to us that they were members of the Committee. Three names fell into Category B because Sands said he was "less sure" that they sat on the Committee and one name was placed in Category C, along with the surname of another possible member—Category C was composed of those who provided financial support for the Committee.

The most important names on the list were those whom Sands had identified as the key figures in the murder conspiracy—Billy Abernethy, Hugh Ross, John McCullagh, Graham Long, David Prentice, Richard Monteith, Will Davidson,[3] Ian Whittle, Robin Jackson and Billy Wright. These were the names of ten key Committee members who, according to their close associate and fervent supporter, Jim Sands, had organised the Loyalist assassination campaign and who had struck terror in the Catholic community right across the entire province in 1989, 1990 and 1991. We had given their names to the RUC because we wished to comply with our legal obligations (subject only to our undertaking to Sands that we would protect his identity) and also because the murder campaign had been continuing right up to the date of the broadcast. We hoped that the information contained in the dossier, especially the above list of names, would help RUC Chief Constable Annesley to take steps to ensure that further killing could be prevented. Channel 4's letter, which accompanied the dossier, had expressed a desire to co-operate with the RUC to the fullest possible extent compatible with the undertakings we had given to our sources. Channel 4 wrote to the Chief Constable:

> As we said at the end of the programme, our paramount concern in handing over this information, is that we respect the undertakings we have given to protect the identity of our sources. Most of the information accompanying this letter has come from our main source, a member of the Ulster [Loyalist] Central Coordinating Committee, whom we describe in this documentation as "Source A."
>
> We have given very careful consideration indeed in preparing and presenting this information. We take the view that, in order to protect our source's identity, we are not in a position to provide you with any further details. However, if you wish to seek clarification of any points, Channel 4 is happy to consider any such request in consultation with the programme-makers.

The Chief Constable's immediate reaction, as we've seen, was an angry denunciation of the programme as an "unwarranted slur" on the good name of his force; his more considered response, announced a few days later, was the creation of the Nesbitt Inquiry. But his most important step was the decision to use the Prevention of Terrorism Act against us, the step which led to the highly publicised High Court proceedings about RUC death squads. However, those proceedings were to produce an unexpected and helpful piece of evidence, which would assist me in my efforts to prove that Sands had, all along, been telling the truth. For the RUC submitted to the High Court an incriminating document which, I believed at the time, strongly suggested that Nesbitt and his colleagues must have known, from an early stage, that the allegations in *The Committee* had been totally accurate. The RUC document is a copy of the list of alleged Committee members, as it appeared in the dossier but with a series of revealing, hand-written annotations; as soon as we noticed this document, we assumed that the hand-writing was that of a member of the Nesbitt Inquiry and, further, that the annotated list had been submitted to the court in error.[4] This document, complete with annotations on other individuals, those presumably also suspected of membership of the murder conspiracy, indicated to me, as soon as I read it, that the RUC "investigators" knew a good deal more about the conspiracy than they would subsequently reveal to Channel 4.

One of the hand-written annotations, scribbled beside a Category C entry on the list—"A senior member of the Ulster Clubs"—reads as follows: "Philip Black, Lurgan, sat chairman one night." When I first read these words, during the High Court proceedings, I felt that the RUC had, quite unintentionally, given us a significant clue that they had turned up new evidence to prove the truth of what Sands had said. The immediate task was to find out more about this Philip Black from Lurgan and to establish what type of event or meeting the RUC thought he had chaired "one night," if it had not been a meeting of Abernethy's Committee.

I soon discovered that Philip Black is a hard-line Loyalist and a prominent figure in his home town, Lurgan; he is also on the staff of Queen's University, Belfast and, more significantly in this context, he is a close friend of two of the Committee's most important members, Richard Monteith and Billy Abernethy. Black turns out to have been a leading figure in one of the Loyalist precursors to the Committee, the Ulster Clubs, a militant grouping once composed of such uncompromising advocates of the Loyalist cause as Richard Monteith, the late Colin Abernethy and a man who, it appears, is well-connected to some of the key murder conspirators, the leader (as he now is) of the Ulster Unionist Party, William David Trimble MP.

Was Black a member of the Ulster Loyalist Central Co-ordinating Committee, as the RUC's annotations suggested? Did he sit as chairman of this body "one night?" Why did the anonymous RUC annotator add his name to the list and suggest that this former member of the Ulster Clubs might also be a member of this Committee? Since I remain convinced that Sands, whatever he might now feel obliged to say, told us the truth back in April 1991, I arranged for a friend and journalistic colleague, Tim Laxton, to telephone Black with some questions. What was his reaction to his name appearing on the RUC document? Had the RUC "interrogators" visited him to probe his possible membership of the murder conspiracy? Does he admit to being a friend of Ross, Monteith and/or Abernethy? Did he ever suspect that any of these men might have been, in some way, connected with the Loyalist assassination campaign centred on his home town, Lurgan, during 1989, 1990 and 1991? This is what Black said when, without any advance warning, he was telephoned in 1996 and asked if he had watched a television programme, *The Committee,* in 1991:

> A: "Ah, you're talking about the one that referred to Hugh Ross . . . I've heard of it [the programme] through articles that were written in *The Sunday Times* . . . I have no reason to believe that it [the Committee] exists.
> Q: Were you interviewed by the police after that programme came out?
> A: Yes, I was.
> Q: How did that come about?
> A: [Long pause] I think that I knew some of the other people who were being interviewed by the police and who were mentioned in your programme.

Q: . . . it wasn't my programme . . .

A: . . . sorry not your programme, the Channel 4 programme . . .

Q: I've been doing some research and, according to two sources who say that they are members of the Committee, they allege that you are also a member of the Committee. Is that true?

A: No, it is not true . . . and I would be very interested to know who is making these suggestions . . . you'd appreciate that you'd probably be wise not to name anyone like myself without having some evidence for it, certainly not on the basis of uncorroborated statements by a couple of people you have been talking to.

Q: I'm a bit bemused as to why you should have been interviewed by the police, really?

A: Ah, em, I think they were. . .[pause]. . .because of the furore that had been created by it, I think they cast their net as wide as possible in order that at the end of their investigation they would be able to say: We can state categorically that there is no truth in this!

Q: But how did they manage to pick, I mean, there is a million and a half people in Ulster . . . they interviewed you as opposed to the other 1.4 million people or whatever?

A: Well, I presume that the people named in the programme would know, I don't know, a hundred, a couple of hundred people who might have been associated with in some way in various political activities . . . the impression from people who watched the programme would have gained from it would have been the untrue impression that Hugh Ross was somehow associated with this Committee.

Q: Do you know the Reverend Hugh Ross?

A: Yes I do.

Q: Do you know Billy Abernethy?

A: [Pause] . . . I . . . well . . . sorry, I'm hesitating because I do know him but I haven't or I did know him would be more correct to say. I mean I haven't spoken to him for three, four, five years.

This short extract from Black's interview with Tim Laxton was, I felt, singularly unconvincing and I felt that this university employee was extremely fortunate that the official RUC "Inquiry" was being conducted by a man who, as we had discovered, knew the nature of the verdict expected of him. Any genuine investigator—someone dedicated to finding out the truth and, ideally, someone possessing a polygraph or "lie detector"—would, I suspect, have rapidly reached the conclusion that there was a very good reason for Black's name appearing on the annotated RUC documents.

The RUC annotations also provided the name of another possible member of the Committee; this name was added to the list just above our entry which, based entirely on what Sands had told us, read as follows: "Man at Akraprint which prints the *Ulster Patriot*;" this is a reference to the magazine published by Ross's Ulster Independence Party and which is printed by a company, Akraprint, located near Portadown, County Armagh. The hand-written RUC annotation reads: "Sammy Abraham, 4 Main Street, Laurelvale, Portadown."[5] Again, after I had read this additional information from the unnamed RUC investigator, I tried to find out more. And when, in 1995, I finally obtained the 213-page transcript of Sands's "recantation" I noticed that, while Black's name had not been mentioned during the "interrogation," Sands had been asked by his RUC "inquisitor" to elaborate on what he knew about alleged Committee member and Akraprint employee, Sammy Abraham. The extract from the "recantation" transcript, printed below, once again gives the impression that these were not entirely spontaneous revelations by Sands, rather that his answers had been given to him in advance by the RUC and were then regurgitated for the benefit of the RUC tape-recorder:

> Q: And they [the Channel 4 dossier] talk about here, the man at Acra-print [*sic*] which prints the *Ulster Patriot*. Do you know this man?
>
> A: Yes.
>
> Q: What's his name?
>
> A: Sammy Abraham.
>
> Q: That's right, yes. Go ahead, and? Was this mentioned, I mean, that Sammy Abraham was part and parcel or what?
>
> A: Well his name and, and address and phone number's on the UIC material which I had given to them, Ben Hamilton.
>
> Q: Right, this is from the notes of the meetings that you gave him?
>
> A: No, this is from magazines and booklets and posters and things like that.
>
> Q: Ah right.
>
> A: Which I had given, his name and address would have been on those . . .
>
> Q: So in actual fact what you're saying to me, the man at Akraprint is Sammy Abraham, Sammy Abraham does all the printing for the UIC and includes the *Ulster Patriot*. Do you know him personally do you?
>
> A: Yes.
>
> Q: Describe him to me roughly just, what sort of a fella he is. Not physically but, I mean ah, give me a wee rough idea, paint a wee sort of a pen picture of him for me.
>
> A: He's about in his fifties.
>
> Q: Right.
>
> Q: And he used to live in Portadown.

Q: Right.

A: Now he lives out at Laurelvale towards Tandragee now.
(*This is exactly what the RUC annotation had stated.*)

Q: Uh huh.

A: And his printing works beside his house.

Q: Right.

A: And.

Q: Could he be in any way described as a terrorist of any shape or form?

A: He couldn't be described as a terrorist.

The "interrogation" of Sands about the extent of his knowledge of Sammy Abraham's character and background carried on for some time until the RUC interviewer had "established" that Sands, who admitted having known Abraham for five or six years, had nevertheless been given this man's name by Ben as part of the "hoax" we had all supposedly played on Channel 4. Sands's account of Sammy Abraham's alleged membership of the Committee, teased out of him by the sympathetic RUC interviewer in his "recantation," is as unconvincing as it is false. For it was Sands who had told Ben of Sammy Abraham's existence and alleged role in the murder conspiracy. So, I asked Tim Laxton to telephone Sammy Abraham to discover what he might have to say.

Q: I'm doing some research into the Ulster Central Co-ordinating Committee and I was hoping you might be able to help me by answering a few questions.

A: Never heard of it.

Q: You've never heard of it?

A: No.

Q: Did you see a Channel 4 programme in October 1991 called *The Committee*?

A: I wouldn't have a clue. 1991, I might have. That's a long time ago.

Q: Well, it's five or six years ago now.

A: That's right.

Q: I've been doing some research into the subject over the last five years and I've been doing a bit more just recently and, according to a couple of sources I've spoken to, they say that you were a member of the Ulster Central Co-ordinating Committee. Is that correct?

A: I really don't know.

Q: Sorry?

A: I don't know.

Q: You don't know whether you were or you weren't?

A: I don't think so.

Q: Well you must know whether you were or not, surely?

A: OK. Then I wasn't.

Q: You don't sound very sure?

A: Well, how much sure do you want me to be rather than say I wasn't?

Q: Just a minute ago you didn't sound as if you were sure whether you were or you weren't, and now you are saying you weren't.

A: I never heard of it. My first comments were that I never heard of it.

Q: Right. Do you know Billy Abernethy?

A: Yes, I do.

Q: Right. Because, you see, he was the chairman of the Committee.

A: Yes. [Pause] Sometimes you'd be involved in a lot of things, you don't even know what they're called and that is the truth. You're there and you're there as a supporter, maybe to support something else and you don't know what it is, you know.

Q: Right. Well have you attended meetings?

A: Not recently.

Q: No? But you have in the past?

A: I don't know. I really don't know because I can't identify it.

Q: Have you attended meetings which have been chaired by Billy Abernethy?

A: No . . .

Q: . . . Were you interviewed by the RUC after that programme came out?

A: Ach, I remember them maybe coming here to talk about something or other. I'm not sure whether it was about that or something. In those days, I suppose, I know it's not all that long ago but certainly it's got a lot quieter since . . . they would have come and yarned and talked to you, maybe in a friendly attitude, not to lock you up but you're always wary of them, regardless of what they come to talk to you about.

Q: Why would they come and talk to you after the programme came out?

A: I don't know whether it was after the programme. I didn't say that, you said that!

Q: So you can't remember? You're not saying they didn't. You're saying you can't remember?

A: That's right.

Sammy Abraham's conversation with Tim Laxton presented me with no great difficulty in believing that this man had been a full member of the Committee. His evasive replies, studied silences and apparent amnesia were what I expected from someone facing the accusation that he had been a conspirator to multiple murder. Abraham may never be asked to take a "lie detector" test but I am confident that, if he were ever to find himself in the witness box in any legal proceedings about his membership of the Committee, he would be no more convincing to a jury than he had been in his conversation with Tim Laxton; a competent lawyer would soon extract the real reason why he had been associating with Abernethy, Ross, Sands and the other conspirators in 1989, 1990 and 1991—namely, to discuss, sanction and organise multiple murder.

Finally, the annotated version of the list of alleged Committee members contains yet another incriminating, hand-written entry. Under "Category A: Businessman" we had entered this name: Charles Moffett (accountant). The annotated version submitted by the RUC to the High Court added these words immediately after Moffat's name: "Yes. Resigned 4 month ago—Moira area." Moira is a small, predominantly Protestant and Loyalist village close to Lurgan. When I read this particular annotation, I knew that it, too, was potentially significant because Charles Moffett's role in the Committee had been discussed at some length by Sands in both his audio and filmed interviews. Again, the RUC annotation suggested that Nesbitt had been, what we might call, economical with the truth when he had reported his "findings" to Channel 4.

Although the transcript of Sands's "recantation" reveals that Charlie Moffett's name, like so many others, was supposedly first mentioned to him by Ben Hamilton, our April 1991 audio tape-recordings tell a rather different story. Charlie Moffett emerges from Sands's 1991 account as an altogether more significant figure. For he appears to have rendered professional accountancy services to the Committee and, so we were told, to have laundered the money which the Committee had used to import weapons into the province from South Africa.

> A lot of the money goes through Mutual Assurance Company of South Africa. I don't know if you've ever heard of it?
> [BH: I certainly have. How do they move the money?]
> Well, they have a sister company or a subsidy (*subsidiary*) Providence Capitol Insurance in Northern Ireland (*Chief Executive, Charlie Moffett!*)
> [BH: And what, they move money from South Africa to here?]
> No. The money comes in here and goes to Providence Capitol . . . They move it through Providence Capitol International and it ends up with the parent company, the Mutual Assurance Company of South Africa.
> [BH: And then the arms come back from there?]
> Uh huh. Then there's money to be made in drugs . . . as well.
> [BH: Is that how some of the money's made?]
> That's how some of the money's made. Like in Northern Ireland, they can lift about £50,000 a month from drugs.

So, having read the RUC's annotation suggesting that Charlie Moffett had "resigned four months ago" from some organisation or other, I decided to obtain his comments on all these matters. Would he admit to his membership of Abernethy's Committee? Had he acted as the Committee's accountant and laundered money through his insurance company to import weapons illegally into the province? What did he make of the RUC's annotation on the list we had submitted to them? This is what he told Tim Laxton:

Sorry, you've got the wrong number.

Though Moffett denies these allegations, I have no reason to believe that Sands was hallucinating when, as he told us during his filmed interview in London, he had seen Moffett at Committee meetings they had both attended in 1989, 1990 and 1991. No wonder, then, that Moffett's name had cropped up during the RUC "Inquiry."

In summary, I accept that the RUC's annotated list of Committee members does not, in itself, prove the truth of all of our allegations. Nevertheless, the contents of that document strongly suggest that Nesbitt and his team possessed information which confirmed, at the very least, the existence of the Committee and which also identified some of its members. The annotations confirm that Nesbitt knew that both Philip Black and Sammy Abraham were members—two names, we should note, which were not contained in the original Channel 4 dossier; and Nesbitt must also have possessed more information about Charles Moffett than we—or he—had learned via Source A, Jim Sands. Taken as a whole, the annotated document suggests that Sands's revelations were as accurate as we would expect from someone who was speaking from personal experience and as a member of the Committee.

(c) The Monteith Libel Actions

On the one and only occasion I met Jim Sands, during his visit to London in April 1991, he had spoken forcibly about the role the solicitor, Richard Monteith, was playing in the Committee's activities. After Abernethy and Ross he was, according to Sands, one of the most ruthless members of the murder conspiracy. I had no reason to doubt this assessment but, as we were not intending to identify anyone in the broadcast, we were advised that we faced no risk of anyone bringing a successful prosecution for libel. As the reader is aware, Monteith's signature appeared on the Witness X statement, which the RUC submitted to the High Court in July 1992—a development which confirmed our suspicions that the Chief Constable's inquiry would turn out to be a bogus exercise. And, as the reader is also aware, I subsequently drew attention to this point in my interview for the BBC's *Inside Ulster*. I did so after being advised that it would be legally safe to do so; my oblique reference to the Portadown solicitor would not, I was assured, allow him to sue me successfully for libel; I believed that then and, in view of the outcome of the two libel actions Monteith subsequently brought against me over this interview, I continue to believe that the words I used in the television interview were, taken on their own, insufficient to identify him.

We have already seen that his action against me—for alleged criminal libel—fell at the first hurdle; Lord Williams persuaded a High Court in Belfast to throw out the case. When Monteith responded to this setback with a second writ—for alleged civil libel—I was already well advanced with my research into his terrorist past; I had discovered that he had been, for many years, an adviser to the strategists of Loyalist terror and, for example, had regularly attended council meetings of the notorious Ulster Defence Association. I had also learned that he had been surprisingly reckless over the years in the degree to which he had associated with Loyalist terrorists, some of whom were known to have attacked and even murdered innocent Catholics.

One such incident, which I investigated in some depth, occurred in Portadown shortly before midnight on February 11th 1984. Monteith had been drinking with a number of well-known Loyalists in one of their favourite watering holes, the Blues Bar in Portadown. A considerable amount of alcohol had been consumed and, as the evening wore on, some of the drinkers were tempted to try to gratify their more primitive tribal instincts; eventually one of them declared his intention to murder the first Catholic he could find. "Let's go and get a Teague," he proposed. His suggestion met with the enthusiastic approval of some of those present, two of whom decided to accompany him in the search for a potential victim. One of these three then left the bar to go and collect a .38 Special revolver, which had been hidden in the pub's back yard. Once he returned, all three Loyalists were then given a lift by their solicitor and drinking companion, Richard Monteith, to a house some distance away.

Two of the three Loyalists, R.J. "Bob" Kerr and Philip "Silly" Silcock, were already notorious terrorists with a string of convictions; so Monteith could have been in no doubt, on the night in question, about the character of the men with whom he was associating and acting as their unpaid taxi driver. The third Loyalist, Ernest McCreanor, had never been involved before in any form of terrorism and would come to regret bitterly his involvement in the incident that was to occur later that night, shortly after Monteith had dropped off the three men and after he had returned to the Blues Bar. McCreanor and his two companions then got into another car and drove to a street in a Catholic district of Portadown, where they selected a suitable target, a young and innocent Catholic on his way home, Paschal Mulholland. McCreanor sat in the car while his two Loyalist companions, Kerr and Silcock, proceeded to launch their attack; they grabbed the young man from behind and, then, one of them fired several shots, wounding him in the back, in the chest and in the head; the two Loyalists ran off, leaving the young man screaming where he lay in the middle of the road. Paschal Mulholland was immensely fortunate to have survived, although fragments of the bullets remain inside his body to the present day.

I investigated this incident in some detail and, if Monteith had not dropped his libel action against me, I would have argued in court that the Portadown solicitor's role in that attack and in subsequent legal proceedings arising from it indicated that he did not have much of a reputation to lose. I soon discovered that there were some extremely disconcerting features about this particular incident and it suggested that collusion between the Loyalists and the RUC had existed long before the creation of Abernethy's Committee. For I learned that McCreanor had sat in the car throughout the period that Kerr and Silcock had been trying to murder Mulholland; he did not aim a single blow at the young Catholic, much less shoot him in the chest, in the back or in the head. Yet, astoundingly, McCreanor was the only one of the three attackers to be placed on trial; he was charged with attempted murder, convicted and sentenced to fourteen years in prison. Both Kerr and Silcock managed to avoid prosecution, according to what Mulholland was told by his solicitor, because they were provided with a cast-iron alibi by one of Portadown's most "respectable" citizens, the man who had acted as their unpaid taxi driver and who later represented the unfortunate McCreanor at his criminal trial, the solicitor Richard Monteith. I also learned that, immediately after McCreanor had been convicted, the trial judge had observed none too discreetly that Monteith had been lucky to escape from finding himself alongside McCreanor in the dock, rather than representing him in court as solicitor for the defence.

Why were Kerr and Silcock not prosecuted? Why was McCreanor the only member of the gang to be put on trial? How could Monteith justify giving the three Loyalists a lift in such circumstances? Why did Mulholland subsequently come under pressure from the RUC not to press charges against Kerr, whom he later recognised as one of those who had attacked him?[6] These were some of the interesting questions that the Belfast libel jury would have been asked to consider, if Monteith had proceeded with his libel action against me. McCreanor is today understandably reluctant to talk about this dark episode in his life but I found it significant that in December 1994, at the time I was investigating Monteith's murky past, the convicted man—who is now a completely reformed character—received a telephone call out of the blue from the Portadown solicitor. Monteith advised his former client that, if he should be approached by any journalist asking questions about the attempted murder of Paschal Mulholland, McCreanor should be careful not to incriminate his former Blues Bar associate and defence solicitor.

So there are good, independent reasons for believing that Richard Monteith would not have been acting out of character, if he had played the role on the Committee attributed to him by Jim Sands. This Portadown solicitor's legal career is, therefore, likely to end in deserved ignominy. For, as he ought to have known, it is normally not possible to pursue a career as a professional lawyer anywhere in the United Kingdom while, simultaneously, helping to run a campaign of sectarian assassination—even if you are acting in concert with senior police officers and a former Assistant Chief Constable with an OBE.

(d) Who was Source A, James Alfred Sands?

Jim Sands told us that he had been, for several years, a close political associate of Abernethy, Ross, Monteith and many others within the Ulster Independence Movement; his intimacy with the murder conspirators and his membership of the Committee were, he claimed, the reasons why he was able to give us such a detailed account of the various assassinations they had carried out. He had given us first-hand testimony about Committee meetings he had attended and about the murder conspiracy in which he had directly participated. But, as we have seen, the RUC subsequently contradicted and ridiculed all these claims; the Nesbitt Inquiry concluded that we had bribed and bullied Sands into helping us to "hoax" Channel 4. Nesbitt told Channel 4, as we've also seen, that Sands was a man "with a serious criminal record," someone whose allegations were utterly worthless, fantasies of the most mischievous kind. How could anyone seriously believe, Nesbitt suggested, that the highly respectable Ulster Protestants named in the Channel 4 dossier as murder conspirators would freely associate with such a disreputable character as Sands? And if Sands's testimony could be safely disregarded, Nesbitt also implied, how could anyone properly criticise the Chief Constable for having denounced as "outrageous" our allegation that some of his senior RUC colleagues had been running death squads?

As soon as I learned the outcome of the Nesbitt Inquiry and, in particular, what the RUC had claimed about Sands, I began to search for independent evidence which would enable me to show which of the two men—our crucially important Source A (Jim Sands) or the RUC's equally important investigator (Jimmy Nesbitt)—was telling the truth. According to Sands, he (Sands) was a long-time associate of Ross,

Abernethy and others in the Ulster Independence Movement; according to Nesbitt, he (Sands) had nothing in common with any of the respectable individuals listed in the dossier, those who had been "appalled and horrified" by Sands's claims that they had been his co-conspirators in multiple murder. Unfortunately, as Sands has been "looked after" by the RUC ever since he "recanted" his story in December 1992, I have had to conduct my search in the knowledge that I would, almost certainly, not be allowed to speak to Sands again or to receive any further assistance from him. My task proved to be extraordinarily difficult because my efforts to obtain documentary evidence which would settle the issue were constantly frustrated. Nevertheless, I eventually succeeded in obtaining the evidence which proves, beyond doubt, that it was Sands—*not* Nesbitt—who had been speaking the truth.

The evidence emerges from Hugh Ross's nomination papers for the House of Commons by-election in the Upper Bann constituency, where he was a candidate in May 1990. It shows that, nearly one year before any of us learned of his existence, Jim Sands was—as he later claimed—a close political associate of those whom he subsequently identified as the organisers of the Loyalist assassination campaign. Ross was nominated by his friend Billy Abernethy, who also paid his election deposit; and, as is required in all elections for the House of Commons, the nomination papers were signed by eight members of the Upper Bann constituency, including several alleged members of the Committee. Most significantly, Ross's nomination papers were also signed by yet another member of the murder conspiracy—*not* one of Nesbitt's "aristocracy of the country"— but the man said to have "a serious criminal record," none other than the supposed hoaxer and fantasist, James Alfred Sands. How had that come about? This is what Ross told Tim Laxton:

> That night there were forty at the meeting [of the Portadown branch of the Ulster Independence Committee]. And we needed so many people to sign and Jim was, yes, in the Portadown branch. There's no crime in that, is there? I honestly know him [Jim Sands] as well as I know you, Tim.[7]

We can safely dismiss this "explanation" as untrue, incredible and disingenuous. For the decision to seek election to the House of Commons is a serious one and it is, I believe, safe to assume that no electoral candidate would wish to have his or her nomination papers signed by a relative stranger. What if that person turned out to have "a serious criminal record" (as Nesbitt later alleged against Sands)? We can, I believe, legitimately assume that Ross took considerable care to choose as signatories only those whom he knew well and trusted absolutely. That is why he asked Abernethy, Sands, and other close political associates to sign his nomination papers. The signatures on Ross's nomination papers, which he does not and cannot dispute, leave no room for doubt, therefore, that Sands was exactly what he claimed to be, a close political associate of this seemingly respectable Presbyterian Minister, the President of the Ulster Independence Party and the Ulster Independence candidate in Upper Bann in May 1990.

Ross could have approached any single one of the many thousands of potential signatories within that constituency but, as the electoral document revealed, he happened to choose a man who would, less than a year later, accuse him of being one of the ringleaders of a murder conspiracy. Jim Sands's signature on Ross's nomination papers strongly suggests that, as a trusted member of Ross's political entourage, he was in a position to know precisely the role the candidate was secretly playing in the ongoing Loyalist assassination campaign.

Obviously, those who sought to discredit our journalism did everything possible to distance Sands from Ross, so that they could give the impression that there was no significant link between them. Barrie Penrose's final report for the *Sunday Express* gave a totally false impression, with no mention of the close political and personal links between the two men, with Sands being portrayed as a harmless "youth leader who, until recently, ran a women's football team" in Portadown;[8] while Nesbitt, who also skated over Sands's intimate involvement with Ross, was also content to dismiss our source as an utterly disreputable character, a well-known criminal and hoaxer. Yet, strangely, Ross himself has recently felt able to admit that he had known Jim Sands for many years and, further, that he had indeed been secretary of the Portadown branch of the Ulster Independence Committee—an admission which completely undermines Nesbitt's effort to discredit Sands as a fantasist and criminal hoaxer.

In summary, the research strategy I followed ever since the Nesbitt "hoax" verdict in February 1993, has been largely successful. I believe that I have demonstrated that Sands's "recantation" is utterly bogus; that its credibility is undermined by his own words, as recorded by Ben Hamilton back in 1991; and that the entire exercise was clumsily executed by his RUC handlers in a desperate attempt to protect the murder conspirators.[9] Nesbitt's activities have been a perversion of his official duties as a member of Her Majesty's constabulary; and they have been exposed as such both by the demolition of the "recantation" and by the other evidence I have managed to obtain since 1993. In short, this evidence includes:

(a) **Corroboration from California**—Inspector Alan Clegg confirmed a crucially important component of Sands's unique testimony about the murder of Sam Marshall. Clegg, who had been in charge of Lurgan RUC station on the night of the murder, reluctantly admitted on oath that the red Maestro car had been on official surveillance duty. Two years before Clegg's admission, Sands had told us that the red Maestro had contained one of the two off-duty RUC Inner Force officers helping the assassin, Robin Jackson. Conclusion: Sands had told us the truth about the murder of Sam Marshall.

(b) The Annotated Document—This document, apparently submitted by the RUC in error to the High Court in 1992, contained fresh information about Committee members and their role in the murder conspiracy. The document is evidence that Nesbitt's "hoax" verdict on the programme was, as he must have known, totally untrue. Conclusion: Sands had told us the truth about Committee members Philip Black, Sammy Abraham and Charles Moffett.

(c) The Monteith Libel Actions—Richard Monteith's involvement with the men who tried to murder Paschal Mulholland in 1984 indicates that this Portadown solicitor was implicated in Loyalist terrorism long before he took his seat on the Committee. Nesbitt could not have been ignorant of this fact. Conclusion: Sands had told us the truth about Committee member Richard Monteith.

(d) Who was James Alfred Sands?—Hugh Ross's nomination papers in the Upper Bann by-election in May 1990 contain the signature of James Alfred Sands. This document showed that Sands was, as he claimed, a close political associate of the man whom, one year later, he identified as a leading member of the Committee. Nesbitt chose to ignore the truth about Sands's proximity to Ross and, instead, told Channel 4 that Sands was a criminal and a hoaxer. Conclusion: Sands had told us the truth about himself.

Long before I had completed my investigations within the four areas outlined above, I was twice called for interview by Michael Beloff QC in September 1993, when I was required, for several hours, to answer questions which had arisen in the course of his Inquiry into the alleged "hoax." Unfortunately I had not, at that stage, acquired either the court documents from California or proved the link between Ross and Sands; and my investigation of Monteith's criminal past was still at an early stage. Still, I had managed to obtain the document from the Channel 4 dossier, as annotated by Nesbitt's "investigators;" and I naturally drew its contents to Mr. Beloff's attention, along with the details contained in the audio and video recordings of Sands's interviews, details which—as I explained—constituted an admission of his involvement in the murder conspiracy. I answered each of Mr. Beloff's questions to the best of my ability and, after the two interviews had ended, I was confident that this skilful and experienced inquisitor would eventually conclude that we had conducted our investigation in 1991 in conformity to the highest editorial standards. Happily, my optimism about the outcome of the Beloff Inquiry proved to be justified when, in November 1993, I learned that each member of the Channel 4 Board had been sent a copy of his final report.

Having been asked to decide, in effect, whether the RUC or Box Productions had told the truth, Mr. Beloff seems to have experienced no difficulty in reaching a judgement. His independent, authoritative and unpublished 100-page report contains a formal "finding" that it was, in his judgement, "inconceivable" that there had ever been *any* truth in *any* of the RUC's allegations against the programme makers.[10] His verdict on the alleged hoaxers at Box Productions reads as follows:

> I inquired myself into the general stance on Irish questions of Sean McPhilemy and Ben Hamilton. If I had to summarise it, I would say it was one of *bien pensant* liberalism sympathetic to the concerns of all sections of the community, Catholic and Protestant; hostile to violence and corruption; desirous that the rule of law be upheld in particular by those whose constitutional task it was to do so. (Both were, coincidentally, educated as philosophers!) I cannot begin to fault Channel 4 either for the process of their own inquiry or for the conclusion to which they came on the calibre and character of the Box personnel. Channel 4, in this instance, were dealing neither with novices nor with the unknown.

Michael Beloff's unequivocal verdict gave Channel 4's Board of Directors all the reassurance they needed. He told them he had found the programme makers to be people of integrity and that Box Productions had complied fully with the legal and editorial standards demanded by its contract with the Channel. In short, he vindicated us completely and dismissed, without qualification, all allegations levelled against us by the RUC and its favoured media outlets, the *Sunday Express* and *The Sunday Times*. Although this happy outcome was exactly what I had expected, the verdict had a greater significance for the Channel 4 Board. For they no longer had to take any matter on trust from their own executives because they now knew that one of Britain's most eminent lawyers had scrutinised every aspect of the affair and had concluded that there were no skeletons in the cupboards either at Channel 4 or at Box Productions.

If the Channel 4 Board had wished, it could have decided to challenge the RUC's "hoax" verdict in two ways. It could have commissioned further research into the subject of collusion, with a view to making a second documentary; or it could, as our barristers Lord Williams QC and James

Price had recommended, have authorised the commencement of libel actions against the two newspapers which had caused so much damage to our reputations. Regrettably, however, the Board decided against pursuing either course of action and preferred instead to draw a line under the affair. After considering the Beloff report, those in control of Channel 4 decided that the time had come to relegate *The Committee* to the past and to move on to a new agenda. They decided that Channel 4 would not commission a second programme, nor would it provide the financial backing to enable us to bring libel proceedings against the two newspapers which had championed the dirty tricks campaign against us.

While Channel 4 could afford to pursue such a course, this was not an option I felt able to take. As a journalist who had helped to uncover a murder conspiracy involving senior RUC and Army officers, I believed that it was my duty to persevere with the investigation until I had discovered everything there was to know about the Committee and its works. I knew that we had not, in 1991, succeeded in discovering the identities of all the conspirators and I also knew that they had organised many more killings than those Sands had told us about. When, therefore, Channel 4 urged me to drop the story and devote my energies to other topics, I indicated that I felt it my duty as a journalist to persevere with my investigation to the end; if I did not, the public would never discover the truth about the conspiracy we had stumbled across in 1991. Besides, as I have already indicated, the media consensus about the programme had already inflicted great damage on the reputation of Box Productions. Outside a small group at Channel 4, nobody knew about the existence of the Beloff Inquiry or that it had vindicated the programme's journalism. So I decided that I would try to restore the fortunes of Box Productions by proving that we had been right all along; if Channel 4 had decided against commissioning another programme, I made up my mind that I would write a book about the affair instead.

While pressing ahead with my investigation, I came to rely ever more heavily on the advice of my solicitor, Geoffrey Bindman. After learning that Channel 4 had declined to support the proposed libel actions, Geoffrey initially advised me to hold back until I saw how events developed; in any case, I was forced to spend much of 1994 and 1995 gathering material to defend myself in the libel action brought against me by Richard Monteith. Gradually, as time passed, it became clear that the broadcast had caused even more damage than I had realised and that my fortunes would not recover until the "hoax" allegations had been publicly retracted by the two newspapers. Early in 1994, therefore, Geoffrey agreed that the time had come to begin proceedings against the *Sunday Express* over the article which had accused me of deceiving Channel 4 about the security threats that had arisen in 1991; but he suggested that I should wait a little longer before deciding whether to take similar action over the more serious allegations in the *The Sunday Times*, those which stated that the entire programme had been a "hoax."

Barrie Penrose and the lawyers acting for the *Sunday Express* huffed and puffed for nearly three years, spending hundreds of thousands of pounds in a futile effort to try to justify what they had published. After discovering that I had told the truth in my affidavit about abandoning my home for security reasons in 1991, the newspaper's lawyers switched to a different line of defence; they tried to argue that I had known all along that there had never been any security threat—supposedly because I had also known that the programme was a "hoax." Even worse, they suggested that I had put my family through the ordeal of moving from our home and living in fear for a year, merely to deceive Channel 4 into believing the programme's allegations. This libel action showed me the lengths to which some lawyers are prepared to go when they have a client foolish enough to underwrite their expensive fantasies. Eventually, at the end of 1996 and only after a firm trial date had been fixed in the High Court, the *Sunday Express* admitted defeat. To avoid the inevitably embarrassing publicity such a trial would have brought, the *Sunday Express* settled out of court. All Penrose's allegations were withdrawn; the newspaper apologised and it agreed to pay me substantial damages, together with all my legal costs. Penrose's reckless "reportage" on behalf of his friends in the RUC had cost his employers an estimated half-million pounds.

This was the first victory I had enjoyed since the programme was broadcast in 1991. When it became clear, during the summer of 1996, that the *Sunday Express* was running out of time and out of remotely plausible arguments, though not out of money, Geoffrey Bindman and James Price QC advised me that the moment had come to launch my second libel action. In August, we served libel writs on Andrew Neil, Liam Clarke and *The Sunday Times*.[11] By then, it was becoming evident that the murder conspirators would be in great difficulty if any of them found themselves subpoenaed to appear in the witness box in a libel trial in London. For the *Sunday Express's* failed attempt to show that the programme had been a "hoax" had forced me to intensify my research into the past activities of the leading murder conspirators. Slowly, gradually, I assembled a dossier on their careers and on their murder conspiracy. For example, I discovered evidence that Billy Abernethy had, back in 1987, used his considerable influence within Loyalist paramilitary circles to recover the proceeds of a robbery from the Portadown branch of the Ulster Bank. Though the bank's most senior managers were (understandably) grateful for his intervention on their behalf, they were alarmed that details of the affair might leak to reveal that the bank was employing a manager known to be involved with Loyalist terrorism. A well-placed source within the back has given me chapter and verse on how the Ulster Bank's little local difficulty in Portadown had been managed and contained, an outcome which left the bank's customers and the wider public—though not the RUC—blissfully unaware of what had really transpired.

In retrospect, I came to see that my victory over Penrose and the *Sunday Express* was a turning point in my struggle to defend the programme, to discredit the dirty tricks brigade, and to vindicate our reputations. Ben Hamilton helped me to celebrate the occasion with a champagne lunch, though we remained well aware that the out-of-court settlement would not receive sufficient publicity in the British press to remedy any significant part of the enormous damage already caused to Box Productions. Nevertheless, having risked everything I possessed and much more to fight the libel case, it was gratifying to witness this national newspaper's lawyer state in the High Court that it was his "pleasure to take this opportunity to apologise to the plaintiff" and that he "acknowledged that [I had been] at all times truthful and [had] acted with complete propriety towards Channel 4." Fortunately, the settlement did receive a fair amount of coverage in the specialist media journals widely read in the television industry and by newspaper journalists. And Channel 4, though it had not supported my decision to bring the libel action, was quick to congratulate me and to mark my victory with a press statement issued by the Director of Programmes:

> I am delighted that the *Sunday Express's* scurrilous campaign to discredit one of the most courageous pieces of journalism of the 1990s has ended in this climbdown. The paper's attempt to rubbish our programme by attacking the integrity of its executive producer was a grubby tactic which has proved completely unsustainable.

This libel victory in December 1996, a full five years after the broadcast, convinced me that if I persevered with my investigation I would eventually succeed in unearthing the full story and in convincing the skeptics that we had been right all along about the Committee and its assassination campaign. It boosted my confidence that I would ultimately triumph. And I became convinced that my new libel action against *The Sunday Times*, though it would be long and costly, would have an identical outcome because that newspaper would, eventually, be forced to recognise that its published allegations were false. I concluded that, if reason rather than emotion prevailed, *The Sunday Times* would see that Jim Sands had compromised all the conspirators when he had spoken freely and frankly to Ben Hamilton, and would appreciate that Sands's intimacy with Ross, Abernethy, King Rat, and the others showed that he had been speaking from the heart.

I certainly have no doubt that Sands was speaking from personal experience when he told us, in great detail, how Ross, Abernethy, Forbes, Monteith, and the other Committee members had organised the eighteen murders described in his tape-recorded and video-recorded interviews. He was neither fabricating nor fantasising when he told us how Ross, bible in hand, had personally "blessed"—though the word is scarcely appropriate— numerous meetings of the Ulster Loyalist Central Co-ordinating Committee before the conspirators settled down to the business of deciding the identities of those whom they planned to murder.

I conclude that our Source A, Jim Sands, told us the truth in 1991; six years later, his allegations against the RUC still stand and they remain unanswered. I also conclude that Nesbitt's "hoax" verdict was the device with which the RUC contained the scandal and suppressed the truth. It follows that the RUC Chief Constable was unjustified when, in August 1992, he attacked me in advertisements in the Irish newspapers for "an outrageous allegation," my assertion that RUC officers were colluding with the Loyalist death squads. For it was not my allegation that was outrageous but the facts themselves.

Notes

1   See Chapter 14.

2   This IRA escaper, John Joseph Smith, was eventually extradited from the United States to Northern Ireland in August 1996.

3   As already explained, we were never sure whether Sands's slight speech impediment had caused us to misspell this man's name; it was either Will or Phil, Davidson or Davison.

4   Ben Hamilton was quick to spot the RUC's mistake and, during the High Court proceedings in July 1992, immediately drew my attention to the annotated list submitted by the RUC.

5   Sands had mentioned Abraham's name to me on the one and only occasion I had met Sands, in 1991. Although I had, since then, known Abraham to be a Committee member, his name was not included in the Channel 4 dossier—an oversight which I have since been unable to fathom.

6   We will see later that R.J. Kerr seems to have enjoyed a degree of immunity from prosecution by the RUC. In 1977, he had helped Robin Jackson to murder a Catholic in Ahoghill but, despite the RUC's full knowledge about those responsible for that murder, neither Kerr nor Jackson were ever prosecuted. [See Chapter 13]

7   Ross was to give a rather different account of his relationship to Sands in a written statement.

8   *Sunday Express*, May 10th 1993.

9   The transcript of the "recantation" reveals that one of the RUC officers

who interviewed Sands after his arrest in December 1992 was Nesbitt's deputy, Chris Webster. We can be sure that Webster shared his superior's enthusiasm for the truth.

10 I was allowed to read the report at the offices of Channel 4's solicitors, where I made a note of Mr. Beloff's main conclusions.

11 These libel proceedings are continuing and, unless this newspaper decides to follow the example of the *Sunday Express* and settle out of court, the case is likely to come to trial in October 1998.

Chapter 13

A GUILTY SECRET

The Beloff Inquiry's verdict, which reassured Channel 4's Board of Directors that they had been right to stand by the programme, had come as no surprise to me. For, by the end of 1993, I was as certain as anyone could be that the broadcast allegations had been true and that the subsequent Nesbitt Inquiry had been primarily interested in suppressing the truth and in limiting the damage we had inflicted on the RUC. I had told Michael Beloff QC that, following the broadcast in 1991 and the High Court proceedings in 1992, the dirty tricks campaign against Box Productions had forced me to immerse myself in the details of long forgotten murders and atrocities, many of which had been the result of collusion between the Loyalists and the security forces. My researches had borne fruit and this new information had confirmed my conviction that we had got the story right and that, despite the frequent and indignant denials by the RUC and the Northern Ireland Office, collusion in murder had been routinely practised by the "security" forces throughout the previous twenty years.

One murder on which I had focused my attention was that of Catholic RUC Sergeant Joseph Campbell, which had taken place on Friday, February 25th 1977, in the small seaside town of Cushendall on the Antrim coast. I had investigated the background to this killing and discovered that the truth had remained deeply buried for many years. This was one of the RUC's best kept and most guilty secrets, one which, ironically, I might never have uncovered but for the campaign against the programme and the effort to destroy my reputation. The RUC's guilty secret, I discovered, was that Sergeant Campbell—one of very few Catholic sergeants in the force in 1977—had been murdered at the behest of the RUC itself and by a man who was subsequently recruited by Abernethy and Ross to be the Committee's principal assassin.

Sergeant Campbell, who had been in charge of the village police station, had stopped work on the fateful weekend and was spending the Friday evening at home with his family. As he preferred to keep his family life separate from his work, he offered no explanation to his wife and children when, after receiving an unexpected phone call that night, he decided to go back to the police station for a short time. His wife and his older, teenage children, who were in the house at the time, realised that something unusual was happening because the policeman had decided to take his regulation RUC pistol with him, as he left the house. Normally, he preferred not to wear a gun. This preference was not as strange as it might, at first, appear because the tranquil village of Cushendall had been largely bypassed by the troubles and Sergeant Campbell had not been greatly concerned about any possible attack by the IRA. After leaving home on that Friday night, he walked the short distance to the police station, having given his family the impression that he would return before long.

But he would never return. For half an hour later, as he was locking the police station's security gates, an unidentified gunman came out of the darkness and shot him in the head. Nobody saw the gunman and, in the commotion which followed the shooting, the killer managed to escape without leaving any clue to his identity. Sergeant Campbell died in the ambulance on the way to hospital. Given that so many other RUC officers had suffered the same fate during the troubles, it was scarcely surprising that rumour quickly spread throughout Northern Ireland that yet another police officer had been murdered by the IRA. The funeral was attended, as was normal in such circumstances, by senior RUC officers and government officials. The mourners included the future Chief Constable, Sir John Hermon. Sir John had a personal interest in this tragic incident because he had trained with Sergeant Campbell, when they had both been young recruits back in the late 1950s; and he also knew Sergeant Campbell's brother, George, who had also served in the RUC for a time before settling in England. Sir John expressed his condolences to the family and the widow, Mrs. Rosemary Campbell, later received a letter of condolence from the then Secretary of State for Northern Ireland, Roy Mason.

> I was deeply shocked to learn of the tragic death of your husband at the weekend. I know my sadness and total revulsion is shared by the great majority of decent people in Northern Ireland. The courage and service to the community of men like your husband deserves and commands the highest admiration.

There is no reason to doubt the sincerity of either Sir John Hermon's or Mr. Mason's expressions of sorrow. For neither of them would, presumably, have had any reason to know, at that time, that the murder had not been committed by the IRA. In the weeks and months that followed Sergeant Campbell's death, the family hoped that the killer would be found but police enquiries proved unsuccessful and, inevitably, the death was soon forgotten by the public as news of other atrocities filled the headlines. The Campbells were left, like so many other families, to mourn their loss in silence and to wait for the culprits to be found.

Mrs. Campbell did her best to recover from the tragedy and to cope with the demands of her large family of eight children. Though she received regular support from the RUC's welfare department, she grew ever more frustrated by the apparent lack of progress in the police investigation of the murder. She had never believed that the IRA had killed her husband because she knew they could have done so at any time. The IRA would not have done it, she believed, because Cushendall was an overwhelmingly Catholic village and her husband had been the popular village bobby. So, frustrated and angry at the lack of progress, Mrs. Campbell insisted on a meeting with the then Chief Constable, Sir Kenneth Newman, to whom she expressed her concerns. When she discovered that RUC Headquarters had virtually no documentation about the killing and saw that the official crime file contained just a few loose sheets of paper, she commented to Sir Kenneth: "There would be more paperwork for a burglary in Cushendall than you've got in that file." Yet her visit to the Chief Constable had not been a complete waste of time because Sir Kenneth indicated that he, too, had concluded that the IRA had not been involved. Mrs. Campbell was intrigued when Sir Kenneth volunteered the information that two men had already been questioned about the murder; and she was dumbfounded when he went on to reveal that both men, though not named, were said to be serving officers in the RUC itself.

Mrs. Campbell's visit to RUC Headquarters had confirmed her growing suspicion that those in charge of the force were being less than candid about what they knew about the murder. She believed that senior officers were deliberately concealing information from her. Even before her meeting with Sir Kenneth, she had discussed her husband's murder with a detective from Ballymena, the divisional station responsible for Cushendall and to which Sergeant Campbell had reported. The Ballymena detective had stoked her suspicions because, while weighing his words carefully, he had allowed himself to venture the opinion that if the truth were ever to come out, the ramifications could be even more serious for the RUC than the murder itself had been. Mrs. Campbell had been aware, therefore, from an early stage that the RUC was keeping information from her but it would be many years before she was to learn the precise nature of the RUC's guilty secret or to discover why she and her family had been kept in the dark for so long.

Three years after the murder, an unexpected development occurred which led Mrs. Campbell to hope that, at last, she might learn what the

RUC was holding back and why its senior officers were so concerned about her refusal to let the matter drop. The development was the arrest, in 1980, of an RUC Special Branch officer based in Ballymena, Sergeant Charles McCormick. McCormick, who had been a frequent visitor to Cushendall and had known Sergeant Campbell well, had emerged as the prime suspect and, to the family's surprise, had suddenly been charged with the murder. This was a puzzling and troubling turn of events for the family because none of them had known of any ill-feeling between McCormick and their late father. Yet they welcomed the proposed trial for they believed that, even if McCormick turned out to be as innocent as he claimed, it was likely that new evidence would emerge. They might, finally, learn the truth and attain peace of mind to let them come to terms with their loss.

Nearly two years after McCormick's arrest, the trial began in Belfast in February 1982. Jury trials had long been abolished in terrorist cases in the province because experience had shown that it was too dangerous for members of the public to serve on a jury; some jurors had been blackmailed and others had been murdered before they had a chance to deliver their verdicts. So, as was normal at the time, the responsibility for determining the accused's guilt or innocence fell on the trial judge, Lord Justice Murray. Mrs. Campbell and her older children attended the High Court where they soon found themselves listening to an amazing story.

McCormick had, ostensibly, been put on trial because he had been accused of the crime by one of his former agents, a Republican whom he had recruited many years earlier to spy on the IRA. This double-agent, Anthony O'Doherty, had accused his former RUC handler because, as he told the court, the policeman had asked him repeatedly to murder Sergeant Campbell. O'Doherty confessed that, with McCormick's enthusiastic support, he had committed an immense variety of crimes, including bank robberies, motor car hijackings and an assortment of terrorist offences—but he had not committed murder. The double-agent told the court that McCormick had been aware that Sergeant Campbell had discovered evidence to implicate him in some of the crimes which he and O'Doherty had committed together. Sergeant Campbell's diligent investigation had constituted a threat to the Special Branch man's continuing career in the RUC; so McCormick had decided to ensure that his superiors would never learn about his unorthodox and illegal conduct. O'Doherty claimed that McCormick had repeatedly asked him to murder Sergeant Campbell but he had, he said, been equally persistent in declining his invitations.

On the night of the killing, he added, he had accompanied McCormick to Cushendall but had sat alone in the police car about three-quarters of a mile from the village, while McCormick had set off, on his own, with a rifle to murder his RUC colleague. Although O'Doherty admitted that he had not actually seen McCormick do the shooting, he was convinced that he had committed the crime. For he had heard the shots and had waited until a breathless McCormick returned to the police car, carrying the rifle and claiming to have eliminated the man who had posed a threat to his continuing career in the RUC.

McCormick's defence team must have been delighted by the testimony of a top ballistics expert, who gave evidence about what he had been able to infer from the injuries suffered by the dead policeman. This evidence allowed the defence to rekindle the original belief that the IRA had murdered the RUC officer. For the ballistics expert told the court that ". . . the shot which killed the policeman could well have been fired by an Armalite weapon in the hands of an IRA marksman." The possibility that it had, after all, been an IRA killing may have created sufficient doubt in the judge's mind about the strength of the case against the accused. The trial ended with McCormick's acquittal on the murder charge and with the possibility reinstated that, despite what the Campbell family had always believed, the RUC sergeant had indeed been murdered by the IRA. After the trial, Mrs. Campbell again found herself in the position that she did not know who had killed her husband or why. She was further mystified by developments which followed the trial. For McCormick, who had been convicted and jailed on bank robbery charges, was subsequently acquitted on appeal, due to an inexplicable decision by the Lord Chief Justice, Sir Robert Lowry. McCormick walked free in January 1984. O'Doherty, his agent-turned-accuser, was also released from prison a few months later, in an equally inexplicable development. He had been granted a Royal Prerogative by the Secretary of State, which cut his sentence by eight years.

Mrs. Campbell, who has continued to live in Cushendall near to the RUC station where her husband was killed, remained determined to learn the identity of those who had made her a widow at a relatively young age. Life for the Campbell family had become a struggle, in the years that followed the trial, because the RUC had been less than generous with financial support. It was as if the force was keeping the family on a leash, controlling their destiny and ensuring that they did not cause any unnecessary embarrassment by asking troublesome questions. The family received regular visits from RUC welfare officers and, occasionally, Chief Constable Sir John Hermon dropped by. He urged Mrs. Campbell to put the episode behind her, look to the future and accept that, though McCormick had not been convicted, she need not look elsewhere to find the culprit. And, when she sought his reaction to her suspicions that the

RUC was holding something back, Sir John dismissed her concerns: "Rosemary, you read too many fairy stories."[1]

Just a few weeks after McCormick's acquittal on the murder charge, a second murder trial opened in Belfast which, on the surface, appeared to bear no relation to the case that had just ended. Two RUC officers were charged with the murder of a Catholic who, like Sergeant Campbell, had also lived within the Ballymena police district. William Strathearn, a thirty-nine-year-old grocer, had been shot dead at his home on April 19th 1977 and, as with the murder of Sergeant Campbell, his family had learned nothing significant about the killing until the sudden arrest of the two policemen, exactly three years after the crime. Again, the evidence was heard by a judge, not by a jury. And the case, which was to last almost two months, also generated some amazing revelations before the verdict was handed down and the two RUC men were given life sentences for the murder.

The most bizarre features of this trial were that the two men who actually committed the murder were not charged, and that the two RUC men in the dock had sat in their police car throughout the attack. The story that emerged in court placed the blame for the murder on the two police officers, Constable William McCaughey and Sergeant John Weir. They were said to have been the instigators and to have recruited the two Loyalists, whom they had provided with a weapon before driving them to the village of Ahoghill, where the victim lived. The two officers had decided to commission Mr. Strathearn's murder because, as the court heard, they believed he had been involved with the IRA. The two Loyalists woke Mr. Strathearn from his bed in the middle of the night and, on the pretext that they needed a medical prescription for a sick child, persuaded him to open the door of his shop. Immediately, they shot him dead and, then, all four conspirators escaped in the RUC car, leaving no clue about why the killing had occurred or about who had been responsible. The court later learned that Mr. Strathearn had been an entirely innocent man and that the rumours, which had allegedly motivated the police officers, had been completely false.

So who were the two Loyalists? And why had neither of them been charged with the murder? The first question is easier to answer than the second. For, as the court was told, the two Loyalists were none other than Robin Jackson and R.J. "Bob" Kerr who, the reader may recall, was one of those whom Richard Monteith would drive from the Blues Bar on the night of the failed murder bid on Pascal Mulholland in February 1984.[2] The only explanation offered in court by the RUC about why they had not been charged was: "operational reasons." Whatever those reasons might have been, they were clearly sufficient to allow both Jackson and Kerr to escape justice. Another bizarre feature of the trial, which may serve as a comment on the quality of justice dispensed in Northern Ireland, was the remark from the trial judge—Lord Chief Justice Sir Robert Lowry—as he passed a life sentence on McCaughey. "Your action, though understandable, was naturally inexcusable." It is easy to agree that it was inexcusable but why the judge found it "understandable" that an RUC officer would organise the murder of an entirely innocent Catholic was not explained.

I discovered that both trials had been arranged by the RUC, three years after the killings, in an attempt to prevent the truth coming out about Sergeant Campbell's murder. For the Catholic sergeant had been murdered by the RUC itself and the gunman they had recruited was the Loyalist hit man, Robin Jackson. Early in 1980, the RUC had grown alarmed that its guilty secret was about to become public. For the RUC officer who had commissioned the killing and accompanied Jackson to Cushendall, Constable William McCaughey, had been so consumed by guilt that he had become unstable and was experiencing a nervous breakdown.

He had begun to talk uncontrollably about his involvement in the murder and about collusion between the RUC and Loyalist paramilitaries. Consequently, a high-level decision was taken within the RUC to have him removed from public circulation before he caused irreparable damage to the force's reputation. McCaughey was arrested, interrogated and charged with the murder of Mr. Strathearn—but, significantly, not with that of Sergeant Campbell.

When McCaughey and Weir were arrested in 1980, they both made full confessions during their interrogation at Castlereagh Barracks in Belfast. Weir immediately admitted his role in the Strathearn murder but told his interrogators that he had simply been acting under orders from RUC Special Branch; the crime had been commissioned by his superiors. As for the Campbell murder, Jackson had asked him to accompany him to Cushendall so that he could assist with the murder but he had declined. McCaughey, who also broke down under questioning, admitted his role in both murders and told the RUC that they had been committed by Jackson; he also revealed that both had been commissioned by RUC Special Branch. In Cushendall, McCaughey and Jackson had teamed up with McCormick, who had left O'Doherty sitting alone in the police car outside the village; McCormick, who had earlier telephoned Sergeant Campbell at his home to set him up, also supplied Jackson with the murder weapon. In Ahoghill, McCaughey had sat with Weir in the police car while Jackson and Kerr had committed the Strathearn murder. So, after Weir and McCaughey had confessed in 1980, the RUC's most senior officers knew the full truth about both murders.

The subsequent trials appear, therefore, to have been carefully stage managed by the RUC so that only a small part of the truth seeped out in the court room. In the Campbell trial, Jackson's name was never mentioned and no hint was given that this Catholic police officer had been murdered on the orders of a group of Special Branch officers, rather than those of a rogue policeman. The court heard nothing about McCaughey's confession to the Campbell murder, nothing about Special Branch's role, nothing about McCaughey's presence alongside Jackson in Cushendall on the night of February 25th 1977. As both Weir and McCaughey had confessed everything about both murders, I have concluded that the Campbell trial was a "fix," designed to pin the blame on a corrupt but subordinate individual (McCormick) and orchestrated to ensure that the force as a whole evaded responsibility for what had been a high-level Special Branch decision. All the elaborate technical evidence about Armalite rifles and the consequent court room speculation that the IRA had been responsible was, it would appear, a cynical exercise to divert attention from the truth.

The RUC's guilty secret is that Sergeant Joseph Campbell was murdered on the instructions of RUC Special Branch because he had discovered that police officers, army agents, double agents and Loyalists were colluding in a wide range of terrorist activities, acting as *agents provocateurs* and running "dirty tricks" operations against Catholics in his police district in an effort to discredit the IRA. Shootings and bombings, which had been attributed to the IRA, had turned out to be "semi-official" low-intensity counter-guerrilla operations run by the security services.[3] Sergeant Campbell's written reports on these incidents had alarmed Special Branch in Ballymena and Belfast, leading to the decision that it would be better if he were removed permanently from the scene.

I discovered that after his arrest McCormick, along with Weir and McCaughey, also confessed everything to his RUC interrogators. It follows that the most senior officers in the RUC were aware, in advance of both trials, about how and why both murders had been carried out. I believe that the meaning of the "operational reasons" mentioned by the RUC in the Strathearn trial, the explanation for their failure to charge Jackson and Kerr with the grocer's murder, can now be easily understood. For, if the RUC had charged Jackson with the Strathearn murder, he would have been able to defend himself by saying that he had murdered both men—Mr. Strathearn and Sergeant Campbell—on the instructions of RUC Special Branch. Further, Jackson would also have been able to prove that the weapons he used in both murders had been provided to him by the RUC. I have learned that Sergeant Campbell had, indeed, been shot with an IRA Armalite—the IRA's preferred weapon—but that it had not, on this occasion, been provided by the IRA. He had been given it by

Ballymena RUC Special Branch, who had kept it at their station following its seizure from a Republican in a police raid. The "operational reasons" why Jackson was not charged with the Strathearn murder could, I suggest, be aptly rephrased as "fears he would reveal that he was merely obeying RUC orders."

From the day McCormick was acquitted until today, the RUC has allowed the Campbell family to remain in ignorance about how their father met his death. Since all the culprits had confessed in 1980, it is reasonable to assume that when the RUC's Chief Constable, Sir John Hermon, visited Mrs. Campbell after the McCormick trial had ended, he knew that he was talking to a very special RUC widow. Her late husband had not been murdered by the IRA but by the RUC itself. Yet, according to Mrs. Campbell's account of her meetings with the Chief Constable, Sir John encouraged her to believe that, despite the court verdict, McCormick alone had been responsible.

Indeed, Sir John's deception extended to another member of the family. When Joe Campbell, who was just nineteen when his father died, wrote to Sir John in 1994 the Chief Constable telephoned him at his home in London to assure him that, if there was anything he could do to help, he would be delighted to do so. By 1994, Joe was well aware of how and why his father had died; and he knew that Sir John, when Chief Constable, had deliberately misled his mother when he had dismissed her worries as mere "fairy stories." Joe, who is not prepared to settle for anything less than the full truth about how his father died, took the matter up with Sir John's successor, Sir Hugh Annesley. He wrote to Sir Hugh to ask whether any effort had been made to substantiate the claim published in a Dublin newspaper, the *Sunday Independent*, that his father had been murdered by Robin Jackson. The RUC replied as follows:

> I refer to your letter of 21 April [1994] last and have to inform you that it is not the Chief Constable's policy to detail what further enquiries have been made in matters of this sort.
>
> Suffice to say that police have not unearthed any new evidence or indeed intelligence to support the claim outlined in the *Sunday Independent* article of 11th July 1993.
>
> Yours faithfully, J E H McIvor, D/Chief Superintendent

More than seventeen years after his father's murder by the RUC's hand-picked assassin, Robin Jackson, Chief Constable Sir Hugh Annesley felt able, via a subordinate, to give the dead policeman's son the brush off. Sir Hugh's reply suggests that the case is currently regarded as officially closed and it indicates that nobody within RUC Headquarters has the slightest intention of sharing its guilty secret with anyone, least of all the young man who bears his father's name. So, in the absence of any co-operation from the RUC, what is publicly known about Robin Jackson which might be of benefit to the Campbell family in their search for the truth? What information emerged from "murder triangle" before Ben Hamilton encountered Jim Sands in 1991?

Perhaps, the best place to begin is with a murder in Banbridge, County Down in October 1973. Patrick Campbell, a thirty-four-year-old shoe factory worker, was at home with his family when his wife answered a ring on the doorbell. She found two men on the doorstep who asked if they could speak to her husband. When Patrick Campbell came to the door, he was immediately cut down by a hail of bullets and died where he fell. His wife, who had seen the faces of both callers, subsequently picked out one of them at an RUC identity parade in the town. The man, who was then charged with the murder, was named in the newspapers as Robin Jackson. He was remanded in custody but, just two months after his first court appearance, the local newspaper reported that the murder charge had, mysteriously, been dropped and that Jackson was being released. No details were given other than the fact that the charge had been withdrawn on the instructions of the Director of Public Prosecutions.

I have investigated this murder and discovered why no-one else has been or is ever likely to be charged with Patrick Campbell's murder. For, in 1973, Robin Jackson was already working for Army Intelligence and RUC Special Branch. I understand that Patrick Campbell's crime, in Jackson's eyes, was that he had made no secret of his desire to see the creation of a united Ireland. This unremarkable political aspiration was sufficient to make him a target and he became Jackson's first publicly known murder victim. I have recently discovered the identity of Jackson's handler within Military Intelligence at that time; the handler recently retired from the Army with the rank of brigadier but my informant met him in Banbridge at the time and established that Jackson had been working for the Army. My informant has also told me that, in the event of any legal proceedings arising from this book, he will testify about the retired brigadier's involvement in these events and about the collusion that enabled this Loyalist hit man to kill an innocent Catholic, twenty-five years ago.

Jackson's next public appearance did not occur until four years later when, in January 1981, he was one of three Loyalists sentenced to seven years jail at Belfast Crown Court for the possession of weapons and ammunition in Lurgan, County Armagh. Interestingly, another of those sentenced was Philip Silcock who, the reader will recall, was one of the three men who tried, in February 1984, to kill the young Catholic, Paschal Mulholland. Silcock must have just been released from jail when he participated in that attack; as we know, Silcock's partner in that attempted murder was R.J. "Bob" Kerr, the very same individual who had been named in court, in 1980, as Jackson's associate when they drove together to Ahoghill and murdered the Catholic grocer, William Strathearn.

My trawl through local newspapers circulating in the "murder triangle" district gave me a glimpse of the personalities who were emerging in the late '70s and early '80s as the main paramilitaries in the Loyalist camp. Robin Jackson, R.J. Kerr and Philip "Silly" Silcock were, by 1984, already well-known Loyalist paramilitaries within "murder triangle." And, as we've seen, two of Jackson's associates—Kerr and Silcock—were Richard Monteith's drinking companions on the night he gave them a lift from the Blues Bar shortly before they tried to murder Paschal Mulholland. It's fair to assume, I believe, that Monteith was on equally good terms with Jackson and would have known about the activities in which he was engaged. My researches indicated that those who would, between 1989 and 1991, serve on Abernethy's Committee had known each other for a long time and that their association with violence dated back, in some cases, virtually to the outbreak of the troubles two decades earlier.

I have interviewed former Police and Army officers who served in Northern Ireland in the '70s and '80s. These officers, who have assured me of their readiness to testify in court in any libel proceedings that may arise from the publication of this book, told me about Jackson's wide-ranging terrorist activities which, for example, included participation in the Dublin and Monaghan bombings in 1974 (when thirty-three people died) and in the notorious Miami Showband massacre in July 1975 (when five people died).[4] They will testify that Jackson was recruited in 1974 by Army Intelligence, which facilitated his activities and trained him in the assassin's art.[5] The 1981 prison sentence, which appears to suggest he was subject to the law, was—I have been told—a ploy to remove him from the sensitive "murder triangle" area and protect him until it was judged safe to use his services again. Former British intelligence agent Fred Holroyd, who was based in Portadown between 1973 and 1975, has no doubts that Jackson's murderous activities were endorsed at a high level and that he became, at that time, a "licensed killer" for the "security services." This is what he told me:

> Whilst serving as a Military Intelligence Officer in the Special Military Intelligence Unit (Northern Ireland) in 1973–75, I became aware of a Protestant paramilitary called Robin Jackson from Portadown. Because of the "need to know" principle and the compartmentalisation of the Intelligence world, officers like myself often had great difficulty in understanding some of the anomalies in operating realities. One of those anomalies was Robin Jackson.
>
> Although he was known by myself and other Army Intelligence persons as an active paramilitary involved in major activities,

Army personnel were not allowed to touch him. The reason we were given was that he was working on behalf of the RUC Special Branch.

After the murder of Mr. (Patrick) Campbell of Banbridge, Robin Jackson was picked out by Mr. Campbell's widow as the man she had witnessed killing her husband, no charges were ever brought against him by the RUC.

The RUC Special Branch "ran" a number of Protestant paramilitaries in the Portadown area that I was aware of, some of them who operated with Robin Jackson. I, like most of my Army colleagues, was disgusted by this but was assured by my senior officers to "go along with it."

It is my considered view that Robin Jackson was a paid informer and agent of the RUC, personally run by a Sergeant of my acquaintance in Portadown Special Branch office.

My investigation of the murders of William Strathearn and Joseph Campbell convinced me that Robin Jackson was, already in 1977, a trained assassin who enjoyed immunity from prosecution because of operations he had carried out on behalf of his Police and Army contacts. The producers of Yorkshire Television's *The Forgotten Massacre*, broadcast in 1992, identified him as a key member of the Loyalist terror gang which bombed Dublin during the rush hour in May 1974. Although that programme did not name him for legal reasons, I have since received confirmation from one of his former associates that he participated in the Dublin bombing and that the material used to make the bombs was supplied to him by his handlers within British Military Intelligence. I also understand that Jackson's role is one of the reasons why the RUC was singularly uncooperative with the Irish Republic's police authorities in their investigation of that terrible crime.

Those who ran the Committee's assassination campaign in 1989, 1990 and 1991—Abernethy, Ross, Monteith et al—would have known all this and much more about Jackson's terrorist career. Given their knowledge that he had, for many years, been contracted to do "dirty work" for both the Police and Army, we can appreciate their confidence that he would be no more likely to face prosecution for the Committee's murders than he would for the murder of Sergeant Campbell. Robin Jackson had been, in reality, a "hit man" for the British security forces during their long war against the IRA; the Committee knew this and they also believed that any work he carried out on their behalf would be treated similarly by the RUC, thereby conferring a degree of protection on the overall conspiracy. We should also recall that Abernethy had been a member of the RUC Reserve and that, according to Sands, eight members of Ulster Resistance and the Ulster Independence Movement (Sands included) sat on the province-wide RUC Inner Force Council, which held its regular meetings just a few days before the fifty to sixty members of Abernethy's Committee assembled to sanction and organise the killings.

The Campbell family, which has co-operated with me for the past few years, is now aware of what happened to their father and in a position to comment on the circumstances of his death. Sergeant Campbell's son, Joe, speaks for the whole family:

> What happened to my father was an outrage. My mother did all she could to persuade the RUC to tell her the truth but she was misled, manipulated and deceived at every turn. As the years went past and various journalists approached the family, we began to realise that the rumours we had heard were true. I now know that my father was murdered by fellow officers in collusion with a Loyalist terrorist. And we have begun to understand why, in the eighteen months leading up to his death, he had become a changed person. He must obviously have uncovered some damning evidence of illegal activities and collusion between the RUC and the Loyalists, a discovery which ultimately led to his death. It is profoundly contemptible that not one senior officer shared his respect for the law or came to his aid. We now want to know who sanctioned his murder because it appears that three successive Chief Constables have conspired to conceal the truth.
>
> My youngest brother was only four when this happened, so he never knew his father; we all did our best but have been a poor substitute. At my eldest brother's wedding, the first big family occasion after my father's death, I looked at the top table and saw my mother sitting on her own; I kept thinking about my father and I know everybody else did too. The same thing happened at my sister's wedding; my dad's brother, George, gave her away. My mother has carried her grief every single day and we don't really know how much she has suffered. The best compliment I can pay my mother is that my father would be very proud of how she's coped.
>
> My father joined the RUC at a time when it was not socially acceptable for Catholics to do that. He did so in the hope that, by his example, barriers would be broken down. Tragically, when people and particularly the Catholic people of Northern Ireland learn what happened to my father, they will not wish to follow his example. His murder puts in question the RUC's claim that it can be trusted to uphold the law, an issue which will only be resolved when those responsible are identified and brought to justice. The RUC has deceived our family for nearly twenty years and this proves they are not worthy of trust.

The Campbell family is united and determined to pursue all those responsible for the murder and the subsequent cover-up. If the family is successful, Sergeant Campbell's killer, Robin Jackson, will have to be arrested and charged with the crime. So, too, will all those in the RUC who conspired with him. If that were to happen, Abernethy and his co-conspirators on the Committee would discover that the immunity they once enjoyed by virtue of Jackson's "untouchable" status as an official hit man was suddenly removed. The Campbell family's quest for justice over the RUC's guilty secret may, therefore, result not merely in the conviction of their father's assassin but in the exposure of those who employed his services in more recent times, the fifty to sixty members of the Ulster Loyalist Central Co-ordinating Committee.[6]

Notes

1   John Stalker, the English policeman who was smeared and discredited in the mid-1980s when he tried to investigate the RUC, provides a revealing insight into the mind of the former Chief Constable, Sir John Hermon. Stalker describes how Hermon took him to lunch on his arrival in Belfast: "During the meal, Hermon handed me a hand-written note, sketched on the back of a flattened out cigarette packet. It outlined my family tree on my mother's side. She is Catholic and her parents were born in the Irish Republic. No mention was made of my father, who is a Protestant from a Liverpool family. Sir John did not say very much about where he had obtained this information, other than to let me know he had been given it at a social function by a man whose name meant nothing to me—indeed, I cannot even remember it. This action took me by surprise, and I was never able to fully fathom why the Chief Constable gave me that piece of flattened cardboard . . . I found it very puzzling; I still do."

2   See Chapter 12, p. 291.

3   Anthony O'Doherty, who participated in many of these "dirty tricks" operations has provided a detailed account of his involvement with British Intelligence and with McCormick. O'Doherty's account was tape-recorded (on behalf of Channel 4) and could prove most useful, in the unlikely event that the British authorities ever agree to hold an independent inquiry into the murder of Sergeant Campbell.

4   Two of the five victims were UVF members who blew themselves up during the attack. One of the two, Wesley Sommerville, had been photographed a few weeks earlier as he stood beside Jackson at the funeral of a leading Loyalist, Billy Hanna. Although Hanna's murder had been blamed on the IRA, it is now known that it was Jackson who committed this murder. Yet, twenty-four years later, the murder remains "unsolved" and the RUC has, presumably, closed the file.

5   Anthony O'Doherty, the double-agent who worked for British Intelligence, told us that he had been given counter-terrorist training at the British Military Intelligence school at Pontrellis, North Wales; interestingly, O'Doherty claimed that one of his fellow students on the same "training course" had been none other than Robin Jackson [The Jackal] himself.

6   Unfortunately, R.J. Kerr will not be able to contribute to any inquiry that may be held into the murder of Sergeant Joseph Campbell. For he was killed in an explosion on the night of Saturday November 8th, 1997 in mysterious circumstances. His sudden death will be a relief to all those with whom he had been involved in Loyalist terrorism and in related crimes which remain officially "unsolved."

Chapter 14

KEN KERR

My investigation of Sergeant Campbell's murder was successful because I was fortunate in finding a unique source, someone in a position to enlighten me about that particular crime and about what had gone on within the RUC before and after the murder. Although this individual had been a member of the RUC in 1977 and had known, at the time, about Robin Jackson's status as a licensed Special Branch assassin, he was unable to answer any of my questions about more recent events; while he helped me to appreciate that collusion between the RUC and the Loyalists had a long history, he was unable to provide any independent corroboration of what Sands had told us or to contribute fresh information about the activities attributed to the Committee. This meant that I had to find a new source, ideally one of Sands's co-conspirators, someone who had attended the same meetings, someone who had witnessed the same events, the selection of targets and the planning of the murders. My search became even more important after I learned, in December 1992, that Sands had, apparently, "recanted" his testimony about the Committee. Though I knew it was highly unlikely that my quest would succeed I felt that, in view of the enormous damage the broadcast had inflicted on my company and my career, I simply had to try. Besides, I remained utterly convinced that Sands had told us the truth as he had understood it, though I suspected that the full picture would turn out to be even more sinister and shocking than the one Sands had painted for us in 1991.

From October 1991 until now—February 1998—much of my professional life has been, necessarily, devoted to the defence of the programme's journalism, to the defence of the libel actions brought against me by Richard Monteith, to the pursuit of my own libel actions against the *Sunday Express* and *The Sunday Times* and, most importantly, to acquiring the evidence which would prove, irrefutably, that what Sands had told us was true. I was determined to establish the identities of the eighteen RUC Inner Force officers who, under the guidance of Trevor Forbes OBE, had devised and implemented the assassination campaign. Inevitably, my research efforts brought me to the attention of the British Intelligence services and I became aware that I was under surveillance during my frequent research trips to the province; such unwelcome attention put me constantly on the alert but it never prevented me from pursuing my research wherever it took me.

I knew I had to be careful in both word and deed because, shortly after the broadcast in 1991, I had learned via Source A that two RUC detectives had been dispatched to London with what must have been a particularly challenging assignment; they had been ordered, I was informed, to explore my presumed links to the Provisional IRA; someone in the RUC must have assumed that, since I had supervised the making of this damaging documentary, I must have been sympathetic to Republican terrorism, an assumption which was totally unfounded because I have always viewed such activity—bombings, shootings, knee-cappings, stabbings and other horrors—as being both morally repugnant and politically counterproductive. I later learned that, after spending a frustrating period at Scotland Yard during which they failed to find any evidence of the desired kind, the two detectives returned home to report that they had found "no known links;" I was contemptuous of this verdict (reported by Source A) because, if the two officers had been tapping our office telephones in October 1991, they would have known that I was in regular professional contact with a number of prominent figures, at least one of whom might well have been a potential target for assassination by the IRA.

Occasionally, the surveillance was amateurish and ostentatious. For example, while waiting to board the shuttle to Belfast in early 1996, I suddenly turned around to find a large, somewhat intimidating, man standing beside me, a physical presence that somehow labelled him as a police officer; a few minutes later, after sitting down in the seat allocated to me, I discovered that this same man was sitting directly behind me. I had been placed in the first row of the aircraft, he in the second—not a coincidence, I assumed. I later discovered from one of my Loyalist sources that this individual was, indeed, a member of the RUC. Trivial incidents like this did not bother me; indeed, if they had any significance at all, they probably reassured me, in a way that was scarcely conscious, that my inquiry was moving along the right track. In truth, I would have been more worried if I had never managed to detect and classify these shadowy figures from the "security" and "intelligence" worlds.

Since Sands had estimated the size of the Committee's membership at between fifty and sixty, I was forced to accept that any approach I might make to any one of them would, almost certainly, be reported to Billy Abernethy. Still, that was a risk I had to take. For if a second member of the Committee were, for whatever reason, to decide to help me, then the dividends could be enormous. It was for that reason that, in April 1996, I telephoned a well-known Loyalist paramilitary, fringe politician and convicted terrorist, Ken Kerr. I had made the call from a public phone in Dungiven, a small town about twenty minutes drive from Derry, where Kerr lives; and I was pleasantly surprised when, after some initial reluctance, he agreed to see me half an hour later. While driving from Dungiven to Derry, I wondered why he had agreed to talk to me and worked out my own strategy for the meeting. I decided that the wisest course was to be open and honest about my motives, to indicate that I knew a great deal about the conspiracy and to tell him that I wished to learn the rest of the story; I also resolved to be properly sceptical about anything and everything he might tell me. For I had already gathered sufficient information about him to suspect that he had been deeply implicated in the Committee's murder campaign from its earliest days.

Kerr, who suffered from a "bad leg"—the result of an injury from his military or paramilitary days—was waiting for me outside the bar of the Waterfoot Hotel in Derry. After the initial greetings, we went inside, ordered a round of drinks and talked for about thirty minutes. I told Kerr, at once, that I knew about Abernethy, Ross, Monteith, Forbes, Moffett, Prentice and various other conspirators, those whom Sands had identified in 1991. Then I said: "I don't know whether you were a member, but I suspect you were." He did not reply at once but, when he did, he was calm and spoke quietly: "Yes. I was a member from the start. What is it that you want to know?" The conversation could not have got off to a more positive or promising start; I had—it seemed—persuaded a second self-confessed Committee member to talk frankly to me about the murder conspiracy. Kerr admitted his involvement in the Committee as readily as he might have told me he was a stamp-collector or a bird-watcher. And he added, quite quickly and with a touch of enthusiasm, that he genuinely admired my persistence and dedication in pursuing this story for so long. "You stuck with it," he commented, as I prepared to leave. "Channel 4 was just fillin' an hour." The meeting seemed too good to be true. And it surely was, as I was to discover just over a year later when I obtained proof that Kerr, despite his plausibility and affability, had been collaborating closely with his co-conspirators on the Committee throughout the entire eighteen-month period he remained in contact with me.

Some weeks after that first meeting, I made another visit to Derry, again meeting Kerr in the bar at the Waterfoot Hotel. On this occasion, he arrived alone but was in an agitated and flustered state. He said that the RUC was aware that he was talking to me, that I had been "tailed" all the way from Heathrow Airport in London and that we ought to keep our meeting as brief as possible. Ten minutes after we began our conversation,

Kerr drew my attention to a man who had just entered the bar, ordered a drink and sat down at a nearby table. "He's an RUC Special Branch man from Limavady," Kerr whispered.[1] Though this visitor, I now presume, would have been one of Kerr's accomplices and, quite possibly, had indeed been an RUC Special Branch man from Limavady, his sudden appearance in the hotel bar was a suitable pretext for Kerr to bring our meeting to an abrupt end. So, after two expensive research trips to meet Kerr in his home town, I had little to show for my investment; for that reason, I decided to invite Kerr and his wife to take a short all-expenses-paid "holiday" in England. I hoped we would be able to talk more freely there.

I invited Tim Laxton to join me in Maidstone in Kent where Mr. and Mrs. Kerr had been booked into a luxury hotel for a long weekend in August 1996. They arrived on a Friday and left on a Monday, with Kerr devoting the entire Saturday afternoon to his conversation with Tim and me. Kerr began by confirming that Jim Sands, though uneducated and indiscreet, had been allowed to participate fully in the Committee because he was vouched for by his boss, "Reverend" Hugh Ross. After the Channel 4 broadcast, said Kerr, there had been a frantic search for the "traitor" but Sands had managed to avoid suspicion because of his close proximity to Ross; Kerr himself had fallen under suspicion, he told us, but he had somehow managed to convince the others that he had never met anyone from Box Productions or Channel 4. We were both encouraged when Kerr admitted that Sands had given us an entirely accurate account of what had transpired at meetings of the Committee.

Kerr's most startling revelation, however, was that he himself had been an even bigger traitor to the Committee than Sands had been. For Kerr explained that he had been, for many years, a paid agent for British Military Intelligence and that, week after week, he had reported to his "handler" about everything that had transpired at Committee meetings. In short, Kerr claimed that he was a British "double-agent" or spy, ostensibly an Ulster Loyalist helping his kith-and-kin to lay the foundations of an Independent Ulster, while secretly reporting in advance to British Military Intelligence about each of the "hits" that the Committee had sanctioned and planned. *If true*, this would have been an astounding revelation because it would have altered decisively the character of the murder conspiracy; it would have meant that the Ulster Loyalist death squads, which had carried out the murders discussed in this book and many other murders as well, had also been British death squads. Kerr asked us to believe that his British Intelligence handler, whose name he gave us, had actually provided him with the names of Republicans the Government wished to see permanently removed from the scene; Kerr told us that he then proposed these names at Committee meetings as "targets" for "hits."

Finally, Kerr assured us that British Military Intelligence had at least one other "double-agent" on the Committee, who would also report directly to his "handler;" the British Government, Kerr was inviting us to believe, had known about and approved of the Committee's assassination campaign from its inception.

It was certainly an interesting story. And Kerr unveiled it to us at great length and with supreme confidence, giving the impression that he was pleased to be getting an enormous weight off his chest. *If the story was true*, Tim and I realised at the time, it was a story with potentially explosive political significance. For the ultimate responsibility for the murders would lie—not with the Committee, nor the RUC Inner Force nor the RUC Inner Circle—but with the British Government. Kerr asked us to appreciate that his complex situation and status—as a public enemy of the IRA, as a well-known Ulster Loyalist paramilitary and as a secret agent of British Intelligence—meant that he risked being murdered by any one of these groups; if his handlers were to discover he was talking to us, he said, an anonymous telephone call to Abernethy or one of his henchmen would undoubtedly have fatal consequences. So why, then, was Kerr telling us all this? After all, he knew why we had invited him to come and talk to us. He knew that I was writing a book and that I proposed to publish everything he said provided, naturally, that I was entirely satisfied that his revelations were true. Even though he knew I had promised him unqualified anonymity, why would he be happy to help me reveal all this in print?

In Maidstone, Kerr's reply was that he was desperate to escape from his plight but that his British Intelligence "handlers" would not allow him to retire to his villa in Spain; he was, he claimed, too valuable as a source about what was happening within the Loyalist camp. Back home in Derry, some months later, he gave me a second, even more urgent explanation but one which was reasonably compatible with the first. He was helping me, he said, because he was suffering from colon cancer and suspected that he did not have long to live. This claim sounded plausible because, since his visit to England, he had lost weight and his long, greying hair had gone; his nearly bald head was, he explained, the result of intensive chemotherapy he was receiving to help him fight the cancer. His looming demise from colon cancer, together with his fears that he could be killed by any of the warring factions—the IRA, the Committee, the British—left him in a state where his peace of mind rested, he said, on the prospect of living to see the full truth become publicly known before his death. I would later discover the *real* reason why Kerr was talking to us and doing his utmost to sound persuasive and convincing.

Kerr had obviously been well briefed before his arrival in Maidstone. After admitting that Sands had told us the truth, he proceeded to give us the names of a further thirty Committee members, many names I had never heard before, including the names of twelve senior RUC officers, two UDR officers and, amazingly, the names of two senior civil servants in the Northern Ireland Office. He claimed to be a close friend of Trevor Forbes and to have been, between 1989 and 1994, the pivotal figure in the Committee's murder conspiracy; he was the link man between the RUC Inner Force and the Loyalist assassins, his military expertise reassuring the key Committee members that the "hits" would be done professionally. He also gave us the names of the Loyalist assassins and RUC officers who, together, had colluded in some of the more spectacular "unsolved" murders. After listening to him for several hours in Maidstone, we told him that we would not be able to use any of his, undoubtedly fascinating, information unless and until we obtained *proof* that it was *true*. Could he give us any documentary evidence? Did he have any official documents, photographs or tape-recordings? How could he convince us that his story deserved to be believed?

He replied that it would be difficult, though not impossible, to obtain what we were looking for. It would, however, take time and require a certain amount of ingenuity because he would have to outwit his Intelligence "handler." Kerr claimed that he had secretly and regularly recorded meetings of the Committee at the behest of his "handler;" after each Committee meeting he had also dictated a brief memo, tape-recorded on a micro-cassette, outlining details of such matters as the next "target" to be "hit," the names of the assassins and RUC Inner Force personnel involved, together with the date and time of the proposed operation. Though he still had access to these tape-recordings, he would have to be careful not to draw attention to himself. He said that he would let us know when Tim ought to visit him in Derry to collect one of these tape-recordings.

After meeting him in Maidstone, we remained in regular contact with him for ten months until, after what seemed an eternity of frustrating delays, Kerr finally signalled that the moment had arrived for the hand over of what we had been waiting for. Tim met him in Derry in May 1997 and, after passing over a brown envelope containing £5000 which I had borrowed from a friend, he returned to England with what promised to be irrefutable evidence of the Committee's murder conspiracy. Supposedly, Kerr had secretly recorded a Committee—or, more accurately, a sub-Committee—meeting in the Seagoe Hotel in Portadown in February 1989, when five Committee members, including Trevor Forbes OBE, had made their final preparations for the planned murder of Belfast solicitor Patrick Finucane. Although Kerr had not specified how much money he wanted, merely that he expected a suitable payment, I had decided to err on the side of generosity with Kerr for two reasons. First, I took the view that, if the tape-recording proved to be genuine, we would have obtained evidence of identified conspirators discussing and planning a notorious and politically salient murder; arrests, charges and convictions would surely follow. Kerr obviously saw the significance with which we viewed his package because, after giving the tape-recording to Tim, he commented with an embarrassed smile: "That should be good for five life sentences." If that had, indeed, proved to be the outcome of the transaction, I would have thought the money well spent. Second, I wished to give Kerr an incentive to obtain a second tape-recording for us, something he promised to do if we were satisfied with the quality and, more importantly, the authenticity of his first offering.

After Tim had returned to England, we met at once and proceeded to open the package Kerr had handed over. It contained a micro-cassette, supposedly a copy of the original tape-recording he had made for his British Intelligence "handler;" he told Tim he had made it immediately after the five Committee members, Kerr included, had settled the logistical details for the planned murder of Patrick Finucane. Kerr's package also contained a hand-written note with the codes he had allegedly used when dictating the tape-recorded memo to his "handler" about his four co-conspirators. Two of the four were said to be prominent businessmen living within "murder triangle" and they were, supposedly, full participating members of the murder conspiracy; why Sands had never mentioned either of these men—in contrast, for example, to his fingering David and Albert Prentice—was not explained. The other two were both said to be RUC officers, Assistant Chief Constable Trevor Forbes OBE and an individual whose name, until then, we had never heard before. Kerr said that the fifth conspirator possessed an unusual, probably unique, name. He was called Ezzard Boyd and was said to have risen through the police force to the rank of Chief Inspector; this senior police officer was, we were told, one of Forbes's most trusted associates within the RUC Inner Force. Boyd and Forbes had—according to Kerr's carefully crafted story—masterminded the killing and, seven years later in 1997, they were still the only people, apart from Kerr himself, who knew the identities of the gunmen who had murdered the solicitor. One of these Loyalist assassins was said to have been an RUC officer, the other to have belonged to the UDR. Kerr, having divulged their names, assured Tim that he was now the only person in the world, apart from Forbes, Boyd, the assassins and Kerr himself, who knew the names of Patrick Finucane's killers.

The tape-recording was of poor quality and we found it difficult to decipher the precise words uttered by the different voices. It seemed, at first hearing, to be a recording of a meeting held in a rather public place, quite possibly a hotel; it contained the sounds of doors being slammed, crockery being handled and intermittent background noises which suggested a degree of activity proceeding while the supposed conspirators planned their murder. After listening to the tape three or four times, Tim and I agreed that—*if the tape-recording was, as it might have been, authentic*—then we had made a sound investment. Abernethy, Ross, Forbes, Monteith and the new conspirator, if he was such—Ezzard Boyd—would, in due course, be in for an almighty shock.

However, neither of us needed to be reminded that the tape-recording might not be genuine nor that Kerr, despite his display of extreme nervousness when giving the tape to Tim a few days earlier, might be a fraudster or worse. It was possible, we both knew, that the tape was a deliberate fabrication, a forgery designed to lure me into committing a catastrophic blunder. I knew that Kerr's real reason for "helping" me might not be his frustrated wish to retire to Spain or his demise from colon cancer but, quite possibly, the desire to discredit my entire investigation into the Committee by feeding me demonstrably false information. So, Tim and I agreed we would have to scrutinise every aspect of Kerr's story before accepting any of it at face value. Fortunately, I could afford to take all the time I wished before reaching any decision about the status of his tape-recording, let alone arriving at a final verdict on the truth of his revelations. Not a single word of Kerr's testimony about the Committee would be included in my book, if I had the slightest doubt about his veracity.

So, in the early summer of 1997, I began at my leisure to test the factual accuracy of Kerr's astounding story. Some obvious questions had presented themselves: Who were the two Portadown businessmen said to have belonged to the Committee?[2] What does Trevor Forbes's voice sound like? Does it match "his" voice on the tape-recording? Did the Seagoe Hotel meeting, if it had occurred at all, take place before or after the Finaghy Orange Hall meeting which, the reader may recall, was the one at which the decision to kill the solicitor was taken, according to Sands's account in 1991? Who is Ezzard Boyd? Is he a Chief Inspector in the RUC? Was his father in the RUC, as Kerr had also told Tim? Where was he on Saturday morning, February 5th 1989, when the five conspirators were said to have met in the Seagoe Hotel? Did the two identified assassins, the RUC and UDR officers, exist and what could we find out about them?[3]

It did not take me too long to discover that Kerr's story had credibility problems. First, I learned that one of Kerr's two businessmen had the same name and nickname as a well-known footballer in Northern Ireland, someone who happened to live in the same town as one of the businessmen, Portadown, Co Armagh. Not a promising start, I thought. My next step was to acquire from Ulster Television in Belfast a video copy of an interview Assistant Chief Constable Trevor Forbes had given the station in 1982, quite some time before his rise to notoriety as a result of the Stalker Affair. None of the five voices on Kerr's tape-recording matched the one that had arrived from Belfast. Next, Tim telephoned the second businessman at his office in Dungannon, Co. Tyrone and made two relevant discoveries. First, his voice was not one of the five recorded on the tape; and second, this gentleman—who made no secret of his extreme Loyalist views—gave the impression that Tim's telephone call had not been entirely unexpected. By this time, around July 1997, Tim and I were tending to the view that Kerr's tape was probably a fake. It did not take much longer for us to obtain information which removed any lingering doubt and which settled the matter once and for all.

By mid-summer 1997 I was exceedingly conscious of the importance of ensuring that every allegation I proposed to make in this book was completely accurate. In particular, I knew that it would be potentially ruinous for me if I were to include in the book any of Kerr's revelations, especially if he had perpetrated a "hoax" on me with the tape-recording he had given to Tim. For, at this time, my lawyers were putting pressure on *The Sunday Times* in the libel case I had brought over its claim that I had bribed Sands to recite a prepared script containing false allegations in *The Committee*. In its defence, if that word is appropriate to the newspaper's desperate response, *The Sunday Times'* lawyers were arguing that their client had never intended to accuse me of participation in any "hoax" of any kind; on the contrary—argued the newspaper's inventive and expensive lawyers—the plaintiff (myself) had been one of the victims of the "hoax," for he had failed entirely to notice that Jim Sands, Martin O'Hagan and Ben Hamilton had conspired to dupe him as well as Channel 4 and its viewers. I realised that this ridiculous scenario would be unlikely to impress any libel jury but that it might, possibly, acquire some degree of plausibility if, six years after the original, supposed "hoax" programme, I were to have been demonstrably "hoaxed" by Kerr; it could, I knew, be catastrophic for me if he duped me into accepting as true the spurious contents of a faked tape-recording. So I appreciated the vital importance of reaching the right verdict on the status of what Kerr had given to Tim.

Suddenly, when my mind was on matters unrelated to Kerr's tape, I came across some documents in my home which had been lying untouched in a box since we had worked on the programme back in 1991. They related to a wide variety of matters pertaining to collusion, the Stevens Inquiry and the Brian Nelson affair. When I started to read one of the documents, a copy of a letter written by an inmate of the Maze Prison outside Belfast about another inmate, my eyes were transfixed and, for a brief moment, I was frozen to the spot. For the letter—significantly, dated February 1991—made it clear that the prisoner referred to was a man who, at that time, had served just about half of a four-year jail sentence for Loyalist terrorism. The name of this convicted terrorist was, incredibly, that of the RUC officer who had—according to Kerr—helped Trevor Forbes in February 1989 to plan the murder of Patrick Finucane, the bizarrely named Ezzard Boyd. The letter also gave the prisoner's home address in Dungannon, County Tyrone. I realised, at once, that I had stumbled across a highly significant piece of information because it was unlikely, to put it mildly, that there could have been, in February 1989, two Ezzard Boyds living in Northern Ireland. But, if Kerr's tape-recording was authentic, this is precisely what the letter meant—there had to be two Ezzard Boyds in Northern Ireland in February 1989, one in the Maze Prison, the other a Chief Inspector in the RUC.[4]

One short telephone call settled the matter beyond doubt. Ezzard Boyd explained that, as far as he was aware, he was the only person in the world with that rare Christian name, one which his father had given him as a mark of respect for an American boxer, now dead.[5] Ezzard Boyd confirmed that, in February 1989, he had been in the Maze Prison serving a four-year term. He assured his caller, Tim Laxton, that neither he nor his father had ever been in the RUC. So, we concluded that there has never been an RUC Chief Inspector Ezzard Boyd and that Kerr's tape-recording was, therefore, a fake.

Why had Ken Kerr taken the trouble to co-operate with me in my investigation over an eighteen-month period? What did he hope to achieve? Who helped him? I believe that plausible answers to these questions can be easily found, if we consider the consequences of my failure to detect the "hoax" tape-recording. If I had accepted the truth of Kerr's revelations and included in my book his account of how Patrick Finucane came to be murdered, the RUC would surely have been delighted. If the only Ezzard Boyd in the world—it's hard to believe there are two people with such a name—could be proven to have been in residence at Her Majesty's Maze Prison in February 1989, what credibility could be given to an author who claimed he was, at that precise time, a Chief Inspector in the RUC? What credibility could the same author claim for any of his other revelations, such as the existence of the Committee, the RUC Inner Force, the RUC Inner Circle and the roles these secret organisations played in the murder of Denis Carville and many others? If I had failed to detect Kerr's deception, I would have allowed him to sabotage my entire six-year-long investigation into collusion between the RUC and the Loyalist death squads; the spurious contents of the faked tape-recording would have utterly discredited this book and left my journalistic career in ruins.

Billy Abernethy, Hugh Ross, Trevor Forbes, Richard Monteith and all the other Committee members, together with all those within the RUC,

UDR and Northern Ireland Office who know the truth about the Committee, would have been celebrating Kerr's achievement between now and the Millennium. The RUC Press Office would have spared no effort to facilitate the efforts of Barrie Penrose, Liam Clarke, Andrew Neil and all other paid-up members of the official dirty tricks brigade. The nineteen murder conspirators identified by Sands, along with the additional thirty or so individuals he saw in attendance at Committee meetings, would have given a collective sigh of relief, as the prospect of murder charges and murder trials receded into the distance before vanishing forever. So I conclude, on the basis of who stood to gain most from the deception, that Kerr was working in close collaboration with other members of the Committee and, probably, with senior police officers belonging to the RUC Inner Force and the RUC Inner Circle.[6]

One of the most revealing moments, during our conversation with Kerr in Maidstone, arose when we were discussing the murder of Denis Carville. When I expressed the opinion that it had been a despicable crime and that the Committee must have known that Denis had been an entirely innocent boy, Kerr merely mumbled the reply: "Not really;" as he spoke, he fidgeted in his chair, looked away from me and led both Tim and me to the same conclusion. We thought it probable that Kerr was so sensitive about this killing because he had been present in the Dolphin Bar in Lurgan on the night Billy Abernethy, Billy Wright and the rest of them laid their plans for that murder.

Since the fake tape-recording proved that Kerr's real motive in talking to me was sabotage, the destruction of my investigation, I have decided that it would be foolish to include any of the new material he provided, without heavy qualification. I suspect, however, that his account of the Committee comprised a mixture of true and false information so that, for example, some of the RUC Inner Force officers he identified had, indeed, participated in the assassination campaign. He may have thought that by feeding me a substantial amount of fresh and accurate details about the Committee and its members that, in my enthusiasm to expose the entire conspiracy, I would fail to discriminate between the wheat and the chaff. Then, following publication of this book, the hard-working RUC Press Office would have been able to show that the particular assassin or RUC officer, identified to me by Kerr as the culprit for a specific murder, could not possibly have committed the crime, for whatever reason. As with Ezzard Boyd so, I suspect, it would have turned out to be with KB and BM, two Loyalists whom Kerr fingered for the two Committee murders discussed below.[7]

After Sands had returned home from his visit to London in early May 1991, he had kept in touch with us up to the date of the broadcast and, as we have seen, well beyond that date. He informed us about two additional murders the Committee had sanctioned and organised during the summer, including one just across the border from Derry in Buncrana, County Donegal in late May, the other in my home town Castlederg, County Tyrone in August. By mid-1996, when we met Kerr in Maidstone, both of these murders—like so many other, indeed *all*, Committee murders—were still, officially, "unsolved;" so we naturally asked our visitor if he could tell us who had been responsible for each. Kerr's response is, I believe, worth reporting because he showed intimate knowledge of both crimes; nevertheless, his account obviously cannot be accepted as the definitive version, given his generally duplicitous conduct and his complete indifference to truth. I suspect that Kerr deliberately injected false information—especially the names of the Loyalist assassins and RUC Inner Force officers involved—into the version of events he gave us but that he was otherwise speaking from direct personal experience. We should remember that it was Sands, *not* Kerr, who had first told us these two murders were the work of the Committee; in which case, it is more than likely that Kerr, the Committee member with most military expertise, had been centrally involved in the planning and the execution of both crimes.

The first murder was that of an elected Sinn Féin councillor, Eddie Fullerton, in Buncrana. He had been shot dead in the middle of the night by a Loyalist squad, which—according to Kerr—was led by a UVF member, BM. He told us that nine Committee members, including BM, had planned the murder at a well-known hotel in Ballymena, County Antrim; among those present, he said, were Abernethy, Forbes, King Rat, Monteith and Kerr himself. BM was said to have led a four-man squad, which was transported in two D-40 Gemini high-speed rubber dinghies by sea across Lough Foyle to Muff in the Republic of Ireland; on arriving at Muff, the four Loyalists were met by two cars which drove them several miles to their destination, Buncrana. Councillor Eddie Fullerton, who was asleep in his bed, was shot dead after the squad burst into his home; following the attack, the Loyalists were driven out of the town at speed, dumped their weapons and clothing at a disused farmhouse at Muff and then split into two separate groups. The two cars, each containing two squad members and a driver, sped off in different directions, one crossing the border at Derry, the other at Strabane in County Tyrone.

The authorities in the Irish Republic may wish to question Kerr about his version of the events that led to the murder of Eddie Fullerton. I would, however, be surprised if the leader of the death squad turned out to be BM because I have independent reasons for believing that this man was a member of the Committee.

Since Kerr's entire rationale for "helping" me turns out to have been a desire to protect all the murder conspirators on the Committee, I know no reason why he would have wished to identify BM as the leader of the Loyalist squad that killed Eddie Fullerton unless, perhaps, BM would turn out to have a convincing alibi on the night in question—as convincing as Ezzard Boyd's would have been for Saturday, February 5th 1989. Perhaps, one day, we will discover the full story of how the Committee organised the assassination of the Sinn Féin councillor.

Three months after the murder of Eddie Fullerton, the Committee sanctioned and carried out another killing close to the border with the Irish Republic. Although we had first heard about this murder from Sands shortly after it happened in August 1991, Kerr claimed—in Maidstone in August 1996—to have comprehensive knowledge about how it had been organised and about those responsible for it. Patrick Shanaghan, a thirty-one-year-old Catholic and Sinn Féin election worker, had been driving to work in the early morning near Castlederg, County Tyrone when a masked man, carrying a machine-gun, stepped into the road, opened fire and riddled his car with bullets. Patrick Shanaghan was mortally wounded and the gunman managed to escape undetected. When Kerr told us his version of what had happened the inquest, which the RUC initiated a full five years after the murder, had just been held in Strabane, County Tyrone and had ended in bitter controversy, with the dead man's family claiming that the RUC was deliberately suppressing the truth about the murder. Halfway through the inquest hearing, the Shanaghan family walked out of the court room protesting at RUC Chief Constable Sir Hugh Annesley's success in preventing the Coroner from holding a full scale investigation into how the murder had occurred.

The Shanaghan inquest had hit the headlines because a local doctor testified in the Coroner's court that, after arriving at the scene of the shooting, he had been prevented by an RUC officer from attending to the victim. The doctor told the court that the RUC officer at the scene of the crime, Inspector Alan Moore, had informed him that Patrick Shanaghan did not need a doctor because he was already dead. Not surprisingly, this testimony proved controversial because, earlier, the inquest had heard from two independent witnesses, who stated that they had arrived at the scene of the shooting just before the doctor and that they had each seen Patrick moving his head. This raised the sensitive question for the Coroner's jury as to whether RUC Inspector Alan Moore had been deliberately keeping the doctor away from Patrick so that he would not recover from his wounds. The court also heard that when the doctor was finally allowed, a full hour after the shooting, to examine Patrick he discovered that he was already dead. The family's anger at the RUC's suspicious conduct had deepened further when they learned that a Catholic priest, called to give the last rites to the dying man, had also been prevented from approaching Patrick until his life had ended.

Patrick's mother, convinced that her son had been murdered as a result of RUC collusion with the unknown assassin, had sought to present a wide range of evidence to the jury in the Coroner's court. For example, thanks to her efforts, the jury learned that a security file containing a photo-montage of her son had been "lost" from the back of a British Army vehicle; and, under questioning by Mrs. Shanaghan's solicitor, an RUC officer told the jury that he had been called to the scene of the shooting twenty minutes *before* it had actually occurred. The inquest was already turning into a public relations disaster for the RUC when the Coroner indicated that he was prepared to allow the jury to hear further evidence—evidence which would, almost certainly, have resulted in yet more embarrassment for the RUC. One of Patrick's friends, a Scotsman, had offered to testify in court about how RUC officers had, in May 1991, threatened to have both Patrick and the friend killed by Loyalist paramilitaries. This development proved too much for the RUC Chief Constable, who promptly dispatched his lawyers to the High Court in Belfast, asking a judge to rule whether it would be proper for the Coroner to hold such an inquiry into how Patrick had come to be murdered. Sir Hugh was not to be disappointed when the High Court's Mr. Justice Kerr came to deliver his ruling.

> It is not a Coroner's function to conduct a wide-ranging inquiry into the broad circumstances in which a person died. It cannot be the case that evidence relating to the quality of police investigations touches upon the means by which Mr. Shanaghan was killed. That goes well beyond the legitimate scope of the Coroner. By the same token, evidence that Mr. Shanaghan had been told [by the police that] he would be killed by Loyalist terrorists is not germane to the facts on which a Coroner must decide as to how the deceased met his death.

When I read this astounding statement, I again recalled Brian Raymond's wry comment on the judiciary when, tutoring me on the realities of the British legal system, he had told me that "judges are just politicians with wigs on." As in London, so it would seem to be in Belfast. Chief Constable Annesley secured all he had hoped for from Mr. "Justice" Kerr[8] and, as a result, the Coroner's jury in County Tyrone was subsequently denied the opportunity of considering the following evidence from Patrick's close friend, Scotsman David Cameron:

> In January 1991, Patrick Shanaghan informed me that while he was being held in Castlereagh [RUC] Interrogation Centre [in

Belfast], he was informed by one of his interrogators that this was
going to be the year of Shanaghan and Cameron.

Then on May 14th, 1991, I was arrested at my home and taken
to Castlereagh Interrogation Centre and was told during one of
the interviews that Paddy Shanaghan and I were responsible for all
the terrorist activities in the Castlederg area and we were going to
be taken out.

I was told our names were to be leaked to a [man] who has
connections with the [Loyalist] Ulster Defence Association.

Deprived of this evidence which, contrary to what Mr. "Justice" Kerr
had to say, could scarcely be more relevant to any consideration of how
and why Patrick Shanaghan was murdered, the jury returned a purely formal and utterly pointless verdict. The Coroner's court had been legally
prevented from inquiring further into how Patrick Shanaghan had come
to be murdered; nevertheless, this did not prevent the Coroner from stating unambiguously that Patrick had been the victim of "a cold-blooded
and cowardly assassination."

So was Patrick Shanaghan's murder sanctioned and planned by
Abernethy's Committee? Did the RUC Inner Force in Castlederg lead the
assassin to the scene of the crime and, following the murder, guide him
safely away? Did the RUC Inner Force's role in the murder affect the quality of the subsequent investigation? We already know the answers to these
questions—yes, yes, yes—from the information passed on to us by Sands
in 1991. When we put the same questions to Kerr in Maidstone, he began
by corroborating what Sands had told us and then proceeded to fill in the
crucial, missing details. He told us that Patrick Shanaghan had been shot
dead by a UFF gunman, KB, a "crack shot" who lives in County Antrim
and that the assassination had been organised by an identified RUC Inner
Force Detective working out of the RUC Station in Strabane, County
Tyrone.[9]

Kerr spoke to us about this murder with ease and conviction, attributes which probably reflect the fact that he was, as with the murder of Eddie
Fullerton, centrally involved in the planning and execution of the crime.[10]
Immediately after learning the names of the two men allegedly responsible for Patrick Shanaghan's murder, we naturally tried to find out what we
could about them. KB proved to be elusive and we did not manage to
speak to him before our discovery that the "Ezzard Boyd" tape was a fake;
after that, once we were satisfied that Kerr was a saboteur, almost certainly
collaborating with Abernethy and company, we did not bother to try to
contact KB again; we also managed to establish that Kerr's identified RUC
Special Branch officer was not based in Strabane but in Waterside RUC
Station in Derry. So we concluded that, as with the murder of Eddie

Fullerton, Kerr had deliberately injected false information into an otherwise accurate version of events. I suspect that, if I had failed to detect Kerr's deception and published the two names he provided for this murder, the RUC would have been able to show that neither of the two men could possibly have been in Castlederg on the morning in question, for whatever reason.

Perhaps, one day, we will discover the *real* names of those involved, the Loyalist assassin and the RUC Inner Force personnel who colluded in the murder of Patrick Shanaghan.[11] Then we will better appreciate why RUC Chief Constable Sir Hugh Annesley was so worried by the developments in the Coroner's court in Strabane that he moved so quickly to prevent the full truth from emerging about the role his RUC officers appear to have played in the murder. Neither Chief Constable Sir Hugh Annesley nor his successor Ronnie Flanagan[12] has, to date, offered any convincing reason why RUC Inspector Alan Moore prevented the local doctor from giving medical assistance to Patrick Shanaghan when, as two independent witnesses have testified, he seemed still to be alive; nor has either Chief Constable, as yet, explained how it could come about that an RUC constable was called to the scene of the shooting, twenty minutes *before* it actually occurred. Until the RUC answers these questions satisfactorily it will, I believe, continue to experience great difficulty in answering the accusations levelled against it by the murder victim's seventy-two-year-old mother, Mrs. Mary Shanaghan.

> This inquest has confirmed my belief that collusion between the security forces and Loyalist paramilitaries was involved in the murder of my son Patrick and that there has been little, if any, effort made to find those responsible for Patrick's murder . . .
>
> What is most distressing for me is the blatant disregard for Patrick's life and the inexcusable refusal of Inspector Moore to allow Dr. Stewart [the local doctor] to provide medical assistance to Patrick as he lay dying. Not the slightest effort was made to call an ambulance. Even Patrick's parish priest, Fr. McGinn, was rerouted and delayed from reaching Patrick in his final moments. As in life, Patrick was, in death, denied the most basic of human rights.

So how many people organised the murder of Patrick Shanaghan? Which RUC officers and Loyalist gunmen, if not those named by Kerr, were responsible? How did the Committee plan and supervise the assassination? Apart from Inspector Alan Moore, the other RUC officers present at the scene of the shooting were Constables Divine, McVicar, Dodds, Sloan and Hicks; were any or all of these men involved in collusion with the Loyalist squad? Until the RUC or, preferably, the British Government agrees to hold a genuinely independent inquiry into Patrick Shanaghan's murder there will continue to be justifiable suspicion that one or more of these officers colluded with unidentified RUC Inner Force members and the Loyalist squad. That suspicion rests on the unexplained events before and after the shooting, together with Committee member Jim Sands's confession in 1991 that the murder had been carried out by the RUC Inner Force and the Loyalists on behalf of the Committee. In these circumstances, Patrick Shanaghan's mother is, not surprisingly, unimpressed by the RUC's response to her allegation of collusion. An RUC press statement read:

> We fully appreciate the intolerable grief of the family circle. We totally refute, however, any suggestion of collusion. The murder was fully investigated and remains open. We invite anyone with new evidence to come forward.

The Shanaghan family organised an independent public inquiry into Patrick's death, which was held in Castlederg in September 1996 by a retired US federal judge, Andrew Somers. This inquiry, which was shunned by the RUC, heard fresh evidence from a witness who had been questioned by RUC detectives at the Castlereagh holding centre in November 1995. Declan Gormley told the inquiry, according to a press report, "that his Castlereagh questioners had "play-acted" various scenes, including one where they urinated on Mr. Shanaghan's grave. The witness further claimed police said no-one would ever be charged with the killing. Mr. Gormley alleged that the RUC told him Mr. Shanaghan had been killed by a man with military experience who was a "crack shot."[13]

Interestingly, that report echoes Kerr's revelation to us in Maidstone that Patrick Shanaghan's assassin was a "crack shot." So, if it wasn't Kerr's "KB," who was it? I suggest that any investigator wishing to find the answer could do worse than begin by interrogating Kerr and Sands before moving on to question those in overall control of *all* the Committee's assassinations, Billy Abernethy, Hugh Ross and Trevor Forbes OBE. It ought not to prove impossibly difficult to find out why RUC Inspector Alan Moore kept the doctor and the priest from attending to Patrick Shanaghan until his short life was over.

In the end, Ken Kerr's determined effort to pollute my investigation with poisoned information was a failure. Fortunately, I established in good time that his tape-recording was a fake, that his most sensitive "revelations"—the names of RUC Inner Force officers and Loyalist assassins—were fabrications and that his professed remorse was bogus; consequently, none of the primary evidence contained in this book about the Committee's murder conspiracy is, in any way, dependent on the contribution or the veracity of Ken Kerr. Nevertheless, his eighteen-month-long involvement with

Tim Laxton and me was by no means a waste of our time or money. For his energetic efforts to sabotage and discredit my inquiry convinced me that his fifty to sixty co-conspirators on the Ulster Loyalist Central Co-ordinating Committee appreciated the potentially devastating consequences they would face, if I were to be successful in uncovering the full truth about their campaign of political assassination in 1989, 1990 and 1991.

Kerr spent many hours with my friend Tim Laxton, feeding him voluminous amounts of detail about the "dirty war" in Northern Ireland, about covert British Army operations against Republicans, about Loyalist/RUC collusion; his "revelations" covered the period from the early 1970s when Kerr's career began in the service of the Crown until the mid-1990s when, despite his attempt to make us believe otherwise, he was a passionate devotee of Ulster Loyalism. Tim and I are convinced that Kerr would not have been able to maintain his elaborate charade so convincingly and for so long, if he had not been able to draw on the memories and the experience of his central role in the Committee's murder conspiracy; his plentiful supply of anecdotes and reminiscences about murders and atrocities, together with his colourful portraits of the conspirators, convinced Tim and me that we had succeeded in one respect at least—we had definitely been talking to a second member of the Committee. Our assessment of Ken Kerr ends, therefore, in a paradox. Though Kerr is an accomplished liar who claimed to be a founding member of the Committee, we have no doubt that he was the brains behind the paramilitary side of the Committee's assassination campaign.[14]

Notes

1. Limavady is a sizeable town about a half-hour's drive from Derry.
2. I do not propose to name them here because they may well turn out to be entirely innocent of *any* involvement with the Committee.
3. Again, I do not propose to name them because, like Kerr's two Portadown businessmen, they *might* be totally innocent—if they exist at all.
4. Before coming across the Maze Prison letter I had, of course, been pondering how best to check Kerr's information about Ezzard Boyd's existence and status. As already explained, I would never have accepted the truth of Kerr's story without independent confirmation.
5. I understand the boxer would, most probably, have been Ezzard Charles.
6. My solicitor, Geoffrey Bindman, reported Kerr's fraud and deception to the new RUC Chief Constable, Ronnie Flanagan, in October 1997. I doubt whether Kerr will be greatly concerned about any RUC "Inquiry" into his activities.

7   Since Kerr is a proven liar, no useful purpose would be served in reporting publicly the names of the two Loyalists whom he accused of murder. However, my solicitor has given the two names, together with all other material supplied by Kerr, to the RUC Chief Constable.

8   As far as I am aware, Mr. "Justice" Kerr is not related to Ken Kerr.

9   The reader will understand why I have decided not to publish the two names mentioned by Kerr.

10   Both Buncrana and Castlederg, the locations for the two murders, are about one hour's drive from Derry, where Ken Kerr lives.

11   My solicitor, Geoffrey Bindman, gave the RUC Kerr's information, including the names of the two supposed assassins when, in October 1997, he reported the fraud involving the "Ezzard Boyd" tape.

12   Sir Hugh Annesley was replaced as RUC Chief Constable by his former deputy, Ronnie Flanagan, in November 1996. It is, I suspect, unlikely that the new Chief Constable will be any more enthusiastic than his predecessor for a public inquiry into how Patrick Shanaghan came to be murdered.

13   *The Irish News*, September 19th 1996.

14   Ken Kerr's claim to have infiltrated the Committee on behalf of British Intelligence was not an implausible one. For we knew, since 1992, that British Intelligence had employed one of Kerr's close associates in the Ulster Defence Association, Brian Nelson, to help organise the murder of suspected members of the Provisional IRA. After Nelson's arrest in 1991 by the Stevens Inquiry team [see page 17] it emerged that he had helped British Intelligence to murder at least fifteen people in Northern Ireland and to attempt the murder of many more. Most of the details of this scandal have been successfully covered up to this day [April 1998] but it is known that Nelson succeeded in facilitating the murder of entirely innocent Catholics. For example, thanks to Nelson, two UDA gunmen burst into the home of Terence McDaid in Belfast in May 1988 and riddled him with bullets. He fell dead in front of his young daughter, and the assassins, having mistaken their victim for his brother who had been their real target, escaped. Nelson's ultimate "handler" within British Intelligence, a mysterious "Colonel J," has not merely managed to escape prosecution for this and other horrific crimes but has been subsequently "decorated" by the British Government for the performance of his official duties. Colonel Gordon J. Kerr is the proud holder of two awards—the OBE, Order of the British Empire, and the QGM, Queen's Gallantry Medal, the latter normally handed out for "conspicuous courage" in time of war.

Chapter 15

THE POLITICAL WING

"It makes you wonder who runs this place, doesn't it?" When Billy Abernethy, posing as a mere "driver" for the shadowy paramilitary group Ulster Resistance, had made this boast to Ben Hamilton in 1991 he was, as we were to discover, speaking from a position of unique power and knowledge about what was actually happening in the province. As chairman of the secret Ulster Loyalist Central Co-ordinating Committee, he had presided over many meetings where the assassination of Republicans and Catholics had been sanctioned and organised. Jim Sands, who had attended most of these meetings, had already told us that the Committee was able to strike anywhere in the province because it could draw on the support and resources of its Loyalist allies within the RUC Inner Force. Abernethy's display of arrogance to the young television researcher may have been unwise but, in the light of what we would later learn, it is difficult to contest the accuracy of his claim. For, by April 1991, the Committee had already eliminated many of those deemed to have been "enemies of Ulster" and was poised to intensify its assassination campaign, emboldened by the fact that its two key assassins, Robin Jackson and Billy Wright, were routinely guided to their targets by their friends in the RUC Inner Force.

Why could Abernethy, Ross, Monteith and the fifty to sixty conspirators be so confident that none of them would ever be made to answer for their crimes? Why would senior RUC officers take the risk of participating in such a conspiracy? Would they not fear that, if the truth were ever to emerge, their elevated status within Her Majesty's constabulary would—in theory, at least—offer them no protection against possible life sentences for murder? Part of the answer to these questions can, I believe, be found by reflecting on the significance of what Sands had told us about the formal, structured and systematic character of the collusion which enabled the Committee to run its assassination campaign. This is what he told us in London in 1991:

> The Central Co-ordinating Committee is sixty in total. There is eighteen from the Inner Force. There's twenty-two from the

Ulster Independence Party, making up the—that's the big proportion. The rest is then divided from various—the rest of the
groups on the Committee, the Ulster Volunteer Force, Ulster
Protestant Action Force, the Ulster Defence Association, the
Ulster Worker's Council, Ulster Freedom Fighters, as well as
prominent individual people who can be [members] of the
Committee, such as solicitors, accountants, people with knowledge of banks as well as prominent businessmen.

Sands may not have been the most articulate of the murder conspirators but he had, nevertheless, sufficient verbal dexterity to be able to make
it clear in his filmed interview that Abernethy's Committee was a unique
entity, quite unlike anything that had existed within Ulster Loyalism before
the signing of the Anglo-Irish Agreement in November 1985. Before that
date, Ulster Loyalism had been fragmented and relatively ineffective, he
explained:

Before then, Ulster people on the Loyalist side were never really
organised. There was wee small groups in various towns [which]
done their own thing. But because of the signing of the Agreement
in 1985, which brought a lot of middle upper classes into Ulster
Loyalism, that these men have, these people have seen that there
is a British withdrawal, gradual but still a withdrawal. And from a
business point of view, they want to look after themselves. They
don't want to be left high and dry with the British withdrawal.
And they're putting their business expertise, their business knowledge to the good of Ulster.

Sands was spelling out for us, as best he could, the reality as he understood it to be in 1991. We should note that Sands, despite his lack of formal educational qualifications, was extremely well placed to speak
knowledgeably and authoritatively about the conspiracy—which is, I am
convinced, the reason why his decision to talk to us posed such a threat to
everyone involved. Sands was secretary of the most important branch of
the Ulster Independence Party—Portadown, the epicentre of extreme, violent Loyalism; he represented that party at regular meetings of the illegal
RUC/UDR Inner Force, which enabled him to appreciate the degree to
which the Loyalists had taken effective control of the locally recruited
RUC and UDR.

The Inner Force themselves say there's a third actually [of the
RUC] who are members of the Inner Force. There's a third, but
there's also the two thirds who are not members but would be
sympathetic to the aims of the Inner Force . . . [And] the Inner
Circle controls the Inner Force. They have manoeuvred through
various ways, they have manoeuvred men with sympathies

towards the Inner Circle in to prominent positions . . . at local police station level, and therefore at divisional level.

Sands had enjoyed a ring-side seat at Ulster Loyalism's preparations for the anticipated "doomsday scenario," the day when the British would betray them—as they were seen to have already done by signing the Anglo-Irish Agreement with Dublin. He had witnessed the formation of the unique coalition of Loyalist forces, covering virtually every significant sector of Loyalist Ulster—the Ulster Workers' Council, "which has been revamped and reorganised . . . and is organised in factories such as Shorts, Harland and Wolff shipyard, the power stations;" the various Loyalist paramilitary groups; middle class professionals and business people; and, most importantly, the RUC and UDR. A coalition encapuslated more succinctly in Abernethy's question: "Makes you wonder who runs this place, doesn't it?"

So, the Committee's fifty to sixty conspirators who met regularly to plan murder knew, as they did so, that those present represented all significant groups within the Ulster Loyalist family; no grouping of any importance had been excluded and, as a result, none of those present felt they had anything to fear from outsiders. That is why the Committee had been able to mobilise and operate the Loyalist death squads in the province throughout 1989, 1990 and 1991.

The corollary of this anarchic reality—the fact that this terrorist Committee could strike "anywhere, at will" and kill with impunity ["no Republican is safe in Ulster"]—was that the same coalition had the power to prevent any of the conspirators from ever having to pay for their crimes; those represented on the Committee, most especially the senior RUC Inner Force officers, could ensure that no conspirator faced any risk of appearing on a murder charge, even if details about the ongoing assassination campaign information were to leak out—as happened in October 1991 when Channel 4 broadcast *The Committee*.[1]

And there is a further reason why the fifty to sixty Committee members felt themselves to be invulnerable. They had taken the trouble to ensure that the political elite within the Loyalist family, the leading Unionist politicians, would be on hand to do their "duty," if a crisis were ever to erupt as a result of the scandal becoming publicly known. As events turned out, the Channel 4 broadcast was the moment when the Committee's political wing, the Unionist politicians linked to the Committee, emerged to take centre stage. One prominent Ulster Unionist MP, as we shall see, was to prove particularly helpful to the conspirators in the days after the broadcast because he appreciated the danger it posed, a danger which he knew would grow alarmingly if the programme's allegations were not immediately and decisively refuted. However, not all Unionist politicians, even though they were aware of the Committee's existence, purpose and murderous record, followed this MP's approach; "Reverend" Ian Paisley MP, for example, kept an uncharacteristic silence, even though he had met Abernethy and his friends only a few months earlier, as the following incident—reported to us by Sands—neatly illustrates.

In 1991, Northern Ireland Secretary of State Sir Peter Brooke was patiently attempting to persuade all the political parties in the province to participate in talks involving the London and Dublin Governments. Abernethy's Committee, pledged to destroy the hated Anglo-Irish Agreement and to resist any further slippage in the direction of a United Ireland, summoned the leader of the Democratic Unionist Party, Ian Paisley MP, to a meeting. Abernethy and his colleague—Committee member and Ulster Resistance commander John McCullagh—began the discussion in a forthright manner: they placed a revolver on the table in front of the Member for Antrim North who—Sands told us—was somewhat taken aback by this unexpected, not to say irreverent, development. [Sands had earlier explained to us that his fellow Committee members did not share the widespread public perception of Paisley as a fearsome figure; in the Committee's eyes, Paisley was an ineffective windbag who talked tough but who went weak at the knees at the thought of activity such as Abernethy's Committee was organising.] The meeting proceeded with McCullagh pointing to the bullet-filled revolver on the table and commenting to Paisley: "Any concession to Dublin and one of those is for you!" Sands, who had described this incident to us with glee, went on to report that Paisley, after he had returned home, telephoned Abernethy and sought to make light of the threat issued by the Ulster Resistance leader. "He sounded as if he meant it," Paisley joked nervously; to which Abernethy dourly replied: "He did!"

So Paisley, as far as I am aware, made no public comment about the programme; perhaps he was indignant at the lack of respect shown by McCullagh and, for that reason, left it to others to defend the conspirators. Similarly, Ulster Unionist Party leader James Molyneaux MP, now Lord Molyneaux, kept a low profile over the controversy even though—according to Sands—he, too, had held secret meetings with Abernethy and other Committee members; he chose to leave the task of defending the conspirators to others.[2] That task, which required a quick response to *The Committee's* revelations about RUC death squads, was enthusiastically performed by a man who, in 1991, was relatively unknown outside Northern Ireland but was already emerging as Ian Paisley's main rival for the political leadership of the Ulster Protestant community, William David Trimble MP.

As we've seen, Trimble had accompanied one of the conspirators, "Reverend" Ross, to the Channel 4 studios in London a few days after the broadcast, when they took part in the *Right to Reply* discussion programme, transmitted on Saturday, October 5th 1991. Before examining what Trimble said on that occasion, we should recall that he had been elected, for the first time, in the Upper Bann by-election less than eighteen months earlier; and a few months after that, as we've also seen, he had reportedly reacted to the murder of his constituent, Denis Carville, with the bizarre comment that "some idiot had taken the law into his own hands."[3] Given that *The Committee* had focused on events within "murder triangle"—where the murders of Sam Marshall, Denis Carville and the three mobile sweet shop victims had taken place—we might have expected a statement from the constituency MP along the following lines:

> I am deeply shocked to learn of the serious allegations made against the RUC by the Channel 4 *Dispatches* programme. These horrific atrocities, committed within my constituency by depraved and heartless people, are an affront to civilised values and to our entire community. I agree wholeheartedly with the words of the Church of Ireland Primate, Archbishop Eames, when he described the brutal murder of my young constituent, Denis Carville, as "a disgrace to Protestants." I condemn these evil murders utterly and without reservation. The perpetrators of these crimes must be hunted down and brought to justice as quickly as possible. The suggestion that members of the security forces, on whom the entire community necessarily relies for protection, have colluded with the killers is deeply disturbing. It must be investigated rigorously and impartially by an outside authority. I call on the Government to set up immediately an independent inquiry into the allegations made by Channel 4.

Such a statement was never likely to cross the lips of David Trimble MP. He was quoted merely as having said there was "no justification for random revenge killings."[4] When he appeared alongside Ross on the *Right to Reply* programme, he showed no sign of distress over this nakedly sectarian murder or shock about how the six other victims featured in the programme, some of them his own constituents, had met their deaths. From the moment the programme had been shown, Trimble's entire effort was devoted to undermining its credibility so that the conspirators— Abernethy, Monteith, Forbes, the "innocent law-abiding" Ross and the rest—could escape responsibility for their crimes.

After Ross had been allowed to deliver on *Right to Reply* his forthright, if startlingly hypocritical, denial that he had any knowledge about or involvement with the Committee, the interviewer moved on to question Trimble about his own reaction to the broadcast. [See Chapter 6]

Interviewer: David, the RUC Chief says: "It's long on accusation, short on credible evidence." Would you agree with that?

Trimble: Yes, I do. I think the Chief Constable's description of this is entirely accurate. I think that what has happened here is that some, possibly naive journalists, have been sold a pup by both paramilitary organisations, primarily by Loyalist paramilitaries. I don't think that people appreciate that Loyalist paramilitaries do have reasons for wanting to discredit the RUC. The RUC is actually extremely, and has been in the past, extremely effective against Loyalist terrorists. For example, Loyalist terrorist murders are five times as likely to be arrested and charged by the RUC as Republicans . . .

Interviewer: The programme was largely based on a silhouetted figure, you think that was not credible, not useable?

Trimble: Well, the evidence seemed to me to lack credibility. I mean, obviously, we do not know exactly what happens inside paramilitary organisations. But it seems to me that the suggestion that Committees of forty to fifty people are planning what they call "hits" lacks credibility. My understanding is, from what the police have told me, over the last year or so, the tendency amongst Loyalist paramilitaries has been to imitate the IRA by operating in a small, tight cellular structure. So I think the programme lacks credibility in terms of what was presented."

Although Trimble did not flatly deny that the Committee existed, he strongly suggested that our central allegation was untrue. Naturally, he gave no inkling that he was on the closest of terms with the Committee's chairman; nor did he reveal that he had been a close political associate of Abernethy's younger brother, Colin; nor that he was a close friend of serving Committee member, Philip Black, once a colleague at Queen's University, Belfast, when Trimble had been on the staff of the Law Faculty. Instead, Trimble sought to give an impression of Olympian detachment from the realities of Loyalist terror—"obviously we do not know what happens exactly within paramilitary organisations"—and reminded viewers of the RUC's response to the programme, suggesting that no reasonable person would give any credence to the allegations it had made. Besides, as he indicated in his next answer, allegations of collusion between Loyalists and the security forces were baseless Republican propaganda.

Trimble: I think you should bear in mind that the Chief Constable is not speaking on a basis of no knowledge. Remember that these allegations have been floating around for years. The Stevens Inquiry, in particular, looked into the suggestion that has been appearing in Republican circles for some time, that there is some sort of Inner Circle and found absolutely no evidence for it.

After doing his best to cast doubt on the programme's principal revelations—the Committee's existence, composition, function and record of assassination—Trimble proceeded to attack the programme makers for exposing innocent individuals, such as his fellow studio guest "Reverend" Ross, to the risk of IRA assassination in retaliation for their alleged crimes. As a former university lecturer in law, Trimble can be presumed to have known that Britain's libel laws prevented his studio opponent, Channel 4's Karen Brown, from explicitly naming the nineteen individuals whom Sands had identified as Committee members; she could not have contemplated doing so unless she knew that Sands would agree to testify publicly against his co-conspirators in any libel proceedings. So Trimble, aware that the anonymous Sands would not come forward to testify, knew he was on strong ground when he accused Channel 4 of dangerous irresponsibility in that it had, quite wrongly, identified "innocent" individuals, especially "Reverend" Ross, as Committee members. The libel laws prevented Karen from telling viewers the full truth, from naming publicly the individuals listed in the Channel 4 dossier or from replying that "Reverend" Ross was indeed a conspirator to murder—guilty of all the crimes attributed to him by his own assistant and fellow Committee member, James Alfred Sands.

> Trimble: That is one thing that very greatly concerns me about the way this programme has gone because it went out in such a way that people automatically associated a number of people with this Committee. By so doing you have made targets of a range of people and you have put their lives at risk in a way that I consider to be irresponsible.
>
> Brown: We take the difficulties and risks very seriously.
>
> Trimble: Sorry, the very clear impression that came over from the programme was that you were associating a number of people, Hugh Ross, was one, others as well, with the terrorist activity.
>
> Brown: That is not correct.
>
> Trimble: Sorry, there was a very clear identification in the programme . . . It has also very clearly identified some people as targets and the way in which it did it, I think, comes very close to inciting the IRA to now attack some of the people that are pilloried in the programme. You have virtually accused someone of murder in that programme.

Trimble's televised defence of Ross as an "innocent, law-abiding" person (Ross's words) was a cynical and duplicitous exercise because the MP can have been in no doubt about the clergyman's true character and status within Abernethy's Committee; nor about the fact that Ross, Abernethy, Forbes and their friends were the individuals who had sanctioned and organised the murder of his own constituents. Trimble's defence of the murder conspirators is, given his status at the time as a Member of Parliament, shocking and scandalous but we ought not to be so greatly surprised because it turns out that Trimble has long been a political soul-mate of some of the leading conspirators, certainly for many years before he became an MP or leader of the Ulster Unionist Party.

Although "Reverend" Ross and David Trimble stood against each other in the Upper Bann by-election in 1990, they had long been political soul mates, both fervently advocating a radical break with the past and the creation of an Independent Ulster. Both men had gone on the record to say that the Anglo-Irish Agreement—or "diktat," as they both called it—had effectively ended the Union between Northern Ireland and Great Britain; and they were both urging their fellow Ulster Protestants to prepare for the creation of a new state, an Independent Ulster. Ross had appeared in *The Committee*, where he had condemned the Agreement:

> The Anglo-Irish Agreement had made us a full colony, under the coalition government of Éire and England. And therefore, as a colony, there was only one way for us to go, and I felt that the only way forward was the way of Independence, so that we could have self-determination . . . leading to self-government.

Trimble had responded to the 1985 Agreement by writing a pro-Independence pamphlet, *What Choice for Ulster?*, published in February 1988. It is worth noting, in passing, that his *curriculum vitae* shows him to have been, at the time, a member of the Executive of the Ulster Clubs Movement, where he was joined by Committee member Philip Black and Billy Abernethy's younger brother, Colin. The pamphlet surveys the pros and cons of five options for the future of the province, four of which— Direct Rule from London, Devolved Government, Integration into the United Kingdom and a United Ireland—are deemed unacceptable, leaving Independence as the only desirable outcome. Trimble's analysis, prescription and language are scarcely distinguishable from those of "Reverend" Ross.

> We have been turned into an internal colony. Worse still, the [Anglo-Irish] diktat has changed the status of Ulster by formally associating a foreign country in the government of Ulster; a foreign country, moreover, which still maintains a formal claim to Ulster.
> . . . the Union as we knew it has ended. It died first in the mind of the [British] establishment some time ago and the [Anglo-Irish] diktat is merely the outward and visible symbol of its determination to bury it.
> The Ulster British people is . . . the only community [in the British Isles] whose very existence is at risk . . . If there is an

orderly transfer of power to an Ulster government, then I am confident that the men of the RUC and UDR could give security to everyone.[5]

Both Trimble and Ross firmly believe that they live in a country called "Ulster;" when they talk of "the people of Ulster," it is clear that they see no role in their Independent Ulster for Irish Nationalists or Republicans, people who view themselves as Irish and many of whom aspire to live in a united Ireland. If Trimble still holds these published views, the prospects for a negotiated settlement in Northern Ireland must be bleak but, for my present purposes, the relevance of Trimble's pro-Independence pamphlet is that it demonstrates his close political affiliation to key Committee members, individuals such as "Reverend" Ross, Billy Abernethy and his former Ulster Clubs Executive colleague, Philip Black.

"Reverend" Ross, Philip Black, Jim Sands and other Independence enthusiasts did not, as the contents of this book reveal, limit their activities to pamphlet writing or speech making. With the Bible in one hand and a sub-machine gun in another, someone else's, they sought to make it more likely that they would, one day, realise their dream of political Independence; they organised the "elimination" of their Republican enemies, some of whom are listed in Appendix Two.[6] Sands told us that Trimble did not, of course, attend any meetings of the Committee; but he assured me that the Upper Bann MP knew all he needed to know about what his friends were up to, both before and after his election in Upper Bann. Even without this inside information, I have no difficulty in believing—on the basis of his published views and his efforts to undermine the programme's credibility—that Trimble knew what Abernethy, Ross, Forbes, Black, Monteith and their fifty or so fellow Committee members were engaged in; and, after the broadcast, I was not alone in judging his efforts on behalf of his friends, the murder conspirators, to be as unconvincing as they were hypocritical.

I conclude, therefore, that David Trimble MP was knowingly associating with and assisting those responsible for the murder of his own constituents, victims of the Committee such as the three innocent Catholic teenagers—Denis Carville, Eileen Duffy, Katrina Rennie and the twenty-nine-year-old customer shot dead as he approached the mobile sweet shop in Craigavon, Brian Frizzell. None of these victims were members of Trimble's "Ulster British nation" but all four of them, like many other Catholics killed in his constituency, were murdered by his friends on the Committee within just one year of his entry to the House of Commons in May 1990.

So, the Member of Parliament for Upper Bann William David Trimble is, in my judgement, as culpable for the terrorist acts of Abernethy's Committee as is the leader of the political wing of the Provisional IRA for that organisation's crimes, Gerry Adams. Arguably, Trimble's conduct is worse than that of the Sinn Féin leader because Adams, at least, has usually admitted responsibility for IRA atrocities; unlike Trimble, he has never sought to deny the existence of the terrorist organisation for which he, too, provides political cover when the occasion demands.

After Trimble's initial, damage limitation appearance on *Right to Reply*, he remained silent about the programme throughout the period in which Channel 4 and Box Productions were resisting the RUC's attempt to extract the name of Source A by legal means; and although, as he would later indicate, he was kept well briefed—presumably by Chief Superintendent Jimmy Nesbitt—on what had been happening in the *in camera* proceedings in Judge Clarkson's court room, he said nothing, even when the case was finally referred to Attorney General Sir Patrick Mayhew in January 1992. And like Sir Patrick, he made no public reference during the British general election campaign in April that year to the fact that Channel 4 and Box Productions had, six months earlier, submitted to the authorities a dossier containing the names of some of those said to be responsible for the murder of Republicans and Catholics in his constituency, as well as for other murders elsewhere in the province. Trimble's silence over these sensitive matters was, we can now appreciate, a sensible one because it later emerged that some of those listed in the dossier—Chief Superintendent Nesbitt's "aristocracy"—were among the MP's closest friends and associates. It was only after Trimble had been safely re-elected to the House of Commons and a mere six weeks before the High Court contempt hearing at the end of July 1992, that the Upper Bann MP made his second public comment on the programme. He made this contribution to a debate in Parliament on June 10th 1992.

> I recall the notorious *Dispatches* programme which alleged the existence of a so-called Inner Circle in which it was said that police and Loyalist terrorists plotted assassinations. What was produced on screen in the way of evidence was singularly unconvincing.
>
> After the programme, in an attempt to bolster their case, those involved in the production of *Dispatches* supplied the RUC with names, some of whom they said were members of the Inner Circle. Some of the names were not even in the RUC, although those involved with *Dispatches* said they were. I believe that the RUC is satisfied that none of those named was so involved.
>
> If the programme makers had consulted any reputable journalist operating in Ulster, they would have been told that the allegations were fantasies. Indeed, some journalists working in Northern Ireland are reluctant to have any dealings with Channel 4 programmers as a result. I understand that the programme cost about £250,000, which is something worth considering.

I suspect that the programme involved more than gullibility. The person who made it was no wide-eyed innocent coming to Ulster for the first time. He was a native of Ulster who, in his student days, was associated with extreme Republican politics.

If the police succeed in their attempts to compel *Dispatches* to disclose its sources, I think that it will be found that essentially that programme had one source—a person who is known to have a Republican political background. We shall then see that the programme was tainted from the outset. The sinister aspect of the programme was that, in addition to smearing the police, it effectively identified members of a mythical Inner Circle and so targeted individuals in the Loyalist community. That is a dangerous consequence of irresponsibility.

By June 1992, Trimble's initial posture of studied scepticism and open mindedness about the programme had, as his statement shows, been replaced by a firm conviction that our allegations had been "fantasies" and that the so-called Inner Circle within the RUC was "mythical." His comments also made it clear that his conclusions were, in part, based on briefings he had received—presumably from the RUC or, quite possibly, the RUC Inner Circle—about facts that had emerged in Judge Clarkson's court room, such as the programme's £250,000 budget. "Some of the names were not even in the RUC" bears an uncanny resemblance to what the RUC had told Judge Clarkson. Trimble was, it appeared, quite content uncritically to accept and to promote the RUC's verdict on the Channel 4 dossier, namely that none of those listed had been involved in a murder conspiracy. Understandably, Trimble chose not to tell his Parliamentary colleagues that some of those listed—Abernethy, Ross, Black, Monteith—were his political allies, those whom he had met regularly to discuss their "mythical" conspiracy and murderous activities, during the period their assassination campaign had been under way, both before and after his entry to the House of Commons in May 1990.

So, in August 1992, the programme had lacked "credible evidence," the result of "possibly naive journalists, hav[ing] been sold a pup by Loyalist paramilitaries;" but, within just a few months, it had become "notorious," a deliberate smear on the RUC and "the person who [had] made it was no wide-eyed innocent" (myself), but a closet Republican, who had invented the entire story; then, aided and abetted by "a person with a Republican political background" (Martin O'Hagan), he had supposedly fooled the gullible broadcaster. Trimble's remarks, as my late solicitor Brian Raymond pointed out, were libellous in that they carried the innuendo that I had been and have remained, since my student days, a supporter of Republican terrorism and, by implication, the Provisional IRA. Brian told me that if Trimble were to repeat such a statement outside Parliament, where he would no longer enjoy the absolute privilege conferred on words spoken in the House of Commons, I could sue him. If he repeats them, maybe I will.

Trimble's other oblique reference was, as the reader will know, a reference to the Belfast-based journalist who had introduced Ben Hamilton to Jim Sands, namely Martin O'Hagan. By identifying and smearing Martin and me in this way, Trimble was, I suspect, echoing his RUC briefings and anticipating the "hoax" verdict which would emerge, some months later and in a more elaborate form, from the Nesbitt Inquiry. The programme had been a hoax "with potentially lethal consequences," Trimble was suggesting, because it had identified Loyalists belonging to a "mythical" Inner Circle, individuals whom we had supposedly turned into potential targets for the IRA. In short, Trimble deliberately misled his Parliamentary colleagues by concealing the truth about his own links to the conspirators, deceiving the House of Commons into believing that the programme had been a malicious, politically-inspired attack on the RUC by two Republican scoundrels, terrorist sympathisers masquerading as responsible journalists.

Trimble's attack provided a foretaste of what was in store for us after the High Court contempt hearing, when the Committee's friends inside the RUC and the Northern Ireland Office launched their "dirty tricks" media campaign. Trimble's various themes—that Channel 4 had got its facts wrong, that it had been "hoaxed," that innocent Loyalists had been identified as murder conspirators, that the Committee had never existed—were later picked up, one by one, and given full orchestral treatment until, after a time, a consensus had emerged in the media that Channel 4 had fought a principled fight over journalistic sources, only to discover—horror-of-horrors—that it had backed a dud programme. Once these fictitious claims, transformed into "hard facts" through repeated and unchallenged assertions, had been firmly embedded in the public mind, the Committee's unofficial representative in the House of Commons rose to his feet a second time. He then delivered what may have seemed the knock-out blow to a programme which, as we have seen, *The Independent* had already said might turn out to be "one of the worst television programmes ever shown in Britain."

Indeed, by the date of his second Parliamentary contribution—December 1992—Trimble was so confident that the programme had been discredited that he even felt able to echo Channel 4's call for an independent investigation. Trimble now called for an inquiry that would investigate both the allegations of collusion ("to put the matter beyond doubt") and the making of the programme ("to dispel the smears on the RUC"). By that time, we should recall, Source A had already been unmasked, interrogated and coaxed into "recanting" his story, all under the supervision of the Chief Constable's "investigators," Nesbitt and Webster.[7] We can, I think, reasonably assume that Trimble, having been briefed by the "investigators" throughout, would have known that Channel 4's informant—Source A [Sands]—had been "turned;" it may have seemed that, as a result, we would never be able to justify any of our allegations from that moment onwards. Trimble began his second Parliamentary contribution as follows:

> . . . I make no apology for returning to it [the programme], partly because it was such a bad programme in sheer journalistic terms and partly because some of the matters that were raised clearly referred to my constituency, and there is a real concern in that respect.
>
> Nearly all the background used in the programme, especially in the crucial second half, was recognisably located in the north Armagh area. Northern Ireland is a small place, so people know the places being shown and quickly recognise them. There was also reference in the programme to terrorist incidents in my constituency, so it is appropriate that I should raise the matter now.

Trimble proceeded to provide a lengthy and seriously inaccurate summary of what the programme had contained, an account which suggested to me, when I read it in Hansard, that the lawyer-turned-politician may well have undergone some training at the Barrie Penrose School of Reporting. For example, Trimble stated: "The second, and more sinister, part of the programme alleged that there existed a secret Loyalist body, which was sometimes referred to as "the Inner Circle" but which the programme as a whole identified as "the Committee." The reader will, I trust, instantly realise that Trimble's conflation of these two, quite distinct, terrorist bodies—one within the RUC, the other drawing on a wider catchment area within the Loyalist terrain—as one and the same organisation, is simply a confusion, a misunderstanding of what the programme alleged. Having failed to grasp these essential distinctions, Trimble then compounded his errors en route to presenting his first substantive complaint against us, namely that the programme had identified and libelled a particular individual when it had stated that the membership of the Committee had included lawyers. After referring to one possible candidate, a lawyer whom he did not name but was said to be a member of "Reverend" Ross's Independence Movement, Trimble continued:[8]

> The other prime candidate is a north Armagh solicitor who specialises in criminal work and is well known for his Loyalist views. He is a former political activist, but he, too, is *a responsible person who I know would not be involved with terrorism.* [my emphasis] He

did not see the programme, but he told me that when he attended court the next day—because he had some cases running in the local courts—he wondered why people were staring at him with a strange expression. He was horrified to discover that all the people present thought that he had been unmasked the night before as the brains behind a murder gang. I am happy to say that he has commenced, or is about to commence, libel proceedings in the matter, and I earnestly hope that there will be a just result.[9]

The solicitor Trimble was referring to was, of course, his old friend and leading Committee member, Richard Monteith. Trimble had no hesitation in assuring the House of Commons that Monteith was "a responsible person" and that there was no justification for his name appearing in a dossier devoted to the realities of Loyalist terrorism. Trimble was, obviously and on his own admission, in regular contact with Monteith, which explains why he was in a position to announce his friend's imminent action for criminal libel against me. We shall see, later, that Trimble's support for Monteith was not limited to speaking on his behalf in a Parliamentary debate but extended as far as providing the solicitor with a sworn affidavit to enable him to brazen his way out of his predicament.

Trimble was equally emphatic about his fellow champion of the cause of Ulster Independence, the individual whom Sands had told us was—along with Abernethy and Forbes—one of the troika which had founded the Committee. What did Trimble tell the House of Commons about this murder conspirator?

> Those two people [the two lawyers he had referred to] were not mentioned by name, unlike the chairman of the Independence Committee, Reverend Hugh Ross, who was interviewed at length. None of those interviews or questions related to a possible involvement with terrorism. He said afterwards that, had he had any idea of the accusations that would be made on the programme, he would have made clear to the interviewer the position of the Independence Committee with regard to terrorism.[10]

When we come to consider this aspect of Trimble's defence of the conspirators, we should keep in mind that, as he spoke, he would have known from many sources within his constituency—Abernethy, Ross, Monteith, Black, the RUC Inner Circle—that Source A [by now unmasked and known to be Jim Sands] had been, for many years, an errand boy for Ross, and that he had also worked for Trimble's Ulster Unionist predecessor in the House of Commons, the late Harold McCusker MP. So, by the time Trimble rose to speak on December 17th 1992, he would have known that the programme's allegations against Abernethy's Committee had emanated, not from a fantasist or hoaxer, but from someone who had long been a fanatical devotee of the Loyalist cause, someone who had also been in a uniquely sensitive position within Ross's political and paramilitary circle.

Given all this, we might wonder why Trimble would have decided to take the risk of offering Ross and the others such unequivocal and public support; as nobody had been convicted for any of the eighteen murders attributed by Sands to the Committee, we might think that Trimble would have paused to ask himself whether his murdered constituents had met their deaths in the way described by Sands on Channel 4. Well we might wonder and we might think; but on the other hand, if Trimble was as knowledgeable about the Committee's existence and activities as I am assured that he was, we can readily understand why he did not pause but, instead, moved into the attack and at top speed. Knowing the enormity of the scandal that *The Committee* had partly uncovered and realising the calamitous implications which further disclosures could have for everyone involved—the fifty to sixty Committee members, including the eighteen RUC Inner Force officers—Trimble obviously felt it imperative to ensure that Ross, the only "aristocrat" featured in the programme, be absolved of any taint of suspicion; hence his swift intervention on the "Reverend" conspirator's behalf.

Trimble was most disingenuous and shamelessly exploitive of his Parliamentary audience's ignorance of the realities of Loyalist terror in north Armagh, when he focused on the role played in the programme by the Loyalist assassin King Rat [Billy Wright]. For, it was an open secret in Lurgan and Portadown in December 1992 that King Rat and Billy Wright were one and the same person; the Channel 4 programme had left little doubt that King Rat had murdered Denis Carville, a fact which Trimble would have known. And it would scarcely have escaped Trimble's notice that this Loyalist assassin had, wisely, chosen not to pursue the matter in the libel courts. Yet, when Trimble stood up to talk about his most notorious constituent, he spoke as if he had no reliable information at all about King Rat and gave the impression that he was dependent on secondhand hearsay about the murderous activities on which this particular constituent had been engaged.[11] Trimble's tone of measured detachment about someone who had murdered so many of his own constituents was less than convincing.

> As evidence for the existence of that Committee, three things were brought forward [in the programme]. The evidence consisted of an interview with a gentleman known as Billy Wright who, if I remember correctly, did not actually refer to "the Committee" but talked generally of the motives of the Loyalist paramilitaries. Although he did not actually confess to personal involvement in any murders, the programme, and indeed Mr. Wright himself, left the impression that he was engaged in paramilitary activities.
>
> I hold no brief for Mr. Wright. I am told that he is a gangster

who tries to cloak his crimes with political motivation, and, to give colour to that motivation, occasionally gets involved in sectarian crimes about which he then boasts to journalists, giving interviews to them regularly. Whether he has committed all the offences of which he boasts, I do not know, but I can hazard a fair guess as to why he collaborated with *Dispatches* and gave credence to the accusation that some RUC officers collude with paramilitaries. The allegation, if true or believed and acted upon, would have a disruptive effect on the police and reduce their effectiveness. He has a clear interest in harming the police force.

We can assume, I think, that few of Trimble's listeners in the House of Commons would have remembered much, if anything, about the programme shown on Channel 4 more than fourteen months earlier. So hardly anyone present would have known that *none* of the programme's revelations depended, to even the slightest degree, on the interview we had conducted with Billy Wright. He had, understandably, denied in his filmed interview that he had murdered Denis Carville or anyone else. Nor would the MPs listening to Trimble have realised that *all* the important revelations, especially the details on how the specific murders had been carried out, had emanated not from Billy Wright but from Billy Wright's old school friend, Jim Sands. Contrary to what Trimble suggested to the House of Commons, Billy Wright had denied that there was any collusion between the RUC and the Loyalist death squads, a denial to which we had given as much credence as we had his assertion that he had not murdered Denis Carville.

Having done as much as he could to protect his friends, Monteith and Ross, and having misled his Parliamentary listeners into thinking that the programme's allegations had been based on "a gentleman known as Billy Wright . . . who I am told . . . is a gangster," Trimble went on to repeat what he had said about me in his first performance as the Committee's Parliamentary spokesman the previous June. He then took up this theme but only after abusing his privilege as an MP by suggesting that the perjury charge against Ben Hamilton should not have been dropped, as it had been a few weeks earlier.

> Channel 4 has invested financial and other capital in the programme. I recall seeing pictures of Sir Richard Attenborough and Michael Grade outside the law courts vowing to support the programme and if necessary go down with it. Did they know at the time that they were defending and supporting a fabrication? Do they know that now? If so, will they support an investigation?
>
> Behind Channel 4 and Box lies the origin of the programme— the person who sold the concept to the programme makers. I refer not to the producer, but to the debate of 10th June. The person

who I suspect was the originator of the programme is a native of Northern Ireland. I understand that he now claims that his life is under threat. I cannot assess the validity of that claim, but I hope that it is as false as some of the others that he peddled through the programme. I understand that he is currently engaged in trying to sell another idea to programme makers in London. Will they be fooled again?

Trimble had moved a long way from his initial position of apparent scepticism and the posture of open mindedness to take upon himself the role of scourge of Channel 4. By December 1992, with Sands in the hands of the RUC and struggling his way through his rehearsed recantation, Trimble felt that he was on sufficiently firm ground to launch an outright attack on the programme and its producer. The *Dispatches* programme's allegations had not merely been false, they had been deliberately fabricated by me. I had "peddled" false claims and duped a gullible Channel 4 into broadcasting them. So confident was Trimble at this point that he felt able to taunt Channel 4 and its top executives, challenging them to support an investigation into how they had been hoaxed into broadcasting a series of false and fabricated smears on the RUC.

We now know that Trimble's robust stand on behalf of the murder conspirators—on behalf of his friends Abernethy, Ross, Black and Monteith, though not their approved assassin Billy Wright—was timed to coincide with the conclusion of the RUC Chief Constable's formal investigation into the programme. For, by December 1992, the Nesbitt "Inquiry" had reached precisely the verdict which Trimble had just spelled out in the House of Commons and which, two months later, Chief Superintendent Nesbitt would personally present to Channel 4.

Whatever we might think of William David Trimble MP and his abuse of his Parliamentary status to defend the murder conspirators, nobody can say that he does not stand by his friends in their moment of need—even when those friends have sanctioned and committed multiple murder. When, as predicted by Trimble in the House of Commons, Committee member Charles Richard Pantridge Monteith launched proceedings for criminal libel against me in December 1992, he was able to call once again on the services of his good friend and his constituency representative. Trimble swore the following statement on behalf of the Portadown solicitor who had, two years earlier, played a central role in devising the plot which had led to the murder of the MP's young Catholic constituent, Denis Carville.

"I, WILLIAM DAVID TRIMBLE of 32 Richmond Court, Lisburn, County Antrim, Member of Parliament, make oath and say as follows:

1. I am the member of Parliament for Upper Bann.

2. I have very considerable knowledge of the Portadown and Lurgan area. I saw the *Dispatches* programme on television and I read the subsequent article in *The Sunday Times* which was published on 2nd August 1992.

3. I had absolutely no doubt that the Solicitor who was referred to as having witnessed the statement of the unidentified witness referred to in the article was Mr. Richard Monteith. I have also no doubt from my conversations with other people that this was a conclusion reached independently by others who took an interest in political, criminal and terrorist activities in the Portadown/Lurgan area.

4. The programme almost exclusively concentrated on the events in the Portadown and Lurgan area. It referred to solicitors being on the Committee. Various people with Protestant paramilitary connections were featured on the programme whom I knew to be clients of Mr. Richard Monteith.

5. I actually rang Mr. Monteith when I read the allegations that had been published to find out his reaction to them. I was aware that Mr. Monteith was very annoyed and upset at the content of the programme and in the light of the murder of the solicitor, Mr. Patrick Finucane, the identification of him was very dangerous for him and his family.

6. Save where otherwise stated or appearing I depose the foregoing facts from my own personal knowledge.

Trimble would have us believe that it was only as a result of viewing *The Committee* that he had become aware of Richard Monteith's alleged membership of the alleged murder conspiracy. Our programme had, as Trimble swore in his affidavit, left him with "absolutely no doubt" that his friend and constituent had been identified as the solicitor we were referring to. Further, the MP's carefully chosen words invited observers to believe that Monteith had always been what he purported to be, an "innocent law-abiding" man. If the reader were to accept this depiction of the solicitor, she or he might be tempted to share Trimble's professed indignation at the jeopardy in which we were said to have placed this "innocent" solicitor; any such temptation can, I suggest, be effectively resisted by recalling that this same solicitor, Richard Monteith, was a leading member of the Committee which, in Finaghy Orange Hall at a meeting held in January 1989 sanctioned the murder of Belfast solicitor, Patrick Finucane. We know this because our source Jim Sands was one of those present.

Regrettably, my lawyers were denied the opportunity to find out how, precisely, William David Trimble MP would respond, when cross-examined under oath, about the contents of his affidavit and about his relationship with Monteith, Abernethy, Ross, Forbes, Black and the fifty or so other conspirators, those who controlled the Loyalist death squads which operated freely within his Upper Bann constituency from before his election in 1990 until the cease fires declared in August 1994. For, as we have seen, Monteith eventually dropped his libel action against me. His attempt to bring proceedings for criminal libel had collapsed at an early stage; and his second action, a civil libel case, was abruptly discontinued after I had made it clear that I would plead justification and prove in court that he was a conspirator to murder.[12]

It is even possible that we might have found out more about Trimble's involvement with the Committee from Monteith's third libel action, proceedings which he brought separately against Channel 4 on the basis that the programme and related publicity material had, he claimed, identified him as a member of the murder conspiracy. This possibility evaporated in mid-summer 1995 when Channel 4 settled this libel action out-of-court, after reaching a confidential agreement with Monteith. I made it clear to Channel 4 that I would not consent, in any way, to the terms of its settlement because I believed then, as I do now, that Monteith is a disgrace to the legal profession and that he ought long ago to have been put on trial for the murder of Denis Carville and others.[13] Monteith's libel victory over Channel 4 is not likely to have reduced his standing among the murder conspirators and, though we have seen that Ken Kerr's testimony on any topic is deeply suspect, I found it not difficult to believe him when he said that the Portadown solicitor was much admired by his co-conspirators for his chutzpah—his shameless claim in his affidavit that we had exposed him to the same risk Patrick Finucane had faced before he was murdered by terrorists.

Trimble was not the only member of the legal profession in Northern Ireland to come to Monteith's aid. Solicitor Drew Nelson swore an identical affidavit to Trimble's. How could Nelson, like Trimble, be so sure that Monteith was the solicitor I had been referring to during my BBC interview?[14] Is it not conceivable that Nelson, like Trimble, already had something more substantial on which to base his inference? I always suspected that I knew the answer to that question and I became even more convinced when I learned that Drew Nelson shares his legal practice with another solicitor whose name, Lewis Singleton, I first heard in 1991, when Jim Sands told me in London that he [Singleton] was a close associate of "Reverend" Ross and a member of Abernethy's Committee. So, I conclude that there is, at least, a reasonable chance that Drew Nelson first learned of Monteith's membership of the Committee, *not* from the programme but from his partner. And it is also possible that Trimble learned about Monteith from Singleton because it turns out that the legal firm which looks after Trimble is none other than the partnership run by Singleton and Nelson.[15]

Trimble's relationship with the Committee might also have been explored further in the High Court in London, if the *Sunday Express* had not capitulated in December 1996, shortly before the date fixed for the libel trial. For nearly three years, that newspaper's lawyers had argued, implausibly, that the Committee had never existed and that I had somehow managed to dupe Channel 4 into believing that it did. If the case had gone to trial, all the evidence relating to the Committee would have been thoroughly aired in the High Court and Trimble might have been subpoenaed and cross-examined on his reasons for rushing, so quickly and so publicly, to the defence of Ross and Monteith. But once the *Sunday Express* finally decided to admit that Barrie Penrose's "reporting" had been, shall we say, "excessively creative," the opportunity to put Trimble in the witness box and grill him about his involvement with the Committee disappeared.

It may not, however, have disappeared altogether because it is possible that, following the publication of this book, all issues relevant to the Committee's murder conspiracy will surface during my libel action against *The Sunday Times*. The trial date in that action has now been fixed for October 1998 and, unless this newspaper follows the precedent set by the *Sunday Express*, we may have an opportunity to hear William David Trimble MP justify his defence of Ross and Monteith and his assertion that *The Committee* was a "fabrication." He would also be given the opportunity to respond to my belief that, in recognition of his efforts to protect the murder conspirators, it is appropriate to enhance his standing as a prominent member of the Orange Order by awarding him the title of leader of the political wing of the Ulster Loyalist Central Co-ordinating Committee.[16]

Notes

1   We should recall that Sands told us that the most senior RUC officer on the Committee was an unnamed Assistant Chief Constable. We can presume that, after the broadcast, this individual did his utmost to contain the scandal. The RUC's attitude to the programme emerges clearly from the extract of Nesbitt's conversation with Penrose, as shown in Appendix 3.

2   Ken Kerr sought to persuade me that every living Unionist politician had heartily endorsed the Committee's campaign; Kerr's effort to convince me of this is, in itself, a powerful reason for scepticism about his claim.

3   Trimble was quoted in the *Lurgan Mail*, October 12th 1990.

4   *Belfast Telegraph*, October 6th 1990.

5   Trimble's claim that Ulster Protestants are an endangered species was also
    one of "Reverend" Ross's themes in his contribution to *The Committee*.
6   Sands did not claim that the eighteen murders he attributed to the
    Committee were the only ones.
7   Ken Kerr sought to persuade me that both Nesbitt and Webster had been
    picked to hold the RUC's "Inquiry" because they had both been members
    of the Committee. Once again, Kerr's enthusiasm for this claim leads me to
    view it with considerable scepticism.
8   The lawyer he did not name is, possibly, Committee member Lewis
    Singleton. [See p. 355]
9   This was a reference to the criminal libel proceedings which Monteith
    brought against me. Trimble's hopes were realised because there was
    indeed, on that occasion, a just result—Monteith lost, having dropped his
    action after I had entered a plea of justification.
10 Ross did, in fact, comment on his movement's attitude to violence; but we
    edited his answer to prevent him from deceiving Channel 4's viewers.
11 By July 1996, with *The Committee* programme long forgotten and apparently
    discredited forever, Trimble felt able to meet King Rat and negotiate with
    him, during the confrontation that arose over the determination of Ulster
    Loyalists to march through a Catholic housing estate at Drumcree,
    Portadown.
12 My lawyers were also denied the opportunity of cross-examining another
    Northern Ireland lawyer who, like Trimble, also swore an affidavit claiming
    that he, too, believed the programme to have identified Monteith as a mem-
    ber of the murder conspiracy. [See p. 355]
13 Monteith also reached out-of-court libel settlements with various newspa-
    pers in Britain and Ireland, which had published the "offending words" that
    both I and Channel 4's spokesman had said about him. I know that he
    picked up £50,000 from *The Sunday Times* (which, in publishing my words,
    had—ironically—told the truth about him) and I have since learned that his
    total takings, from newspapers and television stations, amounted to around
    £250,000—a scandalous outcome in view of his central role in the murder
    conspiracy.
14 See Chapter 9, p.173
15 I do not know why Singleton's name was not included in the Channel 4
    dossier with the list of murder conspirators identified by Sands; it certainly
    ought to have been because Sands was categoric about Lewis Singleton's
    close proximity to Ross and his membership of the Committee.
16 See Appendix 5.

Chapter 16

SO WHO WILL ARREST THEM?

When Ben Hamilton and I began our research, early in 1991, into collusion in Northern Ireland, we knew that we were embarking on a difficult assignment but neither of us envisaged that the resulting documentary—*The Committee*—would immerse us in years of litigation and controversy, which would blight our reputations and lead to the virtual destruction of our television production company, Box Productions. Although Ben has managed to survive the ordeal and to continue with his television career, working as a freelance researcher and director for other production companies, I felt I could not follow that course. As executive producer of the programme, the person ultimately responsible within the company for its editorial content, I felt a duty to persevere with the investigation until I had uncovered and published the full story about the Committee and its works. For the past six years, since October 1991, I have defended our journalism and pursued the story, confident that—sooner or later—I would uncover the truth about the murder conspiracy. Though I am aware that, even now, I have not fully realised that ambition, I have nevertheless made sufficient progress to allow me to reach firm conclusions about where responsibility rests for the deaths that resulted from the Loyalist assassination campaign in 1989, 1990, 1991 and beyond.[1]

Before presenting those conclusions and examining the appropriate response to the revelations disclosed in this book, I believe it is appropriate to pause and reflect on a part of the commentary of *The Committee*, words which I remember writing in the summer of 1991, when the Loyalist assassination campaign was at its height. I wrote them to provide a context which was intended to explain the reasons why the Committee members had felt impelled to act as they did. For we must not forget that the Loyalist terrorism was, in large part, a reaction to the IRA's inhuman and inexcusable conduct over the previous twenty years. The following words were spoken in the film over footage of the funeral of a murdered RUC officer, which showed his weeping family and grieving friends as they prepared to bury yet another member of the Protestant community:

During the past twenty years the Provisional IRA's ruthless terror campaign has brought bloodshed and misery to the people of Northern Ireland.

Atrocity has followed atrocity—a seemingly endless litany of violence and retaliation that has so far claimed almost three thousand lives, Protestant and Catholic.

The Royal Ulster Constabulary has been in the front line in the struggle against IRA terror. Over two hundred and sixty members of the force have been murdered—shot by snipers, blown up by land mines or car bombs. Nearly seven thousand police officers have been injured.

The brutal murders of security force members have left a legacy of suffering and bitterness, not only within their ranks. Ninety per cent of the RUC, and almost all the locally recruited Ulster Defence Regiment are Protestants.

Those words were true in 1991 and they remain true in 1998. It was the prospect of further death and destruction, the certainty of more such RUC and UDR funerals, that led the once respectable, lawful and unremarkable citizens of Portadown, Belfast and elsewhere to volunteer their services in what became a secret Loyalist war against the IRA. Billy Abernethy's brother, for example, was murdered in a spectacularly cruel and cold-blooded manner in 1988; RUC Assistant Chief Constable Trevor Forbes OBE will have attended many funerals such as the one shown in *The Committee*; and I do not doubt that the Reverend Hugh Ross also officiated at the grave side of many IRA victims in County Tyrone. Yet, while we can understand the motivation of those who joined the Committee, it does not alter the fact that they freely and enthusiastically participated in a murder conspiracy. In so doing, Reverend Ross became "Reverend" Ross and he, like his co-conspirators, descended to the same moral plain as those in the IRA who placed explosive devices under car bonnets, raised an Armalite to end a British soldier's life or carried out any of the countless other atrocities which caused so much misery in Ireland and Britain for a generation. The fifty to sixty Committee members and their associates, some of whom are listed in Appendix One, turned themselves into terrorists and adopted exactly the same methods of those whom they so hate and despise, the Provisional IRA.

Evil deeds were committed on all sides during the thirty-year conflict in Northern Ireland. We must bear that in mind as we consider the conclusions which arise from my investigation into collusion between the Loyalists and the British security forces. One day, perhaps, those responsible for the Committee's murder campaign will plead that they would never have resorted to terrorist action, if the Provisional IRA had not tried to bomb the Ulster Protestants into a united Ireland. It will be for others, in due course, to listen to their pleas before passing judgement on their guilt and on their degree of culpability. And, after the law of men has taken its course, each and every one of them will have to answer, as we all will, to that higher authority who commands: "Thou shalt not kill." It has been my task to investigate the Committee's killings, to identify those responsible and to establish the facts about the overall murder conspiracy. Those facts can now be briefly summarised.

A secret terrorist organisation—the Ulster Loyalist Central Co-ordinating Committee—ran a campaign of political and sectarian assassination in the late 1980s and early 1990s. The Committee's fifty to sixty members were drawn from a wide cross-section of the Ulster Loyalist community, including the business and professional elite, the Loyalist paramilitary organisations and, most significantly, the upper echelons of the RUC and the UDR. Collusion between the Loyalists and the RUC/UDR Inner Force was formal, structured and systematic, involving an unknown but sizeable proportion of the locally recruited security services in Northern Ireland.

The Ulstermen in control of the RUC—including two Assistant Chief Constables, one as yet unknown, the other well-known—demonstrated that their primary loyalty was not to the British Crown but to Ulster Loyalism. The eighteen RUC Inner Force members on the Committee effectively placed the resources of both the RUC and the UDR at the disposal of that terrorist organisation. This Inner Force routinely supplied the personnel, equipment and expertise which was used with terrifying effect by the Loyalist death squads, operating under the Committee's control in 1989, 1990, 1991 and beyond. The Committee employed the services of two main assassins—Robin Jackson [The Jackal] and Billy Wright [King Rat]—who, guided by the RUC Inner Force and assisted by other Loyalists, carried out at least nine of the ten murders investigated for *The Committee*.[2]

Although the Committee was primarily dedicated to the murder of Irish Republicans—Provisional IRA activists and Sinn Féin politicians—the Loyalist conspirators were prepared, as and when they felt it necessary, either to murder or to justify the murder of entirely innocent Catholics. Denis Carville, the three "mobile sweet shop" victims—Katrina Rennie, Eileen Duffy, Brian Frizzell—were all murdered, as we have seen, *not* because they were Republican terrorists but because they were Catholics or were presumed to be so. Police officers belonging to the illegal RUC Inner Force participated in the planning and execution of each of these attacks, which is the principal reason why no-one has ever been arrested or charged with any of these crimes. At the date of writing, February 1998, all eighteen Committee murders discussed in this book remained, officially, "unsolved."

Unfortunately, the Committee's assassination campaign was not brought to a permanent end by the Channel 4 broadcast in October 1991. Thanks largely to the appointment of Chief Superintendent Jimmy Nesbitt and Inspector Chris Webster, the RUC managed to contain the scandal and to suppress the truth. The RUC's official, internal investigation exonerated all nineteen Committee members who had been identified by their self-confessed, co-conspirator, Jim Sands. As a result of this RUC cover-up, all fifty to sixty murder conspirators were allowed to remain at liberty and, once they had recovered from the shock of the initial exposure, eventually to resume their murder campaign. Appendix Two lists the Committee's known murder victims, the eighteen Catholics assassinated before May 1991, together with a further thirty-one murdered by Loyalist paramilitaries between May 1991 and August 1996; the Committee's members must, in these circumstances, be regarded as the "prime suspects" for all the "unsolved" murders listed in Appendix Two. Although I have not, as yet, been able to establish the total number of assassinations for which the Committee was responsible, I am satisfied that the RUC's response to the Channel 4 broadcast resulted in the further loss of innocent Catholic lives.[3]

RUC Chief Constable Sir Hugh Annesley must carry responsibility for all Committee murders which occurred while he was in office, those carried out before the broadcast and, especially, those committed afterwards. For, once the RUC had received the Channel 4 dossier containing the names of nineteen Committee members, the killing ought to have been stopped immediately. Instead, as we have seen, the Chief Constable's hand-picked "investigators"—Nesbitt and Webster—proceeded to give their chief the verdict he had himself publicly announced *before* setting up their "Inquiry," a verdict he reiterated in 1992: "the [programme's] allegation of an Inner Circle/Inner Force within the RUC was an invention . . . there is no overall, organised Committee . . . the allegations . . . are without foundation."[4] The Chief Constable's failure to hold a genuinely independent investigation, one which could have established the truth about the murder conspiracy, allowed the guilty to go unpunished and condemned the innocent—the Committee's future victims—to avoidable, violent deaths. The British Conservative Government is equally responsible because, as the ultimate legal authority in Northern Ireland, it could and ought also to have insisted on a thorough search for the truth.

The RUC's verdict that the programme had been a "hoax"—or, in Nesbitt's indelicate phraseology, "a complete and utter lot of balls"—was enthusiastically promoted, as we have seen, in a "dirty tricks" campaign by the *Sunday Express* and *The Sunday Times*. Virulent propaganda against the programme and the programme makers intimidated Channel 4 into a prolonged silence which, in the absence of any further programmes on the Loyalist assassination campaign, allowed a consensus to form in the British and Irish media that *The Committee* had been a deeply flawed exercise in investigative journalism, what one Ireland Correspondent called "[possibly] the worst documentary ever shown on British television." This dismal consensus is now, at last, being challenged and will, I trust, soon be replaced by a more accurate perception, partly as a result of the publication of this book. In 1996, this process of reappraisal gathered momentum when I succeeded in the British libel courts in forcing the *Sunday Express* to retract its strident endorsement of the RUC's "hoax" verdict. This year, it will be the turn of *The Sunday Times* to face its moment of truth in the same courts. I am confident that, in due course, *The Sunday Times* will also be forced to accept that it ought not to have accused me or my company of perpetrating a "hoax" on Channel 4 and on a million British television viewers; I will require that newspaper to recognise publicly that there was never any truth in Nesbitt's report to Channel 4 that "Sean McPhilemy [told Sands] he had done so well [in his filmed interview] he would be given an additional bonus as well as the £5000 originally promised." If *The Sunday Times* does not retract the false statements it published about me in May 1993, the contents of this book will become the subject of an expensive and high profile libel trial in the High Court in London in October 1998.

So what will be the outcome of the investigation into collusion which I have pursued for the past seven years? It would, I believe, be difficult to exaggerate the significance for the RUC of what I have, so far, managed to establish about its misconduct in the late 1980s and early 1990s. For I have discovered and shown in this book that the RUC, the organisation constitutionally obliged to uphold the law and protect the citizen in Northern Ireland, was corrupted to the highest levels during that period. Senior RUC officers, disenchanted by the drift of British Government policy towards Northern Ireland and alienated especially by the signing of the Anglo-Irish Agreement in 1985, had formed themselves into a police force within the police force, an illegal Inner Force which placed itself at the service of the secret Loyalist terror organisation, the Committee. This RUC Inner Force—which was, in turn, controlled by an elite corps of RUC officers, the Inner Circle—routinely assisted the Loyalist death squads to assassinate Republicans and Catholics whom the Committee had selected for elimination.

The unique coalition of forces which constituted the Committee, representing every faction within Ulster Loyalism and enjoying the tacit support of Unionist political leaders, had enabled the conspiracy to function with frightening efficiency in 1989, 1990 and into 1991. The Committee was just beginning rapidly to escalate its rate of assassination when Box Productions and Channel 4 encountered one of its members and persuaded him to talk on national television about the murder conspiracy in which he was participating. This anonymous Committee member, Jim Sands, revealed an immense amount of incriminating detail about the murder conspirators and the murders themselves; fortunately, his first-hand testimony about the nature and scope of the Committee's activities was recorded on audio and video tape; this material was sent abroad before the Channel 4 broadcast and is now available to prove the truth of the allegations I have made against the RUC in this book.

The RUC was so corrupted by Loyalist terrorists, some of them serving and high-ranking officers in the force, that it is impossible now to believe that this body will ever again be trusted by the Catholic community in Northern Ireland. For, as we have seen, RUC officers working at the behest of the Committee selected an entirely innocent boy, Denis Carville, to be murdered by the notorious Loyalist assassin Billy Wright, King Rat. Denis Carville's significance lies in the devastating fact, revealed to us by Sands, that the youth's religious affiliation together with the location he had, by chance, chosen to park his car were the defining criteria set by the Committee for the reprisal murder they had planned. It is clear from what Sands told us that any Catholic in Northern Ireland could, potentially, have suffered precisely the same fate as Denis Carville and for precisely the same reason. We should recall that when the Committee held its first meeting after Denis Carville had been murdered those present, according to Sands, had voiced their approval of the killing even though they knew that the dead youth had not been involved in political activity of any kind.

> . . . because the [RUC] file showed that he had Republican sympathies, that they [the Committee] felt there was nothing wrong with the operation. But, actually at the time when they [the RUC officers] pointed Denis Carville out, they didn't know if there was any Republican sympathies within his family or within himself. They didn't know that at the time. He was just picked out because he was a Roman Catholic in a similar situation as Colin McCullough.

Similarly, the Inner Force's role in the murder of three innocent Catholics at the mobile sweet shop in Craigavon places a question mark over the continued survival of this police force. For, as Sands revealed in his interview in great detail, RUC Inner Force officers helped Robin Jackson [The Jackal] to murder two teenage girls and a young man knowing that Jackson was a person who, when he could not find the target he intended to kill, would instantly decide to kill someone else instead.

The Jackal went into the sweet shop, the owner wasn't there, there was two girl assistants. But then The Jackal decided he wasn't going to go away empty handed, so he shot the two girls, and coming out he then shot a man who was coming across as a customer to the sweet shop. Shot him and got into the van and away. They met up with the car at the entrance to the estate, they in turn then met up with the Inner Force car, who then led them safely back to their houses.

Once the facts about the Inner Force's role in these four killings becomes publicly known and accepted as true—as they will be—it will be impossible, in my judgement, for the RUC to continue to call on the allegiance of the Catholic population, any one of whom could have suffered precisely the same fate as each of these young people. Jim Sands told us about eighteen murders sanctioned by the Committee, facilitated by the RUC Inner Force and carried out by the Loyalist squads; after we had interviewed Sands in London, he informed us about the murders of other Catholics for which his Committee was responsible. Since Abernethy's Committee was, as we now know, the supreme terrorist grouping on the Loyalist side between 1989 and the present day, it is reasonable to suspect that his fifty to sixty colleagues and their known assassins—King Rat, The Jackal and their squads—were, almost certainly, the people responsible for all the other murders of Catholics which occurred between the date of the broadcast and mid-summer 1996.

It does not require an especially fertile imagination to appreciate the degree of panic and fear that must have gripped the conspirators once they learned that one of their number, "the traitor," had revealed details of their crimes to a national television network. Though the conspirators must have been relieved, on viewing the broadcast, to learn that none of them had been named they, nevertheless, knew they had to move quickly if the danger the programme posed was, first, to be contained and, then, to be removed. For, as the murder of Sergeant Joseph Campbell reveals, collusion between the RUC and the Loyalists did not begin with the Committee. This police force had, as we have seen, been sponsoring terrorist murder from the early 1970s when Robin Jackson's career as a political assassin began. Those in charge of the RUC Inner Force, those who know *all* the scandalous activities for which they are responsible, must have realised the urgency of ensuring that *The Committee* would be the last investigative television documentary ever made about their police force.

So, as I look back on the sequence of events which followed the broadcast, I realise that the RUC's primary aim was the prevention of any further damaging revelations or publicity. That goal was, as we know, instantly achieved at the moment the RUC sought and obtained the

Production Orders under the Prevention of Terrorism Act. Once that legal battle had begun in front of Judge Derek Clarkson, the entire affair had become *sub judice* and from then until now we have been fighting a losing battle in the propaganda war. If Channel 4 had pursued the story, commissioned further programmes and broadcast them when legally permitted to do so, the British public would have learned the truth; but once Channel 4 decided to withdraw from the fray, to lick its wounds and to forget about its foray into "murder triangle" the odds against a successful completion of this investigation grew almost impossibly high. I realise now, in a way I certainly did not in early 1991, that anyone proposing to tangle with the RUC ought to recognise at the outset that this organisation, sharpened and hardened by its bitter experiences in fighting the IRA, will do whatever it thinks necessary to come out on top.

What ought to happen now? I have taken my investigation as far as I can. I have publicly identified twenty-four of the Committee's fifty to sixty murder conspirators; Ken Kerr, the Committee's most important paramilitary figure, gave me the names of other supposed members but, for reasons I have already made clear, none of his alleged conspirators should be publicly named, not without further detailed inquiry by an independent investigator. I have also identified eighteen people, all of them Irish Catholics, all of them citizens of the United Kingdom, all of them murdered by the Committee before October 1991 and, most significantly, all of their murders still officially "unsolved;" most of them, as we have seen, were killed by Billy Wright [King Rat] and Robin Jackson [The Jackal], operating under the guidance and supervision of the RUC Inner Force. I have also listed a further thirty Catholics and one Protestant murdered between October 1991 and August 1996; for reasons also already stated, the "prime suspects" for these crimes are the twenty-four Committee members listed in Appendix One.

What ought to happen now is, I suggest, exactly what ought to have happened immediately after the broadcast in October 1991. The British Government should appoint an independent investigator to conduct a thorough inquiry; if the revelations contained in this book prove to be correct, as I am convinced they will, the murder conspirators should be arrested, interrogated and subjected to the due process of law. My lawyers already possess all the research materials I have gathered over the past seven years and these will be available to assist any official investigator who may be appointed to hold an inquiry. I believe that a genuine investigator, someone equipped with the power to compel witnesses to testify publicly and under oath, would quickly establish that Billy Abernethy and his friends were responsible for the Loyalist assassination campaign in Northern Ireland between 1989 and 1996.

The consequences for the RUC are, as I have already made clear, potentially devastating and terminal. Abernethy's Committee could not have conducted its campaign of political assassination without the widespread and systematic collusion described by Sands and documented in this book. It is, perhaps, not surprising that the RUC death squads run by the Committee were supervised by the same police officer who brought the RUC into such disrepute in the early 1980s, Assistant Chief Constable Trevor "shoot-to-kill" Forbes OBE. Forbes's role on the Committee gives us an insight into the true character of the RUC during the long period he ran Special Branch in the 1980s. This insight is reinforced by my discovery of how RUC Chief Constable Sir John Hermon responded to the murder of one of the few Catholic sergeants in his force, Joseph Campbell; Hermon deceived the dead officer's widow over the fact that RUC Special Branch "hit man" Robin Jackson had committed the murder. The RUC shaped and stamped by Hermon and Forbes is the RUC which contained and still contains the Inner Force.

So who will arrest the murder conspirators? Will Abernethy and his friends continue to get away with murder? Will the RUC be able to ride out the storm? The answers will depend on how this book is received. The RUC will respond as before. Just as the programme was a "hoax," so my book will be a "fabrication." My motives, my sources and my revelations will all be challenged. Jim Sands and Ken Kerr will, no doubt, be "interviewed" by Liam Clarke and Barrie Penrose. There will be libel threats and, perhaps, worse. But my reply to the RUC will be simple and short. "Why are all eighteen murders still officially "unsolved"?"

Finally, this scandal has much to teach us about the proper role of the journalist in a democratic society and vividly demonstrates the necessity of having a legal framework which enables the journalist to expose corruption of the kind we found to exist within the RUC. Information about such corruption, especially within the sensitive area of State Security and Intelligence, is only ever likely to be disclosed to a journalist in confidence and, if the law prevents the journalist from giving a source an absolute guarantee of confidentiality, the corruption is likely to continue unchecked; if, in 1991, we had not promised Sands that we would keep his name secret, he would not have agreed to the interview—and, as a result, the Committee's assassination campaign would have continued unhindered. So it was right to give Sands the undertaking he demanded and, having done so, it would have been wrong to betray him by disclosing his name after the broadcast—even if a different police force had been appointed to hold a *genuine* inquiry.

It would, of course, have been doubly wrong to betray him to a *bogus* inquiry team. For, as we now know, there was never the remotest prospect that the Nesbitt Inquiry would publish the truth about the Committee or RUC/Loyalist collusion. The reader will recall Nesbitt's hypocritical performance in court as, under oath, he sought to persuade Judge Clarkson that the RUC was, despite the judge's express misgivings on the matter, genuinely investigating itself. The reader may recall his cross-examination by the Crown's barrister, Mr. David Calvert-Smith, who suggested to him that our defence of Source A was a scandalous obstruction of vigorous law enforcement.

> *Calvert-Smith*: What about Source A and his importance or otherwise to the investigation?
> *Nesbitt*: Source A is crucial to the investigation, your Honour.
> *Calvert-Smith*: Because?
> *Nesbitt*: Because, your Honour, he alleges that he had knowledge of and took part in the planning of acts of murder and other terrorist crimes; that he had knowledge of other persons who had taken part in these crimes and of members of the Royal Ulster Constabulary who were also accomplices in these matters.

We can now see that, with those answers, Nesbitt was deceiving the court into believing that he was holding a genuine inquiry when, in fact, he was doing his utmost to help the conspirators, the "aristocrats" who had been, in his own words, "planning acts of murder and other terrorist crimes."[5]

My discoveries about the real nature of Nesbitt's "Inquiry" have reinforced my conviction that we were, in 1992, totally justified in refusing to betray Source A, as Lord Woolf, Mr. Justice Pill and the Crown Prosecution Service's Mr. (now Mr. Justice!) Andrew Collins had all urged us to do. How embarrassed these distinguished lawyers ought to be when they realise that they were urging us, indeed punishing us, for our failure to assist the RUC officer in charge of protecting the murder conspirators! We should recall their learned contributions in the High Court and remind ourselves that not one of them voiced any concern over the obviously unsatisfactory fact that the RUC was being allowed to "investigate" itself; all three condemned us for failing to participate in what was a fresh scandal, the RUC's own cover-up of the original murder conspiracy.

> Mr. Andrew Collins:
> The net result of what has happened is that there has been presented to the British public as fact, "conclusive evidence" were the words used, very grave allegations against the integrity of the Royal Ulster Constabulary. Those allegations may be *complete rubbish and probably are*, but nonetheless it is essential that they be investigated because if there is any truth in them a very serious situation is disclosed . . . My Lord . . . the failure to disclose the

relevant information to enable the investigations properly to be carried out has—and this was the evidence of Chief Superintendent Nesbitt before the learned judge—resulted in the situation that the wrongdoing cannot properly be discovered and rooted out if it exists . . . It . . . nullifies the whole purpose of the investigation if this attitude is adopted. [my emphasis]6

Lord Woolf:
Both companies must have appreciated what would be the consequences of the programme, that almost inevitably there would be an inquiry as a result of the programme and [Source] A's role would be crucial . . . That the immediate effect of the programme would be to undermine the confidence of the public, particularly in the Province of Northern Ireland, in the RUC and an inquiry would be essential if the damage to that confidence was to be kept within limits. It was, and should have been, obvious that if the investigations into the RUC took place . . . the security forces would inevitably want to identify [Source] A and follow up his involvement. This would be necessary if [Source] A was speaking the truth to eradicate a canker within the RUC and it would be necessary if he was not speaking the truth to show the RUC had been gravely slandered to the disadvantage of the Province . . .

Mr. Justice Pill:
The result of the respondents' contempt of court is that the authorities and the courts have been *deprived of the opportunity to investigate the extremely serious and inflammatory allegations which have been made.* If the allegations are true, urgent and thorough investigation is required. Prosecutions would be likely. If the allegations are untrue, they should be exposed for the dangerous and pernicious falsehoods they are . . . The danger to society if falsehoods of this kind go uncorrected needs no underlining. Neither does the degree of concern to be felt if Source A is telling the truth. The respondents should not have so conducted themselves as to place themselves in the position they have, for the reasons given by My Lord [Woolf]. [my emphasis]7

All three men—Lord Woolf, Mr. Justice Pill and Mr. (now Mr. Justice) Andrew Collins—had condemned us for our refusal to give Source A's name to the RUC; not one of them seemed in any way bothered by the fact that the RUC was "investigating" itself; nor was any one of them prepared seriously to entertain the possibility that the RUC was so corrupt, so thoroughly imbued with Loyalist sentiment, that the official RUC "investigator" was in league with the murder conspirators. Now, as Nesbitt's own words reveal, we know—with all due respect to Mr. Justice Pill—that Nesbitt was *not* "deprived of an opportunity to investigate" but was prevented from coming to the "hoax" verdict that he was to reach much later when, unfortunately, he eventually managed to get his hands on Source A, Jim Sands. And we can now also appreciate the irony of Lord Woolf's observation, quoted above, that we should have known that "an inquiry would be essential if the damage to confidence [in the RUC] was to be kept within limits." How right he was! Contrary to what Mr. Justice Pill had to say, prosecutions were *never* likely to result from Nesbitt's "investigation;" if we had co-operated with Nesbitt's "Inquiry," we might as well have posted Source A's name directly to Committee chairman, Billy Abernethy. If we had not defended our sources, the Committee's fifty to sixty members would, almost certainly, have escaped justice forever and the world would never have learned about the RUC death squads.

Notes

1   I hope that the next edition of this book will contain the names of all fifty to sixty members of the Committee.

2   Billy Wright murdered: Denis Carville, Dwayne O'Donnell, John Quinn, Malcolm Nugent, Thomas Armstrong; Robin Jackson murdered: Eileen Duffy, Katrina Rennie, Brian Frizzell, Sam Marshall, RUC Sergeant Joseph Campbell, William Strathearn and Patrick Campbell. Neither Billy Wright nor Robin Jackson were ever charged with any of these murders.

3   Committee member Ken Kerr sought to persuade me that the Committee was responsible for an additional sixteen murders of Catholics and Republicans, all carried out between January 1989 and October 1991; in view of my discovery that Kerr was trying to sabotage my investigation, I have not included any of those sixteen specified murders in this book.

4   RUC Press Release, August 2nd 1992; Compare these reassuring words with the transcript of John Coulter's interview with his anonymous RUC Inner Circle member. [See Appendix 4]

5   Compare Nesbitt's posturing in front of Judge Clarkson with the transcript of his tape-recorded conversation with the *Sunday Express*'s Barrie Penrose. [See Appendix 4]

6   Mr. Collins declined to offer any reason for his expressed belief that the programme's allegations had "probably" been "complete rubbish." His remarks have certainly not induced any scepticism in my mind over the truth of Brian Raymond's aphorism that judges are just "politicians with wigs on."

7   I hope Mr. Justice Pill now realises that our "extremely serious and [allegedly] inflammatory allegations" were absolutely true.

POSTSCRIPT

A PUBLIC INQUIRY?

The RUC has succeeded for the past six years in containing the scandal, which was partially exposed when *The Committee* was broadcast in October 1991. Publication of this book will, I expect, reopen the controversy over the murder conspiracy and will probably provoke a further round of legal actions against me. Whatever may happen, I will continue to pursue the same strategy I have followed for the past seven years, to document the facts and to publish the truth. Fortunately, those most likely to contemplate action against me may be presented with an opportunity, sooner than they might wish and in a forum well beyond their control, to reply to the allegations I have made against them. For my libel action against *The Sunday Times* is well advanced and unless that newspaper's lawyers decide, between now and October 1998, to admit that its "hoax" allegation is false, we may witness the spectacle of leading Committee members and their associates appearing under subpoena in the High Court in London; they will be required to testify under oath about the political assassinations they organised between 1989 and 1996. If, however, *The Sunday Times'* lawyers manage to avoid a full-scale libel trial, that does not mean that the RUC will be able to escape responsibility for its involvement with Abernethy and his friends; the families and friends of all those murdered by the Committee will demand to know everything possible about this scandal.

An Official Inquiry led by an independent figure, who would sit in public and have the power to compel witnesses to testify under oath, will be necessary if the full story about the RUC death squads is ever to emerge. For this unprecedented scandal in the short and troubled history of Northern Ireland is far worse now, in 1998, than it was back in 1991, when *The Committee* was screened. For, since then, many more innocent Catholics lost their lives as a direct result of the RUC's effort to discredit the programme's allegations and to suppress the truth. If those whom Sands had identified as his co-conspirators in murder had been promptly arrested, the Loyalist death squads would have been unable to function as they had before October 2nd, 1991. So we can readily identify a number of specific tasks that any investigator would immediately face: to establish the reasons why RUC Chief Constable Sir Hugh Annesley failed to stop the killing; to learn how it came about that Nesbitt and Webster were allowed to hold a bogus investigation; to establish how Jim Sands, following his arrest in December 1992, was induced to "recant" his televised confession and to admit his involvement in a "hoax." Once the investigator gives us the answers to these questions, we will be well on the way to understanding the reasons why the RUC allowed the Committee's fifty to sixty murder conspirators to remain at liberty. Then, with these dimensions of the scandal charted, the investigator could probe deeper into the mystery surrounding the many further "unsolved" murders of Catholics by the Loyalists, those which occurred between October 1991 and the cease fires in August 1994.[1]

We should recall that Jim Sands—our unique source with the Ulster Independence Committee, the Ulster Loyalist Central Co-ordinating Committee and on the RUC Inner Force (which he attended as an observer for the UIC)—told us in 1991 that every single assassination by the Loyalists had to be sanctioned by Abernethy's Committee and was organised by the RUC Inner Force. He told us:

> The Loyalists will not move without the Inner Force giving the okay . . . The Inner Force is organised on an all Ulster basis. Therefore, they're able to move throughout Ulster. They can move anywhere at will. People from within the Inner Force boast that no terrorist is safe, no Republican is safe in Ulster. The terrorists can be removed at will, if and when the Inner Force decide.[2]

We have already seen that the Loyalists were not excessively scrupulous in discriminating between Republican activists and politically uninvolved Catholics. Sands made it clear that, though killing an identified Republican had been the Committee's preference, murdering a Fenian— Loyalist parlance for a Catholic—was a perfectly acceptable alternative when circumstances required.[3] Between 1991 and 1996, the Loyalist death squads controlled by the Committee were allowed by the RUC to murder many Catholics, nearly all of whom were just as innocent as Denis Carville had been. Though the world at large has forgotten these atrocities, the families of those who lost their lives have not—and, having met some of the grieving relatives, I know they never will. I have selected just three Loyalist attacks which took place during this period, the same period in which Nesbitt, Webster and Hetherington were coaxing Sands into his admission of a "hoax," were helping the *Sunday Express* and *The Sunday Times* to mislead the public about the truth of the programme's allegations and were simultaneously allowing the Committee's solicitor, Richard Monteith, to sue me in the libel courts. Nine innocent Catholics were murdered in these three attacks and, as with all the murders investigated in our documentary, the assassins escaped amid allegations of collusion which, as usual, the RUC indignantly denied. All nine murders remain officially "unsolved;" the victims would, almost certainly, still be alive if those in control of the Loyalist assassination campaign had been arrested and charged in October 1991.

(1) The Murders of Gerard and Rory Cairns

Just over two years after *The Committee* had been broadcast, the Loyalist assassination campaign had resumed with undiminished ferocity and the Catholic population living within the notorious "murder triangle" had, once again, been singled out for attack. All Catholics in that area were vulnerable and none more so than those who openly expressed their Irish identity and who made no secret of their love of Irish culture—traditional music, the Gaelic language and such sports as hurling and Gaelic football. It was, we must assume, the uninhibited enjoyment of their Irish culture and pride in their Irish identity which turned the Cairns family into a target for those who sent the Loyalist murder squad to attack them, after darkness had fallen on the night of October 28th 1993. For, as we shall see, this Irish Catholic family was remarkable only in the fact that its evident Irish identity and character had turned it into an offensive symbol in the eyes of the group of "Ulster British" Loyalists who, on that night, had decided to engage in a bout of ethnic cleansing.

Eamon and Sheila Cairns, who lived in a modest and isolated house in the country five miles from Lurgan, County Armagh, had spent the early evening happily with four of their five children; the parents had been holding a birthday party for their eleven-year-old daughter and youngest child, Roisin. Their three sons—Gerard, a twenty-two-year-old lorry driver; Rory, an eighteen-year-old joiner; and Liam, aged fourteen—had all enjoyed the party and each had taken photographs of other family members with their young sister. Paula, aged twenty-one, is the only family member who had not been present; she was living in England where she was completing a degree in business and economics. Shortly after the party had ended, the parents had driven to an evening class in Lurgan, where they were learning the Gaelic language. Liam had gone out to see a friend who lived about sixty yards down the road, leaving Roisin at home with her two older brothers. Not one member of the Cairns family suspected, as Roisin's birthday party ended, that they would never enjoy together such a happy occasion again.

Shortly after the parents and Liam had left the house, Roisin was alone in the kitchen, while Gerard and Rory were sitting in the adjoining living room, watching television. Roisin told her parents what happened after they had left and her father, Eamon, has provided me with a written account which describes, in some detail, the sequence of events that occurred on that night:

> At approximately eight o'clock Roisin got up from where she was sitting. At this point the back door, which leads directly into the kitchen, opened. Two men dressed in black boiler suits and faces covered with masks entered through the unlocked door. Initially, Roisin thought it was a Halloween prank by some of Gerard's or Rory's mates. One man ran into the living room to where the boys were sitting, whilst the other stood in the kitchen staring at Roisin and raising his finger signalling Roisin to keep quiet. The other then signalled him and he followed into the living room and started shooting. They carried a rifle each. One gunman shot Rory where he sat in front of the television. One shot passed up through his head and another three through his body. Gerard must have managed to stand up when alerted, trying to protect himself with his arm. Three bullets skimmed his arm before entering his body. Death must have been instantaneous in both cases. Rory was slouched in his chair whilst Gerard lay on the floor in front of the sofa. The two gunmen then ran back out through the kitchen, one stopping momentarily to stare at Roisin.
>
> Roisin then ran to the living room in a state of extreme shock. She saw Rory's eyes were closed. Seeing Gerard with his eyes open, she asked Gerard what was wrong with Rory, not realising they were both dead. She ran out screaming for help and down the road to the neighbour's house where Liam was visiting to raise the alarm.

After the alarm was raised, the RUC and British Army arrived at the house but, by then, the Loyalist squad had already escaped, leaving few clues behind. There had been two men involved; one was the same size as a suspicious character whom Eamon and Sheila Cairns had seen, some weeks earlier, lurking near their home; Eamon noticed that some twigs had been broken near the back fence which separates his garden from that of his neighbour, suggesting that the two gunmen may have arrived by jumping over the fence. All this information and much more was passed to the RUC which, despite the passage of over four years, has since then made no apparent progress in finding the killers.

Naturally, the parents of the dead brothers have tried to discover what effort the RUC made to track down the culprits and what facts, if any, the police had managed to uncover. Suspicions of collusion between the RUC and the Loyalists arose shortly after the murders when Eamon Cairns discovered that, as he puts it, "during one interview with a neighbour . . . one detective remarked that they knew an attack was going to take place but they didn't think it would be so soon." The family grew sceptical about the true status of the RUC's investigation into the murders and, even before learning from me about the existence of the Committee, suspected that the murders had been organised by people whom the RUC, if given any choice in the matter, would never touch.

In assessing the RUC's failure to solve these two murders, we must bear in mind the enormous effort Nesbitt and his team made to prevent the truth emerging about the existence and role of Abernethy's Committee. And we should recall what Sands told us in 1991, namely that "the Loyalists will not move without the Inner Force giving the okay." So the obvious questions to be asked about the murders of Gerard and Rory Cairns, should there ever be a genuinely independent inquiry into their deaths, include: did Abernethy's Committee sanction and organise the killings? Was the RUC Inner Force involved? Were the two assassins drawn from Billy Wright's "rat pack" or from Robin Jackson's gang?

Given what we have learned from Sands about the Committee's central role in organising Loyalist terrorism, we are justified in assuming that Abernethy and his co-conspirators should still be regarded as the "prime suspects" for these murders. And given what we know about the role of the RUC Inner Force, it is highly likely that these murders will forever remain in the RUC file marked: "Unsolved." If Eamon and Sheila Cairns were to succeed in securing a public inquiry they would, I believe, make two crucial discoveries—first, that those ultimately responsible for the murder of their sons have been known to the RUC since October 1991; and second, that if the RUC had arrested the conspirators at that time, their two boys would probably still be alive.

(2) The Murder of Kathleen O'Hagan

Paddy O'Hagan is lucky to be alive. He would certainly have been shot dead along with his wife, Kathleen, if he had been at home with her on Saturday night, August 7th 1994, when a Loyalist squad arrived at their remote farmhouse in the Sperrin mountains in County Tyrone. On that night, Paddy had gone out for a late night drink and a game of pool with friends, leaving his five young children, all under the age of eight, in the care of his wife who was pregnant with their sixth child. When he returned home in the early hours of the morning, he encountered a scene of pure horror. His terrified children came rushing out to meet him shouting: "Mammy's dead. Mammy's in heaven. Bad boys came and broke the glass. They've shot mammy and she's in heaven."[4]

Paddy rushed into the house and made his way to the bedroom. "I think the light was on where she was lying. I put my arms round her. She was still warm but I saw there was nothing I could do for her. That's a wee picture you'd never forget."[5]

As Kathleen O'Hagan's body was lowered into the grave a few days later, a local woman grabbed the microphone through which the funeral service had been relayed to a large crowd outside the church. "The RUC colluded in the murder of Kathleen O'Hagan," she told the mourners, many of whom applauded eagerly. They also welcomed a family statement, read aloud, which claimed that the death was "the end product of years and years of endless organised harassment of our family." But the RUC dismissed all the criticisms, rejecting the collusion charges as "ritual statements and less than constructive," and asserting that this "savage, barbaric and cold-blooded murder" would be vigorously investigated.

It will not surprise the reader to be told that, despite the professed intention to track down the killers, the RUC's detective efforts appear to have come to nought. More than three years after this killing, which the priest at the funeral described as "unnaturally obscene," nobody has been arrested or charged with Kathleen O'Hagan's murder. And it is not at all likely that anyone ever will be. For Kathleen's husband of nine years, Paddy O'Hagan, is not someone for whom the RUC would have much sympathy; he had spent eight years in prison for IRA terrorist offences before his release and marriage in 1985. In fact, he had met his future wife for the first time when she was visiting her Republican brother, who had lost a leg in a premature bomb explosion, an incident which eventually led to his sharing a prison cell with Paddy O'Hagan.

Kathleen O'Hagan's murder hit the headlines because the Loyalist terrorists, in murdering this five-month pregnant woman in front of her five infant children, had sunk to an abyss which most people who heard about it, no matter what their political viewpoints, could recognise as an uniquely depraved and foul deed. Yet, as the wife of a former IRA terrorist, Kathleen O'Hagan was soon forgotten and, as a result, there can be few who seriously believe that the RUC, left to its own devices, will ever locate or prosecute the culprits. We can be fairly confident that Kathleen O'Hagan's murder will forever remain officially "unsolved."

Was it a Committee killing? Who gave it the go-ahead? Was the RUC Inner Force involved? Was the Loyalist squad led by King Rat, by The Jackal or by somebody else? Was Kathleen O'Hagan murdered because she was the mother of a large Catholic family, because she was a symbol of the population trend the Ulster Loyalists fear? We are unlikely to learn the answers to any of these questions unless and until a public inquiry, instituted along the lines outlined above, is able to interrogate Abernethy, Ross, Forbes, Monteith and the other members of the Committee. Before any investigator decides to cross-examine these people about this particular murder, they could profitably recall what Jim Sands told us in his filmed interview about the nature of the Committee's murder conspiracy: "It's run as a business, with business expertise being given by experienced people . . . Nothing happens now without actually getting the go-ahead from the central Committee." Did Billy Abernethy give the "go-ahead" for the murder of Kathleen O'Hagan?

(3) The Loughinisland Murders

In the summer of 1994 millions of people in Britain and Ireland greatly enjoyed the spectacular progress of the Irish Republic's football team in the World Cup in the USA; it was a source of pride not just for the Irish but also for the British because the hero of the hour was the team's English manager, Jackie Charlton. And when, on June 20th, the Irish team defeated the soccer loving Italians by one goal to nil, cheers erupted in many thousands of pubs, clubs and homes throughout the British Isles.

Tragically, the joyous emotions stirred by this sporting triumph were instantly crushed when television viewers in Britain and Ireland were shown pictures of what had happened in a pub in County Down at the time the football players were on the field. For shortly after the match had begun, a Loyalist squad had burst into O'Toole's bar in Loughinisland and opened fire with a machine gun, spraying the customers with bullets. O'Toole's bar had, as the Loyalists would have known, a largely Catholic clientele and it was crowded with regulars who had arrived to watch the live television coverage of the match. Six people were murdered, five Catholics and one Protestant—the bullets did not discriminate on the basis of religion or age or anything else. Six more families were plunged into misery and the Loyalist squad, having achieved their objective, escaped undetected.

Most of those murdered in the attack were in the prime of life—Patrick O'Hare, Malcolm Jenkinson, Dan McGreanor, Eamonn Byrne, Adrian Rogan; one of the dead, Barney Green, was in his eighties. The television pictures of the carnage, the blood-splattered bar and the heart-broken relatives managed to convey the intensity of the hatred and the horror of the sectarian conflict, which has driven ordinary human beings into barbarism. Loughinisland is now a word which stands for the images we saw that night in June 1994.

I remember wondering, when I first heard about that attack and saw the images on my television screen, whether the Committee could possibly have been responsible. "Kill the fish and poison the water" had been the Committee's strategy for eliminating the IRA and intimidating the Catholic population in Northern Ireland. The attack on O'Toole's bar in

Loughinisland had fitted in with that strategy. Could it possibly be the case, I asked myself, that these six harmless men had been murdered by those very individuals whose names I had learned from Jim Sands in 1991?

When Tim Laxton and I eventually met and talked with Committee member Ken Kerr in Maidstone in 1996, I asked him about the Loughinisland murders. Two years on from that attack, the images had faded in my mind but I knew that the atrocity would remain an acutely painful memory for many thousands of people, especially the Catholic population in Northern Ireland. So who was responsible for Loughinisland? Did Billy Abernethy give it the go-ahead? Was the RUC Inner Force involved? Were those six murders the result of collusion between the RUC and the Loyalist squad?

Ken Kerr claimed that the attack had been sanctioned and organised by the Committee. And he gave us the name of the RUC Inspector who, he said, had supervised the killings. For the reason I have already given—Ken Kerr's attempt to discredit my investigation—I have decided not to name this RUC officer publicly at this stage. But if Kerr's information about this RUC Inspector turns out to be true, it will explain why these murders, almost four years after the attack on O'Toole's bar, remain officially "unsolved." The Committee's involvement would be shocking but no more shocking than the fact that those identified by Jim Sands in 1991 as the architects of Loyalist terror continue to enjoy immunity for their crimes.

Early in 1998, I obtained fresh information about these three atrocities. I believe that, if they were to be probed by an independent investigator, it will be discovered that:

> (1) Rory and Gerard Cairns were murdered by a member of Billy Wright's "rat-pack" and that the RUC has known the person's identity since the day the crime was committed. The assassin's identity is known to me.
>
> (2) Kathleen O'Hagan was murdered by another of Wright's "rat-pack" and, again, the identity of the assassin has long been known to the RUC.
>
> (3) The Loughinisland atrocity was carried out by the Loyalist assassin who has been an RUC "hitman" since 1973, the Committee's Robin Jackson.

****

In late 1997 I was trying to arrange meetings with some of the leading figures in the Loyalist assassination campaign in an effort to discover whatever I could about more of the Committee's "unsolved" murders. I had made tentative arrangements to meet R.J. Kerr who, though not a member of the Committee, had helped Robin Jackson to murder William

Strathearn in 1977, had participated in the attempted murder of Paschal Mulholland in 1984 and had been involved—albeit at a low level—in Loyalist sectarian killings over a period of nearly thirty years. He was in a position to fill in many gaps in my knowledge of Loyalist terrorism and had grown disenchanted by developments within the paramilitary underworld. Shortly after I had learned of his willingness to talk to me, the news reached me of his death in a mysterious explosion, reportedly an accident. I had also taken initial steps towards arranging a meeting with Billy Wright in prison where he was serving an eight-year sentence—not for murder, not even for attempted murder, but for threatening to kill a woman in his home town, Portadown. I was told he would see me but I did not really expect to make any significant breakthrough in my research from such a steely and ruthless terrorist. Before any date was fixed for the meeting, he was murdered by a Republican splinter group on December 27th, 1997. And my hopes of securing an interview with the Committee's other key assassin, Robin Jackson, were also dashed when, in January 1998, I learned that he was dying of lung cancer.

Though I have been forever denied the opportunity of face to face interviews with these assassins, there remains—at least in theory—considerable scope for securing confessions from those who planned and organised the murders. But it is highly improbable that any of these Committee members will talk. On the other hand, it is certain that I will persevere in my efforts to expose what they have done.

Notes

1   By choosing this date, August 1994, I do not wish to suggest that the Committee and its assassins were idle after that date. For the Loyalists have continued to murder Catholics right up to the present day (February 1998).

2   See Chapter 4 p. 38.

3   See Chapter 4 p. 42.

4   These tragic events are movingly described in an article by Susan McKay in the *Sunday Tribune*, "The Life and Death of Kathleen O'Hagan." August 14th 1994.

5   Same article, *Sunday Tribune*, August 14th 1994.

Appendix 1

The Committee

Twenty-four identified or suspected Members and four Associates of the Ulster Loyalist Central Co-ordinating Committee. This terrorist organisation—The Committee—controlled the Loyalist death squads which murdered, among others, the eighteen Republicans and Catholics listed in Appendix Two. These are some of the "prime suspects" for the murders of Republicans and Catholics between October 1991 and mid-1996, as listed in Appendix Two; Source A, Jim Sands, told us that the Committee had a membership of between fifty and sixty people. All those listed below deny membership. Almost all of the alleged Committee members were interviewed by the RUC, which declared them all innocent.

24 Alleged Committee Members

Billy Abernethy	Chairman, Ulster Loyalist Central Co-ordinating Committee—"The Committee;" Ulster Bank executive; ex-RUC Reserve
Hugh Ross	Presbyterian Minister; President, Ulster Independence Committee
Trevor Forbes OBE	RUC Assistant Chief Constable and Head of Special Branch (retired)
James Sands	"Source A;" Hugh Ross's "messenger"
John McCullagh	Representative, Ulster Resistance paramilitary organisation
Isobel McCulloch	Performed secretarial services, booked halls etc.
Graham Long	ex-British Army, Loyalist paramilitary
Nelson McCausland	Belfast City Councillor; Ulster Unionist Party
David Prentice	Businessman; Prentice Garages, Portadown, Co. Armagh
Albert Prentice	Businessman; Prentice Garages, Portadown, Co. Armagh

Charles Moffett	Accountant, laundered money for arms shipments
Richard Monteith	Solicitor, Belfast and Portadown, Co. Armagh
Cecil Kilpatrick*	Member, Ulster Independence Committee; Hillsborough, Co. Down; ex-RUC Reserve
Lewis Singleton	Solicitor; Ulster Independence Committee [*See below, Drew Nelson and William David Trimble MP*]
Philip Black	Staff member, Computer Science Department, Queen's University, Belfast
Sammy Abraham	Businessman; Akraprint Ltd, Tandragee, Co. Armagh
Will Davidson	Major, Ulster Defence Regiment; UDR Representative on Inner Force; former Chairman, Banbridge District Council [Ulster Unionist Party]; former B Special; former Justice of the Peace!
Alec Jamison	Inner Force
Robin Jackson	Assassin; nickname The Jackal
Billy Wright	Assassin; nickname King Rat
Dean McCullough	Portadown/Lurgan Ulster Volunteer Force
Alec Benson	Assassin; Loyalist Retaliation and Defence Group, Lisburn, County Antrim
Ken Kerr	ex-British Army, Loyalist paramilitary [*See Chapter 14*]
Ian Whittle	RUC Inner Force, Portadown Representative

*Sands has a slight speech impediment, which explains why this name appeared as "Kirkpatrick" in the Channel 4 dossier.

4   C o m m i t t e e   A s s o c i a t e s

Alan Clegg	RUC Inspector and Head of Lurgan RUC Station when Sam Marshall was murdered by Robin Jackson in March 1990
William David Trimble	Member of Parliament for Upper Bann; Leader, Ulster Unionist Party since 1995; Member of the Privy Council, which advises the Queen of England; briefed by Committee leaders while assassination campaign was under way; swore affidavit in libel proceedings brought by Committee member Richard Monteith; defended Committee member Hugh Ross on *Right to*

	Reply; attacked *The Committee* programme in speeches in the House of Commons; legal representatives: Lewis Singleton and Drew Nelson [*See above and below*]
Frazer Agnew	Politician, Ulster Unionist Party; ex-Mayor of Carrickfergus, Co. Antrim; associate of Trevor Forbes [*See above*]
Drew Nelson	Solicitor; Dromore, Co. Down; Partner in Legal Practice with Lewis Singleton [*See above*]; Signed affidavit on behalf of Richard Monteith in his unsuccessful criminal libel action against the author

Ken Kerr gave me the names of at least twenty more people who, allegedly, attended meetings of the Committee or who, while judging it prudent not to attend, had fully supported its murderous acivities. These included four senior RUC Special Branch officers, two senior civil servants in the Northern Ireland Office and a Lieutenant Colonel in the Ulster Defence Regiment. Given Kerr's failed attempt to sabotage my investigation and, therefore, the dubious status of *all* his revelations, I have decided not to identify in this book any of the additional alleged conspirators or assassins whose names he gave me. Nevertheless, I hope that further research will enable me to identify all fifty to sixty Committee Members and Associates, and to give a comprehensive list of the Committee's victims, in the second edition of this book.

Appendix 2

THE MURDER VICTIMS

The eighteen murders listed immediately below were sanctioned and organised by the Ulster Loyalist Central Co-ordinating Committee. In 1991, Source A [Jim Sands] provided Britain's Channel 4 Television with details on seventeen of these murders, all committed between 1989 and 1991; some time after the murder of Patrick Shanaghan in August 1991, Sands confirmed to us that this killing had also been sanctioned and organised by the Committee.

February 1989   Patrick Finucane, Belfast
        [*See Chapter 4*] No-one charged or convicted for the murder.

March 1990   Sam Marshall, Lurgan, Co. Armagh
        [*See Chapter 4*] None of those who carried out the killing has been charged or convicted for the murder—one UVF terrorist was convicted for aiding and abetting the crime. [*See below, "Malachy Trainor" murder*]

October 1990   Denis Carville, Lurgan, Co. Armagh
        [*See Chapter 1 and Chapter 4*] No-one charged or convicted for the murder.

October 1990   Tommy Casey, Cookstown, Co. Tyrone
        57-year-old Sinn Féin member shot dead by Loyalists in front of his wife, at a friend's house near their home. Collusion suspected but not proved. No-one charged or convicted for the murder.

March 1991   Dwayne O'Donnell, Cappagh, Co. Tyrone
        John Quinn, Cappagh, Co. Tyrone
        Malcolm Nugent, Cappagh, Co. Tyrone
        Thomas Armstrong, Cappagh, Co. Tyrone.
        [*See Chapter 4*] No-one charged or convicted for the murders.

[Note: The anonymous RUC Inner Circle officer, interviewed for us by John Coulter, clearly knew the identities of those responsible for these four murders. ". . . and the people at Cappagh, when four Republicans were killed, but in that incident they didn't get the real man they were after." *See Appendix 4*]

March 1991	Eileen Duffy, Craigavon, Co. Armagh
	Katrina Rennie, Craigavon, Co. Armagh
	Brian Frizzell, Craigavon, Co. Armagh
	[*See Chapter 4*, p. 52–53] Only one member of The Jackal's gang was convicted for the murders.
April 1991	John O'Hara, Belfast
	42-year-old taxi driver shot dead by a squad of at least four UFF gunmen. No involvement in politics or paramilitary activity. Collusion not suspected at the time. No-one charged or convicted for the murder.
May 1991	Eddie Fullerton, Buncrana, Co. Donegal
	[*See Chapter 14*] No-one charged or convicted for the murder.
August 1991	James Carson, Belfast
	33-year-old Catholic newsagent shot by two Loyalist gunmen because he sold *Republican News* in his shop. Collusion not suspected at the time. No-one charged or convicted for the murder.
August 1991	Thomas Donaghy, Kilrea, Co. Derry
	38-year-old Sinn Féin member, shot seven times in the face, head and neck, while on his way to work, by two UFF gunmen. Victim released from jail in 1988 after he had served ten years of a nineteen-year sentence for attempted murder, IRA membership and firearms offences. Collusion alleged but not proved. No-one charged or convicted for the murder.
August 1991	Patrick Shanaghan, Castlederg, Co. Tyrone
	[*See Chapter 14*] No-one charged or convicted for the murder.
August 1991	Martin O'Prey, Belfast
	28-year-old Republican activist and senior member of the paramilitary Irish Peoples' Liberation Organisation, IPLO. Shot by UVF gunmen and hit by at least sixteen bullets, as he played with his two young daughters at his home. Collusion suspected at the time but not proved. No-one charged or convicted for the murder.

September 1991 Bernard O'Hagan, Magherafelt
Sinn Féin councillor and college lecturer shot dead by
UFF gunmen as he arrived for work. Collusion alleged
by Sinn Féin but denied by Secretary of State Sir Peter
Brooke, who said that no credence should be given to
allegations that British Secret Service agents were
involved in the assassination of Sinn Féin activitists. No-
one charged or convicted for the murder.

31 LOYALIST MURDER VICTIMS
October 1991—August 1996

Thirty of the thirty-one victims listed below were murdered by Loyalist
death squads between the date of the Channel 4 broadcast, October 2nd
1991 and the ceasefires in August 1994; the thirty-first murder occurred
in August 1996. All of the victims were Catholics except for Malcolm
Jenkinson, a Protestant, who was shot dead at O'Toole's bar in
Loughinisland on June 20th, 1994. [*See below*] Since the Ulster Loyalist
Central Co-ordinating Committee controlled the Loyalist death squads
throughout this period, the twenty-three Committee Members listed in
Appendix One can also be regarded as being among the "prime suspects"
for most, if not all, of the murders listed below.

[Note: In June 1994 a Loyalist terrorist, 31-year-old Laurence George
Maguire, was given five life sentences for his role in the murder of the five
Catholic victims marked with an asterisk below. Abernethy's Committee
was not mentioned at Maguire's trial but this does not mean that the
Committee was uninvolved; it will be the task of a public inquiry to establish what role the Committee may have played in these and the other murders listed below.]

Sean Anderson	Pomeroy, Co. Tyrone	October 25, 1991
Desmond Rogers	Factory worker	November 14, 1991
Fergus Magee	Factory worker	November 14, 1991
John Lavery	Factory worker	November 14, 1991
Kevin McKearney	Butcher, Moy, Co. Tyrone	January 3, 1992
John McKearney	Butcher, Moy, Co. Tyrone	January 3, 1992
James Gray	Portadown, Co Armagh	
Terence McConville*	Musician, Portadown	March 29, 1992
Peter Clements	Portadown	April 1, 1992
Charles Fox*	Moy, Co. Tyrone	September 7, 1992
Teresa Fox*	Moy, Co. Tyrone	September 7, 1992

Sheena Campbell	Belfast	October 16, 1992
Peter McCormack	Castlewellan, Co. Down	November 19, 1992
Patrick Shields*	Dungannon, Co. Tyrone	January 3, 1993
Diarmuid Shields*	Dungannon, Co. Tyrone	January 3, 1993
Martin McNamee	Cookstown Co. Tyrone	January 28, 1993
Eugene Martin	Ballyronana, Co. Tyrone	February 2, 1993
Thomas Molloy	Loughgall, Co. Tyrone	February 11, 1993
Gerard Cairns	Bleary, Lurgan, Co. Armagh	October 28, 1993
Rory Cairns	Bleary, Lurgan, Co. Armagh	October 28, 1993
Rose Anne Mallon	Dungannon, Co. Tyrone	May 8, 1994
Gavin McShane	Keady, Co. Armagh	May 18, 1994
Shane McArdle	Markethill, Co. Armagh	May 19, 1994

The following six people were shot dead while watching television in O'Toole's Bar in Loughinisland, Co Down on June 20, 1994. They were viewing a televised football match between Ireland and Italy, when a Loyalist squad burst in and sprayed the bar with gunfire.

Patrick O'Hare
Malcolm Jenkinson
Dan McGreanor
Barney Green
Adrian Rogan
Eamonn Byrne

Kathleen O'Hagan	Omagh, Co. Tyrone	August 7, 1994
Michael McGoldrick	Lurgan, Co. Armagh	July, 1996

KEN KERR'S LIST OF ADDITIONAL COMMITTEE VICTIMS

Committee Member Ken Kerr told Tim Laxton and me in 1996 and 1997 that the fifteen Catholics listed below were also murdered by the Committee. Since Kerr was, as we have seen, attempting to sabotage and discredit my investigation, we cannot attribute any of these, mostly unsolved murders, to the Committee at this stage; further, independent investigation will be needed. [*See Chapter 14*]

January 1989	Ian Catney, Belfast
	27-year-old shop assistant shot in the head by Loyalist gunman. Victim not involved in politics or paramilitary activity. No-one charged or convicted for the murder.
January 1989	Tony Fusco, Belfast
	33-year-old glazier shot dead in central Belfast by motor-cycle gunmen, while on his way to work. Victim not

involved in politics or paramilitary activity. No-one charged or convicted for the murder.

February 1989   John Davey, Cookstown
Sinn Féin councillor, late 50s, shot dead by Loyalist gang in the laneway of his home near Maghera, Co. Derry. RUC collusion widely suspected but not proved. No-one charged or convicted for the murder.

April 1989   Gerry Casey, Rasharkin, Co. Antrim
29-year-old IRA member shot dead in front of his wife by Loyalist gunman. RUC collusion alleged but not proved. No-one charged or convicted for the murder. [Note: The anonymous RUC Inner Circle officer, interviewed for us by John Coulter, expressed his pleasure over this murder. *See Appendix 4*]

May 1989   Malachy Trainor, Rathcoole, Belfast
34-year-old Catholic joiner from Kilkeel, Co. Down shot dead in a mainly Loyalist housing estate, after he had arrived to start work. Victim was not involved in politics or paramilitary activity. In June 1992, two Loyalists— UVF gunman Victor Graham, aged 32, and William Haythorne—were jailed for life for this murder. Graham also received a life sentence for aiding and abetting the murder of Sam Marshall; he had helped hold a family hostage while their car, the red Rover, was used in the killing. No mention of the Committee was made during Graham's trial.

July 1989   John Devine, Belfast
37-year-old Catholic shot dead in front of his 13-year-old son when three Loyalist gunmen burst into his home. Victim was not involved in politics or paramilitary activity. No-one charged or convicted for the murder.

September 1989   Paddy McKenna, Belfast
43-year-old Catholic shot dead by two UVF gunmen, one of whom was then shot dead by a British Army undercover team shortly after the murder; the other UVF gunman, David McCullough, aged 22, was jailed for life for his part in the murder. Victim was not involved in politics or paramilitary activity.

July 1990   Martin Hughes, Lisburn, Co. Antrim
33-year-old Catholic shot dead by UFF gunmen. Victim was not involved in politics or paramilitary activity. No-one charged or convicted for the murder.

July 1990   John Judge, Belfast
34-year-old Catholic shot dead outside his home, after a birthday party for his five-year-old son, Kevin. Victim was not involved in politics or paramilitary activity. No-one charged or convicted for the murder.

October 1990   Francis Hughes, Dungannon, Co. Tyrone
61-year-old Catholic taxi-driver. Shot dead by Loyalists after he had picked up a tall, well-dressed female passenger at a hotel in Dungannon. His charred remains were found in his burnt-out taxi after the killing. No involvement in politics or paramilitary activity. No-one charged or convicted for the murder.

November 1990   Malachy McIvor, Stewartstown, Co. Tyrone
42-year-old Catholic mechanic, shot by Loyalists while working on a car. No involvement in politics or paramilitary activity. Collusion not suspected. No-one charged or convicted for the murder.

January 1991   Sean Rafferty, Belfast
44-year-old scaffolder shot at his home while preparing a meal with his teenage daughter, Geraldine. No involvement in politics or paramilitary activity. Collusion not suspected. No-one charged or convicted for the murder.

February 1991   Peter McTasney, Newtownabbey, Belfast
26-year-old youth worker shot by UVF gunmen. Victim had no involvement in politics or paramilitary activity. Two self-confessed UVF members were jailed in 1993 for their part in the crime—one received a life sentence for murder, the other eighteen years for assisting the killers; no mention of the Committee during the trial.

August 1991   Francis Crawford, Belfast
57-year-old retired joiner shot dead by UFF. No involvement in politics or paramilitary activity. Collusion suspected but not proved. No-one charged or convicted for the murder.

September 1991   Seamus Sullivan, Belfast
24-year-old Catholic employed by Belfast City Cleansing Department. No involvement in politics or paramilitary activity. Collusion not suspected. No-one charged or convicted for the murder but, in 1992, a Belfast taxi driver was jailed for two years for witholding information about the killers, who had hijacked his car to carry out the attack.

Appendix 3

The Nesbitt/Penrose Conversation

Sunday Express reporter Barrie Penrose tape-recorded his telephone conversations with RUC Chief Superintendent Jimmy Nesbitt who led the official "inquiry" into the Channel 4 programme. The transcript of one conversation shows that Penrose made it clear to Nesbitt, from the outset, that he had no interest in discovering the truth about the Committee's existence or about any of the murders it was alleged to have organised. Penrose's "reporting" strategy was to let Nesbitt know that he shared wholeheartedly the RUC's antipathy to the programme makers and that he was prepared to co-operate fully in an all-out attack on the programme's credibility—by writing articles which would, as he put it, "blow them out of the water."

The transcripts show that Nesbitt, quite improperly, disclosed to Penrose the contents of the confidential affidavits which we had submitted to the High Court. He quoted extensively from my affidavit and gave Penrose the names of several people whom Source A had identified as his fellow murder conspirators on the Committee. For example, Billy Abernethy's name cropped up at an early stage. Naturally, Nesbitt was careful to ensure that Penrose did not learn the truth but was told only what he wanted to hear—namely, information which he could use to attack the programme makers.

Nesbitt: Abernethy?
Penrose: Abernethy, yes. Did he meet them?
Nesbitt: Oh yes.
Penrose: He did?
Nesbitt: Oh yes. Oh, they interviewed Abernethy.
Penrose: Right.
Nesbitt: Yes.
Penrose: But the interview wasn't used?
Nesbitt: No, the interview wasn't used. They interviewed him, you see, as a member of the Ulster Independence Committee.
Penrose: Right.

Nesbitt: He's one of the Reverend Hugh Ross's cohorts.
Penrose: Right, right.
Nesbitt: Ulster Independence Committee.
Penrose: And he, yes, and he's got no form of any kind or . . .?
Nesbitt: He's got no form of any kind, you see. They're putting him down as an ex-policeman . . .
Penrose: Right.
Nesbitt: . . . who is a member of the Inner Circle.
Penrose: Oh, I see.
Nesbitt: Well, he served in the RUC part-time Reserve.
Penrose: Right.
Nesbitt: From 1973 to 1976.
Penrose: Right.
Nesbitt: It's a long time ago.
Penrose: Sure.
Nesbitt: You know . . .
Penrose: He's in his fifties now, is he, I mean?
Nesbitt: Oh yes he is.
Penrose: Yeah.
Nesbitt: Yeah, yeah.

The above excerpt indicates that, in August 1992, Nesbitt had already set-tled on a cover story which would, he hoped, succeed in protecting the murder conspirators. We can see that Nesbitt encountered no difficulties from the less-than-inquisitive Penrose, when he misled the *Sunday Express*'s "Investigations Editor" into believing that Abernethy and Ross were merely fringe politicians engaged in the perfectly legitimate business of peacefully promoting an Independent Ulster. Penrose would faithfully reflect this official line in his subsequent articles. And, in return for Nesbitt's assistance, Penrose offered to provide what help he could to enable the RUC to prove that I had never taken the threats against me at all seriously, that I had deceived Channel 4 about them—in short, that I was a scoundrel and a perjurer. Nesbitt quoted extensively from my affi-davit and Penrose, as we will now see, rushed to the conclusions which, once published, landed him in an expensive libel action.

Nesbitt: . . . have you got the violin music playing?
Penrose: Right.
Nesbitt: Video music playing . . . [*He begins to quote my affidavit.*] "When Liz Forgan, Channel 4 director of programmes was informed in August of the report of the recruitment of the mercenary . . ."
Penrose: Yes.

Nesbitt: "She asked me if I wished to continue with the project. I was deeply troubled and concerned at the time for my family's safety."

Penrose: Em.

Nesbitt: "But Liz Forgan made it clear that there was no pressure upon me from Channel 4 to continue with this project if I did not wish to do so."

Penrose: Yes.

Nesbitt: "After discussing the matter with my wife, I decided that despite this serious threat I had a duty to ensure that what we had discovered was brought to the public attention."

Penrose: Isn't that wonderful?

Nesbitt: Isn't it? "Ben Hamilton agreed, having paused for similar reflection on the security threat that had arisen [and] also decided independently to continue working on the project. We all felt that, if we abandoned the project, the Committee's murder campaign would continue and more innocent lives would be lost." Now, this is the bit you want . . .

Penrose: Yes.

Nesbitt: [*Nesbitt then explains, at some length, that I had moved out of my home in May 1991, several months before the programme was completed and broadcast.*] . . . since May 1991.

Penrose: Oh! I see. Not May of this year, May of last year.

Nesbitt: No, since May of 1991.

Penrose: Oh really. The violins, the violins get even louder.

Nesbitt: Yes. "My family and I therefore have been living in rented accommodation . . ."

Penrose: Right.

Nesbitt: "At some considerable expense . . ."

Penrose: What a bloody liar! What a liar! It's absolutely deep, I mean deeply flawed man this because, you know, I mean, and by the way em, of course, he's been seen by the odd person who's around the area, you see. But anyway, the Estate Agent, the woman, whose name I'll get you, em, she em, is absolutely loud and clear that they've been living there. She's been there when they've been there and that's it!

Nesbitt: Been living there, yes.

Penrose: And er, but he does go and live in Oxford as well. But he's got, you know, his phone is on there and they live there sometimes, often at the weekends they're there.

Nesbitt: Yes. Yes.

Penrose: Er because, you see, the Loyalist gangs, they never attack at the weekend. They only attack Monday to Friday.

Nesbitt: Monday to Friday. Nine to Five.

Penrose: Nine to Five. It's wonderful, isn't that?

Nesbitt: It is. It really is.

Penrose: . . . I mean it's quite clear that em, you know, this perjury, you know in his Affidavit, I'm talking about the chap with the farm.
 [McPhilemy]
Nesbitt: Yes
Penrose: Em obviously, the [*Sunday Express*] reader will make it, will see very clearly that this is a criminal conspiracy I mean, you know, it's absolutely plain as a pike staff.
Nesbitt: Yes.
Penrose: We shall put that question to him, you know, that you've been defrauding Channel 4.
Nesbitt: Yes. Yes.
Penrose: Em, and we shall see what he says . . . So . . . if you're near a telephone tomorrow . . . you can call me and I'll let you know exactly what we're doing.
Nesbitt: OK.
Penrose: And the responses they make. But it will be something along the lines that these Channel, not Channel 4 but the Box Production people, that an investigation, you know, I'm talking about our investigation, the *Sunday Express* one . . .
Nesbitt: . . . yes? . . .
Penrose: . . . has, has found evidence of criminal conspiracy.
Nesbitt: Yes. Yes.
Penrose: Right.
Nesbitt: Right.
Penrose: And obviously it follows that em, they could face charges, I mean er, in due course. I mean it, it follows that, as we've established that they are out and out liars and that they've done it, obviously, for advantage to themselves.
Nesbitt: Yes. Yes.
Penrose: And I think, in particular, as the so-called safe accommodation . . .
Nesbitt: Yes.
Penrose: Obviously, we'll say in the piece that they could face charges for this because . . .
Nesbitt: . . . Right. You know, the only problem with that, Barrie, is...
Penrose: Right . . .
Nesbitt: That we need a complainant in the first place.
Penrose: Right.
Nesbitt: We need an injured party. We need Channel 4 to come up and say: "We want to make a complaint. We . . ."
Penrose: Right. Well. I'll tell you that after this weekend, they will be . . .
Nesbitt: Channel 4 don't say that, you see. We can't just wallow about and . . .

Penrose: Ah, I'm with you. I'm with you. Well, in fact . . .

Nesbitt: If somebody steals your money, you have to report it.

Penrose: Yes, of course, and if you don't want the chap to be questioned, the that's it. I've got your point. The thing, of course, is that I'll be talking to the Channel 4 people later on, this afternoon.

Nesbitt: Yes.

Penrose: And tomorrow, with these questions, and obviously when the evidence is presented, they will have to, then, have an immediate inquiry themselves, and that will obviously lead to em, you know, to bringing the police in.

Nesbitt: Yeah.

Penrose: Don't forget, of course, that em, I mean. I know you probably have got a slightly different view but er, Michael Grade and Attenborough and Liz Forgan, they're in show business and, you know, for them, they've gone on to a moral platform . . .

Nesbitt: Ah well this is it, I can see that alright.

Penrose: Do you see that?

Nesbitt: I firmly believe that, right from the very outset, that they [Channel 4] were totally deceived.

Penrose: Yes . . . but, of course, the moment that the pendulum swings the other way, they'll join that so quickly to disassociate themselves from Box.

Nesbitt: Well, they'll have to, otherwise I would have imagined that Michael Grade's job must be on the line.

Penrose: Yes, of course, it would be if, because, I mean, it's not just Michael Grade, I mean it'll be the Board it'll be, I mean once they know that the game's up, I'm talking about once they know that Box has been caught out.

Nesbitt: Yes.

Penrose: They will eventually, they'll swing to the other, they'll swing to the angels.

Nesbitt: They'll have to. They'll have to abandon them.

Penrose: Yes, of course they will.

Nesbitt: They will have to.

Penrose: Of course they will.

The early conversations between Penrose and Nesbitt indicate that the two men, newspaper "reporter" and police "investigator," were pooling their resources so that they could come up with a knock-out blow to the programme. Penrose seems to have played a central role in helping Nesbitt to reach the bizarre conclusion that Channel 4 had been duped by Box Productions—bizarre because Channel 4's David Lloyd had been in overall editorial control throughout and, as I witnessed on the day before trans-

mission, he had amended and approved the final commentary for the programme just minutes before it was recorded. Partly thanks to Penrose,
therefore, Nesbitt rapidly reached the verdict that Channel 4 had been
"hoaxed" even though, as we shall see, he could not make up his mind
about who precisely had done the "hoaxing."

The transcripts show that immediately after the first *Sunday Express's*
first article, published on August 2nd 1992, Penrose was back on the
phone to Nesbitt, fishing for compliments and shamelessly cultivating the
"investigator" to obtain information for his next story.

Penrose: Did you see the piece?
Nesbitt: I did indeed Barrie. I thought it was terrific.
Penrose: Well ha ha, there's nothing like flattery to make me agree, you
know, em . . .
Nesbitt: No, no. I really did. I thought it was really terrific.
Penrose: Well, we didn't have much time, may I say, obviously because I
was running. But we were lucky or I was lucky enough to em, to get some
of the ne'er do wells who were interviewed to talk and they always had the
same story, you know.
Nesbitt: Yeah, yeah, yeah. Oh no, I mean it's genuine enough, Barrie. I
mean I wouldn't have misled you on it.
Penrose: No, no, absolute, absolutely. But, you see, the thing is em, I put
up the idea here on Tuesday that we should really look at this Channel 4
film because it didn't have—*I'd not seen it at the time*—I saw the video later
and I, it looked, it looked flakey. [my emphasis]
Was there anything . . . that I missed . . . because I'd like to do a hard-hitting piece for this coming week, Sunday.
Nesbitt: Yeah, yeah.
Penrose: Because there are people, I mean, Trevor [Forbes] is one of them
who was mentioned by name. I mean, he should sue. I mean he's keen on
suing actually.
Nesbitt: Yeah. There's a difficulty there, Barrie. Some of the other people
we have spoken to were keen to sue and they'd gone along to see about it.
Penrose: Yeah.
Nesbitt: And I suppose, you see, to mentioning them in public, they hand-
ed their names to us [the RUC] in a confidential dossier.
Penrose: Of course.
Nesbitt: So they're going under the old ploy of, they were going around,
they got information about these people [who have] been involved in ter-
rorism and they passed it on to the police . . .
Penrose: Yes.
Nesbitt: . . . so that they could investigate it.

Penrose: Yes.

Nesbitt: They did their public duty.

Penrose: Yes.

Nesbitt: You know, so I don't know whether they have a case [for suing] or not.

Penrose: No. Sure. It's just that, that's a private thing, I mean.

Nesbitt: Yeah.

Penrose: I know that Trevor [Forbes] feels incensed. He's delighted with the *Sunday Express* piece.

Nesbitt: Oh, I was absolutely delighted with it!

Penrose: Yes.

Nesbitt: Because I thought it was terrific.

Penrose: Because we didn't have much time. Incidentally, who was the solicitor, obviously just between ourselves, who, you know, who represented the Mr. X?

Nesbitt: That's Richard Monteith.

The transcripts reveal that Penrose is so grateful to Nesbitt for the confidential information he has received that he offers the detective various ideas which might help the RUC to track down the elusive Source A. "Would-be-detective Barrie Penrose" then suggests that Nesbitt ought to try to find the actor whom Box Productions employed to disguise the words spoken by Source A.

Penrose: Did you ever track down the actor who did the voiceover?

Nesbitt: I can get you those details. We got those from the records we seized from them [Box Productions].

Penrose: . . . That would be helpful . . . You see, it just crossed my mind that, if you got a transcript and you've got an actor reading the words, you might just get the actor to sit in [on the interview].

Nesbitt: Yeah?

Penrose: Isn't that possible?

Nesbitt: That's possible. That's very possible. In fact, they could have put the cleaner from Channel 4.

Penrose: Yes, they could. But they needed someone with the right accent.

Penrose, having won Nesbitt over to the idea that Box/Channel 4 had employed an actor to read a prepared script, then went a stage further. He suggested that Source A was, most probably, a former UVF commander in Co. Armagh, a Loyalist called Jackie Whitten whom Nesbitt had earlier said had been paid "six or seven thousand pounds" by the programme makers.

Penrose: If Whitten gets the £6000, he's the most important player, isn't he?
Nesbitt: He is, yeah.
Penrose: If you think about it, I mean, he could be, therefore, the most important part of Source A.
Nesbitt: Right.
Penrose: . . . They could have had an actor to sit in [with Whitten] as well.

By this stage in the conversation, Penrose appears to have forgotten completely that he is a mere newspaper reporter and has temporarily become a junior member of the Nesbitt "Inquiry" team. Nesbitt, for his part, is so grateful for Penrose's speculative suggestions that he takes the reporter into his confidence and reveals something which he knows to be quite shocking, namely that, in the effort to identify Source A, the RUC has even gone so far as to recruit the services of the proscribed Loyalist terrorist organisation, the Ulster Volunteer Force, the UVF.

Nesbitt: Barrie, now just between you and I.
Penrose: Yeah, sure.
Nesbitt: The UVF down there [in Portadown], they also have carried out their own enquiries.
Penrose: Right.
Nesbitt: And they will do it more forcefully than we would.
Penrose: Yeah.
Nesbitt: But they had [Jackie] Whitten in the frame for it.
Penrose: Yeah.
Nesbitt: And they had [Graham] Long in the frame for it.
Penrose: Right.
Nesbitt: And the message that we got back was that they [the UVF] were satisfied that it were neither of them.

Penrose—ever-the-optimist—responded immediately by suggesting that, if Nesbitt was satisifed with the UVF's negative verdict on Whitten and Long, he might like to consider the possibility that Source A had been "a conglomeration, amalgamation or call it what you will;" in other words, he was suggesting that the programme makers had invented their Source A and, having prepared a script on the basis of discussions with numerous Loyalists, had given it to an actor to read in front of the camera, as if he were a unique Source on this non-existent Loyalist Committee. This far-fetched suggestion met with a surprisingly favourable response from Nesbitt.

Nesbitt: Yeah, yeah. That's what it looks like to me.

Penrose: Now, if that came out, if that is established, that is a devastating piece of evidence.

Nesbitt: It is! It is! You see, what strikes me is that Michael Grade is coming on television and so forth and so on but the Channel 4 people . . . never met Source A and they don't know who he is . . . Barrie, my understanding is that McPhilemy never met him either!

Penrose: He [McPhilemy] is lying!

The transcripts of the Penrose-Nesbitt conversations show that, if there had been a genuine investigation to find the truth, the contribution from the *Sunday Express's* amateur sleuth would have been a time-wasting distraction. But we can see that Nesbitt manipulated Penrose skilfully and managed to turn the *Sunday Express* into an effective propaganda tool in the RUC's battle with Channel 4.

Appendix 4

An Interview with the RUC Inner Circle

Box Productions commissioned John Coulter, a journalist in Northern Ireland, to interview his anonymous contact within the illegal RUC Inner Force/Inner Circle. John Coulter had previously published interviews he had conducted with this man in 1988 and 1989.

Q: What does the Inner Circle think of the talks process?
A: The Foreign Office [FO] people at Whitehall and the English civil servants in the Northern Ireland Office [NIO] desperately want to bring the doves of Sinn Féin to the negotiating table and turn them into a Workers Party type outfit. But the English military people want a three to four week campaign spearheaded by the SAS [Special Air Service] to take out at least one hundred and twenty people on both sides, including politicians, which would be Sinn Féin councillors. This would free the constitutional politicians on both sides to get on with the "wheeling and dealing," that is the talks process. Martin McGuinness and Alex Maskey are regarded as hawks in the Republican movement and they would be two politicians from Sinn Féin who would be eliminated. The SAS had already drawn up this plan three or four years ago.[1]
Q: What is the RUC's reaction to the Brooke talks?
A: There are enough men in the RUC who don't see themselves being forced into a united Ireland by any government, British or Irish. The RUC opinion of the Brooke talks is that they wanted to see it succeed and regard the posturing on the Unionist side as being exactly that, and of no real substance. They want to see all brands of Unionism putting their act together as a united political initiative, not as a three man initiative. The RUC don't regard the Brooke talks as a failure, but a stock and take operation. Annesley was right when he said that it was imperative that the politicians did succeed. The question is being asked, would you accept Sinn Féin at the negotiating table? The reality is, so far as the FO and NIO are concerned, there will not be any useful progress until Sinn Féin is at the conference table. Twelve months ago, John Hume was on TV with representatives from the

Shankhill Road, working class Loyalists. What they said was that if he was prepared to sit down and do business, they'd come a long way and be more flexible. The feeling in the Unionist camp is that they're fed up with the whole thing; they are not going into a united Ireland, but they wouldn't mind if there was an initiative, even if it was power sharing. In the Maze prison there are three strands of the IRA body; first, the avid IRA man doing his time for ten to fifteen years, who never had a wife and kids and wants that because he's done his bit. He has no military interest and very little political interest. Second strand is the IRA man who sees the future going into the political Sinn Féin bandwagon. Strand Three, the IRA man who is purely a psycho who will kill and kill again. In Loyalist terms, there are those who will do their time, get out and will fade away, and a small percentage who want to pursue the armed struggle—about twenty to twenty-five per cent of Loyalist inmates.

Q: What future does the Inner Circle see for the talks process?

A: The FO and the NIO want to get Sinn Féin off the hook. There are those within that organisation who want to go political. Look at the secret Sinn Féin Ard Fheis in Dublin. There is no longer the hype that there was five years ago, and a lot of serious questions have to be faced up to by the Republican movement; and that's coupled by the mood of the prison population. A lot of Sinn Féin's thinking is promoted and instigated by the political prisoners. A document produced by Sinn Féin had been sent into the prison and it was purely to get a reaction from inside the higher command as to the future policy and the path that it should take. This document was to formulate a policy of where the Republican movement was going to in the next ten years.

Q: What will the Inner Circle's future strategy be?

A: *The objective of the Inner Circle will be basically to ensure that the hawks in the Republican movement are killed and this will leave the talkers.* A feud in the Republican movement would also see the hawks kill the talkers. Just look at history at what happened between the pro-Treaty and the anti-Treaty factions in the Twenties. All the hits that are being carried out at the moment are against the hawk wing of the Republican movement. There is no way that the talkers could come out into the open because they would be executed. Adams would go totally political and I think he would be spared. McGuinness is a hawk and he would have to go. McGuinness took part in a firing party that ambushed Army patrols and has been credited with two kills. Morrison too is on the military wing, but Adams is being left alone.

Q: How will the Inner Circle implement this strategy?

A: The hawks have to be made ineffective. They must be discredited in the hope that their own people would do them in anyway. There was an initiative floated by the doves in response to political statements made by Brooke, but this was stifled by McGuinness. You could see a terrorist campaign to take out the hawks, or you get an IRA feud going. The Roman Catholic people as a whole are fed up with the terrorists because they've suffered a lot from random killings. There has also been the random killings of RCs to let the IRA know that the Prods can kill RCs, too. Pressure is being brought to bear on the IRA, and the RC people are saying to their priests—"My husband would not have been dead if the IRA hadn't killed that Prod businessman."

Q: Is the Inner Circle now killing people?

A: It has taken the Prod paramilitaries twenty years to reach the situation that the IRA were at in the early Seventies—Cappagh, Buncrana, and several other incidents, including the lawyer Finucane. He was one of the Provos' out and out spokesmen to the extreme. Whoever did him, did society a favour. I have always been sceptical of the leaking of police information in any great quantity. The UDR has a good system and they'd be more versatile because the UDR vetting system is not as extreme as the police.[2]

Q: How do the security force commanders view the present killings being claimed by the Loyalists?

A: I am sure the higher echelons of the RUC and Army see the Prod attacks on Sinn Féiners as serving a purpose. The Prod gunmen are now trained to a higher level. As for Coagh, Loughgall and Strabane, these were hard gunmen to locate, so the security forces did them themselves. There has also been a stifling of IRA funds brought about by the tightening of laws regarding black taxis, registration of clubs, and having to show returns, and the failure of some clubs to be relicensed. The IRA is now doing armed robberies to get cash. The Republican movement is now facing the same crisis as faced the ANC in South Africa. If it wants to come into the political arena, it will have to be more democratic, but to do this means a war with the hawks.

Q: Is there much support within Inner Circle for Independence?

A: I don't think there ever was really too much support for independence because you only need to look at the Queen's visit and the number of people in the establishment who went to the garden party. There is a powerful groundswell of opinion that might not like the British Government, but still supports the monarchy and the Throne; they see it as part of their heritage and they won't relinquish it. I can't see how the establishment, titled people in Northern Ireland, heads of the judiciary, heads of the TA, UDR, RUC and regular Army would tolerate a position where Northern Ireland would be handed over.

Q: What view does the Inner Circle take of the so-called doves in Sinn Féin?

A: The Republican movement don't know themselves what way they are travelling. With the advent of Germany being united, the reduction in strategic weapons—where does that leave the IRA? They are now struggling to find an identity and a viable policy that will be acceptable to the Nationalist people. The dove element in Sinn Féin needs a political boost, and what better for them than to be invited to the talks, but to get them there, you must get rid of some of the hawks, and you need the rank and file supporter. There are those within the FO and NIO who want the Republican movement there lock, stock and barrel. But if it is the will of the British to get the Republican movement there, let's take advantage of the situation by removing the hawk, and all that would arrive at the conference table would be a Sinn Féin more akin to the old Irish Independence Party of John Turnley. Such an IIP-type Sinn Féin would certainly be more than politically neutered, and it would be only a matter of time before it was then killed off by the even more constitutional SDLP. The ordinary Roman Catholic is crying out for a political initiative. A lot of northern Roman Catholics see the demands of Hume as being unrealistic, even though he has the support of the Éire Government. The Prods will not accept and cannot accept all that Hume wants. There would be business done in the morning if Articles Two and Three of the Éire constitution were removed. Maybe in itself, that block doesn't count for much, but the articles are a major stumbling block. But I can't see much movement at the moment, it needs a breath of spring from south of the border; it needs Éire to do something. Haughey is not pragmatic and is too staid in his ways. I think MacSharry is the man to deal with. As for the Unionist side, Trimble and Robinson would deal a lot quicker if Paisley and Molyneaux were out of the way. MacSharry is a cut and thrust politician and would get the job done. The rest are just posturing.

Q: What scenario do you see developing involving the Sinn Féin "doves?"

A: I would say sixty to sixty-five per cent of Sinn Féin is made up of doves but they would be stifled if they tried to make a move on their own. There has to be some form of limited military solution, if not eradication. There must be selective internment to take them out of circulation, but I don't see that happening before the next General Election. The people to take out are the hawks and the re-offenders who plot and take part in active military action. Unless and until we either eradicate or intern the bombers, we will still be existing at the same level for the next ten years and we'll still be putting up with it. Sentencing should be longer and re-offenders should get their licences revoked.

Q: Does it not seem strange that the Inner Circle would be appearing to help an element of the Republican movement, namely the Sinn Féin "doves?"

A: This should not be seen as giving in to Sinn Féin, but there is an element in Sinn Féin that is not gunmen or bombers, but represents a section of the Nationalist community and for us not to recognise that fact is to bury our heads in the sand. There is a problem to be tackled. How much or how little you give them is a matter for the conference table.

Q: What future for the political process does the Inner Circle envisage?

A: I'd have to be realistic and say that while Articles Two and Three remain, there will never be any settlement, and while they claim jurisdiction over Northern Ireland, there'd be no way the talks could succeed.

Q: Let's look again at [Ulster] Independence. Why could this notion find support in the first place?

A: Certainly, the Independence lobby will increase and people will be looking more seriously at the Independence option now. The main objection to Independence is that it is contrary to the spirit of Unionism. It is supported because of the frustration with the Irish and British governments, especially with British Government ministers; secondly, there is support for Independence because of the lack of democracy in Northern Ireland; thirdly, and the main reason, is the fact that the majority community in Northern Ireland are always being made out to be the bad guys and the fact that the minority community have never played their role as citizens in Northern Ireland, that is, they have always regarded themselves as citizens of another state. Fourthly, the ineffectiveness, or lack of will by the British Government to deal with the problem of terrorism. Fifthly, the dream that having the country in their own hands, they would be masters of their own affairs and those not willing to play their full parts as citizens of that country would be dealt with accordingly.

Q: Could the Inner Circle ever see Independence actually coming about?

A: If the situation of Independence ever arose, with all the people who had been trained by the various wings of the security forces, the Loyalists would have a ready made Army to defend the Province. It's not the security situation that is the problem, it's the economic situation. But links with countries such as South Africa, Norway, Switzerland and Israel would in fact hold out the possibility of making Northern Ireland a very viable and attractive investment situation on the edge of Europe.

Q: Is the Inner Circle happy about the present security strategy of the Army and Police commanders?

A: No, definitely not because intelligence is not of a high enough standard and they're too hide bound by bureaucracy, and too scared of offending the South, and if anything happens, the British Government is too scared of Seamus Mallon squealing his head off, and Gerry Collins shouting about the UDR. Until Éire takes the thing seriously in terms of an effective security policy . . . what you need is to go in and root out the terrorists, if you have any information on them at all, and put them out of the way. The Inner Circle came into being through frustration that the job was not being done. They know the people who should be arrested and put behind bars, but the security forces on the ground's [*sic*] hands are tied by politicians and the NIO and FO. But I think the Inner Circle's influence will decline because you will see the job being done by the paramilitaries. Loyalist intelligence is becoming more professional. This information on Republican activists is not being leaked from the police, but would come from the regular Army at the moment.

Q: What activities do you see the Inner Circle now initiating?

A: The Inner Circle is dormant at the moment because the Loyalist paramilitaries are becoming more active, and because the Loyalist paramilitaries are getting their own information, such as in Donegal which was entirely UFF from start to finish.[3] The Loyalist paramilitaries are developing their own ethos. Ulster Resistance will probably become the military wing of the Independence politics, just as the IRA is the military wing of Sinn Féin.

Q: How could the Inner Circle help such a campaign?

A: Inner Circle could certainly aid a Loyalist campaign by feeding information and intelligence. The Inner Circle could, in fact, pass on details of target movements; they could also cover the tracks of those involved in the assassinations, and could assist in training. But again, I stress, the recent killings are because of a growing professionalism within the Loyalist paramilitaries in recent years. Since the death of a Protestant businessman in Belfast, the business community is contributing funds to pay for hitmen. The business community is now talking of getting the terrorists off their backs and getting on with the job of commerce. The business community is angry with the assassination of businessmen just because they are selling food and doing contracts for the security forces. They are also anxious because it doesn't seem to them that the security forces can do the job, so that someone has to be brought in to take out the terrorists. The business community has a lot of scores to settle and a few thousand pounds would be regarded by the business community as a cheap price to pay. The other aspect is that by paying a few thousand now to take out some of the Republican hit men, it would save the lives of a number of men in the business community in the years to come.

Q: What killings would lead you to give this answer?

A: Look at Casey in Rasharkin, Fullerton in Buncrana and the people at Cappagh when four Republicans were killed, but in that incident, they didn't get the real man they were after.[4]

Q: How are the Loyalists becoming so accurate in their supposed targeting?

A: The Loyalist paramilitaries are now using men who have trained themselves in assassination techniques to a high degree and would not be seen

[at] or frequent the traditional Loyalist drinking clubs and pubs, therefore, they would go largely undetected by the security forces or by Republican moles. The hitmen could also be ex-SAS who know the country and are prepared to do the job they were hindered from doing by the FO.

Q: If this is the case, why does the Inner Circle not disband?

A: The command structure of the Inner Circle is still in place, but there's no need at this point in time to activate any action because the paramilitaries are doing it very well themselves.

After John Coulter had given us this transcript of his conversation, he told us in a filmed interview that this RUC Inner Circle member had first approached him in 1986. The police officer, who was wearing his RUC uniform and supervising a Loyalist parade during the marching season, indicated that he was willing to talk about the illegal Loyalist cell which had formed within the RUC. John Coulter has continued since 1991 to insist that the anonymous individual whom he interviewed on our behalf was, as he claimed, an experienced police officer belonging to the illegal RUC Inner Circle.

Notes

1   The Loyalists tried to "eliminate" Alex Maskey in 1987, when he was shot in the stomach after answering a knock on his front door. The would-be-assassin managed to escape before the RUC arrived to investigate.

2   The RUC Inner Circle representative is here referring to six people murdered by the Committee—four at Cappagh, Eddie Fullerton in Buncrana, Co. Donegal and Belfast solicitor Patrick Finucane.

3   This is another reference to the murder of Eddie Fullerton in Buncrana, Co Donegal. It is evident that the RUC Inner Circle officer knew more about this murder than he was prepared to disclose to his interviewer.

4   These murders are listed in Appendix 2. It is again obvious that the RUC Inner Circle member knew more about some of these murders than he wished to reveal.

Appendix 5

The Orange Order

The Loyal Orange Institution of Ireland—the Orange Order—is dedicated to "the glorious and immortal memory of William of Orange, 1690" and, in 1963, published a short booklet which describes the appropriate manner in which its rituals and ceremonies are to be conducted. The Orange Order's anti-Catholic ethos is seen at its most explicit in the initiation ceremony for new members. All candidates wishing to join the organisation are asked to make the following promise:

> Do you promise, before this Lodge, to give no countenance, by your presence or otherwise, to the unscriptural, superstitious, and idolatrous worship of the Church of Rome? And do you also promise never to marry a Roman Catholic, never to stand sponsor for a child when receiving baptism from a priest of Rome, nor allow a Roman Catholic to stand sponsor for your child at baptism? And do you further promise to resist, by all lawful means, the ascendancy, extension and encroachments of that Church; at the same time being careful always to abstain from all unkind words and actions towards its members, yea, even prayerfully and diligently, as opportunity occurs, to use your best efforts to deliver them from error and false doctrine, and lead them to the truth of that Holy Word, which is able to make them wise unto salvation?

It is, perhaps, not entirely surprising that several members of Abernethy's Committee are members of this venerable body and that two of them—Nelson McCausland and Cecil Kilpatrick—are members of the so-called "Education Committee" of the Grand Orange Lodge. It would appear that the promise "to abstain from all unkind words and actions" towards Catholics did not weigh too heavily on the consciences of those Orangemen on the Committee who shared in the decisions to murder the Catholics listed in Appendix Two.

The Orange Order organises a full-blown Lodge within the RUC itself, a fact which not only helps to explain the emergence of the (illegal) RUC Inner Circle and RUC Inner Force but demonstrates the anti-Catholic traditions and character of a police force which is understandably viewed with great suspicion by the Catholic community in Northern Ireland.

Index